THE

The Complete Guide to Sporting Firearms:

GUNNER'S

Rifles, Shotguns, Handguns and their Accessories

BIBLE

Revised Edition

Bill Riviere

DOUBLEDAY & COMPANY, INC., GARDEN CITY, NEW YORK

ISBN: 0-385-02423-1
Library of Congress Catalog Card Number 73–77415

Printed in the United States of America
9 8

Contents

Chapter I

A BALLISTICS PRIMER

Daily practice with a given gun over a period of several weeks will make you a better than average marksman, at least with that particular gun. Some pistol coaches even require that team members fire only every other day to avoid going stale. The fact remains that, whether you shoot daily or only every second day, you'll develop some degree of skill which can't be matched by a shooter who fires only occasionally. This skill will come to you even if you don't grasp what goes on within a firearm when you shoot it.

However, if you'll combine consistent practice habits with some understanding of ballistics —the science of projectiles—you'll become truly expert in less time and your shooting fun will be multiplied hundredfold. When you understand the "why" of shooting, the "how" becomes easier.

Caliber

"Caliber" is the term applied to the interior diameter of a rifle or pistol barrel or to the diameter of a bullet. In English-speaking countries this is indicated in hundredths or thousandths of an inch (.30) or (.308).

Sometimes caliber indicates bore diameter—that is, measurements made from the top of the lands or raised surfaces between the rifling grooves within a barrel. A typical example of this is the .30 Remington which, if measurements were made from the bottom of the rifling grooves, would be .308. The same is true of other .30 calibers irrespective of manufacturer and what it boils down to is that a .30 caliber is actually .308 inches in diameter!

Many .30 caliber loads exist, of course, including the .30/30, .30/06 Springfield, .300 Holland & Holland, .300 Savage, .308 Winchester, and others. Bullets for these loads may be interchangeable since they all use projectiles .308 inches in diameter, but the cartridges themselves may be fired only in rifles specifically designed for particular loads due to variations in the shape and powder capacity of the shells. In other words, a .30/06 cartridge cannot be fired in a .30/30 rifle—even if both are .30 caliber.

Even the date of original issue is sometimes included in caliber designation as is the case with the .30/06 Springfield. The ".30," of course, indicates bore diameter. The "06" is an abbreviation of the year (1906) during which the load was issued to the U. S. Army and "Springfield" is the name of the rifle, taken from the armory where the guns were manufactured. The Rock Island Armory also turned out these weapons.

Often, too, commercial developers of cartridges have given their names to calibers so that the latter have become household words among shooters. Among these are the .30 Remington, .270 Winchester, .300 Savage and .300 Holland & Holland.

Calibers originating in countries where the metric system of measurement prevails are likely to be indicated in millimeters. The 8/57 R mm, for example, has an 8-millimeter-diameter bullet. The second figure, 57, is the length of the cartridge case or shell given in millimeters while the "R" is applied to a shell whose base is rimmed. Foreign calibers are also associated with their originators by adding the latter's name, as is the case with the 8 mm Mauser.

The confusion of calibers carries into the pistol field, too. The .38 Special fires a bullet .357 inches in diameter so that, in reality, the .38 is a .35! Confusion was further compounded with the appearance, some years ago, of the .357 Magnum firing a bullet .357 inches in diameter. However, a .38 Special load may be fired in a .357 handgun since the bullets are identical in diameter but mechanical design and pressures prevent the firing of a .357 in a .38 Special revolver.

Ballistics

The word "ballistics" has a forbidding sound, reminiscent of dry textbooks and dull formulas. The report of a gun and the smell of gunpowder have much more appeal, so why bother with the technical aspects of shooting? As a matter of fact, ballistics is a fascinating field which, when learned step by step, is easy to grasp. Surprisingly, too, it's only once removed from the early morning duck marshes, the endless golden plains, towering mountain skylines, rolling hillsides, the serenity of deep woodlands and the pageantry of competitive shooting ranges. Take the trouble to learn about the "innards" of your gun while you're learning to shoot and it will pay handsome dividends.

Ballistics deals with three phases of the behavior of a cartridge. *Interior* ballistics is concerned with what happens within a gun when the trigger is pulled. *Exterior* ballistics applies to the behavior of the bullet or shot charge as it travels through the air. *Terminal* ballistics, usually a military phase but important to hunters, has to do with the reactions set up when the charge strikes its target.

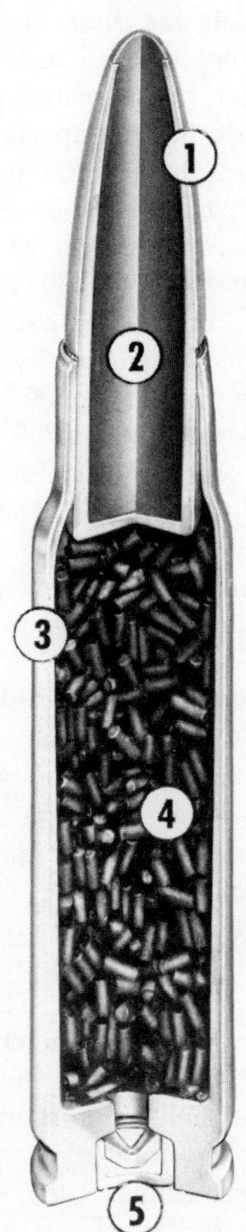

Cutaway view of center-fire rifle cartridge showing (1) bullet jacket, (2) lead core, (3) case, (4) powder, (5) primer. (FEDERAL CARTRIDGE CORP.)

What Is a Cartridge?

The first step is to know the parts of a cartridge and their functions. Take a rifle cartridge, for example, made up of a brass shell or case, a primer, a powder charge and a bullet. Target range and military shooters refer to a loaded and ready-to-fire cartridge as a "round." Hunters are more likely to say, "I've got one 'shot' left." TV heroes—and the "bad guys"—call a cartridge a "bullet," and they are inaccurate, since a bullet is only one part of the cartridge.

When You Pull the Trigger

When a gun is cocked the firing pin is drawn back and held under spring tension until released by the pulling of the trigger. This frees the pin, which is then driven into the cartridge primer. The latter explodes, sending a tiny flame through the flash hole in the cartridge base into the powder compartment. Contrary to popular opinion, the powder *does not* explode. It burns rapidly, building up gas pressure. When this pressure reaches sufficient intensity, the bullet is dislodged from the mouth of the shell and is driven out through the barrel.

The walls of a rifle or pistol shell have some degree of flexibility so that, as the gas pressure mounts, the shell expands to fit snugly into the gun's firing chamber. This prevents gas from blowing back by the shell and escaping through the action, possibly injuring the shooter. After the charge has left the barrel and the pressure has been dissipated, the shell contracts to almost its original size so that it can be extracted easily. The cartridge case alone could never stand such pressures—which commonly run to 40,000 pounds per square inch—were it not for the great strength built into the actions and breeches of modern guns.

Pressure within the barrel, however, doesn't make up the entire picture of interior ballistics. Rifle and pistol barrels are "rifled," that is, spiraling grooves are cut or pressed into their inner surfaces. As the bullet is pushed toward the muzzle, it is gripped by these grooves and by the barrel surfaces between the grooves. The latter are called "lands." The diameter of a barrel measured from the bottom of the grooves is then slightly greater than that measured from the land surfaces. This is known as "groove diameter" or "bore diameter" as the case may be. Bullets are manufactured at close to groove diameter so that they will fill the grooves as they move forward in the barrel. This confines gases and the pressure against the base of the bullet. This grip on the bullet by the lands and grooves causes it to spin, and by the time it leaves the barrel it is spinning at great speed. This gives the bullet lateral stability so that it cannot tumble, or turn end-over-end. In other words, a bullet's accuracy stems from the stability in flight created by this spinning. The longer a bullet in relation to its diameter the faster it must spin for ultimate stability. The rate of spin is governed by the degree of "pitch" of the grooves. Some rifles are bored with a greater number of grooves than others.

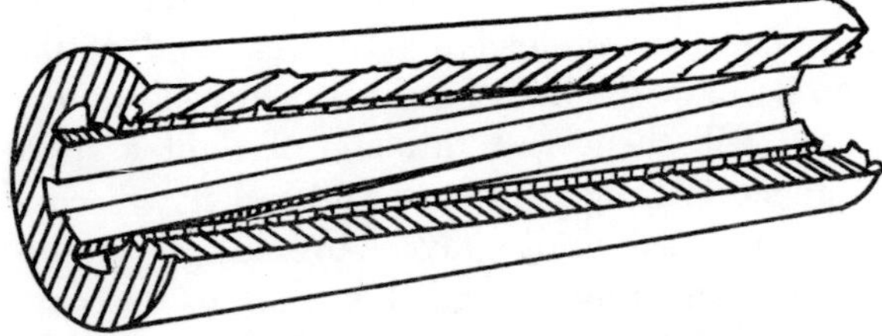

"Rifling" or grooves in a rifle or pistol barrel cause the bullet to spin as it travels toward the muzzle.

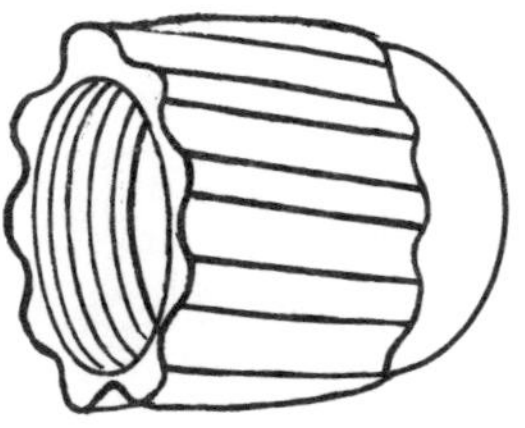

Rifled slug for shotguns. Note hollow base, spiraling grooves.

Shotgun barrels are not rifled, since they are designed to shoot a number of small pellets which would be deformed by rifling and then tend to scatter erratically. However, because many hunters, particularly deer hunters in areas where rifles are illegal, want to fire a solid slug in shotguns, these slugs are manufactured with spiraling lands and grooves along their sides. Most hunters believe that these slugs are given a spinning effect as a result of these grooves pressing against the smooth inner bore of the shotgun barrel. While the matter is still in some contention, recent research seems to be proving that these slugs *do not spin.* This may come as quite a shock to many shooters, as it did to me and you may ask, "How, then, can slugs be accurate?" Slugs have a hollow base so that the nose is heavier than the tail and this is what gives them the necessary lateral stability in flight to produce the surprising accuracy they have!

Just before the American Revolution, Patrick Ferguson, a Scotch officer in the British 70th Foot Regiment, devised one of the early military weapons whose barrel was rifled. The gun was also a breechloader—that is, it could be loaded through the action rather than through the muzzle, a decided advantage for a military weapon.

The so-called Kentucky rifle originated in Pennsylvania in about 1730 as a smoothbore, although some were built with straight rather than spiral rifling. Later spiral rifling was introduced and small gun shops throughout Tennessee, the Carolinas, Virginia and Kentucky began to turn them out in growing numbers. It was these later models that could match the shooting range of the Ferguson. British Commander Sir William Howe complained bitterly of the deadly accuracy of these rifled Kentuckies in the hands of American sharpshooters and is reported to have sent a captured Kentucky rifle to England to prove his point.

The famous Kentucky rifle which originated in Pennsylvania and was also made in several surrounding states.

Getting back to ballistics: When the bullet and the gas pushing it strike the atmosphere at the muzzle, a strong backward thrust is set up so that the gun is shoved briskly against the shooter's shoulder, or hand in the case of a pistol. Technically, this thrust starts the moment the bullet escapes the grasp of the cartridge case but it isn't actually felt until the bullet leaves the barrel. Since this thrust is directed against the shooter and is somewhat absorbed by him, it is not completely free and therefore causes the muzzle to jump upward. This is known as recoil or kick.

Since the full effect of this recoil is not manifested until after the bullet has left the barrel, it has little or no effect on the bullet's path of flight. You can't blame a miss on recoil, unless the kick you expect causes you to flinch, something we'll go into later. Recoil varies in relation to the weight of the bullet, the powder charge and the gun's weight. For example, a heavy bullet fired by a large powder charge in a lightweight rifle will cause much greater recoil than will a small bullet fired by a light powder charge in a heavy rifle.

Recoil can be painful, physically and psychologically. One of the phenomena you'll discover is that recoil which occurs while you're shooting at game is rarely noticed but, while firing the same gun and load at a stationary target, you'll get the full treatment!

The Bullet in Flight

Once the charge has left the barrel, you're dealing with exterior ballistics. So far as shooting skill is concerned, this is a more important phase of ballistics because the bullet's behavior in flight will make the difference between a hit and a miss.

A bullet, even though it flies so fast you can't see it, is affected by the pull of gravity. As a boy, dreaming of my first gun yet to come, I used to think that a bullet fired into the air just kept right on traveling! Actually, it's little different from a baseball in that it must come to earth. If you could stand in a vacuum on a large flat area and fire a rifle whose barrel was horizontal, and at exactly the same moment you could drop an identical bullet from your other hand, both bullets would strike the ground at the same moment, though several hundred feet apart.

In order to offset this pull of gravity the barrel of a gun must be elevated at the muzzle if you're going to hit a distant target. The muzzle will then actually point *above* the target so that the bullet's path of flight becomes an arc from the muzzle to the point of impact. This is called trajectory.

Of course, you can't sight along this trajectory. You will look through the gun's sights in a direct line to the target, known as the line of sight. Most rifles and some pistols have rear sights which can be adjusted. Raising the rear sight has the effect of lowering the rear end of the barrel below the line of sight. When you fire, the bullet will then cross this line of sight a short distance in front of the muzzle and it will continue upward until gravity overcomes its upward momentum. It will then start to descend, still traveling in an arc, until the line of sight and the bullet's trajectory meet exactly on target and you'll have a bull's-eye, providing your sights were correctly set for the range and that you sighted accurately. With guns having fixed sights, you'll have to guess and hold the front sight slightly above the target. The longer the range, the more allowance you'll have to make. This allowance is termed elevation.

Gravity, however, isn't the only natural force affecting the flight of a bullet. Wind, even a slight breeze, will drive a bullet off its aimed path, and the longer the range, the farther off its course the bullet will deviate. For this reason, better sights are adjustable laterally to compensate for this "wind drift" of a bullet. Shooters refer to this adjustment as windage. For short-range shooting or for woods hunting this is rarely necessary but for competitive target shooting and long-range hunting shots, such windage adjustments are a must. A 300-yard shot, for example, may well require a lateral compensation of as much as 12 to 14 inches.

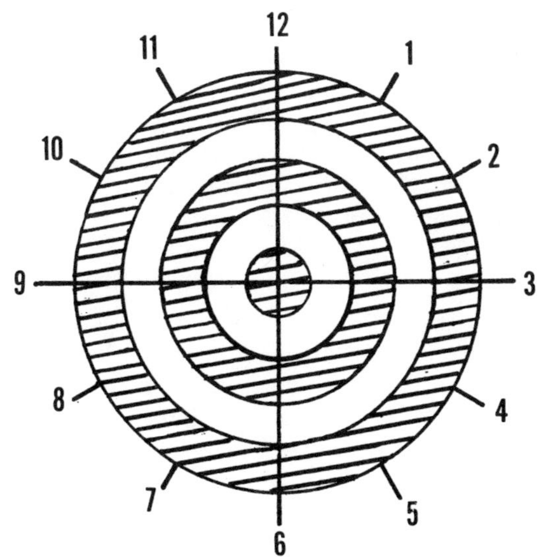

Learn to think of a target as the face of a clock. Someone can then "spot" or "call" your shots.

In connection with elevation and windage adjustments, learn to think of your target as the face of a clock with the bull's-eye located at the joining of the hands and the target's outer rim as the circular row of hour numerals. Since you can't see the bullet holes in the target when shooting at long ranges, someone should "spot" your shots through a powerful spotting scope. If your spotter were to tell you that your shot was "high and left," you would really have only a vague idea of the location of your hit. On the other hand, if the spotter tells you that your shot struck at "ten o'clock in the seven ring," you can see in your mind's eye exactly where the bullet struck in relation to the bull's-eye.

When the wind is blowing from your right as you face your target, it is blowing from "three o'clock" and your bullet will tend to drift to the left or toward "nine o'clock." To offset this, move the rear sight to the right, which in effect moves the rear of the gun barrel to the left of your line of sight. The muzzle will now point slightly upwind or toward three o'clock. The bullet will leave the barrel headed to the right of the target but the pressure of the wind will carry it back toward the line of sight and the target's center. As in the case of elevation, the bullet's path and the line of sight will coincide on the bull's-eye, providing, of course, sight adjustments and sighting were accurate. Basically, this is windage.

Bullet velocity, or rate of speed, has a sharp bearing upon the degree of elevation and windage adjustment required to send a bullet accurately to its target. The faster a bullet travels, the farther it will get before gravity or wind pressure force it seriously off its intended course, and this is why high-velocity ammunition is known to have a flat trajectory. Gravity pulls just as hard at a high-velocity bullet as it does at a slower missile but it has less time in which to pull the bullet downward from its path. Hence, with high-velocity ammunition, fewer and smaller elevation and windage adjustments are required.

"Foot seconds" is a term you'll encounter frequently in dealing with ammunition. This is

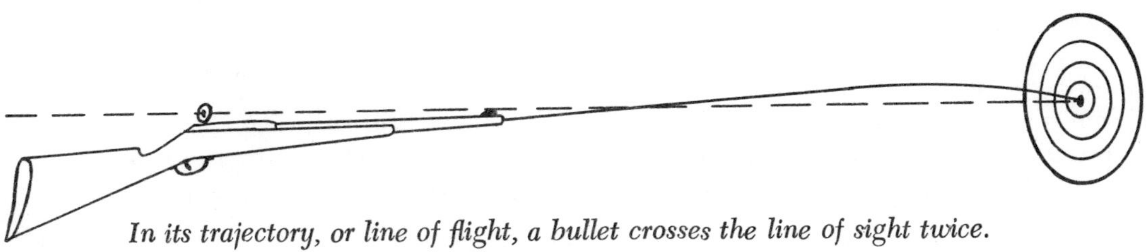

In its trajectory, or line of flight, a bullet crosses the line of sight twice.

simply the number of feet a bullet will travel in one second. A bullet said to have a velocity of 2700 foot seconds will travel that distance in one second.

Velocity, however, is not a stable quality. As a bullet travels toward its target it loses momentum continually until it finds its goal or falls to the ground. Therefore, we have the term "muzzle velocity," the speed at which a bullet leaves the gun, as compared to velocity at 100, 200 and 300 yards. Because of this progressive loss of velocity, a bullet's trajectory is not a perfect arc from gun to muzzle. As the bullet slows, the downward arc is steeper than the ascending arc. Therefore, the high point of the trajectory above the line of sight is not necessarily at exact mid-range between the gun and target. Ballistics charts indicate trajectory by the number of inches below or above the line of sight at regular intervals, usually 100, 200 and 300 yards.

The velocity of a bullet is governed by the type and weight of the powder load, weight and type or shape of the bullet, and to some degree by barrel length. Too little powder in a cartridge will decrease velocity and certain loads such as "mid-range wad-cuttters" used in target shooting, are loaded lightly for lower velocities, less recoil and greater accuracy. An overloaded cartridge not only results in possibly dangerous pressures but also in erratic bullet flight. The weight and shape of bullets will determine their susceptibility to wind and air resistance, thus affecting velocity. It's probably apparent to you now that interior and exterior ballistics are closely related.

The weight of a bullet is denoted in grains, with the variety ranging from as little as 15 grains in the shooting gallery .22 Short rim-fire to 500 grains in double-barrel elephant gun ammunition. There are 480 grains to one ounce, troy weight.

The Bullet's Impact

The third phase, "terminal ballistics," deals with the impact effects of a bullet striking its target, usually of greater concern to the hunter than to the target shooter or "plinker." Terminal ballistics is more commonly associated with military projectiles, but it concerns the hunter who wants to kill as quickly and as humanely as possible with a minimum destruction of edible meat. In the case of dangerous game such as the Alaskan brown bear and the many African species, concern about meat doesn't enter the picture. Destructive impact is what counts.

The energy of a bullet is measured in foot pounds, an engineering unit denoting force that will move a one-pound object one foot. As in the case of velocity, energy diminishes as the bullet travels from the muzzle.

Energy, or killing power which occurs upon impact, is the result of a combination of bullet weight, type, shape and velocity. Bullets, made for killing game, are a type designed to expand upon impact, thus creating greater tissue damage and shock. Such bullets often have hollow points or a soft nose with a partial jacket of harder metal so that they mushroom upon striking flesh and bone, frequently more than doubling their original diameter. This may seem to contradict the hunter's wish to damage as little meat as possible while still effecting a clean kill but the primary concern of any true sportsman should be the latter.

The opposite type of bullet is the military missile which is completely jacketed and designed to kill or wound without unnecessary damage to flesh. Such bullets expand very little, if any, upon striking flesh and they are likely to fly right through the body, mushrooming or expanding only if they strike bone. It follows, then, that military ammunition should not be used on game. Terminal ballistics bears out the fact that a shot which may kill a man instantly will only wound a wild animal.

For many years there has been conflict between hunters who prefer heavy, slow-moving bullets and those who have advocated lighter missiles traveling at high velocities. Shooters of slow-moving heavy bullets claim these have time

Perfectly "mushroomed" bullet recovered after impact. Note that its diameter has almost doubled. (NOSLER PARTITION BULLET CO.)

to expand and damage flesh before coming to a stop in a game animal's body. The high-velocity bullets, they say, are often dissipated by exploding upon impact and before proper penetration has taken place. The high-speed bullet shooters are likely to counter with the claim that their ammunition creates greater shock which is the killing factor. Of recent years, the development of Magnum and heavy high-speed loads has introduced a third faction into the argument—those who shoot moderate to heavy bullets at high velocities. Actually, there is something to be said in favor of all three general types of ammunition because the bullet most likely to succeed in hunting is the one which develops enough *energy upon impact* to down the quarry being hunted. Fortunately, this factor can be evaluated, even before you own a gun, by means of ballistic tables.

Ballistic Tables

These are issued by ammunition manufacturers and they represent a statistical picture of the behavior of various calibers, bullets and powder loads. The tables usually include the caliber, trade or popular name of the cartridge, bullet weight and type, velocity and energy at the muzzle as well as at 100, 200 and 300 yards, along with mid-range trajectories at these same ranges. Some tables, dealing with long-range ammunition, include statistics covering 400- and 500-yard ranges. Not only will these tables afford you direct help in choosing a gun and caliber combination, but they're fascinating to read. Ballistic tables, too, are frequently used to settle discussions regarding the merits of various pistol and rifle loads.

For a "dry run" through the tables, take the .30/06 Springfield 180-grain bullet and you'll note that the muzzle velocity is 2700 foot seconds (usually abbreviated "fs."). At 100 yards, velocity has diminished to 2470 foot seconds; at 200 yards it is down to 2250 foot seconds; at 300 yards, it is 2040 foot seconds.

For purposes of comparison, examine the ballistics of the .30/30 Winchester 170-grain bullet. Its comparative velocities are 2220 foot seconds, 1890 foot seconds, 1630 foot seconds and 1410 foot seconds.

Now, to consider energy. The .30/06, 180-grain bullet, has a muzzle energy of 2910 foot pounds (abbreviated ft. lbs.), dropping to 2440 foot pounds at 100 yards. It then drops to 2020 foot pounds at 200 yards and develops 1660 foot pounds at 300 yards.

The muzzle energy of the 170-grain .30/30 bullet, on the other hand, is 1860 foot pounds at the muzzle, with corresponding drops at 100, 200 and 300 yards to 1350 foot pounds, 1000 foot pounds, and 750 foot pounds.

Next the chart compares trajectory. This shows that the .30/06 mid-range trajectory, with the 180-grain bullet, is 0.7 inches at 100 yards, 3.1 inches at 200 yards and 8.3 inches at 300 yards. The corresponding trajectories of the .30/30 are indicated as 1.2 inches, 4.6 inches and 12.5 inches. It's obvious, then, that the .30/06 develops greater velocity, has a flatter trajectory and a higher energy quotient at all ranges. You might conclude, possibly, that the .30/06 is a better load but this isn't necessarily so.

The ballistic table has shown you the comparative behavior of the two bullets and that's as far as a ballistic table can go. You can reasonably conclude, however, that the .30/06 is a better choice for long-range shooting and that the .30/30 is limited to comparatively short-range work. Here, however, a general knowledge of gun types should enter the picture before a final choice is made.

For example, while the .30/06 is a better choice for long ranges, its recoil is greater and the rifle is likely to be heavier than the one shooting a .30/30 bullet. True, the .30/30 has more stringent range limitations, but it is available in lightweight carbine models, its recoil is light, ammunition less expensive and its 100-yard 1360 foot pounds energy isn't to be sneered at for woods hunting. In fact, the .30/30 has probably killed more deer than any other caliber! Winchester has manufactured three and a half million Model 94s, most of them chambered for the .30/30.

Many hunters who have no knowledge of ballistics are inclined to attribute fantastic or even impossible qualities to their favorite rifles. I once met a hunter who told me that his newly purchased 8 mm Mannlicher-Schoenauer was "flat-shooting up to one mile!" I didn't disillusion him.

Chapter II

.22 RIFLES

Nearly every shooter has fond memories of his first .22 rifle, and no matter how varied his battery of heavier guns may now be, that first gun quite likely holds a choice spot in the gun rack. During the earlier days of the .22's popularity in America it was pretty much a boy's gun. Today, it's a rifle everyone, Mom, Dad, Sister and Brother, all enjoy shooting together. Its report is negligible, a mere "splat!"; there's no recoil and it still costs little to shoot.

.22 Ammunition

First, however, you should understand the make-up, advantages and limitations of the .22 rim-fire shell. This is the smallest of our firearms ammunition and the term "rim-fire" is derived from the fact that the primer is located in a tiny rim about the base of the shell, as opposed to a center-fire cartridge whose primer is centered in the base. Rim-fire cartridges cannot be reloaded and are discarded. Their cost is so low that even if they could be reloaded, the process would not be economical.

The three most popular rim-fire .22s are the Short, Long and Long Rifle loaded at standard and high-speed velocities. The Short is loaded with bullets ranging from 15 grains up to 29, including a bullet which disintegrates upon impact for use in shooting galleries. Trick shooting is sometimes faked with this bullet because its spattering effect appears to be a direct hit despite a near miss. Some .22 Shorts are used for target work and certain fine target pistols are chambered for these. Generally, however, the .22 Short is a "plinking" load or one used for the smallest game. Because it's the most economical it finds wide favor among young shooters.

The .22 Long seems to have little reason for its continued existence. It is loaded with a 29-grain bullet which offers only slightly more velocity than does the Short. There is some inclination among manufacturers to discontinue it, but as of this writing, it is still available.

It's the .22 Long Rifle which is the world's most popular cartridge, available in standard, high-velocity and match loads with varying bullet weights. With the 36-grain hollow-point bullet, a shooter has a fine load for small game which can reach out 100 yards to pot a crow in

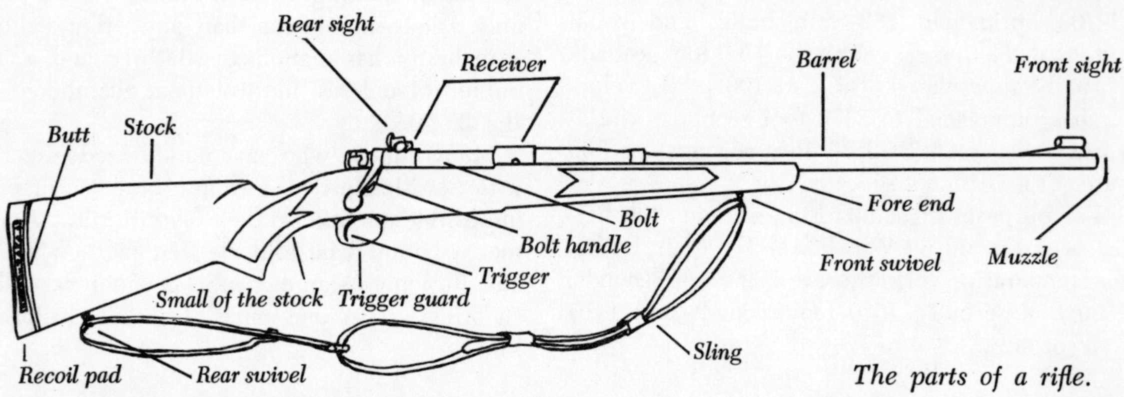

The parts of a rifle.

Ballistics Tables for .22 Caliber Rim-Fire Ammunition

Cartridge	*Bullet Wt. (Grains)*	*Velocity Muzzle*	*Velocity 100 Yds.*	*Energy Muzzle*	*Energy 100 Yds.*	*Mid-Range Trajectory 100 Yds.*
Short	29	1125 fs.	920 fs.	81 ft. lbs.	54	4.3"
Short	27	1155	920	80	51	4.2"
Short (Gallery Ammo.)	15	1710		97		
Long	29	1240	965	99	60	3.8"
Long Rifle	40	1285	1025	147	93	3.4"
Long Rifle	36–37	1315	1020	142	85	3.4"
Long Rifle Shot	Loaded with #12 shot					
Winchester Rim Fire (WRF)	45	1450	1110	210	123	2.7"
Remington Special	45	1450	1110	210	123	2.7"
5 mm Remington Magnum	38	2100	1605	372	217	*
Winchester Magnum Rim Fire	40	2000	1390	355	170	1.6"
Short (Target Load)	29	1045		70		5.6"
Long Rifle (Target Load)	40	1145	975	116	84	4.0"
Long Rifle (Spec. Target Ld.)	40	1120	950	111	80	4.2"
Winchester Automatic	45	1055	930	111	86	4.6"

* With rifle sighted in at 100 yards, point of impact at 150 yards is —4.3 inches. Unless otherwise designated, the above ballistics are based on Winchester tables.

the cornfield. The standard 40-grain bullet load, on the other hand, offers a good all-round load for informal plinking and target shooting at 1335 foot seconds velocity. Match or target loads are made up for serious competition with a 40-grain bullet loaded at about 1100 foot seconds, for greater accuracy. This is the load for the small-bore precision shooter.

Despite repeated warnings, there still exist misconceptions about the .22. Parents sometimes say, "We bought Johnny a 'little' .22," implying that the gun is safe by virtue of its small bore. Nothing could be farther from the truth. Used carelessly, the little bullet is highly dangerous, and in the hands of skilled marksmen, has downed practically every species of game on earth! Few realize its great range, for example. It isn't safe to shoot it over water or among rocks where it might ricochet. Hold a .22 rifle at about 30 degrees from the horizontal and a Long Rifle bullet will travel over a mile!

Plinking is the favorite sport with .22 shooters. This is simply informal shooting at tin cans, wooden blocks, mothballs, balloons or other inexpensive or valueless targets. Bottles, too, are popular, but should not be used as targets unless you plan to clean up the debris afterwards. Perhaps the greatest advantage of the .22 is its light report, making it suitable for indoor shooting with a safe backstop or bullet trap.

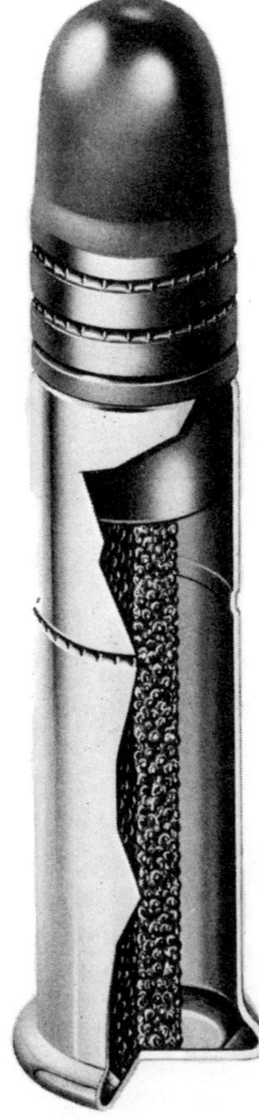

Cutaway view of .22 Long Rifle rim-fire cartridge. (WINCHESTER/WESTERN)

Single-shot .22 bolt-action rifles, excellent "first guns"— Remington Model 580, Marlin Model 101, Glenfield Model 10, Harrington & Richardson Model 750, Winchester Model 310, Stevens Model 73.

How Old Should a Boy Be?

There is no arbitrary age at which a youngster may be given his first .22 with any assurance that he or she will use it properly. Under experienced supervision a young shooter can be started as soon as he or she can understand the mechanics of firing the rifle, including the ability to hold it properly, to sight and to squeeze the trigger. It's foolhardy to allow a youngster to shoot if he is not old enough to hold the gun with ease. Further, a youthful trainee should be impressed with the fact that shooting is serious, adult fun during which pranks or carelessness have no place.

As to the proper age at which to start a young shooter, a booklet issued by the Sporting Arms and Ammunition Manufacturers Institute states the case well: "Chronological age is no yardstick. Some youngsters start at eight, some at fourteen. The real measure is that of responsibility. Will you leave your youngster in the house alone for two or three hours? Would you send him to the grocery store with a shopping list and a ten dollar bill? If the answer is 'Yes,' he is ready for a gun, under proper supervision."

Fathers who have had no shooting experience frequently undertake to train their offspring on the assumption that "common sense" is all that's needed. This can be dangerous, because an untrained adult can't possibly be aware of all accident-inducing situations, nor is he being fair to his son or daughter when there are available free or very inexpensive training courses conducted by experts. Among the finest training programs are those set up by the National Rifle Association, usually through a local sportsmen's club or high school physical education department. So vital and effective are these programs, that many states will not issue a hunting license to older boys and girls if they plan to hunt alone unless they have completed such a course.

The Single-Shot Bolt-Action .22

These are not precision guns, by any means. In fact, some of them have considerable trigger "creep" and others rather heavy trigger pull, but they are reliable, safe and sturdy firearms, ideal for training and as birthday and Christmas gifts. One of these I presented my own son on his twelfth birthday—a Model 67 Winchester. Frankly, I probably chose this particular gun because it was an earlier version which had been *my* first gun.

I'm a firm believer in the single-shot rifle for a first gun, if only to impress upon a young shooter the importance of making the first shot count. Too many shooters, even adults, carrying magazine rifles are careless with the first shot or two because there's more firepower in reserve. This results in sloppy shooting habits and haphazard hunting technique. Knowing that the first—and only—shot must count, has made a deadly marksman out of many a youngster. The safety features of the single-shot rifle, of course, are obvious.

Most must be cocked manually so that a shooter is made much more conscious that his gun *is* loaded and ready to fire—a definite asset during training intervals. I don't like to have youngsters depending upon safety devices for the prevention of accidental discharges. Too

Embodying the traditional style of "western" guns, the Ithaca Model '49 "Saddlegun" is an ideal boy's rifle.

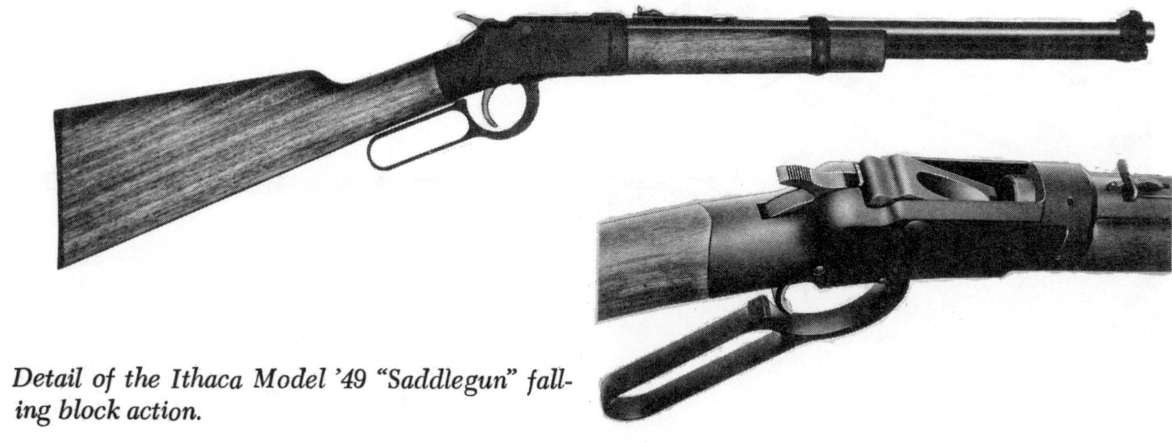

Detail of the Ithaca Model '49 "Saddlegun" falling block action.

Single-Shot Bolt-Action Rim-Fire .22s

Make	*Model*	*Barrel Length*	*Weight (lbs.)*	*Over-all Length*
Harrington & Richardson	750	22″	5	39″
Marlin	101	22″	4½	40″
Marlin	G-10	22″	4½	
Mossberg	320-B	24″	6½	43½″
Remington	580	24″	4¾	42⅜″
Remington	580BR (Youth's)	24″	4¾	41⅜″
Savage	63K	18″	4	36″
Savage/Stevens	73	20″	4¾	38½″
Savage/Stevens	73Y (Youth's)	18″	4¼	35″
Winchester	310	22″	5⅝	39½″

often, during the early stages of their training, they forget whether or not the safety *is* engaged, and just as often the safety mechanism is not obvious enough to a youngster under the tension and excitement of his first days with a gun.

Although my choice of a first gun for my son was a Winchester Model 67, I'm sure that both he and I would have been equally happy with any of the many similar models on the market. These include those listed above. All, unless otherwise indicated, are chambered for the .22 Short, Long and Long Rifle.

The Single-Shot Lever Action

One of the great disappointments of my life was the failure to acquire, back in the late 1920s, a Stevens Favorite single-shot .22. As I recall, it cost somewhat over $4 in those days, about $3 more than I could raise!

During 1971 Savage re-created the Stevens Favorite, an exact replica except for updated metallurgy. Issued in honor of Joshua Stevens, "the father of .22 hunting," the 1971 versions are fast becoming collector's items.

In 1972 Savage then brought out "field grade" versions in the Model 74 Little Favorite, and the Model 72 Crackshot. All three models feature a falling block action activated by a lever.

Another single-shot lever-action .22 is Ithaca's Model 49 "Saddlegun," closely resembling the famed Winchester Model 94. It too has a falling block action, handling all of the .22 rim-fires, with a special model chambered for the .22 Winchester Magnum.

Single-Shot Lever-Action .22s

Make	*Model*	*Barrel Length*	*Weight (lbs.)*	*Over-all Length*
Ithaca	49	18″	5½	34½″
Savage	74	22″ (Rd.)	4½	37″
Savage	72	22″ (Octagon)		37″

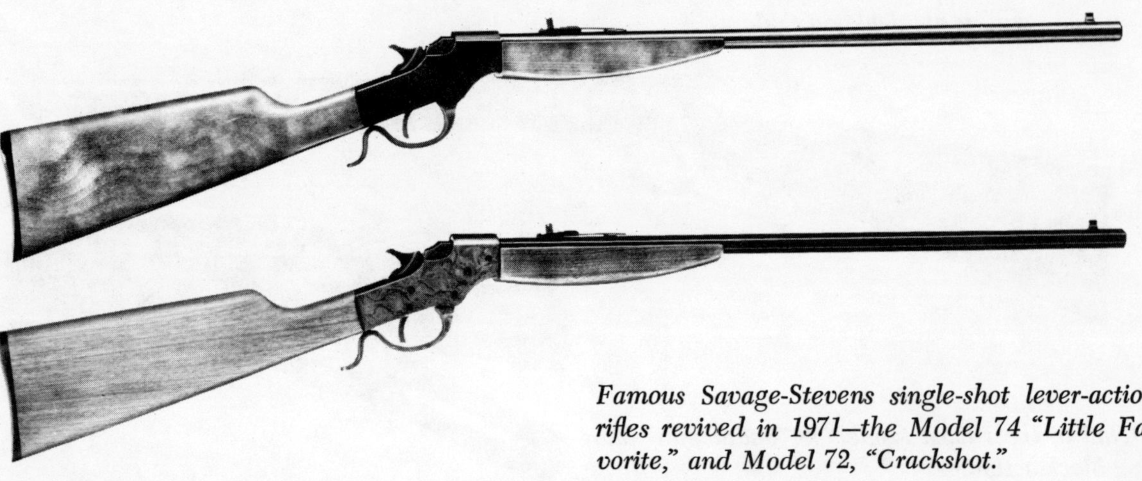

Famous Savage-Stevens single-shot lever-action rifles revived in 1971—the Model 74 "Little Favorite," and Model 72, "Crackshot."

*Bolt Action .22 Clip Repeaters Field Grade or Sporters**

Make	*Model*	*Barrel Length*	*Weight (lbs.)*	*Magazine Capacity*	*Over-all Length*
Browning	T-2	24″	6	5	41¼″
Harrington & Richardson	865	22″	5	5	39″
Marlin	780	22″	6	7	41″
Glenfield (Marlin)	20	22″	5½	7	
Mossberg	340M	18½″	5¼	7	38½″
Mossberg	340K	24″	6½	7	43½″
Mossberg	342K	18″	5	7	38″
Remington	581	24″	4¾	6	42⅜″
Savage	65	20″	5	5	39″
Savage/Anschutz	164	24″	6	5	40⅜″
Savage/Anschutz	54	23″	6¾	5	42″
Savage/Stevens	34	20″	5	5	39″
Winchester	320	22″	5⅜	5	39½″

* Field-grade or sporter-type rifles are designed for hunting, plinking, or informal target shooting, as opposed to more highly refined target models. Field-grade or sporter rifles, however, are accurate far beyond the average shooter's ability as a marksman.

The .22 Bolt-Action Clip Repeater

In appearance the clip repeater is much like the single-shot bolt-action rifle. The clip magazine, a boxlike container, holds five to eight shells, feeding them into the receiver from within the forearm just ahead of the trigger guard. A spring pops the cartridges upward automatically when the bolt is drawn back to eject a fired case. Some models have large capacity clips available, holding up to ten shots. These protrude below the forearm somewhat but do not interfere with shooting. Most such repeaters will handle Short, Long and Long Rifle ammunition in standard and high-speed grades.

You can best take advantage of these rifles by buying one or two extra clips. Reloading the rifle then is just a matter of pulling out an empty clip and slipping in a freshly loaded one—a matter of three to five seconds. Because this type of rifle is capable of a more rapid rate of fire, most models are self-cocking—that is, the hammer and firing pin are drawn back automatically as the bolt is opened or closed. All have manual or automatic safeties.

The field or sporting grades, which are listed below, are excellent for small-game hunting, plinking or informal target shooting. They are, in fact, accurate enough to tax the ability of many experts. They will weigh between five and seven pounds with iron sights. Most of them, too, are tapped and drilled for mounting telescope sights.

The advantages of a repeater are obvious. There's always a second or third shot—or even more—for fast shooting at running game, and the nuisance of reloading after each shot is eliminated. This is the rifle for the shooter who has passed the early stages of training and is ready for the added responsibility and fun that go with shooting a repeater.

Of the repeaters, though, the bolt action is probably the slowest, since operating the bolt requires an awkward motion. The bolt handle must be raised then drawn toward the shooter. As the empty shell is ejected and a fresh load moves into the receiver, the bolt is then thrust forward and turned down into shooting position. This motion is likely to throw off your line of sight somewhat, also, requiring a little more time for resighting for the next shot. With practice, however, you can learn to shoot a bolt action rapidly and efficiently but almost never with the speed and smoothness of other types of repeaters.

Clip magazine, bolt-action repeaters—Remington Model 581.

Glenfield Model 20.

Harrington and Richardson Model 865.

Marlin Model 780.

Mossberg Model 340K.

Mossberg Model 342K carbine.

Savage Model 65.

Savage/Anschutz Model 54 Sporter.

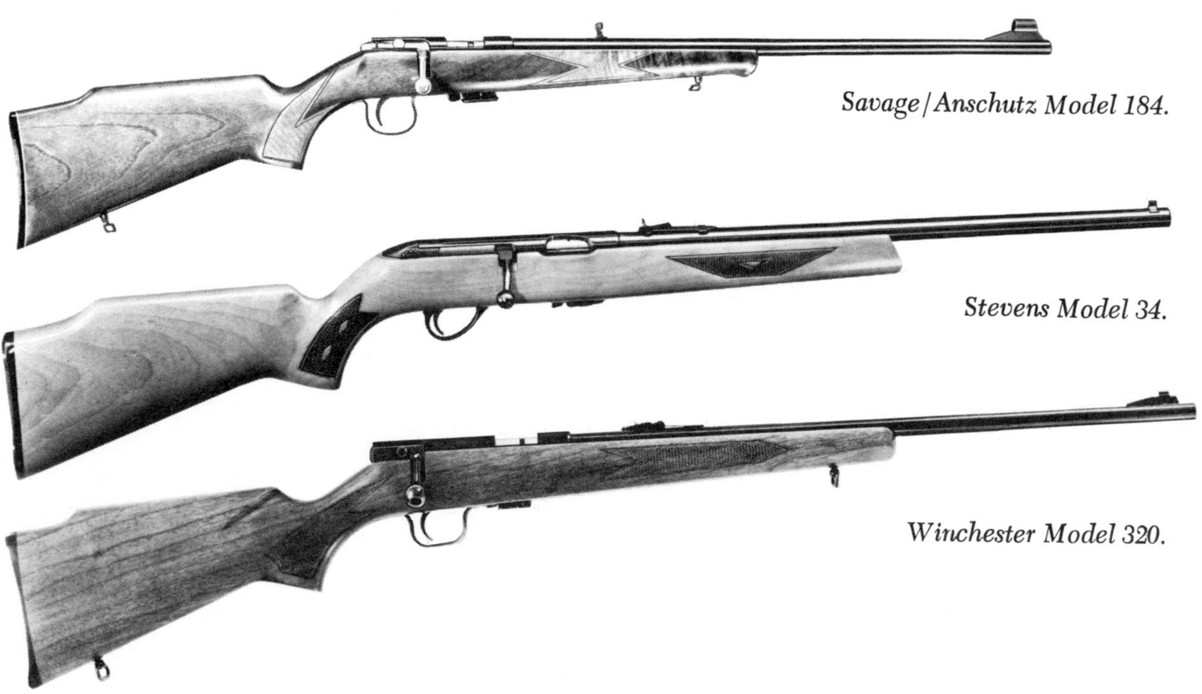

Savage/Anschutz Model 184.

Stevens Model 34.

Winchester Model 320.

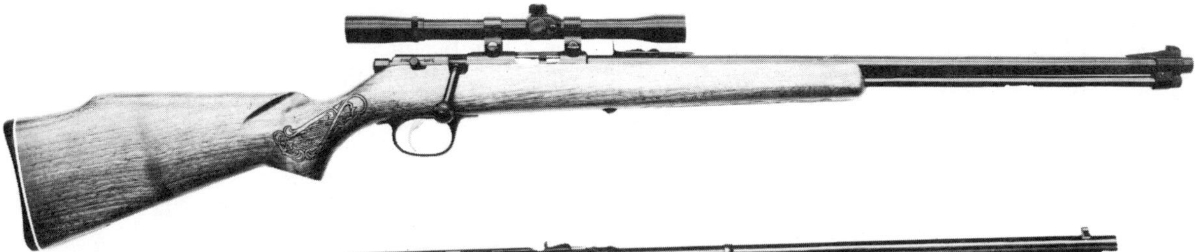

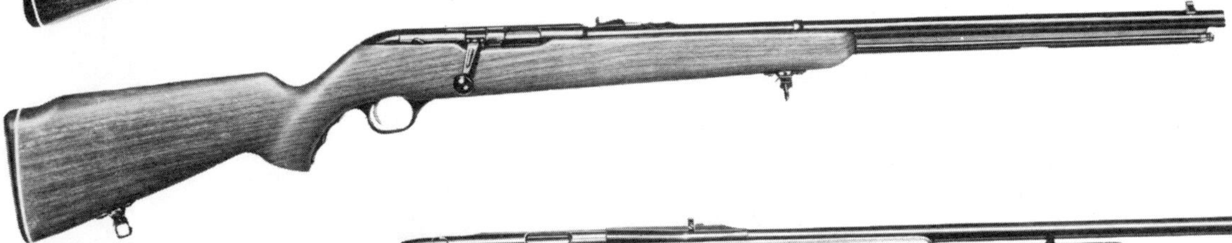

Tubular magazine, bolt-action .22 repeaters with loading capacities up to twenty-five rounds—Marlin Model 781, Mossberg Model 346K, Remington Model 582, Stevens Model 46.

Bolt-Action .22 Tubular Magazine Repeaters

Make	*Model*	*Barrel Length*	*Weight (lbs.)*	*Magazine Capacity**	*Over-all Length*
Marlin	781	22″	6	25 S 19 L 17 LR	41″
Mossberg	346K	24″	6½	25 S 20 L 18 LR	43½″
Remington	582	24″	5	20 S 17 L 14 LR	42⅜″
Savage/Stevens	46	20″	5	22 S 17 S 15 LR	39″

* S, Short; L, Long; LR, Long Rifle

The .22 Bolt-Action Tubular Repeater

The bolt-action tubular magazine repeater is essentially the same as the clip magazine repeater except for adaptations for handling .22s as they are fed into the action from a tubular magazine located under the barrel. Such magazines load from the front or through a small port at one side of the tube, and a coil spring drives the shells into the action as they are fired and ejected. Since the cartridges are loaded "in line" rather than one above the other, magazine capacity depends upon whether you're shooting Short, Long or Long Rifle ammunition. Magazines also vary in length, some holding up to 15 Long Rifle shells and up to 25 Shorts. The great capacity of these rifles makes them favorites among plinkers and informal target shooters, as well as hunters of fast-moving small game.

.22 Lever-Action Tubular Magazine Rifles

The lever-action .22 rifle is a popular choice for a number of reasons, the most prominent of which is probably the speed and ease with which a lever-action rifle can be operated. It's among the fastest, out-gunned only by the pump or slide action—and some shooters will question this! Most of the new .22 lever-action rifles are of the

Lever-Action .22 Tubular Magazine Repeaters

Make	*Model*	*Barrel Length*	*Weight (lbs.)*	*Magazine Capacity*	*Over-all Length*
Browning	BL-22	20″	5	22 S 17 L 15 LR	36¾″
Marlin	39-D	20½″	5¾	21 S 16 L 15 LR	36½″
Mossberg	402	20″	4¾	18 S 15 L 13 LR	36½″
Winchester	150	20½″	5	21 S 17 L 15 LR	39″
Winchester	250	20½″	5	21 S 17 L 15 LR	39″
Winchester	9422	20½″	6½	21 S 17 L 15 LR	37⅛″

Speed of action and large-capacity magazines make these lever-action models favorites as "plinkers"—Marlin Model 39D, Mossberg Model 402, Winchester Model 250, Winchester Model 150, Winchester Model 9422, a .22 version of the famed Model 94.

"short throw" type, meaning that the lever can be worked in some cases, without removing the right hand's complete grip from the gun. Flipping the lever downward and back up again to eject and reload is a natural motion for either right- or left-handed shooters and doing this creates a minimum of disturbance of the general sight alignment. The lever-action rifle is more compact and more easily carried than the bolt-action type. Quite often, too, it is lighter.

Designing rifles to look like the famed Winchester Model 94 was a basic approach to gun sales during the 1960s and continues into the 1970s. Browning produced its Model BL-22 .22-caliber, lever-action tubular magazine rifle, a handsome and fun-to-shoot little gun. And since John M. Browning, then working for Winchester, levised the Model 94 action, Browning certainly cannot be criticized for capitalizing on the 94's popularity. Its BL-22 is a superb .22.

Winchester, however, early in 1972, went one step further. It reproduced the Model 94 in .22 caliber (and in .22 Magnum). When I first saw the M94 in 30/30 caliber side by side with the new 9422, I couldn't tell which was which. I have a penchant for old-time guns. That was enough to draw me to the 9422. Following a series of test-firings, in the field and in the Winchester indoor test range, I came to the conclusion that the little 9422 Winchester is probably the finest field-grade or sporter-type .22 ever built. I rarely recommend a specific gun to a reader, but for a shooter beyond the raw-beginner stage, I consider the Winchester 9422 the ultimate in .22 rifles for plinking, hunting or informal target shooting.

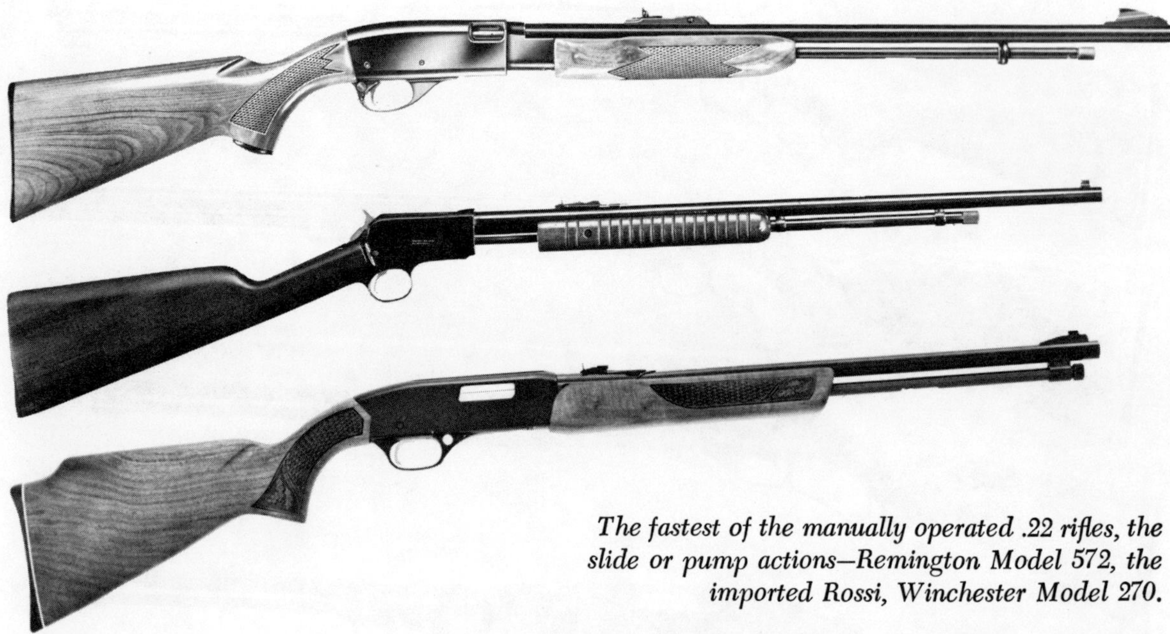

The fastest of the manually operated .22 rifles, the slide or pump actions—Remington Model 572, the imported Rossi, Winchester Model 270.

Slide-Action .22 Rifles

Make	*Model*	*Barrel Length*	*Weight (lbs.)*	*Magazine Capacity*	*Over-all Length*
High Standard	8006	24″	5½		41¾″
Remington	572-A	24″	5½	20 S 17 L 14 LR	42″
Rossi	Gallery		5¾	20 S 16 L 14 LR	
Winchester	270	20½″	5	21 S 17 L 15 LR	39″

Pump, Slide or "Trombone" Action .22s

These are all the same rifle and the names derive from the sliding forearm which, when pulled back, ejects the fired shell and cocks the rifle. Pushing the forearm forward, back into firing position, feeds another shell into the chamber. It's a toss-up as to whether the slide action or the "short throw" lever action is the fastest of the manually operated rifles. Like flipping the lever action, sliding the forearm back and forth is a natural motion for both right- and left-handed shooters and can be effected with speed that would lead a nearby observer to think that the shooter is firing an automatic. Since all slide-action .22s have tubular magazines of considerable capacity, a skilled rifleman can lay down a deadly barrage. It's possible, too, to keep the sights roughly "on target" while working the action, thereby increasing still further the gun's rapidity of effective fire.

The Automatic .22 Rifle

This is not a true automatic rifle, but rather a self-loading or semi-automatic gun which fires one shot with each pull of the trigger, with the action ejecting the empty shell and loading a fresh one into the firing chamber and, at the same time, cocking the rifle—all without any effort on the part of the shooter except pulling the trigger! A fully automatic gun is a military or police machine gun that continues to fire as long as the trigger is held back and the magazine contains ammunition.

The automatic—the name persists, so I'll use it

The "automatics" with clip magazines fire as rapidly as the trigger can be pulled. They are—Marlin Model 989, Mossberg Model 350K, Mossberg Model 352K, Remington Model 77, Ruger 10/22 with ten-shot rotary magazine.

Clip Magazine .22 "Automatics"

Make	*Model*	*Barrel Length*	*Weight (lbs.)*	*Magazine Capacity*	*Over-all Length*
Marlin	989M2	18″	4½	7	37″
Mossberg	352K	18½″	5	7	38″
Mossberg	350K	23½″	6	7	43½″
Remington	77	19⅝″	4	5	38½″
Ruger	10/22	18½″	5	10 (Rotary Magazine)	37″

Tubular Magazine .22 Automatics

Make	*Model*	*Barrel Length*	*Weight (lbs.)*	*Magazine Capacity*	*Over-all Length*
Browning	Auto	19¼″ (LR)	4¾	11 (LR)*	37″ (LR)
Browning	Auto	22¼″ (S)	4¾	16 (S)*	40″ (S)
Colt	Courier			15	
Colt	Colteer			15	
Colt	Stagecoach			13	
High Standard	8005	22¼″	5½	21	42¾″
High Standard	8002	18¼″	5½	21	38½″
Marlin	49DL	22″	5½	19 LR	40½″
Marlin	99C	22″	5½	19 LR	40½″
Marlin	99M1	18″	4½	9 LR	37″
Mossberg	430	24″	6¼	18 LR	43½″
Mossberg	432	20″	6	15 LR	39½″
Mossberg	351C	18½″	5½	15 LR*	38½″
Mossberg	351K	24″	6	15 LR*	43″
Remington	66MB	19⅝″	4	14 LR*	38½″
Remington	66AB	19⅝″	4	14 LR*	38½″
Remington	552	23″	5¾	20 S 17 L 15 LR	42″
Remington	552C	21″	5¾	20 S 17 L 15 LR	40″
Savage	90	16½″	5¾	10 LR	37½″
Savage	60	20″	6	15 LR	40½″
Savage	88	20″	5¾	15 LR	40½″
Winchester	290	20½″	5	17 L 15 LR	39″
Winchester	190	20½″	5	17 L 15 LR	39″

* Tubular magazine located in butt stock.

Large magazine capacity and rapid fire are combined in the tubular magazine "automatics."

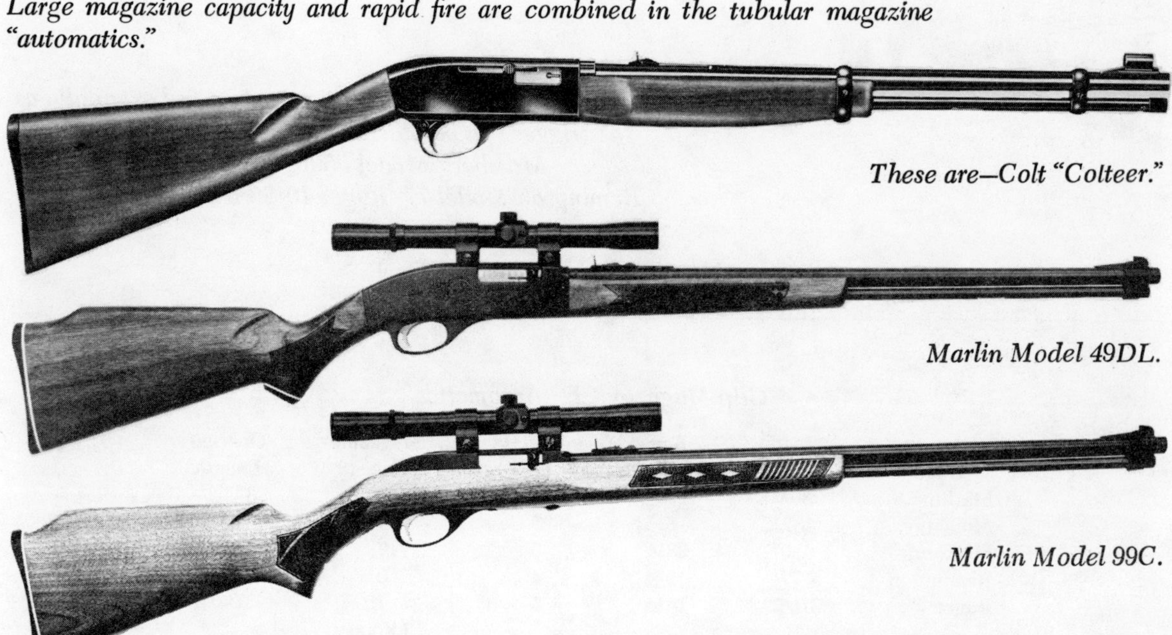

These are—Colt "Colteer."

Marlin Model 49DL.

Marlin Model 99C.

Mossberg Model 351K with stock-loading magazine.

Mossberg Model 430.

Mossberg Model 351C, also a stock loader.

Remington 552.

Remington Model 66.

Savage Model 60.

Stevens Model 88.

Winchester Model 290.

Winchester Model 190.

too—is the fastest of the sportsmen's firearms—and quite often the most wasteful, except in the hands of a cool and skilled rifleman. The beginner is apt to be careless about sighting the first shot. This is not a condemnation of the automatic. I'm simply pointing out that with such reserve firepower there is a strong temptation to spray the general target area in the hope of a hit.

Its greatest advantage, of course, is that a shooter can keep pouring shots at a target without moving the sights, or his finger from the trigger.

Several models are available with five- to seven-shot clip magazines, while the Ruger boasts a ten-shot rotary magazine. A still greater variety of "automatics" feature large-capacity tubular feeds.

.22 Target Rifles

Target rifles can be used for hunting or plinking, of course, but this would be like taking a leisurely drive on back roads in a supercharged racing car. These rifles are precision-built shooting machines of extreme accuracy with weights ranging from eight to eleven pounds—certainly not guns to be toted merrily over hill and dale in quest of game or tin cans to puncture. While weight would be a burden in a hunting rifle it helps a shooter to hold more steadily on the target range.

All .22 target rifles are either single-shot or clip magazine models designed to handle Long Rifle match or specially loaded ammunition in order to utilize the utmost accuracy built into these guns. Invariably they are bolt-action rifles, proven the most accurate—and such guns have been known to place fifty shots within a three-quarter-inch group at 50 yards! Actions are beautifully smooth and triggers have no creep or slack. Some have adjustable triggers with pulls as light as three pounds as compared to the four- to six-pound pull found on standard rifle triggers.

Such guns are often used for bench-rest shooting, firing being done from a sitting position at a specially constructed bench or table with the rifle's forearm resting in a padded fork or stand, minimizing as much as possible the element of human error in sighting. Target rifles used for bench-rest shooting are often "tuned up" by their owners and may have such refinements as heavy target-type stocks, oversized barrels, thick forearms, full pistol grips, thumb rest, high comb and special no-slip butt plates. Frequently the

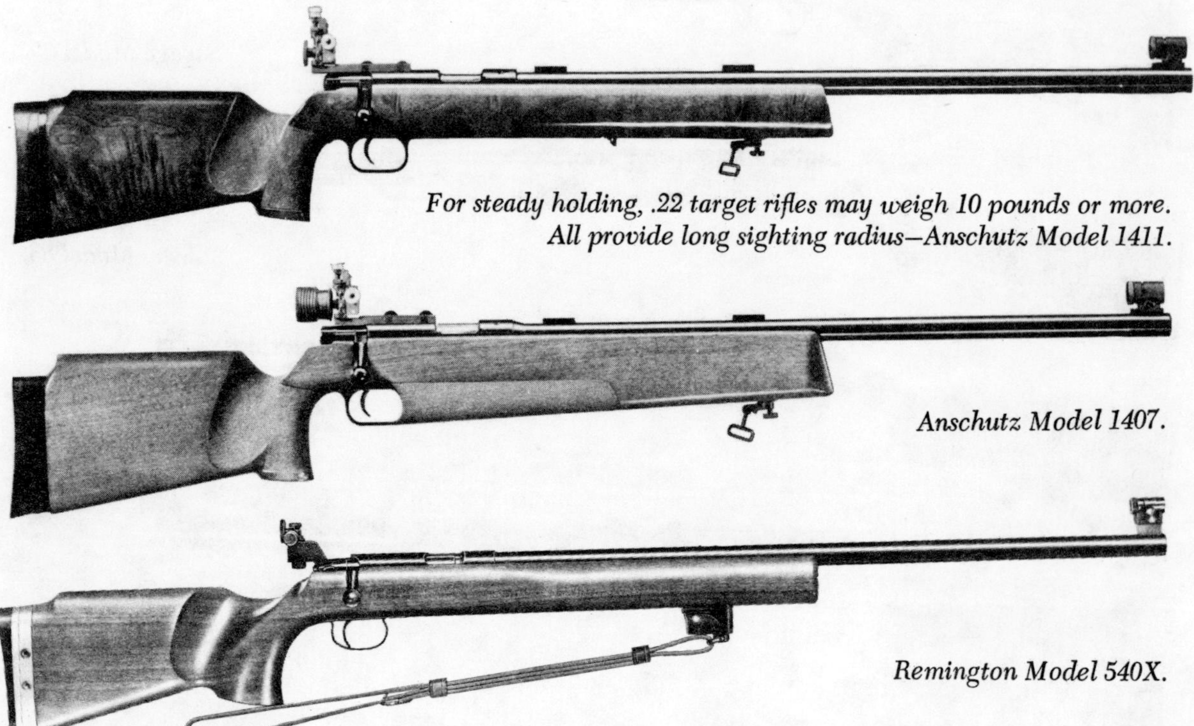

For steady holding, .22 target rifles may weigh 10 pounds or more. All provide long sighting radius—Anschutz Model 1411.

Anschutz Model 1407.

Remington Model 540X.

Mossberg Model 340B.

Mossberg Model 144LS.

Mossberg 320B, a beginner's target rifle.

Savage/Anschutz Model 64-S.

Savage/Anschutz Mark 10-D.

Winchester Model 52 standard weight.

Winchester Model 52 heavy.

.22 Caliber Target Rifles

Makes	Model	Barrel Length	Weight (lbs.)	Magazine Capacity	Over-all Length
Mossberg	144LS	26″	8	7 (Clip)	43″
Mossberg	340B	24″	6½	7 (Clip)	43½″
Mossberg	320B	24″	6½	Single Shot	43½″
Remington	540X	26″	8	Single Shot	43½–47″
Remington	40-XB	28″	10¾ (Standard)	Single Shot	47″
Remington	40-XB	28″	12 (Heavy)	Single Shot	47″
Savage/Anschutz	Mark 10	26″	8½	Single Shot	44″
Savage/Anschutz	64	26″	7¾	Single Shot	44″
Savage	1407 Match 54	26″	10	Single Shot	44½″
Savage	1411 Match 54	27½″	11	Single Shot	46″
Winchester	52D (Standard)	28″	9¾	Single Shot	46″
Winchester	52D (Heavy)	28″	11	Single Shot	46″

forward sling swivel is adjustable. Many are custom-made.

High-grade peep sights are often standard equipment, but target rifles are also offered without sights so that a shooter may mount his own pet style. These sights are so critical that adjusting them one "click" or notch will change the bullet's point of impact only ¼ inch at 100 yards. For some matches and often for bench-rest shooting, telescope sights are added. Both American and imported target rifles are likely to be expensive, as compared to the field grades, but mass production methods of American firms have made possible precision target rifles that are moderately priced and more than adequate for any shooting but the most highly competitive international matches. A few models are available in lighter weight smaller versions for Boy Scout and youth training as well as competitions.

The Free Rifle

Some shooting matches permit the use of almost any type of .22 with few restrictions as to design or accessories. Here you see the "free rifle," actually a manually operated shooting machine. Originated in Europe, but now made by Savage, Remington and Winchester, the free rifle has such embellishments as adjustable stocks, special forearm grips, fitted combs, hand-fitting pistol grips that include a thumb hole for a firmer hold and adjustable trigger pull. The inherent accuracy of these rifles far outdistances the ability of most rifle shooters.

Using one of the first ten off the assembly line at Winchester in 1969, my son fired a .35″ ten-shot group at 50 yards with a Model 52 International Match. At that time, Bill's experience had been limited to informal plinking and target shooting with field-grade .22'!

Remington's Model 1413 Super Match 54 is also available in the 7.62 NATO and .30/06 calibers for "big bore" matches.

The Super .22s

These are the "souped up" .22s which allow a shooter to reach out 50 or more yards beyond the normal range of the .22 Long Rifle. While velocities and energy considerably overshadow those of the regular .22s, there is little perceptible recoil from these, and the report, while somewhat louder, is far from objectionable. Essentially these offer a flatter-shooting bullet up to 100 yards or so. Beyond that, the trajectory falls off rather rapidly.

For small-game hunting or pest shooting, they pack two to three times the wallop of the Long Rifle .22, at the muzzle and at 100 yards or more.

In choosing a rifle for these loads, bear in mind that the .22 Winchester Rim-Fire and the .22 Remington Special can be fired in a rifle chambered for the .22 Winchester Magnum, but not conversely!

These "free rifles" are precision shooting machines—Anschutz Model 1413, Remington International Match, Winchester International Match Model 52.

Rifles Chambered for Winchester .22 Magnum Rim-Fire Ammunition

Make	*Model*	*Magazine Capacity*	*Type of Magazine*	*Action*	*Barrel Length*	*Weight (lbs.)*
Ithaca	49	Single Shot		Lever	18″	5½
Marlin	783	13	Tubular	Bolt	22″	6
Marlin	782	7	Clip	Bolt	22″	6
Mossberg	640M	5	Clip	Bolt	20″	6
Mossberg	640K	5	Clip	Bolt	24″	6
Remington (5 mm Rem)	591	5	Clip	Bolt	24″	5
Remington (5 mm Rem)	592	11	Tubular	Bolt	24″	5½
Savage	63KM	Single Shot		Bolt	18″	4
Savage	65M	5	Clip	Bolt	20″	5
Savage	34M	5	Clip	Bolt	20″	5
Savage/Anschutz	164M	4	Clip	Bolt	24″	6
Winchester	9422	11	Tubular	Lever	20½″	6½

NOTE: These rifles are not pictured since their exact counterparts in regular .22 calibers have been included in this chapter.

Chapter III

VARMINTER RIFLES

Generally speaking these are rifles suitable for one-shot kills at long ranges. The name "Varminter" derives from "varmint," of course—a derivative of "vermin." Varmint hunting can be assessed as target shooting at estimated ranges at live, elusive, often difficult to approach game. The ultimate in such sport requires a knowledge of the quarry's habits, shooting ability and understanding of the ballistic behavior of various calibers and loads.

One shooter's opinion of what makes a good varminter rifle is likely to differ considerably from another's, particularly if they live and hunt in different parts of the country. The westerner, with millions of acres of wild uninhabited land, may favor the super-high-velocity loads despite their loud reports. The easterner, confined to more limited areas of hunting such as pastureland where farmers may object to the noise of the heavier guns, will favor lighter loads with a less prominent report.

Some "inner sanctum" varmint shooters insist that the only suitable varminter rifle is custom-made—probably built around an F.N. (Fabrique Nationale, Belgium) action with a barrel somewhat heavier than those of regular hunting rifles. Heavy barrels, they say—and they're probably correct—make for greater consistent accuracy which, for ultra varmint shooting requires one-inch groups at one hundred yards. To this gun they're likely to add a custom-made stock, "form-fit" in every sense. A gunsmith may tinker the trigger seat, so that a light touch of the finger will set it off without nudging the sights off the target. One of the fine eight- to twelve-power Unertl, Lyman or Weaver scopes will be set atop the rig. This is the ultimate in varminter rifles, really a high-grade target rifle modified for field use.

It stands to reason, of course, that a finely honed shooting machine is going to outshine a standard factory field-grade rifle when it comes to long-range, precision shooting. However, such fine rifles are not inexpensive.

If financial limitations restrict you to a factory-produced varminter, or even to a field-grade hunting rifle, you can enjoy varmint hunting by choosing a rifle chambered for the best possible varminter load.

This rules out the .22 rim-fires, with the possible exception of the .22 Winchester Magnum and the .22 Remington Special, either suitable up to about 150 yards. However, these have limited application.

A true varmint load should be as flat-shooting as possible up to 300 yards or more. Ballistics tables will enlighten you on this point. The load should also resist the effects of wind, which causes long-range bullets to drift off course. High velocity helps minimize much of this problem, since the faster a bullet travels a given distance, the less time the wind has to force it off its normal trajectory. Also vital is the bullet's impact, its ability to kill quickly, with one shot. Velocity provides energy, combined with the bullet's weight. But bullet design is important too. Varminter loads are provided with bullets that strike with maximum force, dissipating most of their energy *in* the target.

Calibers which qualify as varminter loads are fairly numerous but keep in mind that the choice should be governed by the area in which it will be used. Don't pick a .22 Winchester Magnum, for example, for a long-range coyote load. By the same token, the .25/06 Remington may be out of place in settled countryside.

Below are listed calibers which qualify, in varying degrees, as varminter loads, though not necessarily in all bullet weights. Ballistics details of these are included in the next chapter.

.22 Winchester Magnum	.243 Winchester
.22 Remington Special	.25/06 Remington
.17 Remington	.257 Weatherby
.222 Remington	6.5 Remington Magnum
.22-250 Remington	.264 Winchester
.223 Remington	.270 Winchester
.224 Weatherby	.270 Weatherby Magnum
.225 Winchester	.280 Remington
6 mm Remington	.284 Winchester
.240 Weatherby	.30/06 Springfield

New in 1971, the center-fire .17 Remington is loaded with a 25-grain hollow-point bullet, actual diameter .1725 inches, with a muzzle velocity of 4020 foot seconds, our fastest commercially loaded ammunition. The .17 caliber is not entirely new. It reigned first as a necked-down version of the Winchester .218 Bee, then later and more successfully in cases necked down from various .222s. Remington's version is necked down from its .223 but with the shoulder moved back to provide a long case neck.

With a rifle sighted in for 200 yards, its mid-range trajectory is a mere +1.2 inches. At 300 yards it has fallen only 6.3 inches.

At 100 yards its velocity is still 3290 foot seconds; at 200 yards, 2630; at 300 yards, 2060.

Energy is similarly impressive, 600 foot pounds at 100 yards; 380 at 200; and 230 at 300. There is certainly little doubt about the little .17 Remington qualifying as a varminter load. Best of all, for shooters in settled areas, its report is merely a snappy "splat!"

A heftier load is the .222 Remington with a 50-grain hollow-point bullet propelled at a muzzle velocity of 3200 foot seconds, but since little killing is done at the muzzle, it's the 340-pound energy quota at 300 yards that helps qualify it as an effective varminter. Its trajectory, too, is quite flat, 2.5 inches at 100 yards.

The .223 Remington, with a 55-grain bullet, has a slightly flatter trajectory, somewhat more velocity, and substantially more energy. This is the case from which the .17 Remington evolved.

Among the popular, commercially loaded "fodders," I would consider the .22-250 Remington the No. 2 varminter load. This handles a 55-grain bullet, leaving the muzzle at 3810 foot seconds, and still wheeling along at 2320 foot seconds at 300 yards. As for energy, its impact at 300 yards is almost equal to that of the .30/30! Sighted in for 200 yards, its mid-range trajectory is only 1.6 inches.

Another superb varminter load is the .224 Weatherby, with a choice of 50- or 55-grain expanding-type bullets. Ballistics between the two vary only slightly. Mid-range trajectory, sighted in for 200 yards, is 1.7 inches. Energy at 300 yards is 509 and 629 foot pounds respectively.

Almost identical in performance is the .225 Winchester. In fact, fired side by side in similar rifles, it would take an expert with three degrees in physics to tell one from the other.

With the 6 mm Remington, we venture among the "big guns" of the varminter field. With a choice of 80-grain bullets, leaving the muzzle at 3540 foot seconds, impact at 300 yards is more than 1000 foot pounds! Sighted in at 200 yards, trajectory is +1.3 inches at 100 yards, and down 6 inches at 300.

Another 6 mm whopper is the Weatherby .240 Magnum. Available with 70-, 87- or 100-grain expanding-type bullets, this is probably the most powerful, flattest-shooting 6 mm load. Weatherby claims this, at least. And ballistics tables seem to substantiate the claim.

When I first started dabbling in .22s, the .257 Roberts was then a "hot" load. Regrettably, the .257 reached its zenith and waned during my shooting years. However, in recent years, California's Roy Weatherby managed to keep a limited interest alive in this caliber by developing his .257 Magnum. Whether or not it is a true varminter load is open to question, but certainly it qualifies as a combination varminter/hunting load.

It offers a choice of 87-, 100- or 117-grain bullets, at muzzle velocities ranging from 3825 to 3300 foot seconds respectively. It's the 100-grain bullet, however, that's likely to catch the eye of the varminter shooter. Initial velocity is 3555 foot seconds, which eventually powers a 1388-foot-pounds blow at 300 yards, with a mid-range trajectory of 4.4 inches when sighted in at 300 yards. For an "old-timer" this is action requiring little sales pitch!

Given a choice among all of the varminter loads, I would lean heavily toward the .25/06 Remington. This is not a load for plinking in the suburbs. It speaks with authority. The "06," of course, refers to the case, that of the .30/06, necked down to .25. The .30/06 was never a

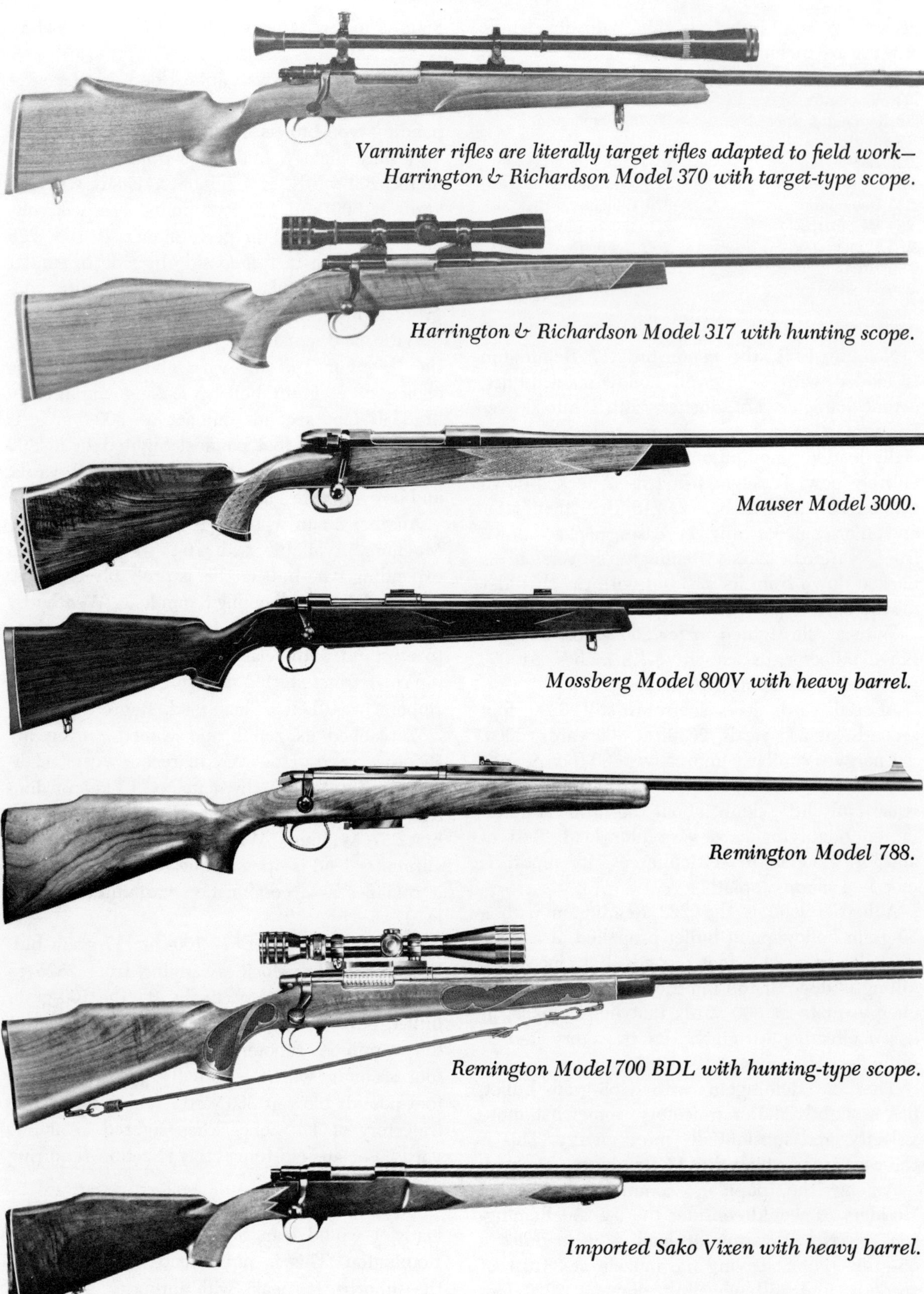

Varminter rifles are literally target rifles adapted to field work—Harrington & Richardson Model 370 with target-type scope.

Harrington & Richardson Model 317 with hunting scope.

Mauser Model 3000.

Mossberg Model 800V with heavy barrel.

Remington Model 788.

Remington Model 700 BDL with hunting-type scope.

Imported Sako Vixen with heavy barrel.

Savage Model 340 in .222 caliber.

Recently introduced Savage Model 110-D.

Winchester Model 760.

Winchester's versatile Model 70 adapted to varminter specifications.

gentle load, at either end of the rifle. Propelling a .25-caliber bullet, it is still a man's gun.

I recall my Border Patrol days in El Paso when we had to qualify with .30/06 Springfields. The Springfield in those days had a pump handle for a stock, one that cracked cheekbones, lacerated shoulders and splintered the collarbones of unwary shooters. Since then the innocuous letters "06" have meant pain to me.

With my first shot at the Winchester range, I flinched as I pulled the trigger of a new Model 70, chambered for the .25/06. The target revealed a flyer—a wild shot. But my shoulder was intact, my cheekbone unbruised. I settled down to some serious shooting, my fears dispelled.

Lest you are puzzled about my discussing the .25/06 *Remington* while shooting at the *Winchester* range, allow me to explain that major gun companies recognize each other's triumphs. Remington's .25/06 was one of these recognitions by Winchester, just as Remington's recognition of Winchester's .270 resulted in the chambering of Remingtons for a Winchester load.

At any rate, targeting the .25/06 through a Winchester Model 70 proved a delight. I shot no record scores, came up with no astonishing groups. But I fell in love with the .25/06! Following an hour on the shooting range, ballistics are a dull subject, but they help prove a point. Propelling a 90-grain expanding-type bullet, this load leaves the muzzle at 3500 foot seconds. At 300 yards, it is still traveling at better than 2400 foot seconds. And at a 300-yard point of impact, it strikes with the force of 1170 foot pounds!

Combine this velocity and energy quotient with 1.8-inch trajectory when sighted in at 200 yards (4.7 inches at 300 yards) and you have close to the ultimate in a varminter load.

I have cited the Winchester Model 70 simply because this was the rifle used in my own testing of the .25/06. However, don't overlook the Remington 700 BDL, one of several others chambered for the .25/06.

Other calibers might qualify as varminter loads—the 6.5 Remington, .264 Winchester, .270 Winchester, .270 Weatherby Magnum, .280 Remington, .284 Winchester and the .30/06 Springfield. Ballistics for these border on the varminter qualifications. And if you are restricted to one rifle for all-round use, these are worthy of consideration. You may have to hold a little higher at long ranges, and they may prove somewhat noisy in pastoral neighborhoods, but they will do the job. What's more, you can use them on your annual deer, bear, elk or antelope hunt.

Not all of us can afford to shoot a .25/06 solely at woodchucks. For this reason I have included some of the borderline calibers under the varminter classification. This is true, too, of the rifles themselves. True varminter rifles, beautiful shooting machines that they are, are expensive. With a little extra stalking skill, careful sighting and a steady squeeze on the trigger, you can convert field-grade hunting rifles into precision varminters!

Varminter Rifles

Make	*Model*	*Calibers Available*
Browning		.222, .22–250, .243, .270, .30/06, .308, 7 mm
Sako	Vixen*	.222, .223
Sako	Forester	.22–250, .243, .308, .25/06, .264, .270, .30/06, 7 mm Magnum
F. N. Mauser		.243, .270, .308, .30/06, .264, 7 mm
H & R	300	.22–250, .243, .270, .30/06, .308, 7 mm
H & R	317*	.17 Remington, .222, .223
H & R	370*	.22–250, .243, 6 mm
Ithaca	LSA55	.22–250, .243, .308
Ithaca	LSA65	.270, .30/06
Mauser	3000	.243, .270, .308, .30/06, 7 mm
Mauser	4000*	.222, .223
Mauser	660	.30/06, .308, .270, .243
Mossberg	810	.30/06
Mossberg	800	.308, .243, .22–150
Mossberg	800VT*	243, .22–150
Remington	788*	.222, .22–250, 6 mm, .243, .308
Remington	700	.17 Remington, .22–250, .222, 6 mm, .243, .25/06
Remington	700BDL*	.222, .223, .22–150, 6 mm, .243, .25/06
Savage	110D*	.30/06, .243, .270, .25/06, 7 mm
Savage	340*	.222
Smith & Wesson	A	.270, .30/06, .308, .243, 7 mm, .22–150
Smith & Wesson	B	.270, .30/06, .308, .243
Weatherby	Varmint-master*	.224, .22–250†
Weatherby		.240 Magnum†
Weatherby		.257 Magnum†
Weatherby		.270 Magnum†
Weatherby		7 mm Magnum†
Weatherby	Mark V	.30/06†
Winchester	70	.225, .243, .270, .308, .30/06, .222, .22–250, .25/06, .264
Winchester	70A*	.22–250, .222, .243, .270, .308, .30/06, 7 mm Magnum, .25/06, .264 Magnum, .300 Magnum
Winchester	670	.243, .30/06

* Specifically suggested by manufacturer as a varminter rifle.

† Except for .22-250 and .30/06, these are special Weatherby calibers designed for use in Weatherby rifles only.

With knowledge that comes from experience, chances are you can reload ammunition that will outperform factory loads in some instances. Sometimes, loading a bullet slightly heavier than the factory missile, *ahead of a suitable powder charge*, will cut velocity somewhat but may well increase energy output and accuracy. However, don't become hypnotized by the velocity syndrome, whether you reload or shoot factory fodder. All loads have a "twilight zone" where most accuracy, greatest energy and suitable velocity combine to form the best load. This can be determined only by you, through trial and error, *in your own rifle.*

Varminter Scopes

If you plan to use your varminter rifle as a dual-purpose gun—for deer, elk, bear, antelope and varminter shooting—consider mounting a variable-power scope sight. These are available in models that adjust 2½–4 power up to 10 and 12 power. Thus, in one instrument, you will have an excellent hunting sight, as well as a more than adequate varminter long-range scope.

To use iron sights for varminter shooting is to handicap yourself to the extent that you'll lose interest in the sport. After all, at 200 yards, a woodchuck is a mighty small critter, so small, in fact, that the front sight bead will hide him completely.

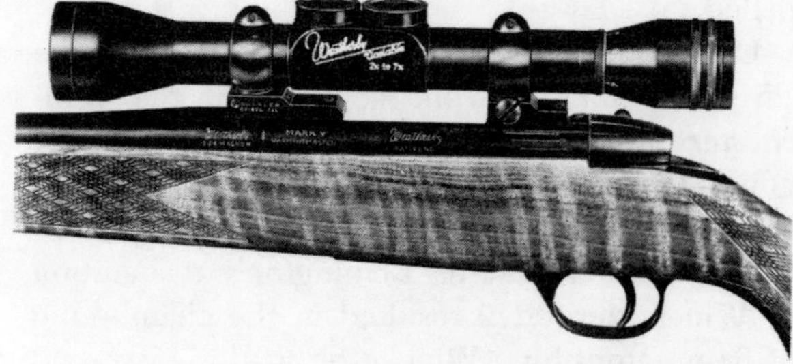

The "eyes" of a varminter rifle—a Weatherby Imperial 2X–7X variable power scope mounted on a Weatherby .224 Varmintmaster with Buehler mounts.

Chapter IV

CENTER-FIRE RIFLE AMMUNITION

While the previous chapter discussed center-fire ammunition more or less suited to a specialized type of hunting, this section will point out the fascinating aspects of the wide range of calibers and loads available for *all* types of shooting, except the small-bore .22s. Of the nearly one hundred commercially loaded calibers on the market, all somewhat overlap their neighbors so that it's impossible to say, for example, "this load is just right for moose hunting and this one is best suited for woodchucks." There are as many opinions among shooters as there are loads.

This may seem like double-talk, but consider the .30/06 to prove a point. Load it with a 110-grain bullet at 3370 foot seconds and it's a pretty fair ammunition for a long-range varmint shooting—not the best perhaps, but certainly suitable. However, load that same case with a 180-grain soft-nose or open-point bullet at 2700 foot seconds, and you have potent medicine for moose. Yet both can be fired from the same rifle.

In the general field of center-fire ammunition (so named because the primer is located in the center of the shell base) there is a seemingly endless variety of shooting possibilities. Velocities, for example, range from as little as 1460 foot seconds in the .25/20 Winchester—scarcely outrunning the peewee .22 rim-fire—up to the phenomenal .17 Remington's 4020 foot seconds.

Energy variations are equally great. Again citing the .25/20, its energy quotient at 100 yards is a mere 265 foot pounds. Compare this to the walloping .460 Weatherby Magnum with its 6025 foot pounds impact at the same range.

To the ingredients puzzling a would-be shooter, add the factors of recoil, type of action, weight of gun and shooting costs. It's no wonder that making a choice can be bewildering.

To make matters worse, even the experts disagree. Many agree that there may be an ideal rifle and load for the average shooter who wants only to hunt deer, for instance, but they can't get together on a *particular* rifle and caliber. And this is only natural, for what it boils down to is that a shooter must decide for himself after a thorough study of *his own needs*.

Perhaps you're thinking, "This guy isn't going to be much help!" If you're considering your first center-fire rifle, chances are you'll have to make your decision much as I made mine more than twenty-five years ago. I read what the experts had to say; I studied ballistic charts until I could quote shooting statistics more accurately than the American League standings of the day. I talked with shooting friends and tried some of their guns. I haunted sporting goods stores. My den was knee deep in catalogs. Finally I boiled the choice down to three calibers, the 7 mm, .270 Winchester and the .30/06. I wanted a rifle that would knock out woodchucks across a wide pasture and I wanted to hunt deer with it. Too, I had dreams of bigger game, possibly bear, moose or elk and I didn't know when I could buy a second rifle—for this was during the Great Depression. I finally chose the .270, and I've never regretted the choice. Someone else in similar circumstances might have picked the .30/06 or 7 mm with equally happy outcome.

Shooting magazines carry considerable information on "wildcat" cartridges—"homemade" loads not available over the counter and usually developed by reloaders and gunsmiths from standard cases. Many of today's outstanding commercial loads were once wildcats—the .17 Remington, for example, and the .25/06. As long as we have experts who are dissatisfied with today's loads, we'll have continued improvements in ammunition via the wildcat route. However, for the average shooter, do-it-yourself wildcat loads are impossible. These require considerable technical know-how and skill as a gunsmith. Wildcat loads and rifles can be purchased, of course, but usually a shooter will find factory loads more than adequate.

New guns, as they become available, are passed on to several of the country's shooting experts, who then try them out on the target range and in hunting country. Usually, their reports, made public in shooting publications, are enthusiastic and justifiably so, for the modern high-power rifle is rarely a failure *at the job for which it was designed.* It's rare indeed, though, that such trials and field testing bring forth an "all-round" gun.

The "All-Round" Rifle

Such a rifle is called upon to take a variety of game—deer, bear, elk, antelope, mountain sheep or moose—a big order for any rifle. And it may have to double as a varminter. Obviously, there is no one rifle and/or caliber which is ideal for all of these chores. The best approach is to buy a rifle that is ideally suited to your favorite type of hunting. Other uses, if you are limited to one gun, must be a compromise.

Some calibers come close to qualifying as "all-round" loads, thus lessening the degree of compromise. One of these is the .30/06. It's been around for more than sixty-five years and is still going strong. Its 110-grain bullet is a pretty fair varminter load, but if you have your eye on a big muley buck across the canyon, you simply adjust your sights, slip in a 150-grain bullet load, capable of a 1660 foot pounds wallop at 300 yards, with a 6-inch trajectory. If you have a moose in mind, charge up with the 220-grain bullet with its 2320 foot pounds impact at 100 yards, or 1910 foot pounds at 200. (You'll rarely knock over a moose at ranges beyond this!) Obviously, there's much to be said for the .30/06 as an all-round load.

But before charging down to the gun store with your checkbook, look into the disadvantages of the .30/06. The 110-grain bullet lacks the excellent sectional density of some of the better varminter loads due to its short length in relation to its diameter. In settled areas, the rifle's booming voice is not easy on the ears. And, if you're a person of slight build, you'll notice the recoil!

It follows, then, that the all-round rifle may be elusive. To find it, evaluate your own shooting needs—not those of "experts" who have access to a dozen rifles and calibers. This is the only way you can arrive at your all-round rifle! The following list includes calibers and loads which may be candidates:

All-Round Calibers

Cartridge	*Bullet Weight (grains)*	*Energy (ft. lbs. 300 yds.)*	*300 yd. Mid-Range Trajectory (inches)*
.243 Winchester	100	1190	5.5
6 mm Remington	100	1300	−6.5*
.240 Weatherby Mag.	100	1495	4.4
.25/06 Remington	120	1480	−6.8*
.257 Weatherby Mag.	117	1315	6.8
6.5 Remington Mag.	120	1520	−6.6*
.264 Winchester Mag.	100	1440	4.2
.264 Winchester Mag.	140	1910	4.9
.270 Winchester	100	1215	4.8
.270 Winchester	130	1660	5.3
.270 Winchester	150	1550	6.3
.270 Weatherby Mag.	100	1317	4.3
.270 Weatherby Mag.	130	1776	4.5
.270 Weatherby Mag.	150	1967	5.0
.280 Remington	150	1680	−7.8*
.280 Remington	165	1420	−9.3*
.284 Winchester	125	1480	5.3
.284 Winchester	150	1550	6.3
7 mm Remington	125	1660	−5.7*
7 mm Remington	150	1990	−6.3*
7 mm Remington	175	2290	−6.7*
7 mm Mauser	175	1100	9.5
7 mm Weatherby Mag.	139	1877	4.9
7 mm Weatherby Mag.	154	1994	5.0
7 mm Weatherby Mag.	175	2301	5.2
.30/06 Springfield	125	1340	5.6
.30/06 Springfield	150	1510	6.1
.30/06 Springfield	180	1660	7.0
.30/06 Springfield	220	1560	9.2
.300 Savage	150	1080	8.0
.300 Savage	180	1250	9.2
.303 British	180	1440	8.2
.308 Winchester	125	1300	5.9
.308 Winchester	150	1400	6.5
.308 Winchester	180	1130	8.9
.308 Winchester	200	1400	9.0
.300 Weatherby Mag.	110	1750	3.7

* Point of impact below line of sight with rifle sighted in at 200 yards.

The famous Winchester Model 94 which, in .30/30 caliber, has probably downed more deer than any other rifle. More than 3½ million Model 94s have been produced.

The Woods Loads

Despite the growing popularity of high-velocity, flat-shooting ammunition for open-country shooting, there persists a great demand for slower-moving, heavier "brush" or "woods" loads. Proof lies in the continuing production of rifles chambered for the .30/30, .32 Special, .35, .44 Magnum and the Marlin .444. My own enthusiasm for zippy loads has simmered down over the years. I now tote into the deer woods a Winchester 94, chambered for the .30/30. The load is close to fifty years older than I am! Winchester's production of the Model 94 in .30/30 and .32 Special calibers has exceeded the 3½ million mark, with no sign of slackening. And virtually every other maker of center-fire rifles includes these calibers. The two, in fact, have probably downed more deer than all others put together.

Most eastern deer hunting is done in heavy cover or close to thickly forested areas. Long shots are the exception. A 60-yard shot is considered "reaching out." Flat trajectory is of no importance. Don't worry about a deer outrunning your "low"-velocity missile. Ballistics and the experience of thousands of hunters speak volumes for slower loads.

Heavier bullets, at slow to moderate velocities, plow through brush to find their mark. This is the prime advantage of woods loads, as opposed to lighter and zippier missiles, which frequently disintegrate, or are deflected, upon striking a twig.

Another advantage of woods loads is the availability of lightweight, easy-to-carry rifles handling these, including the short, highly maneuverable carbines. And you can purchase ammunition in almost any country store.

Woods Loads

Cartridge	*Bullet Weight (grains)*	*Velocity (ft. sec. 100 yds.)*	*Energy (ft. lbs. 100 yds.)*
.270 Winchester	150	2620	2290
.280 Remington	150	2670	2370
.280 Remington	165	2510	2310
.284 Winchester	150	2620	2290
7 mm Mauser	175	2170	1830
7 mm Remington	175	2720	2870
.30/30 Winchester	150	2020	1360
.30/30 Winchester	170	1890	1350
.30 Remington	170	1820	1250
.30/40 Krag	180	2120	1790
.30/40 Krag	220	1990	1250
.30/06 Springfield	150	2620	2280
.30/06 Springfield	180	2330	2170
.30/06 Springfield	220	2120	2190
.300 H & H Mag.	180	2670	2850
.300 Savage	150	2390	1900
.300 Savage	180	2160	1860
.303 Savage	180	1810	1310
.303 Savage	190	1680	1190
.303 British	180	2300	2120
.303 British	215	1900	1720
.308 Winchester	150	2520	2120
.308 Winchester	180	2250	2020
.308 Winchester	200	2210	2170
.32 Winchester Spec.	170	1870	1320
.32 Remington	170	1800	1220
8 mm Mauser	170	2140	1730
.348 Winchester	200	2220	2190
.35 Remington	150	1960	1280
.35 Remington	200	1710	1300
.351 Winchester	180	1560	975
.358 Winchester	200	2210	2160
.358 Winchester	250	2010	2230
.45/70 Government	405	1160	1210
.44 Magnum	240	1350	970
.444 Marlin	240	1845	1815

The Giant Killers

In this group are classified the loads which will kill any game on the North American continent, as well as heavy African and Indian species

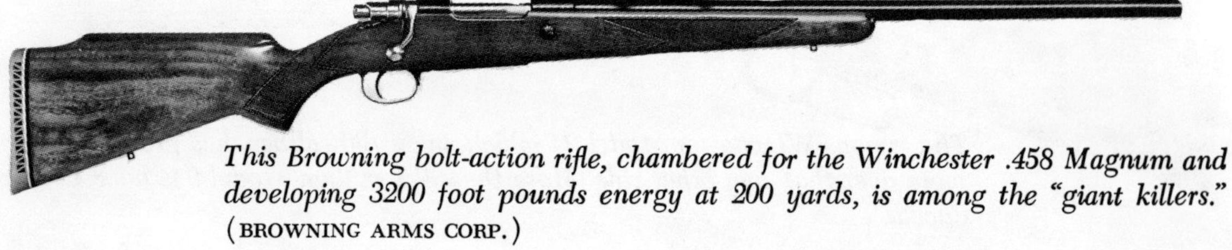

This Browning bolt-action rifle, chambered for the Winchester .458 Magnum and developing 3200 foot pounds energy at 200 yards, is among the "giant killers." (BROWNING ARMS CORP.)

The Giant Killers

Cartridge	*Bullet Weight (grains)*	*Velocity (ft. sec. 200 yds.)*	*Energy (ft. lbs. 200 yds.)*	*200 Yd. Mid-Range Trajectory (inches)*
.264 Winchester Magnum	140	2700	2270	2.0
.270 Winchester	150	2380	1890	2.5
.270 Weatherby Magnum	130	2720	2183	1.8
.270 Weatherby Magnum	150	2675	2385	2.0
7 mm Remington Magnum	150	2700	2430	1.5
7 mm Remington Magnum	175	2630	2700	1.7
7 mm Weatherby Magnum	154	2640	2384	2.0
7 mm Weatherby Magnum	175	2383	2207	2.4
.280 Remington	150	2450	2000	2.0
.280 Remington	165	2220	1810	2.3
.284 Winchester	150	2380	1890	2.5
.30/06 Springfield	180	2250	2020	2.9
.30/06 Springfield	220	1980	1910	3.7
.300 Winchester Magnum	150	2730	2480	1.9
.300 Winchester Magnum	180	2640	2790	2.1
.300 Winchester Magnum	220	2270	2520	2.1
.300 H & H Magnum	150	2580	2220	2.1
.300 H & H Magnum	180	2440	2390	2.4
.300 H & H Magnum	220	2150	2260	3.1
.300 Weatherby Magnum	150	2890	2783	1.5
.300 Weatherby Magnum	180	2705	2925	1.9
.300 Weatherby Magnum	220	2385	2757	2.5
.308 Winchester	180	1940	1500	3.4
.308 Winchester	200	1980	1750	3.6
.338 Winchester Magnum	200	2410	2580	2.4
.338 Winchester Magnum	250	2180	2640	3.0
.338 Winchester Magnum	300	1910	2430	3.7
.340 Weatherby Magnum	200	2615	3038	2.1
.340 Weatherby Magnum	250	2325	3000	2.7
.348 Winchester	200	1940	1670	3.6
.350 Remington Magnum	200	2130	2000	–5.1*
.350 Remington Magnum	250	1980	2180	–6.4*
.358 Winchester	200	1910	1610	3.6
.358 Winchester	250	1780	1760	4.4
.375 H & H Magnum	270	2210	2920	2.9
.375 H & H Magnum	300	2040	2770	3.3
.378 Weatherby Magnum	270	2600	4053	2.0
.378 Weatherby Magnum	300	2380	3774	2.5
.458 Winchester Magnum	500	1700	3210	4.8
.458 Winchester Magnum	510	1600	2900	5.1
.460 Weatherby Magnum	500	2005	4465	3.3

* Point of impact below line of sight at 200 yards with rifle sighted in for 100 yards.

—in the hands of a competent shooter. Killing power can never substitute for rifle skill. No matter how powerful a rifle may be, it's useless—even dangerous—in the hands of a gunner who can't place his shots.

In 1958 I made motion pictures of a western buffalo hunt, part of the thinning operation of a government-owned herd. Although my work was primarily with the cameras, the professional hunters allowed me to kill one buffalo with my .270, loaded with 130-grain bullet loads which I carried just in case. I'm not a particularly outstanding marksman, so with the pros looking on and contributing little with their jibes, I sighted carefully at a two-year bull of some 1500 pounds heft which had been picked for me to knock down. A buffalo's vulnerable spot lies between the ear and eye and this is where I held the sights. When I "touched 'er off," the .270 rocked me slightly and its report was muffled by the vastness of the open prairie. The bull dropped, his legs seeming to dart upwards as he died instantly, even before falling.

Later that same day, a visiting state official was also allowed to shoot a bull. Using one of the guide's rifles, a .30/06 loaded with 220-grain ammunition, he brought the rifle up quickly and threw a quick shot. The big animal reared back, spun about like a dog chasing its tail, then bounded across the prairie—toward us. Fascinated, I kept the camera grinding but the two professional hunters each poured a single shot into the enraged animal and dropped it. Never before, had the contrast between careful and sloppy shooting been so clearly demonstrated before me! A haphazard shot on the rifle range means only a blown score, but in hunting country it can mean the loss of game or even danger. Careful shooting is at least as important as killing power on big game.

The giant killers can, of course, be used on smaller game such as deer and black bear, but they're at their best on heavier and sometimes dangerous game. They are characterized by comparatively heavy bullet loads propelled at moderate to high velocities, creating a high-energy impact for quick, humane and safe kills. To a hunter accustomed to lighter loads and rifles, their recoil may seem as destructive as the bullet's impact and it takes an experienced shooter to handle these guns efficiently and he's not likely to lie in the sun some Saturday afternoon plinking tin cans with this kind of firepower.

In the list of giant killers you will again find an overlapping of loads. Figures deal with velocity and energy at 200 yards along with mid-range trajectories at that range. This is because it's what a bullet does upon striking game that counts, not what it can do at the muzzle where, surprisingly, very little game is knocked down!

Long-Range Loads

For open country, prairie and above-timberline hunting of such species as mule deer, antelope, mountain goat and sheep, elk, the long-range flat-shooting, high-velocity loads come into their own. These are the hunting weapons of the present-day West, including Mexico, the Rockies and the Canadian mountains. Flat trajectories are important because of the difficulty for the average hunter of estimating accurately ranges beyond 150 yards. Even with such flat-shooting loads, however, the ability to guess ranges is important. Using such rifles without telescope sights of three to six power is a serious handicap. Long-range hunting calls for the clearest possible view of the target to assure consistent hits.

The list of suitable long-range loads which follows is based upon 300-yard ranges, the ultimate for average hunters, although experts have been known to down big game at ranges up to 450 and 500 yards.

Ballistic Tables

The following pages contain ballistic tables issued by a few of our leading ammunition manufacturers. As I have stated earlier, study these tables carefully, but only after you have studied your guns and the use to which you will put them.

Long-Range Loads

Cartridge	*Bullet Weight (grains)*	*Velocity (ft. sec. 300 yds.)*	*Energy (ft. lbs. 300 yds.)*	*300 Yd. Mid-Range Trajectory (inches)*
.25/06 Remington	90	2420	1170	4.7
.25/06 Remington	120	2360	1480	5.5
6 mm Remington	100	2420	1300	−6.5*
.240 Weatherby Magnum	87	2550	1256	4 4
.240 Weatherby Magnum	100	2595	1495	4.4
6.5 Remington Magnum	100	2320	1190	−6.3*
6.5 Remington Magnum	120	2390	1520	−6.6*
.257 Weatherby Magnum	87	2450	1160	4.4
.257 Weatherby Magnum	100	2500	1388	4.4
.257 Weatherby Magnum	117	2250	1315	6.8
.264 Winchester Magnum	100	2550	1440	4.2
.264 Winchester Magnum	140	2480	1910	4.9
.270 Winchester	100	2340	1215	4.8
.270 Winchester	130	2320	1550	5.3
.270 Winchester	150	2160	1550	6.3
.270 Weatherby Magnum	100	2435	1317	4.3
.270 Weatherby Magnum	130	2480	1776	4.5
.270 Weatherby Magnum	150	2430	1967	5.0
7 mm Remington Magnum	125	2450	1660	−5.7*
7 mm Remington Magnum	150	2450	1990	−6.3*
7 mm Remington Magnum	175	2430	2290	−6.7*
7 mm Weatherby Magnum	139	2465	1877	4.9
7 mm Weatherby Magnum	154	2415	1994	5.0
7 mm Weatherby Magnum	175	2434	2301	5.2
.280 Remington	150	2250	1680	−7.8*
.280 Remington	165	1970	4120	−9.3*
.284 Winchester	125	2310	1480	5.3
.284 Winchester	150	2160	1550	6.3
.30/06 Springfield	125	2200	1340	5.6
.30/06 Springfield	150	2130	1510	6.1
.30/06 Springfield	180	2190	1900	6.7
.30/06 Springfield	220	1790	1560	9.2
.300 Winchester Magnum	150	2430	1970	4.8
.300 Winchester Magnum	180	2440	2380	5.3
.300 Winchester Magnum	220	2060	2070	6.9
.300 H & H Magnum	150	2300	1760	5.2
.300 H & H Magnum	180	2220	1970	5.8
.300 H & H Magnum	220	1940	1840	7.7
.300 Savage	150	1890	1190	7.6
.300 Savage	180	1770	1250	9.2
.300 Weatherby Magnum	150	2615	2279	3.9
.300 Weatherby Magnum	180	2475	2448	5.2
.300 Weatherby Magnum	220	2150	2257	6.7
.303 British	180	1900	1440	8.2
.308 Winchester	125	2160	1300	5.9
.308 Winchester	150	2050	1400	6.5
.308 Winchester	180	1970	1540	7.4
.308 Winchester	200	1770	1400	9.0
.338 Winchester Magnum	200	2170	2090	6.0
.338 Winchester Magnum	250	1940	2090	7.4
.338 Winchester Magnum	300	1690	1900	9.5
.348 Winchester	200	1680	1250	9.0
.358 Winchester	200	1640	1190	9.4
.375 H & H Magnum	270	1990	2370	7.1
.375 H & H Magnum	300	1830	2230	8.3

* Point of impact below line of sight with rifle sighted in for 200 yards.

Ballistics Tables for Weatherby Magnum Ammunition

Caliber	Bullet Wt. (grs.)	Velocity (ft. sec.) Muzzle	100 Yds.	200 Yds.	300 Yds.	Energy (ft. lbs.) Muzzle	100 Yds.	200 Yds.	300 Yds.	Mid-Range Trajectory (inches) 100 Yds.	200 Yds.	300 Yds.
.224	50	3750	3160	2625	2140	1562	1109	765	509	0.4	1.7	4.7
.224	55	3650	3150	2685	2270	1627	1212	881	629	0.4	1.7	4.5
.240	70	3850	3395	2975	2585	2304	1788	1376	1038	0.3	1.5	3.9
.240	87	3500	3165	2852	2550	2363	1931	1572	1256	0.4	1.7	4.4
.240	100	3395	3115	2850	2595	2554	2150	1804	1495	0.4	1.8	4.4
.257	87	3825	3290	2835	2450	2828	2087	1553	1160	0.3	1.6	4.4
.257	100	3555	3150	2815	2500	2802	2199	1760	1388	0.4	1.7	4.4
.257	117	3300	2900	2550	2250	2824	2184	1689	1315	0.4	2.4	6.8
.270	100	3760	3265	2825	2435	3149	2363	1772	1317	0.4	1.6	4.3
.270	130	3375	3050	2750	2480	3283	2686	2183	1775	0.4	1.8	4.5
.270	150	3245	2955	2675	2430	3501	2909	2385	1967	0.5	2.0	5.0
7 mm	139	3300	2995	2715	2465	3355	2770	2275	1877	0.4	1.9	4.9
7 mm	154	3160	2885	2640	2415	3406	2847	2384	1994	0.5	2.0	5.0
7 mm	175	3070	2850	2637	2434	3663	3157	2702	2301	0.5	2.1	5.2
7 mm	175*	3070	2716	2383	2083	3663	2867	2207	1685	0.5	2.4	6.1
.300	110	3900	3466	3057	2677	3716	2927	2283	1750	0.3	1.5	3.75
.300	150	3545	3195	2890	2615	4179	3393	2783	2279	0.4	1.5	3.9
.300	180	3245	2960	2705	2475	4201	3501	2925	2448	0.4	1.9	5.2
.300	220	2905	2610	2385	2150	4123	3329	2757	2257	0.6	2.5	6.7
.340	200	3210	2905	2615	2345	4566	3748	3038	1442	0.5	2.1	5.3
.340	250	2850	2580	2325	2090	4510	3695	3000	2425	0.6	2.7	6.7
.378	270	3180	2850	2600	2315	6051	4871	4053	3210	0.5	2.0	5.2
.378	300	2925	2610	2380	2125	5700	4539	3774	3009	0.6	2.5	6.2
.460	500*	2700	2300	2005	1730	8095	6025	4465	3320	0.7	3.3	10.0

* Round-nose bullet. All others are point-expanding type.

Ballistics Tables for Remington-Peters Center-Fire Ammunition

Explanation of bullet-style abbreviations: H.P., Hollow Point; S.P., Soft Point; P.S.P., Pointed Soft Point; M.C., Metal Case; L., Lead; B.P., Bronze Point.

			Velocity (ft. sec.)				Energy (ft. lbs.)				Point of Impact Inches above (+) or below (−) line of sight. Rifle sighted for 100 yds.		
Cartridge	Wt. (grs.)	Bullet Style	Muzzle	100 Yds.	200 Yds.	300 Yds.	Muzzle	100 Yds.	200 Yds.	300 Yds.	50 Yds.	200 Yds.	300 Yds.
.17 Remington	25	H.P.	4020	3290	2630	2060	900	600	380	230	−0.1	−2.4	−9.9
.218 Bee	46	H.P.	2860	2160	1610	1200	835	475	265	145	+0.2	−6.4	−25.9
.22 Hornet	45	S.P.	2690	2030	1510	1150	720	410	230	130	+0.3	−7.8	−30.5
.22 Hornet	45	H.P.	2690	2030	1510	1150	720	410	230	130	+0.3	−7.8	−30.5
.222 Remington	50	H.P.	3200	2690	2230	1830	1140	800	550	370	0.0	−4.0	−15.0
.222 Remington	50	P.S.P.	3200	2660	2170	1750	1140	785	520	340	0.0	−4.0	−15.7
.222 Remington Mag.	55	H.P.	3300	2830	2400	2010	1330	975	700	490	0.0	−3.5	−13.1
.222 Remington Mag.	55	P.S.P.	3300	2800	2340	1930	1330	955	670	455	0.0	−3.6	−13.8
.22–250 Remington	55	H.P.	3810	3330	2890	2490	1770	1360	1020	760			−5.3*
.22–250 Remington	55	P.S.P.	3810	3270	2770	2320	1770	1300	932	655			−5.8*
.223 Remington	55	H.P.	3300	2830	2400	2010	1330	975	700	490	0.0	−3.5	−13.1
.223 Remington	55	P.S.P.	3300	2800	2340	1930	1330	955	670	455	0.0	−3.6	−13.8
6 mm Remington	80	P.S.P.	3540	3130	2750	2400	2220	1740	1340	1018			−6.0*
6 mm Remington	100	P.S.P.	3190	2920	2660	2420	2260	1890	1570	1300			−6.5*
.243 Winchester	80	P.S.P.	3500	3080	2720	2410	2180	1860	1320	1030	−0.1	−2.8	−10.2
.243 Winchester	80	H.P.	3450	3050	2675	2330	2115	1650	1270	965	−0.1	−2.9	−10.6
.243 Winchester	100	P.S.P.	3070	2790	2540	2320	2090	1730	1430	1190	0.0	−3.5	−12.2
.244 Remington	90	P.S.P.	3200	2850	2530	2230	2050	1630	1280	995	−0.1	−3.4	−12.3
.25/06 Remington	87	H.P.	3500	3070	2680	2320	2370	1820	1390	1040			−6.3*
.25/06 Remington	120	P.S.P.	3120	2850	2600	2130	2590	2160	1800	1480	0.0	−3.4	−11.2
.25/20 Winchester	86	L.	1460	1180	1030	940	405	265	200	170	+2.1	−23.9	−79.4
.25/35 Winchester	117	S.P.	2300	1950	1680	1460	1370	985	730	555	+0.5	−8.2	−28.6
.250 Savage	100	P.S.P.	2820	2500	2210	1940	1760	1390	1080	835	+0.1	−4.8	−16.5
6.5 mm Remington Mag.	100	P.S.P.	3450	3070	2690	2320	2640	2090	1610	1190			−6.3*
6.5 mm Remington Mag.	120	P.S.P.	3220	2900	2630	2390	2780	2240	1840	1520			−6.6*
.257 Roberts	117	S.P.	2650	2280	1950	1690	1820	1350	985	740	+0.2	−5.7	−20.6
.264 Winchester Mag.	100	P.S.P.	3700	3260	2880	2550	3040	2360	1840	1440			−5.5*
.264 Winchester Mag.	140	P.S.P.	3200	2940	2700	2480	3180	2690	2270	1910			−6.1*
.270 Winchester	100	P.S.P.	3480	3070	2690	2340	2690	2090	1600	1215			−6.3*
.270 Winchester	130	P.S.P.	3140	2850	2580	2320	2840	2340	1920	1550			−7.0*
.270 Winchester	130	B.P.	3140	2880	2630	2400	2840	2390	1990	1660			−6.5*
.270 Winchester	150	S.P.	2800	2440	2140	1870	2610	1980	1520	1160			−9.5*
.280 Remington	150	P.S.P.	2900	2670	2450	2250	2800	2370	2000	1680			−7.8*
.280 Remington	165	S.P.	2820	2510	2220	1970	2910	2310	1810	1420			−9.3*
7 mm Remington Mag.	125	P.S.P.	3430	3080	2750	2450	3260	2630	2100	1660			−5.7*
7 mm Remington Mag.	150	P.S.P.	3260	2970	2700	2450	3540	2940	2430	1990			−6.3*
7 mm Remington Mag.	175	P.S.P.	3070	2850	2630	2430	3660	3150	2700	2290			−6.7*
7 mm Mauser	175	S.P.	2490	2170	1900	1680	2410	1830	1400	1100	+0.3	−6.4	−22.4

.30 Carbine	110	S.P.	1980	1540	1230	1040	955	575	370	260	+1.0	−14.1	−51.8
.30/30 Winchester	150	P.S.P.	2410	1960	1620	1360	1930	1280	875	615	+0.4	−8.3	−29.5
.30/30 Winchester	170	H.P.	2220	1890	1630	1410	1860	1350	1000	750	+0.7	−8.2	−29.6
.30 Remington	170	S.P.	2120	1820	1560	1350	1700	1250	920	690	+0.6	−9.5	−33.8
.30/40 Krag	180	S.P.	2470	2120	1830	1590	2440	1790	1340	1010	+0.3	−6.4	−23.4
.30/40 Krag	180	P.S.P.	2470	2250	2040	1850	2440	2020	1660	1370	+0.3	−6.1	−20.2
.30/06 Springfield	125	P.S.P.	3200	2810	2480	2200	2840	2190	1710	1340			−7.4*
.30/06 Springfield	150	P.S.P.	2970	2670	2400	2130	2930	2370	1920	1510			−7.5*
.30/06 Springfield	150	B.P.	2970	2710	2470	2240	2930	2440	2030	1670			−7.5*
.30/06 Springfield	180	B.P.	2700	2480	2280	2080	2910	2460	2080	1730			−8.5*
.30/06 Springfield	180	S.P.	2700	2330	2010	1740	2910	2170	1610	1210	+0.2	−5.6	−19.2
.30/06 Springfield	180	P.S.P.	2700	2470	2250	2040	2910	2440	2020	1660			−9.0*
.30/06 Springfield	220	S.P.	2410	2120	1870	1670	2830	2190	1710	1360	+0.3	−6.7	−23.6
.300 Savage	150	S.P.	2670	2270	1930	1660	2370	1710	1240	915	+0.2	−5.9	−20.4
.300 Savage	150	P.S.P.	2670	2390	2130	1890	2370	1900	1510	1190	+0.2	−5.4	−17.9
.300 Savage	180	S.P.	2370	2040	1760	1520	2240	1660	1240	920	+0.4	−7.5	−25.3
.300 Savage	180	P.S.P.	2370	2160	1960	1770	2240	1860	1530	1250	+0.4	−6.5	−22.3
.300 H & H Mag.	180	P.S.P.	2920	2670	2440	2220	3400	2850	2380	1970			−7.6*
.300 Winchester Mag.	150	P.S.P.	3400	3050	2730	2430	3850	3100	2480	1970			−6.1*
.300 Winchester Mag.	180	P.S.P.	3070	2850	2640	2440	3770	3250	2790	2380			−6.9*
.303 Savage	180	S.P.	2140	1810	1550	1340	1830	1310	960	715	+0.6	−10.0	−33.8
.303 British	180	S.P.	2540	2300	2090	1900	2580	2120	1750	1440	+0.2	−5.8	−19.0
.303 British	215	S.P.	2180	1900	1660	1460	2270	1720	1310	1020	+0.6	−9.1	−30.2
.308 Winchester	150	P.S.P.	2860	2570	2300	2050	2730	2200	1760	1400			−8.5*
.308 Winchester	180	P.S.P.	2610	2390	2170	1970	2720	2280	1870	1540	+0.3	−5.0	−17.8
.308 Winchester	180	S.P.	2610	2250	1940	1680	2720	2020	1500	1130	+0.2	−6.0	−20.8
8 mm Mauser	170	S.P.	2570	2140	1790	1520	2490	1730	1210	870	+0.3	−6.6	−24.7
.32 Remington	170	S.P.	2120	1800	1540	1340	1700	1220	895	680	+0.6	−9.5	−33.3
.32 Winchester Special	170	H.P.	2280	1920	1630	1410	1960	1390	1000	750	+0.5	−8.5	−29.8
.32–20 Winchester	100	S.P.	1290	1060	940	840	370	250	195	155	+2.8	−30.1	−97.2
.348 Winchester	200	S.P.	2530	2140	1920	1570	2840	2030	1470	1090	+0.3	−7.1	−23.7
.35 Remington	150	P.S.P.	2400	1960	1580	1280	1920	1280	835	545	+0.4	−8.1	−30.7
.35 Remington	200	S.P.	2100	1710	1390	1160	1950	1300	855	605	+0.7	−10.9	−39.4
.350 Remington Mag.	200	P.S.P.	2710	2410	2130	1870	3260	2570	2000	1550	+0.2	−5.1	−18.0
.350 Remington Mag.	250	P.S.P.	2410	2190	1980	1790	3220	2660	2180	1780	+0.4	−6.4	−21.5
.351 Winchester Self L.	180	S.P.	1850	1560	1310	1140	1370	975	685	520	+1.0	−14.5	−51.8
.375 H & H Mag.	270	S.P.	2740	2460	2210	1990	4500	3620	2920	2370			−9.8*
.375 H & H Mag.	300	M.C.	2550	2180	1860	1590	4330	3160	2300	1680			−12.5*
.38–40 Winchester	180	S.P.	1330	1070	960	850	705	455	370	290	+2.7	−29.1	−93.7
.444 Marlin	240	S.P.	2440	1845	1410	1125	3070	1815	1060	675	+0.6	−9.6	−36.7
.44/40 Winchester	200	S.P.	1310	1050	940	830	760	490	390	305	+2.8	−29.6	−95.2
.44 Remington Mag.	240	S.P.	1750	1360	1110	980	1630	985	655	510	+1.4	−17.5	−64.5
.45/70 Government	405	S.P.	1320	1160	1050	990	1570	1210	990	880	+2.4	−25.1	−81.2
.458 Winchester Mag.	500	S.P.	2130	1910	1700	1520	5040	4050	3210	2570	+0.6	−8.9	−29.4
.458 Winchester Mag.	510	S.P.	2130	1840	1600	1400	5140	3830	2900	2220	+0.6	−9.2	−32.1

* Point of impact below line of sight with rifle sighted in for 200 yards.

Ballistics Tables for Winchester-Western Center-Fire Rifle Ammunition

Explanation of bullet-style abbreviations: H.S.P., Hollow Soft Point; P.S.P., Pointed Soft Point; S.P., Soft Point; F.M.C., Full Metal Case; H.P., Hollow Point; O.P.E., Open Point Expanding; St.Exp., Silvertip Expanding; F.M.C.B.T., Full Metal Case Boat Tail; P.E.P., Positive Expanding Point.

			Velocity (ft. sec.)				*Energy (ft. lbs.)*				*Mid-Range Trajectory (inches)*		
Cartridge	*Wt. (grs.)*	*Bullet Style*	*Muzzle*	*100 Yds.*	*200 Yds.*	*300 Yds.*	*Muzzle*	*100 Yds.*	*200 Yds.*	*300 Yds.*	*100 Yds.*	*200 Yds.*	*300 Yds.*
.218 Bee	46	O.P.E.H.P.	2860	2160	1610	1200	835	475	265	145	0.7	3.8	11.5
.22 Hornet	45	S.P.	2690	2030	1510	1150	720	410	230	130	0.8	4.3	13.0
.22 Hornet	46	O.P.E.H.P.	2690	2030	1510	1150	740	420	235	135	0.8	4.3	13.0
.22–250 Remington	55	P.S.P.	3810	3270	2770	2320	1770	1300	935	655	0.3	1.6	4.4
.220 Swift	48	P.S.P.	4110	3490	2930	2440	1800	1300	915	635	0.3	1.4	3.8*
.222 Remington	50	P.S.P.	3200	2660	2170	1750	1140	785	520	340	0.5	2.5	7.0
.225 Winchester	55	P.S.P.	3650	3140	2680	2270	1630	1200	875	630	0.4	1.8	4.8
.243 Winchester	80	P.S.P.	3500	3080	2720	2410	2180	1690	1320	1030	0.4	1.8	4.7
.243 Winchester	100	S.P.	3070	2790	2540	2320	2090	1730	1430	1190	0.5	2.2	5.5
.25/06 Remington	90	P.E.P.	3500	3090	2730	2420	2450	1910	1490	1170	0.4	1.8	4.7
.25/06 Remington	120	P.E.P.	3120	2850	2600	2360	2590	2160	1800	1480	0.5	2.0	5.5
.25/20 Winchester	86	Lead	1460	1180	1030	940	405	265	200	170	2.6	12.5	32.0
.25/35 Winchester	117	S.P.	2300	1910	1600	1340	1370	945	665	465	1.0	4.6	12.5
.250 Savage	87	P.S.P.	3030	2660	2330	2060	1770	1370	1050	820	0.6	2.5	6.4
.250 Savage	100	St.Exp.	2820	2460	2140	1870	1760	1340	1020	775	0.6	2.9	7.4
.256 Winchester Mag.	60	O.P.E.	2800	2070	1570	1220	1040	570	330	200	0.8	4.0	12.0
.257 Roberts	87	P.S.P.	3200	2840	2500	2190	1980	1560	1210	925	0.5	2.2	5.7
.257 Roberts	100	St.Exp.	2900	2540	2210	1920	1870	1430	1080	820	0.6	2.7	7.0
.257 Roberts	117	S.P.	2650	2280	1950	1690	1820	1350	935	740	0.7	3.4	8.8
.264 Winchester Mag.	100	P.S.P.	3700	3260	2880	2550	3040	2360	1840	1440	0.4	1.6	4.2
.264 Winchester Mag.	140	S.P.	3200	2940	2700	2480	3180	2690	2270	1910	0.5	2.0	4.9
.270 Winchester	100	P.S.P.	3480	3070	2690	2340	2690	2090	1600	1215	0.4	1.8	4.8
.270 Winchester	130	S.P.	3140	2880	2630	2400	2850	2390	2000	1660	0.5	2.1	5.3
.270 Winchester	130	St.Exp.	3140	2850	2580	2320	2850	2340	1920	1550	0.5	2.1	5.3
.270 Winchester	150	S.P.	2900	2620	2380	2160	2800	2290	1890	1550	0.6	2.5	6.3
.284 Winchester	125	S.P.	3200	2880	2590	2310	2840	2300	1860	1480	0.5	2.1	5.3
.284 Winchester	150	S.P.	2900	2620	2380	2160	2800	2290	1890	1550	0.6	2.5	6.3
7 mm Mauser	175	S.P.	2490	2170	1900	1680	2410	1830	1400	1100	0.8	3.7	9.5
7 mm Remington Mag.	150	S.P.	3260	2970	2700	2450	3540	2940	2430	1990	0.4	2.0	4.9
7 mm Remington Mag.	175	S.P.	3070	2720	2400	2120	3660	2870	2240	1750	0.5	2.4	6.1
.30 Carbine	110	H.S.P.	1980	1540	1230	1040	955	575	370	260	1.4	7.5	21.7
.30–30 Winchester	150	O.P.E.H.P.	2410	2020	1700	1430	1930	1360	960	680	0.9	4.2	11.0
.30–30 Winchester	170	S.P.	2220	1890	1630	1410	1860	1350	1000	750	1.2	4.6	12.5
.30 Remington	170	St.Exp.	2120	1820	1560	1350	1700	1250	920	690	1.1	5.3	14.0
.30/06 Springfield	110	P.S.P.	3370	2830	2350	1920	2770	1960	1350	900	0.5	2.2	6.0
.30/06 Springfield	125	P.S.P.	3200	2810	2480	2200	2840	2190	1710	1340	0.5	2.2	5.6
.30/06 Springfield	150	S.P.	2970	2620	2300	2010	2930	2280	1760	1340	0.6	2.5	6.5
.30/06 Springfield	150	St.Exp.	2970	2670	2400	2130	2930	2370	1920	1510	0.6	2.4	6.1
.30/06 Springfield	180	S.P.	2700	2330	2010	1740	2910	2170	1610	1210	0.7	3.1	8.3

.30/06 Springfield	180	St.Exp.	2700	2470	2250	2040	2910	2440	2020	1660	0.7	2.9	7.0
.30/06 Springfield	180	F.M.C.B.T.	2700	2520	2350	2190	2910	2540	2200	1900	0.6	2.8	6.7
.30/06 Springfield	220	S.P.	2410	2120	1870	1670	2830	2190	1710	1360	0.8	3.9	9.8
.30/06 Springfield	220	St.Exp.	2410	2180	1870	1670	2830	2320	1910	1560	0.8	3.7	9.2
.30/40 Krag	180	S.P.	2470	2120	1830	1590	2440	1790	1340	1010	0.8	3.8	9.9
.30/40 Krag	180	St.Exp.	2470	2250	2040	1850	2440	2020	1660	1370	0.8	3.5	8.5
.30/40 Krag	220	St.Exp.	2200	1990	1800	1630	2360	1930	1580	1300	1.0	4.4	11.0
.300 Winchester Mag.	150	S.P.	3400	3050	2730	2430	3850	3100	2480	1970	0.4	1.9	4.8
.300 Winchester Mag.	180	S.P.	3070	2850	2640	2440	3770	3250	2790	2380	0.5	2.1	5.3
.300 Winchester Mag.	220	St.Exp.	2720	2490	2270	2060	3620	3030	2520	2070	0.6	2.9	6.9
.300 H & H Mag.	150	St.Exp.	3190	2870	2580	2300	3390	2740	2220	1760	0.5	2.1	5.2
.300 H & H Mag.	180	St.Exp.	2920	2670	2440	2220	3400	2850	2380	1970	0.6	2.4	5.8
.300 H & H Mag.	220	St.Exp.	2620	2370	2150	1940	3350	2740	2260	1840	0.7	3.1	7.7
.300 Savage	150	S.P.	2670	2350	2060	1800	2370	1840	1410	1080	0.7	3.2	8.0
.300 Savage	150	St.Exp.	2670	2390	2130	1890	2370	1900	1510	1190	0.7	3.0	7.6
.300 Savage	180	S.P.	2370	2040	1760	1520	2240	1660	1240	920	0.9	4.1	10.5
.300 Savage	180	St.Exp.	2370	2160	1960	1770	2240	1860	1530	1250	0.9	3.7	9.2
.303 Savage	190	St.Exp.	1980	1680	1440	1250	1650	1190	875	660	1.3	6.2	15.5
.303 British	180	S.P.	2540	2300	2090	1900	2580	2120	1750	1440	0.7	3.3	8.2
.308 Winchester	110	P.S.P.	3340	2810	2340	1920	2730	1930	1340	900	0.5	2.2	6.0
.308 Winchester	125	P.S.P.	3100	2740	2430	2160	2670	2080	1640	1300	0.5	2.3	5.9
.308 Winchester	150	S.P.	2860	2520	2210	1930	2730	2120	1630	1240	0.6	2.7	7.0
.308 Winchester	150	St.Exp.	2860	2570	2300	2050	2730	2200	1760	1400	0.6	2.6	6.5
.308 Winchester	180	S.P.	2610	2250	1940	1680	2720	2020	1500	1130	0.7	3.4	8.9
.308 Winchester	180	St.Exp.	2610	2390	2170	1970	2720	2280	1870	1540	0.8	3.1	7.4
.308 Winchester	200	St.Exp.	2450	2210	1980	1770	2670	2170	1750	1400	0.8	3.6	9.0
.32 Winchester Special	170	S.P.	2280	1870	1560	1330	1960	1320	920	665	1.0	4.8	13.0
.32 Remington	170	St.Exp.	2120	1760	1460	1220	1700	1170	805	560	1.1	5.3	14.5
.32–20 Winchester	100	S.P.	1290	1060	940	840	370	250	195	155	3.3	15.5	38.0
8 mm Mauser	170	S.P.	2570	2140	1790	1520	2490	1730	1210	870	0.8	3.9	10.5
.338 Winchester Mag.	200	S.P.	3000	2690	2410	2170	4000	3210	2580	2090	0.5	2.4	6.0
.338 Winchester Mag.	250	St.Exp.	2700	2430	2180	1940	4050	3280	2640	2090	0.7	3.0	7.4
.338 Winchester Mag.	300	S.P.	2450	2160	1910	1690	4000	3110	2430	1900	0.8	3.7	9.5
.348 Winchester	200	St.Exp.	2530	2220	1940	1680	2840	2190	1670	1250	0.7	3.6	9.0
.35 Remington	200	S.P.	2100	1710	1390	1160	1950	1300	860	605	1.2	6.0	16.5
.351 Winchester	180	S.P.	1850	1560	1310	1140	1370	975	685	520	1.5	7.8	21.5
.358 Winchester	200	St.Exp.	2530	2210	1910	1640	2840	2160	1610	1190	0.8	3.6	9.4
.358 Winchester	250	St.Exp.	2250	2010	1780	1570	2810	2230	1760	1370	1.0	4.4	11.0
.375 H & H Mag.	270	S.P.	2740	2460	2210	1990	4500	3620	2920	2370	0.7	2.9	7.1
.375 H & H Mag.	300	St.Exp.	2550	2280	2040	1830	4330	3460	2770	2230	0.7	3.3	8.3
.375 H & H Mag.	300	F.M.C.	2550	2180	1860	1590	4330	3160	2300	1680	0.7	3.6	9.3
.38–40 Winchester	180	S.P.	1330	1070	960	850	705	455	370	290	3.2	15.0	36.5
.44 Mag.	240	H.S.P.	1750	1350	1090	950	1630	970	635	480	1.8	9.4	26.0
.44–40 Winchester	200	S.P.	1310	1050	940	830	760	490	390	305	3.3	15.0	36.5
.45–70 Government	405	S.P.	1320	1160	1050	990	1570	1210	990	880	2.9	13.0	32.5
.458 Winchester Mag.	500	F.M.C.	2130	1910	1700	1520	5040	4050	3210	2570	1.1	4.8	12.0
.458 Winchester Mag.	510	S.P.	2130	1840	1600	1400	5140	3830	2900	2220	1.1	5.1	13.5

* Discontinued caliber, included only for comparison purposes.

Ballistics Tables for Norma Center-Fire Rifle Ammunition

Explanation of bullet-style abbreviations: S.P., Soft Point; F.J., Full Jacket; H.P., Hollow Point; S.P.B.T., Soft Point Boat Tail.

Cartridge	Wt. (grs.)	Bullet Style	Velocity (ft. sec.) Muzzle	100 Yds.	200 Yds.	300 Yds.	Energy (ft. lbs.) Muzzle	100 Yds.	200 Yds.	300 Yds.	Point of Impact Inches above (+) or below (–) line of sight. Rifle sighted at 150 yds. 50 Yds.	100 Yds.	200 Yds.
.22 Hornet	45	S.P.	2690	2030	1510	1150	720	410	230	130	+0.9	+1.5	–4.3
.220 Swift	50	S.P.	4110	3611	3133	2681	1877	1448	1060	799	–0.4	+0.1	–0.9
.220 Swift	50	F.J.	4110	3460	2850	2295	1877	1329	902	585	–0.3	+0.2	–1.1
.222 Remington	50	S.P.	3200	2650	2170	1750	1137	780	520	340	+0.1	+0.7	–2.2
.222 Remington	50	F.J.	3200	2610	2080	1630	1137	756	480	295	+0.1	+0.7	–2.3
.223 Remington	55	S.P.	3300	2900	2520	2160	1330	1027	776	570	+0.4	+1.3	0.0*
.22–250 Remington	50	S.P.	3800	3300	2810	2350	1600	1209	885	613	–0.3	+0.3	–1.2
.22–250 Remington	55	S.P.	3650	3200	2780	2400	1637	1251	944	704	–0.2	+0.3	–1.3
.243 Winchester	75	H.P.	3500	3070	2660	2290	2041	1570	1179	873	–0.1	+0.4	–1.5
.243 Winchester	80	S.P.	3500	3080	2720	2410	2177	1686	1316	1032	–0.1	+0.4	–1.4
.243 Winchester	100	F.J.	3070	2790	2540	2320	2090	1730	1430	1190	0.0	+0.6	–1.8
.244 Remington	75	H.P.	3500	3070	2660	2290	2040	1570	1180	875	–0.1	+0.4	–1.5
.244 Remington	90	S.P.	3200	2850	2530	2230	2050	1630	1280	995	0.0	+0.5	–1.7
6 mm Remington	100	S.P.	3190	2920	2660	2420	2260	1890	1570	1300	0.0	+0.5	–1.2
.250 Savage	87	S.P.	3030	2660	2330	2060	1770	1370	1050	820	+0.1	+0.7	–2.0
.250 Savage	100	S.P.	2820	2514	2223	1956	1769	1404	1098	850	+0.3	+0.8	–2.4
.257 Roberts	100	S.P.	2900	2588	2291	2020	1870	1488	1166	906	+0.2	+0.8	–2.2
.257 Roberts	120	S.P.	2650	2405	2177	1964	1865	1542	1263	1028	+0.4	+1.0	–2.6
6.5 Japanese	139	S.P.	2428	2280	2130	1990	1820	1605	1401	1223	+0.6	+1.1	–2.9
6.5 Japanese	156	S.P.	2067	1871	1692	1529	1481	1213	992	810	+1.3	+1.9	–4.7
6.5 × 54 Mauser	77	S.P.	3116	2731	2369	2036	1662	1274	960	710	+0.1	+0.6	–2.0
6.5 × 54 Mauser	139	S.P.	2575	2420	2270	2120	2056	1808	1591	1388	+0.4	+1.0	–2.5
6.5 × 54 Mauser	156	S.P.	2461	2240	2033	1840	2098	1738	1432	1173	+0.6	+1.2	–3.1
6.5 Carcano	156	S.P.	2000	1810	1640	1485	1386	1135	932	764	+1.5	+2.1	–5.0
6.5 × 55 mm.	77	S.P.	2725	2362	2030	1811	1271	956	706	562	+0.4	+1.0	–2.8
6.5 × 55 mm.	77	S.P.	3116	2730	2370	2040	1664	1275	961	712	+0.1	+0.6	–2.8
6.5 × 55 mm.	139	S.P.	2788	2630	2470	2320	2402	2136	1883	1662	+0.7	+1.8	0.0*
6.5 × 55 mm.	156	S.P.	2493	2271	2062	1867	2153	1787	1473	1208	+0.6	+1.1	–3.0
.270 Winchester	110	S.P.	3250	2966	2694	2435	2578	2150	1773	1448	+0.3	+1.2	0.0*
.270 Winchester	130	S.P.	3140	2884	2639	2404	2847	2401	2011	1669	+0.4	+1.3	0.0*
.270 Winchester	130	F.J.	3140	2944	2753	2568	2847	2502	2188	1904	+0.4	+1.2	0.0*
.270 Winchester	130	S.P.B.T.	2525	2296	2080	1878	1836	1516	1244	1014	+0.6	+1.1	–2.9
.270 Winchester	150	S.P.B.T.	2800	2616	2436	2262	2616	2280	1977	1705	+0.8	+1.8	0.0*
.270 Winchester	154	S.P.	2800	2622	2450	2284	2679	2350	2052	1783	+0.2	+0.7	–2.1
7 × 57	110	S.P.	3067	2792	2528	2277	2300	1904	1561	1267	0.0	+0.6	–1.8
7 × 57	150	S.P.	2756	2539	2331	2133	2530	2148	1810	1516	+0.3	+0.8	–2.3
7 × 57 mm.	175	S.P.	2490	2170	1900	1680	2410	1830	1400	1100	+0.7	+1.3	–3.3
Super 7 × 61 mm.	160	S.P.	3150	2973	2801	2634	3526	3141	2788	2465	+0.3	+1.2	0.0*

7 mm Remington Mag.	150	S.P.	3260	2970	2700	2450	3540	2945	2435	1990	+0.3	+1.2	0.0*
7 mm Remington Mag.	175	S.P.	3070	2900	2740	2590	3660	3269	2918	2607	+0.4	+1.3	0.0*
7 mm Remington Mag.	175	S.P.	3070	2720	2400	2120	3545	2876	2240	1747	+0.6	+1.6	0.0*
.30 Carbine	110	F.J.	1970	1595	1300	1090	948	622	413	290	+2.0	+2.7	—7.0
.30/30 Winchester	150	S.P.	2410	2075	1790	1550	1934	1433	1066	799	+0.8	+1.4	—3.7
.30/30 Winchester	170	S.P.	2220	1890	1630	1410	1860	1350	1000	750	+1.2	+1.8	—4.5
.308 Norma Mag.	180	S.P.	3100	2881	2668	2464	3842	3318	2846	2427	+0.4	+1.4	0.0*
.308 Winchester	130	S.P.	2900	2590	2300	2030	2428	1937	1527	1190	+0.2	+0.8	—2.2
.308 Winchester	150	S.P.	2860	2570	2300	2050	2725	2200	1760	1400	+0.2	+0.8	—2.2
.308 Winchester	180	S.P.	2610	2400	2210	2020	2725	2303	1952	1631	+0.4	+1.0	—2.6
7.62 Russian	180	S.P.	2624	2415	2222	2030	2749	2326	1970	1644	+0.4	+1.0	—2.6
.30/06 Springfield	130	S.P.B.T.	3280	2951	2636	2338	3108	2514	2006	1578	+0.3	+1.2	0.0*
.30/06 Springfield	150	S.P.B.T.	2970	2680	2402	2141	2943	2393	1922	1527	+0.6	+1.7	0.0*
.30/06 Springfield	150	S.P.	2410	2037	1708	1432	1930	1378	968	681	+0.9	+1.5	—4.0
.30/06 Springfield	150	S.P.	2970	2680	2402	2141	2943	2393	1922	1527	+0.6	+1.7	0.0*
.30/06 Springfield	180	S.P.B.T.	2700	2494	2296	2109	2914	2487	2107	1778	+0.9	+2.0	0.0*
.30/06 Springfield	220	S.P.	2410	2197	1996	1809	2840	2358	1947	1599	+0.7	+1.2	—3.2
.300 H & H	180	S.P.B.T.	2920	2706	2500	2297	3409	2927	2499	2109	+0.6	+1.6	0.0*
.300 H & H	220	S.P.	2620	2400	2170	1986	3367	2814	2301	1927	+1.1	+2.3	0.0*
7.65 Argentine	150	S.P.	2920	2630	2355	2105	2841	2304	1848	1476	+0.2	+0.7	—2.1
.303 British	130	S.P.	2790	2483	2195	1929	2246	1780	1391	1075	+0.3	+0.9	—2.5
.303 British	150	S.P.	2720	2440	2170	1930	2465	1983	1569	1241	+0.4	+0.9	—2.6
.303 British	180	S.P.B.T.	2540	2340	2147	1965	2579	2189	1843	1544	+0.5	+1.0	—2.8
.303 British	215	S.P.	2180	1947	1733	1541	2273	1810	1434	1134	+1.1	+1.7	—4.3
7.7 Japanese	130	S.P.	2952	2635	2340	2065	2513	2004	1581	1231	+0.2	+0.7	—2.1
7.7 Japanese	180	S.P.B.T.	2493	2292	2101	1922	2484	2100	1765	1477	+0.6	+1.1	—2.9
7.7 Japanese	215	S.P.	2264	2023	1802	1603	2448	1954	1550	1227	+1.0	+1.6	—3.9
8 × 57 JR	196	S.P.	2362	2045	1761	1513	2428	1820	1530	996	+0.9	+1.5	—3.9
8 × 57 JRS	196	S.P.	2395	2074	1795	1535	2497	1873	1402	1026	+0.8	+1.4	—3.8
8 × 57 JS	123	S.P.	2888	2515	2170	1857	2277	1728	1286	942	+0.3	+0.8	—2.4
8 × 57 JS	159	S.P.	2724	2362	2030	1734	2618	1970	1455	1062	+0.4	+1.0	—2.8
8 × 57 JS	159	F.J.	2560	2208	1903	1631	1790	1332	990	727	+0.6	+1.2	—3.3
8 × 57 JS	165	S.P.B.T.	2855	2563	2285	2028	2984	2405	1912	1506	+0.2	+0.8	—2.3
8 × 57 JS	196	S.P.	2526	2195	1894	1627	2778	2097	1562	1152	+0.6	+1.2	—3.3
8 × 57 JS	198	H.P.B.T.	2624	2416	2216	2028	3031	2567	2160	1808	+1.1	+2.2	0.0*
8 × 57 JS	227	S.P.	2329	2085	1855	1650	2737	2192	1735	1373	+0.9	+2.2	—3.7
8 × 57 J	196	S.P.	2526	2195	1894	1627	2778	2097	1562	1152	+0.6	+1.2	—3.3
8 × 58 RD	196	S.P.	2230	1927	1656	1426	2164	1614	1193	884	+1.1	+1.7	—4.5
.358 Norma Mag.	250	S.P.	2800	2493	2231	2001	4322	3451	2764	2223	+0.3	+0.8	—2.4
.358 Winchester	200	S.P.	2530	2210	1910	1640	2843	2170	1621	1195	+0.6	+1.2	—3.3
.358 Winchester	250	S.P.	2250	2010	1780	1570	2811	2243	1759	1369	+1.0	+1.6	—4.0
9.3 × 57 mm.	286	S.P.	2067	1818	1595	1404	2714	2099	1616	1252	+1.4	+2.0	—5.0
9.3 × 62 mm.	232	H.P.	2624	2304	2009	1742	3551	2735	2080	1564	+0.5	+1.1	—3.1
9.3 × 62 mm.	286	S.P.	2362	2088	1873	1612	3544	2769	2144	1651	+0.8	+1.4	—3.7
.375 Holland & Holland	270	S.P.	2740	2459	2207	1987	4502	3620	2920	2368	+0.3	+0.9	—2.5
.375 Holland & Holland	300	S.P.	2550	2280	2040	1830	4333	3464	2773	2231	+0.6	+1.1	—3.0

* Rifle sighted in for 200 yards.

*Ballistics Tables for Federal Center-Fire Rifle Ammunition**

All bullets are soft-point style.

	Bullet	Velocity (ft. sec.)				Energy (ft. lbs.)				Mid-Range Trajectory (inches)		
Cartridge	Wt. (grs.)	Muzzle	100 Yds.	200 Yds.	300 Yds.	Muzzle	100 Yds.	200 Yds.	300 Yds.	100 Yds.	200 Yds.	300 Yds.
.222 Remington	50	3200	2660	2170	1750	1140	785	520	340	0.5	2.5	7.0
.22–250 Remington	55	3810	3270	2770	2320	1770	1300	935	655	0.3	1.6	4.4
.223 Remington	55	3300	2800	2340	1930	1330	955	670	455	0.5	2.3	6.1
.243 Winchester	80	3500	3080	2720	2410	2180	1690	1320	1030	0.4	1.8	4.7
.243 Winchester	100	3070	2790	2540	2320	2090	1730	1430	1190	0.5	2.2	5.5
.270 Winchester	130	3140	2880	2630	2400	2840	2390	1990	1660	0.5	2.1	5.1
.270 Winchester	150	2800	2440	2140	1870	2610	1980	1520	1160	0.6	2.9	7.6
7 mm Mauser	175	2490	2170	1900	1680	2410	1830	1400	1100	0.8	3.7	9.5
7 mm Mauser	139	2710	2440	2190	1960	2280	1850	1490	1190	0.7	3.0	7.8
7 mm Remington Mag.	150	3260	2970	2700	2450	3540	2940	2430	1990	0.4	2.0	4.9
7 mm Remington Mag.	175	3070	2720	2400	2120	3660	2870	2240	1750	0.5	2.4	6.1
.30 Carbine	110	1980	1540	1230	1040	955	575	370	260	1.4	7.5	21.7
.30–30 Winchester	150	2410	2020	1700	1430	1930	1360	960	680	0.9	4.2	11.0
.30–30 Winchester	170	2220	1890	1630	1410	1860	1350	1000	750	1.2	4.6	12.5
.30–06 Springfield	125	3200	2810	2480	2200	2840	2190	1710	1340	0.5	2.2	5.6
.30–06 Springfield	150	2970	2670	2400	2130	2930	2370	1920	1510	0.6	2.4	6.1
.30–06 Springfield	180	2700	2430	2180	1940	2910	2360	1900	1500	0.7	3.1	7.6
.300 Winchester Mag.	150	3400	3050	2730	2430	3850	3100	2480	1970	0.4	1.9	4.8
.300 Winchester Mag.	180	3070	2850	2640	2440	3770	3250	2790	2380	0.5	2.1	5.3
.300 Savage	150	2670	2390	2130	1890	2370	1900	1510	1190	0.7	3.0	7.6
.300 Savage	180	2370	2160	1960	1770	2240	1860	1530	1250	0.9	3.7	9.2
.303 British	180	2540	2300	2090	1900	2580	2120	1750	1440	0.7	3.3	8.2
.308 Winchester	150	2860	2570	2300	2050	2730	2200	1760	1400	0.6	2.6	6.5
.308 Winchester	180	2610	2250	1940	1680	2720	2020	1500	1130	0.7	3.4	8.9
8 mm Mauser	170	2570	2140	1790	1520	2490	1730	1210	870	0.8	3.9	10.5
.32 Winchester Special	170	2280	1920	1630	1410	1960	1390	1000	750	1.0	4.8	4.8
.35 Remington	200	2100	1710	1390	1160	1950	1300	855	605	1.2	6.0	16.5

* The Federal Cartridge Company lists these ballistics as "Approximate" (which is probably true of all ballistics tables).

Chapter V

CENTER-FIRE RIFLES

In the field of center-fire rifles you see a wondrous world of guns at their best, some sleek and beautiful, others ugly and misshapen in design—but all interesting. Never before has the variety been so wide in bolt, lever, slide and automatic models. Which, then, should you buy? Generally, woods hunters lean toward the lever, slide and automatic rifles, while western hunters in open country tend to buy bolt actions. There's no reason, however, why you should conform to this pattern. Buy the model which will do the best job for *you* and which *you'll* enjoy shooting, but buy only after you've made a rather thorough study of the various types available.

A popular misconception is that a long-barreled rifle will shoot farther and flatter. To comply with the law, a shoulder gun must have at least an 18-inch barrel, but any length beyond that will give you little, if any, additional power. A 24-inch barrel will average some 10 foot seconds more velocity per inch than a 20-inch barrel, a difference which is impossible to detect without a chronograph. Many feel that a short barrel results in greater muzzle blast, but this is likely to be hypothetical to a great degree. What's more, the shorter bore is handier to swing in brushy terrain and, of course, easier to carry. Many standard 24-inch barrel rifles are also available in carbine style with 20-inch barrels for just such hunting. On the other hand, used with iron sights, a long barrel offers a greater sighting radius, hence the long barrels on target models.

The Single Shot

This is not a widely used rifle but its popularity is great enough to warrant several models by Ruger. These have a lever-activated falling block action. Among the calibers available are:

.243 Winchester	6 mm Remington
.30/06 Springfield	.25/06 Remington
.270 Winchester	.375 H & H Magnum
7 mm Remington Magnum	.458 Winchester Magnum
.300 Winchester Magnum	.45/70 Government
.22–250 Remington	

If you can afford a magazine rifle, by all means buy one, but don't go without the shooting fun a single-shot center-fire rifle will provide. For one thing, you'll develop sound shooting habits and stalking skill since there'll be no quick second shot.

Double Rifles

These are European guns, little used in this country although one is available here as a Mauser-Bauer import in calibers that include .243, .270, .30/06 and .308. It is an over-and-under (one barrel atop the other) and a beautiful rifle of its type.

Combination Rifles

The product of the practical European mind, these combination rifle-shotguns are sometimes known as "drillings." Two shotgun barrels are usually set over a center-fire rifle barrel, often in combinations of 16-gauge shotgun barrels and .30/30, .30/06 or 8 mm rifle barrel. Some models have a single shotgun barrel only. Such guns were designed for hunters who took whatever game they encountered, whether four-footed or winged. I have as yet to see one in use in America, nor is this likely since their cost is

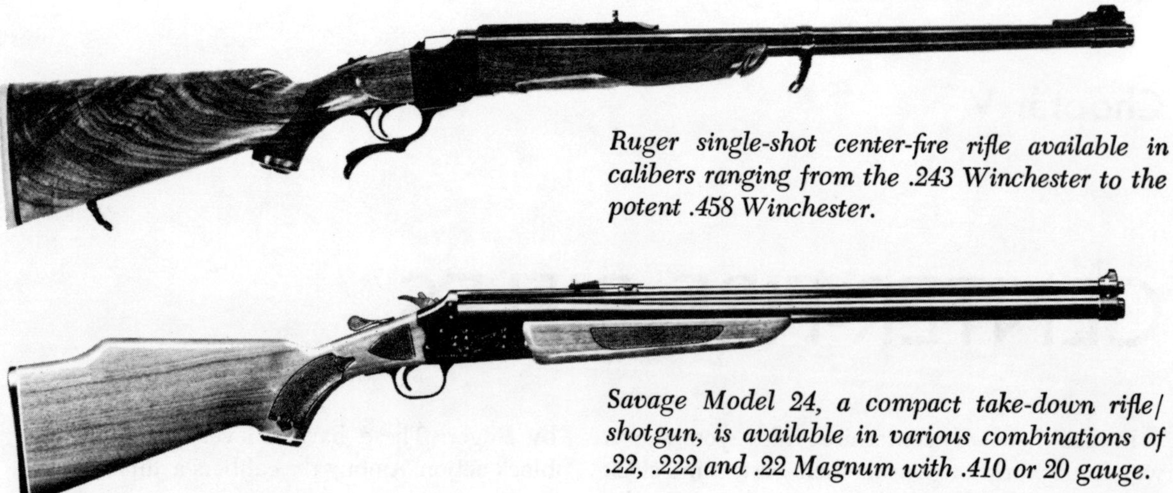

Ruger single-shot center-fire rifle available in calibers ranging from the .243 Winchester to the potent .458 Winchester.

Savage Model 24, a compact take-down rifle/shotgun, is available in various combinations of .22, .222 and .22 Magnum with .410 or 20 gauge.

prohibitive for the average American sportsman.

A more practical version for American hunting is the Savage Model 24, to my knowledge the only true combination rifle/shotgun made in this country. It's available in the following combinations:

.222 and 20 Gauge
.22 Long Rifle and 20 Gauge
.22 Long Rifle and .410
.22 Magnum and 20 Gauge
.22 Magnum and .410

This is a single-trigger gun with barrel selector. An ideal "pot gun" for small game, whether it runs or flies. It is also an excellent "first gun." The upper barrel (rifled) is grooved for scope mounting.

Not truly a combination gun but worthy of a second look in this field is the Harrington & Richardson Model 158. This is a break-open, single-shot .30/30 rifle, with an optional interchangeable barrel in 20 gauge. Essentially two guns in one, it does not, however, allow a quick choice of rifle or shotgun in the field. The barrels must be shifted.

The Bolt-Action

The continued popularity of the bolt-action rifle is understandable. It offers the greatest variety of loads and calibers—possibly more than all of the other actions put together—all the way from the .17 Remington up to the potent Weatherby Magnums. It's identified with big-game hunting, the dream of most shooters limited to deer trips once a year. It's easy to load, and with the "trap-door" magazines, is the simplest and safest to unload, since the action need not be worked to eject the unfired cartridges. What's more, all of the new, high-velocity and flat-shooting loads are handled by one or another of the many bolt-action rifles on the market.

Despite its great appeal, though, it might well be the wrong type of rifle for *your* needs. In the deer woods of the North and the Northeast, it's likely to take a back seat to the lever-action because it's slower to operate and heavier to carry. Presently Savage is the only American manufacturer offering left-handed models.

Today's assortment of bolt-action rifles is an astounding one, especially in the light of their availability twenty years ago. American makers are turning out a greater variety of models and calibers than ever and European imports seem to grow daily, with both domestic and imported models all tapped and drilled for American telescope mounts. Some shooters believe they can save money by buying European guns, while others believe these to be superior in quality and workmanship. If this were ever true, it no longer is. Imports are priced high enough to make American shooters take a second and more careful look at American guns, and as to quality and workmanship, I'm not sure how many American guns I've owned during the past twenty-five years, but my arsenal has ranged all the

Favorite American bolt-action center-fire rifles—Harrington & Richardson Model 330, Mossberg Model 800D, Remington Model 700 BDL, Ruger 77 Magnum, Smith & Wesson Model MB, Weatherby Vanguard, Winchester Model 70 Deluxe, Winchester Model 70 African.

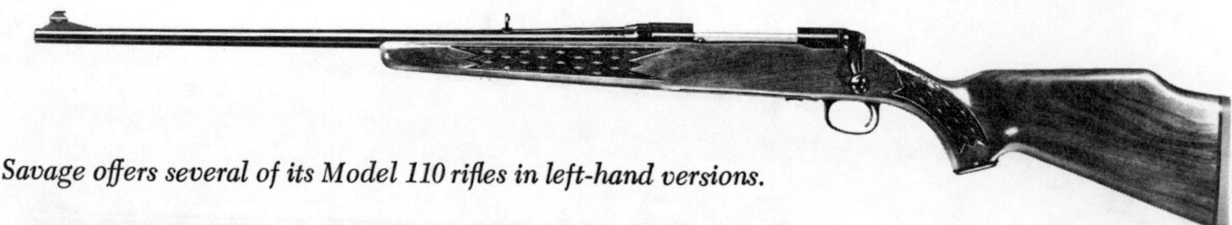

Savage offers several of its Model 110 rifles in left-hand versions.

way from five-dollar .22s to the finest in standard-grade center-fire rifles and *not once have I ever had to run to a gunsmith for repairs.*

Many shooters, once they've smelled enough burning gunpowder get the urge to build their own rifles, or have them built to their specifications and these are invariably bolt-actions. Some American manufacturers now supply their actions for this purpose and, of course, there are the famed Mauser actions, along with the Finnish Sako and the Belgian F.N. or Fabrique Nationale.

The average shooter and especially the beginner buying his first high-power rifle will do well to stick to one of the American brands, at least until he "gets his feet wet" in this shooting game.

Bolt-action center-fire rifles imported from Europe and chambered for popular American calibers—F.N. (Fabrique Nationale, Belgium) Mauser, Mauser Musketeer, Sako Forester, Sako Vixen, Sako Finnbear.

The woods hunter's favorite, a lever-action center-fire. Among these are: Browning BLR, Sako Finnwolf, Marlin Model 444 designed for the potent .444 Magnum, Savage 99, most popular of all American hammerless lever-actions, Winchester Model 88 also available as a carbine, Winchester Model 64, once discontinued and recently revived, Winchester Model 94.

These you can see, feel and try out at a neighboring sporting goods store. If your thinking, however, is toward a European rifle, buy one of the well-known rifles such as Sako, BSA (English) or the Husqvarna from Sweden.

Modern American and European bolt-action rifles are chambered in the following calibers:

.17 Remington	.270 Weatherby Mag.
.22–250 Remington	7 mm Remington
.222 Remington	7 mm Weatherby Mag.
.222 Remington Mag.	.284 Winchester
.223 Remington	.30/06 Springfield
.224 Weatherby Mag.	.300 Winchester Mag.
.225 Winchester	.300 Weatherby Mag.
6 mm Remington	.308 Winchester
.240 Weatherby Mag.	.308 Norma Mag.
.243 Winchester	.338 Winchester Mag.
.25/06 Remington	.340 Weatherby Mag.
.257 Weatherby Mag.	.350 Remington Mag.
6.5 mm Remington	.375 H & H Mag.
.264 Winchester Mag.	.378 Weatherby Mag.
.270 Winchester	.458 Winchester Mag.
	.460 Weatherby Mag.

The Lever-Action

The 1866 Winchester triggered the popularity of the lever-action. It has fluctuated over the years but is now at an all-time high. It is popular enough to warrant the reintroduction in 1972 by Winchester of its Model 64 after an absence of fifteen years. This is a rifle version of the most famous of all lever-actions, the Winchester Model 94. But Winchester has by no means a monopoly. The entire Marlin center-fire line is concentrated on lever-actions, and Savage's famed Model 99 continues to be a favorite.

Some models have visible hammers, such as the Winchester 64 and 94, as well as the Marlins. Winchester's Model 88 and the Savage 99 are "hammerless." Some feature tubular magazines, others a box feed.

Lever-actions present some minor drawbacks. Those which eject a shell upward interfere with the use of a scope sight. Side ejection eliminates this problem. Also, hammer models may be difficult to cock if a low-mounted scope is used, but here again, ingenuity by the Williams Gun Sight Company has produced a side extension for the hammer.

Whether or not slings are practical on a lever-action gun depends upon the type of hunting involved. For quick woods shots, leather may prove a nuisance except for carrying. In open country, where stalking and more deliberate aiming are possible, the sling can be an asset.

Early lever-actions were restricted to conservative loads developing comparatively low breech pressures. Modern versions handle much "hotter" loads—the .243, .284, .308, .300 Savage, even the potent .444 Marlin.

Generally, lever-action rifles and carbines are good "saddle guns," since they are flat and compact. They're not limited to being carried by horsemen, however. Guides, trappers and other professional woodsmen, especially older ones, are fond of the lever-action while the general run of deer hunters favor them, too. They're faster to shoot than bolt-actions and they're suitable for either right- or left-handed shooters. The short-barreled or carbine models, most of them having 20-inch barrels, make ideal woods guns because of their lightness and the speed and ease with which they can be brought up for snap shots at short ranges. Magazine capacities range from four to seven shots.

Certain lever-actions are available either as carbines with 20-inch barrels or as rifles with 24-inch barrels. Calibers available in lever-actions include:

.243 Winchester	.308 Winchester
.250/3000 Savage	.32 Winchester Spec.
.284 Winchester	.35 Remington
.300 Savage	.44 Magnum
.30/30 Winchester	.444 Marlin

The Slide-Action

The slide-action, also known as "pump" or "trombone," makes possible rapid fire and quick sighting, since activating the forearm is a natural motion, even at high speed, that does not seriously disturb sight alignment, an advantage on running game. Being hammerless, slide-actions have smooth receiver lines that make possible low scope mounting. They are adaptable to either right- or left-handed shooters.

Only two American firms turn out slide-actions—Remington and Savage. Remington's Model 760, available as a rifle with a 22-inch barrel or as a carbine with an 18½-inch barrel, is chambered for the 6 mm Remington, .270 Winchester, .30/06, .308 Winchester and the .243 Winchester.

The Savage Model 170, also featuring a 22-inch barrel, handles .30/30 Winchester loads.

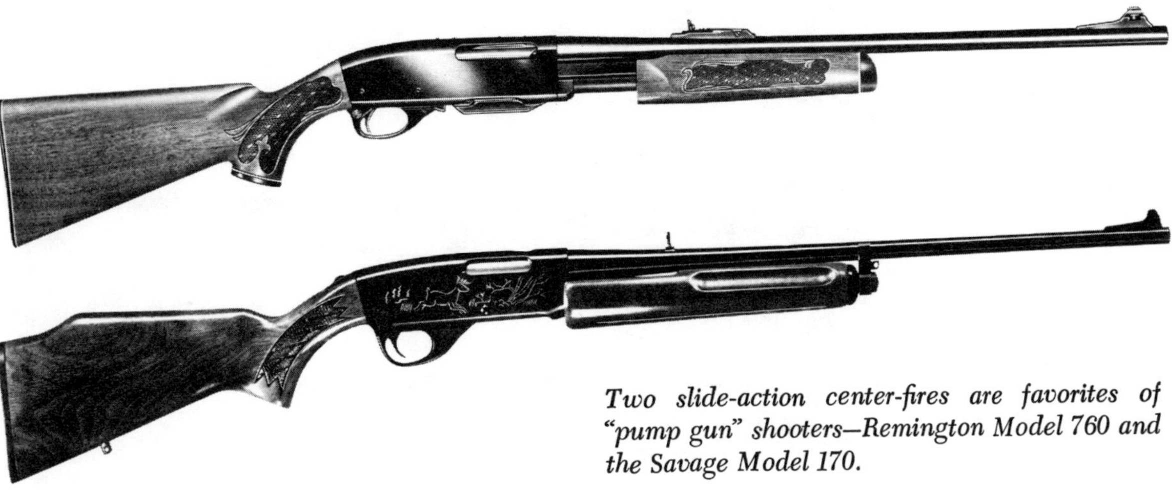

Two slide-action center-fires are favorites of "pump gun" shooters—Remington Model 760 and the Savage Model 170.

The Automatic

As explained in the case of the .22 automatics, this is really a semi-automatic or self-loading rifle (or carbine, a short-barrel version of a rifle) which will fire one shot with each pull of the trigger, loading and cocking itself automatically. It's the fastest of all sportsmen's guns. I've always felt that the incredibly fast rate of fire which is possible with an automatic is completely unnecessary in hunting and I suspect that many users depend upon firepower rather than upon accuracy of sighting.

However, my lack of enthusiasm for center-fire automatics has not detracted from their popularity. The following are available:

Make	*Model No.*	*Calibers*
Browning	BAR	.243 Winchester, .270 Winchester, .30/06, .308 Winchester, 7 mm Remington Magnum, .300 Winchester Magnum, .338 Winchester Magnum
Harrington & Richardson	360–361	.243 Winchester, .308 Winchester
Remington	742	.243 Winchester, 6 mm Remington, .280 Remington, .308 Winchester, .30/06
Sturm-Ruger	44 Carbine	.44 Magnum
Winchester	100	.243 Winchester, .284 Winchester, .308 Winchester

Center-Fire Target Rifles

Unlike some .22 target rifles which can be used for informal shooting such as plinking or even small-game hunting, center-fire target rifles are specialized guns. A rifle weighing 10 to 13 pounds doesn't get toted very far afield as a hunting weapon!

The two foremost American center-fire target rifles are the Winchester Model 70, chambered for .308 (7.62 NATO) or the .30/06 Springfield, and the Remington 540XB, also chambered for the .308.

These rifles find their way into target matches such as the Palma event at Camp Perry where competition is at 800, 900, even 1000 yards. Such rifles are also used in international matches and for bench-rest shooting. Most such rifles are built in compliance with requirements set up by the International Shooting Union.

They are not as sophisticated as the so-called "free rifle," but they are nevertheless precision shooting machines. Winchester, for example, offers a 26-inch heavy barrel with the action bedded in glass to fit the stock perfectly, trigger tension that can be adjusted without removing the action, and a forearm rail for accessories. Remington's version also has a heavy barrel of stainless steel. The Model 70 has a five-shot clip, while the 540XB is available either as a repeater or as a single shot.

As a repeater, the Remington may be ordered

Autoloading center-fires are increasing in popularity, especially the Browning Auto, Harrington & Richardson Model 361, Remington Model 742, Ruger .44 Magnum carbine, Winchester Model 100, also available as a carbine.

chambered for .308 Winchester, .222 Remington, .222 Remington Magnum, .243 Winchester, 6 mm Remington, .22-250 Remington and 6.5 Remington Magnum. In the single-shot version these same calibers are available, plus the .25/06 Remington, 7 mm Remington Magnum and .300 Winchester Magnum.

A few other rifles with heavy barrels are rated "target" rifles by their makers but these are really varminter-grade guns, hardly in the same class with the Model 70 and the Model 540XB.

Military Surplus Rifles

The workmanship in most military weapons made during peacetime is likely to be quite good and parts made to tolerances that allow the interchange of parts even on the battlefield. Weapons turned out hurriedly, in the desperation of wartime, may not be of such high quality. Would-be purchasers overlook the fact that military weapons, designed to withstand hand-to-hand combat, may be clumsy and awkward to carry on hunting trips. Most have very long barrels and the stocks are generally ill-fitting. You should remember, too, that they are being discarded because they are obsolete, as well may be the ammunition for which they are chambered.

Many sportsmen buy such rifles with the intention of converting them to "sporters," and many such conversions result in highly efficient and beautiful rifles, as is often the case with Springfield conversions.

A skilled amateur gunsmith can do a passable job of converting a military rifle to a sporter but before attempting the chore, obtain a copy of *How to Convert Military Rifles* by the Williams Gun Sight Co. Conversion instructions include the 30 M-1 Carbine, Springfield, 1917 Enfield, U.S. Krag, Garand, Model 95 Winchester, the British SLME, all Mausers, the Italian Carcano, the 7.7 Japanese, 6.5 Japanese, the 7.62 Russian and numerous others.

The Winchester Ultra Match Model 70 which has been breaking match records in recent years is admired by the author at the Winchester plant. The heavy barreled target model is available in .308 Winchester and 30/06 Springfield calibers.

Superb center-fire accuracy is represented by these three target rifles: Remington Model 40XB, Winchester Model 70 International Match, Winchester Model 70 Target.

Chapter VI

IRON SIGHTS

The term "iron sight" applies to any that does not contain glass and it doesn't necessarily mean that the sight is actually made of iron. Most are of alloys that combine lightness and ruggedness.

Despite the ever mounting production of telescope sights, there are still millions of shooters, especially woods hunters, who stick to iron sights —and with some justification. Many are still to be convinced of the superiority of the scope in forest cover. Also, get caught out in a snow or rain storm with a scope sight and you'll have to be very careful not to get the outside surfaces of the lenses wet. Telescope sight makers now turn out scopes that will not "fog" from interior moisture condensing on the lenses. By means of nitrogen gas and tight seals, modern scopes are practically fogproof—from the inside. However, let a single snowflake or raindrop light on an exterior lens surface and the image will be blurred.

Iron sights generally are less susceptible to damage than scopes. A surprisingly great number of rifles ride in pickup trucks and cars, sometimes year-round and are subject to abuse which would quickly ruin a scope sight. Only the simplest and most rugged sights can withstand this treatment.

I fail to agree with them, but many woods hunters, guides, trappers and loggers of the old school, maintain that iron sights are much faster than the scope. Insofar as they are concerned, they're probably right. Using a scope in the woods requires long practice which few hunters have the patience to carry out. Nevertheless, iron sights *are* fast.

Another advantage of the iron sight is its low cost, especially when compared with that of a high-quality scope. You can buy an excellent open rear sight, fully adequate for woods or short-range hunting, for about $3.00, and the finest micrometer receiver peep sight for about $20.

Open Sights

Also known as a "sporting rear sight" this type is nothing more than a blade set crosswise atop the rifle barrel forward of the receiver, with a notch cut into its upper edge. The shooter lines up the front sight in this notch with the target. Such sights vary considerably in design but all operate on the same principle. Some are known as "semi-buckhorn" or "full buckhorn," with flaring outer edges that help the eye to "slide" automatically and quickly into the sighting notch. Nearly all open sights are adjustable for elevation by means of a sliding bar with graduated notches for raising or lowering. Sighting notches vary in shape, too—some in the form of a *V*, *U* or a square-bottomed *U*. Some are adjustable for windage—especially those used on target pistols —but generally open rear sights on rifles rarely are adjusted laterally. Because of their location forward of the receiver, such sights are also known as "middle sights," as opposed to the receiver mounting of peep or aperture sights.

Hunters seldom adjust the sights for elevation, once they've sighted in the rifle. For long shots, they merely raise the front sight so that more of it is visible in the rear-sight notch. Although this method invariably causes the front sight to hide at least a part of the target, some old-time hunters are uncannily accurate at this type of shooting. "Taking a full sight" is about as accurate as this type of sighting equipment can be. Another shortcoming is the short sighting radius afforded by the sight's location—sighting radius being the distance between the front and rear sight. The longer the radius the more accurate is likely to be the shot, all other factors being equal.

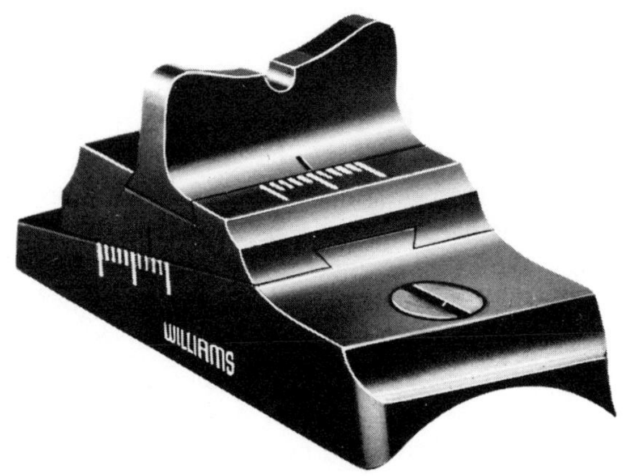

Williams Guide, a calibrated open rear sight. (WILLIAMS GUN SIGHT CO.)

One of the most ingenious open rear sights is the Williams Guide open sight which is adjustable for windage and elevation. Designed for use with a ramp-type front sight, adjustments can be made simply by turning a single screw which locks securely at any set elevation or windage.

The Receiver Sight

Also known as the "peep" or aperture sight, this is the ultimate in sighting equipment short of the scope sight. Many an old-time woodsman will disagree violently but the receiver sight is faster than the open sight. Here is why. With an open sight, you must make three conscious alignments, the rear sight, the front sight and the target. With a peep receiver sight, you merely *look through* the aperture and line up the front bead on the target, actually aligning two objects instead of three.

Inexperienced shooters, looking at a peep sight for the first time are a little appalled at the small aperture, which may be only .022 inches. Normal reaction is "with such a tiny aperture, sighting must be slow!" However, put the sight to your eye in normal shooting position and the entire target field comes into view much like a ball game through a knothole in the fence.

An opposite reaction then sets in. "This hole is too big!" The target field at first appears to wobble all through the sight aperture. However, *your eye will automatically center itself* in the aperture! If you try deliberately to center your eye, you may well be off to one side or the other, too high or too low, but if you concentrate simply on lining up the front sight on the target, your eye will do its job automatically and with amazing accuracy. This is what makes the peep receiver sight faster than the open sight.

The peep-sight aperture is located at the center of a removable disc which may be replaced with others having apertures of varying diameters for different types of shooting. These may vary from .022 inches up to .125 inches. For hunting where snap shots are expected, or in poor light, some hunters remove the disc altogether and sight through the tapped hole! For target shooting or hunting in good light, smaller apertures are used.

While elevation and windage adjustments with open sights depend much upon estimates, receiver peep sights make these changes with machine-like precision through a system of micrometer "clicks." Usually a knurled screwhead is turned, which "indexes" itself either audibly or by feel for elevation, and a similar knob adjusts windage. These "clicks" change the point of impact as little as ¼ inch at 100 yards. A full inch adjustment at 100 yards is one minute of angle in shooting terminology, so that a ¼-inch adjustment would be ¼ minute of angle.

Not all receiver sights, however, have click adjustments. Some have slotted units which slide up or down for elevation and sideways for windage. Both types, though, can be locked into position once satisfactorily adjusted. Although the sliding type is not as easily adjusted, and involves some degree of guesswork, they are surprisingly efficient.

Most receiver sights have a minute-of-angle scale and one model has an additional blank scale on which a shooter can inscribe his own calibrations. Many receiver sights can be removed from their bases and later replaced without changing the point of impact. This makes possible the use of a removable telescope sight on the same rifle.

Receiver or peep sights are usually associated with bolt-action rifles and it's for this type of rifle that the greatest variety of such sights are made, but there are also excellent models for lever action, both hammer and hammerless, and for slide and automatics. Most manufacturers issue charts which make the otherwise complicated process of buying new sights for a rifle a simple one.

Aperture-type Williams Guide rear sight, Williams Foolproof receiver sight with calibrations for windage and elevation.
(WILLIAMS GUN SIGHT CO.)

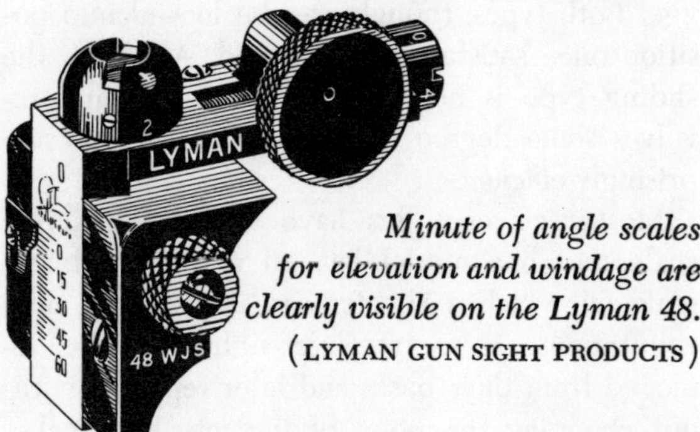

Minute of angle scales for elevation and windage are clearly visible on the Lyman 48.
(LYMAN GUN SIGHT PRODUCTS)

Front Sights

Chances are that when your new rifle comes from the factory it will be equipped with a "gold" bead or ivory-colored front sight. Near the muzzle, or atop a small ramp, there is a dovetail cut into which this sight is inserted. The front sight has been matched to the rear sight as to proper elevation in relation to the bore of the barrel so that the gun will place your shots where you point the sights. Should you decide to change the open sight for a receiver peep your rifle may then shoot slightly high even with the rear sight depressed as far as it will go, because the relative heights between the front and rear sight have now been changed. Also affecting the point of impact will be any change in sighting radius. The remedy is a new front sight, to match the substituted rear sight.

First you'll have to remove the old front sight by sliding it from its dovetailed slot. Since it is inserted rather snugly, you'll have to force it out; but don't strike it with a metal hammer, lest you miss and mar your new barrel. Instead, place a hardwood block against the sight base and strike the wood light but sharp blows with the hammer.

Gun-sight manufacturers have tables indicating front sight elevation corrections for just such situations.

For target shooters there are hooded front sights, too. Some of these have interchangeable discs made of light green or amber—or sometimes clear—plastic. Others are made of light sheet steel. Such inserts are provided with posts and various sizes of apertures to help concentrate vision on the bull's-eye and to utilize as much light as possible on dark days. For use in bright sunshine, some of these hooded front sights have a "sun-shade," really an extension of the hood. I once mounted such a front sight on an inexpensive .22 rifle—hardly a target model —yet I found my scores improving immediately. "Tinkering" the sights of a pet rifle can be a fascinating hobby in itself and one that will pay off, at least in better scores and more hunting hits—if not financially!

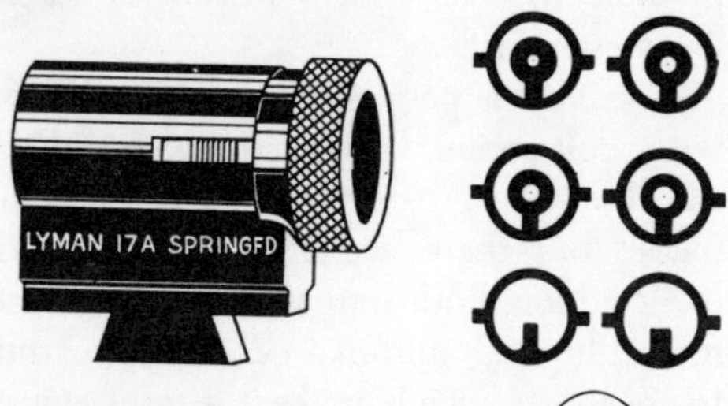

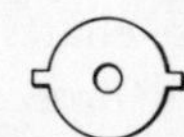

The Lyman 17A hooded front sight uses a variety of interchangeable sighting disc inserts for different light conditions.
(LYMAN GUN SIGHT PRODUCTS)

Chapter VII

TELESCOPE SIGHTS

Telescope sights got off to a bad start in this country. Prior to World War I, most were imported from Germany, and although of fine optical quality, the mounts then available were crude and set the scopes too high above the bore of a rifle so that a shooter had to crane his neck. Also, they were expensive and delicate. It was American manufacturers who brought scope prices down within reach of the average rifleman and lowered the mounting systems to their present efficient level. In addition, scopes were toughened. They are no longer knocked out of kilter by a slight accidental rap.

The optical system of a telescope sight utilizes an objective lens (front) to produce an upside-down and reversed image at a station within the scope tube called a focal point. An erector lens system then rights and corrects it as to right and left. The eyepiece, at the rear of the scope, magnifies this image and the human eye, actually becoming a part of the scope's ocular system, sees the target image. This is an oversimplification of a scope's workings but it will serve as a start toward understanding the "innards" of today's fine telescope rifle sights.

The most obvious reason for using a scope, of course, is that the field of view and the target are magnified and that's as far as most scope buyers go. However, there's more. For example, the scope is the fastest of all rifle sights, once you become accustomed to it. I've already pointed out how two points must be aligned in using the peep sight, and three with open sights. Telescope sights, however, allow focal plane sighting—there is no apparent third dimension. When sighting through a scope, you merely look through the tube and place the post or cross-hair reticle ON the target. You are not conscious of the several hundred feet which may separate you from your target. Because of this, it takes less time to get on target with a scope than with any form of iron sight.

This doesn't mean that if you've been shooting with iron sights for several years, you'll be delighted with your first scope. Rather, you're likely to cuss it, until you become accustomed to it, after which you'll probably never revert to iron sights. It takes getting used to! Don't buy a scope a week before the deer season opens and expect it to work wonders for you. Buy it in the spring and practice through the summer with it, on targets or varmints.

Apart from sighting speed, there are other advantages to using a scope. The lens system can correct a shooter's poor eyesight, including near- and farsightedness, simply by focusing the instrument. Thus an elderly hunter, or one with failing eyesight, need not give up hunting. Even for a hunter with 20/20 vision, the scope is a boon because of its light-gathering qualities, allowing earlier and later hunting under poor light conditions that would balk an iron-sight user. A scope sight does not obscure a part of the target, as do iron sights and, because of this, it's a safety factor. You can tell quickly whether your target is a deer, for example, or another hunter!

A scope will be at a slight disadvantage in a snow- or rainstorm, as I've pointed out, but other than this, I know of nothing detrimental that can be said about a *good* scope properly mounted. True, a hunting scope and its mount will add about one pound to a rifle's over-all weight, but that's a small price to pay for the sighting efficiency and increased shooting range made possible by the glassware.

Telescope sights are not all alike in quality, however, as is evidenced by the wide price ranges. The crudest open sight is a better rig

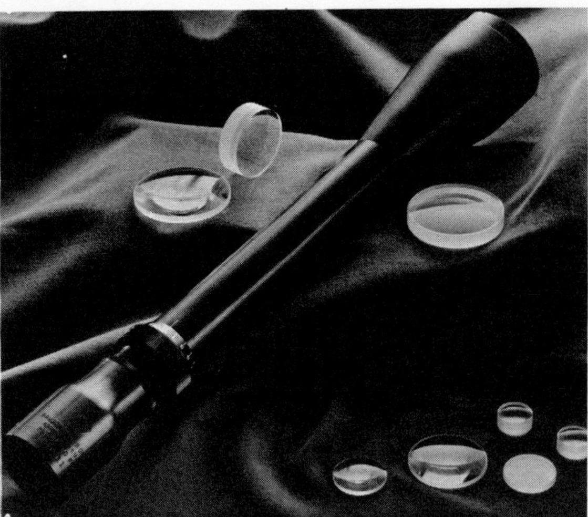

The optical elements that go into the making of a fine telescope sight. (BAUSCH & LOMB)

than a poor scope and you might as well reconcile yourself that a $19 "bargain" in glassware is a bad investment. Fortunately, the general run of American-made scopes is very good and *some* of the imports are of surprising quality.

Ruggedness. A hunting scope is exposed to considerable abuse, no matter how careful its owner may be. Heavy recoil, of course, jars it and occasionally a scope-mounted rifle is dropped or hit accidentally against a rock, tree or car. Also, the rifle may ride over rough roads in a jeep or truck, or over rough trails in a saddle scabbard. It is taken from the 70-degree warmth of a hunting camp into below freezing temperatures. Under this normal but still substantial abuse, the lens system must remain firmly in place and the scope must retain its zero, or sighted point of impact. Lenses in medium-priced scopes are mounted in gaskets of Canadian balsam or synthetic cements. The more expensive scopes have their lens systems mounted solidly against metal. Exterior tubes which house the components are made of light steel or aluminum alloys, with the steel tougher than the alloy.

Fogproofing. Fogging was one of the failings of early telescope sights. Interior lens surfaces became blurred through condensation of moisture that had worked its way into the scope tube, with this likely to occur when the rifle was taken from a warm camp into the cold outdoors. Some present-day scopes are assembled in moisture- and dust-controlled rooms and their tight assembly is such that moisture cannot enter the completed scope, short of its being damaged. Other scopes, lower-priced but still highly efficient, are assembled within a nitrogen-gas-filled tube which eliminates fogging. If the construction isn't absolutely tight, of course, the nitrogen gas may escape and moisture enter. Therefore, sound construction is needed in addition to the nitrogen gas.

Coated Lenses. Practically all scopes today have their lenses coated with magnesium fluoride to cut down light reflections and to improve light transmission. Usually visible as a purplish tinge on the lens surface this coating is applied to all surfaces of interior as well as exterior glass, at least in the better scopes. For some twelve years I guided deer hunters in the Maine woods, using a scope-sighted rifle every year except one. That was the year I tried a scopeless lever-action rifle—and it turned out to be my poorest season! I had trained myself to use a scope by year-round shooting (except for the dead of Maine's bitter winter) at varmints until sighting became second nature. It didn't matter about the range, and brush bothered very little. Sighting with the scope had become an automatic motion. This is when the scope can beat the iron sight!

While returning from an afternoon of high-power plinking, my partner and I spotted a big woodchuck feeding at the edge of a field, farther away from his hole than any woodchuck has any business being! Shooting an open-sighted .30/30, my partner got off the first shot and missed at some 50 yards. A second shot only sent the chuck scurrying faster for his den. In the meantime, I'd brought up my scope-sighted .270. Seeing the chuck clearly enough to distinguish his left eye as he ran, I swung the cross hairs slightly ahead of him and touched the trigger. He toppled over —decapitated! This was *not* a case of superior shooting skill, for my partner was no slouch with his .30/30, but open sights on a running woodchuck just were not adequate. Following the animal in the scope was easy.

Eye Relief. This is the distance between a shooter's eye and the ocular or rear lens. A scope designed for .22 shooting may have eye relief as short as one inch, since there's no recoil to drive

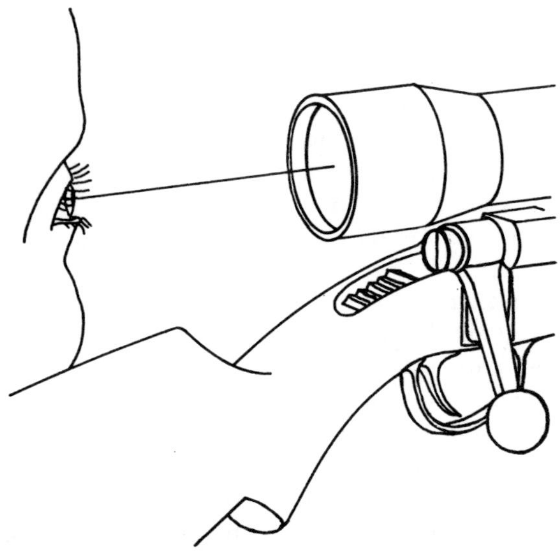

Eye relief is the distance between a shooter's eye and the rear or ocular lens.

the scope back into his eye or forehead. To avoid a black eye with a heavy recoil rifle, however, an eye relief of three to five inches is required.

If your scope is properly mounted and the comb of your stock is correct for your natural shooting stance, you'll have no trouble with this three to five inch eye relief limitation. In order to see 90 per cent of the field of view you have a leeway, backward and forward, of about one inch. An hour's practice, even in your living room sighting through a window, will have you bringing up the rifle to your shoulder so that you automatically find the correct eye relief for a maximum view through the scope. If you find that you must place your eye too close to the scope, exposing yourself to recoil abuse, loosen the mount rings slightly and slide the tube ahead slightly. On the other hand, you may have to slide the scope *back* slightly if it's too far forward to give you a full view of the target area. You may also encounter some difficulty with centering your shooting eye directly back of the scope, and raising the height of the comb will likely cure this trouble. By all means, if the scope forces you to assume an uncomfortable stance, don't try to change your shooting habits to conform. Instead change the position of the scope or the height of the comb to fit *your* stance.

Field of View. This represents the width of the area visible through the scope, usually expressed in feet at 100 yards. The greater the scope's power or magnification, the smaller or narrower will be the field of view. In scopes where magnification may be varied, the field will vary accordingly. For a hunting scope you'll want as wide a field as possible, the more easily to pick out running game or to search out a wooded area for a skulking animal. A 30- to 40-foot field of view at 100 yards is considered ample for most hunting. In a target scope the field of vision is comparatively unimportant since the target is a stationary one and the scope line of sight is concentrated within a small target area. Greater magnification, then, is possible for the target shooter.

Magnification. Magnification is more popularly termed "power," indicated by an X following the scope's designation such as 4X or four-power, meaning that the glass magnifies four times. Magnification is figured mathematically by dividing the diameter of the objective lens by the diameter of the exit pupil, both dimensions usually given in millimeters, although some scope makers are now indicating these in inches or fractions thereof. By holding a telescope sight a foot or so away from the eye you will see a concentration of light in the center of the eyepiece. This is the exit pupil.

For target shooting, scopes of ten to thirty power are used to show the target more clearly and to reduce aiming error. Such high-power scopes must be used with a rest, however, since the shooter's natural body movements, even heartbeat, would otherwise be magnified in accordance with the scope's power. Aiming would be impossible. A steady rest eliminates transmission of body tremors to the rifle and scope.

For varmint hunting, target techniques and equipment are, to some degree, applied to hunting tactics and scope power may vary from as little as four up to as much as twenty, with eight- to twelve-power scopes the most popular. Running shots are more difficult with such scopes, of course, but much of the shooting in this type of hunting is at standing animals at long ranges. The problem of body-tremor magnification still exists here, but varminter shooters are likely to offset this by steadying their bodies against a log, fence, tree or rock to cut down "shimmy."

For long-range hunting, particularly for antelope, mountain sheep and goats, scopes of six to eight power are proving amazingly successful, but it takes an experienced rifleman to use them, taking advantage of the steadying influence of a sling or using natural body rests to steady the aim. The latter are particularly necessary under the excitement and tension of trophy hunting or in view of heartbeat acceleration that may be caused by climbing at high altitudes in mountain hunting.

In the case of woods hunting or short-range open country work, the two-and-a-half- to four-power scope is the best choice, especially if running or jump shots are likely to be the order of the day, as they well may be in deer hunting. For speed in sighting, it's difficult to beat a four-power scope in the hands of a rifleman who has learned to use it!

Probably the ultimate in scope sights for field use are the variable-power models. These can be likened to the zoom lens on a movie camera. A twist of the finger shifts the power from 1.5X to 4.5X, for example; or from 4X to 12X. And this has a highly practical application. For quick shots at relatively close range, high power is not important but a wide field of view is, and, as we have noted, the lower the power, the wider the field of view. On the other hand, where a long, deliberate shot is called for, power *is* vital, but the field of view less critical. In other words, such a scope sight serves for various forms of hunting.

Definition. This is rather a vague term, although bandied about quite freely in scope advertising. It applies to the clarity of the image and its sharpness of detail as seen through the scope. Definition is dependent upon the quality of the lens system. All lenses, even those of the highest quality, are subject to certain shortcomings. Optical technicians don't deny this. In fact, they admit to the existence of no less than six standard faults, or "aberrations," which must be overcome or rectified. When you consider that a scope has several lenses and that each is subject to these faults, only then can you realize the tremendous task that faces ocular technicians who produce the sharp clear images reflected into a shooter's eye through a high-grade scope. The subject is highly technical but of this you can be certain: No telescope sight offered at $25 is going to match the quality of the ocular system in a $95 scope!

Definition can be seen when examining a scope only in the form of a clear image, sharp in all its detail and lacking in even the slightest degree of haziness or fogginess. If there's such a fuzziness, even around the rim of the lens or target picture, the scope is *not* of the best quality.

Relative Brightness. Scope makers would have you think that they can pin-point relative brightness with mathematical precision, and possibly they can. I'm neither an optician nor a mathematician. But the fact remains that the amount of light introduced into a telescope sight is governed largely by the size of the objective (front) lens, and to a lesser degree by the quality of the lenses, their coating or lack of it. Generally, the higher the scope's power, the larger the objective lens.

Focusing. Practically all scopes made today can be focused and a wide berth should be given any instrument claiming a "universal" focus. There is no such thing. Focusing a scope is simply a matter of turning a ring sleeve or dial until the reticle is in clear focus. This should automatically bring the target, no matter what its range, into clear and sharp view. Focusing does not change the point of impact; once it is accomplished, the focusing ring can usually be locked into position.

Reticle. The reticle, sometimes spelled "reticule," is the "sight" within the scope tube, which is placed "on target." Popular reticles today are the cross hairs, the cross hairs with tapered post and the dot suspended on fine cross hairs. Cross hairs are made of silk, spider webbing, spun glass, platinum, tungsten, silver, copper and stainless steel wire.

Some scopes offer a "range finder" cross-hair reticle, in the form of a single vertical cross hair and two or more horizontal cross hairs, the latter spaced to distend 6 inches at 100 yards. A hunter must know the approximate size of the game he is hunting or the target at which he is shooting in order to use these effectively. If, in sighting, the two horizontal cross hairs appear to border a 3-inch area for example, the hunter knows the target is at 50 yards, or if the space appears to be 12 inches, the target is then 200

new Lyman reticules

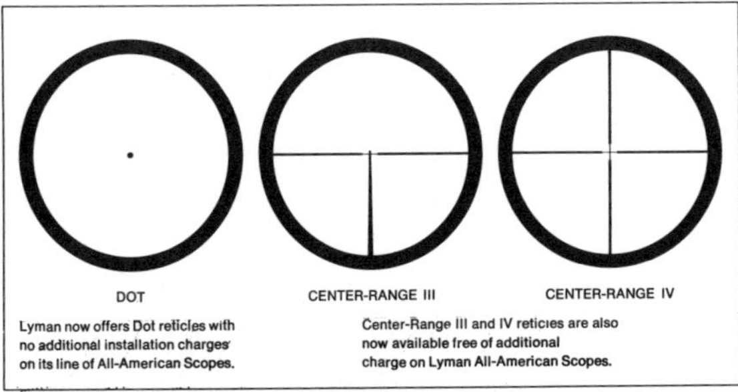

Telescope sight reticles of more recent design: Williams Guide scope (WILLIAMS GUN SIGHT CO.), *Lyman Dot and Center Range types* (LYMAN GUN SIGHT PRODUCTS), *Tasco 33/30 range calculator* (TASCO IMPORTS).

yards. A knowledge of trajectories then comes into play and the shooter holds accordingly.

The post-type reticle is most popular in the West. It resembles roughly the front sight of a pistol as seen by its shooter. Such posts may be a straight flat top, tapered or with a pointed top, generally with a single horizontal cross hair. Posts are not as well suited for fine shooting since they tend to obliterate at least a small part of the target.

Another range-finder type of reticle is the famous "dot," invented by the late T. K. Lee, for whom early dots were named. A dot is suspended on fine cross hairs with a "one-minute dot" subtending one inch of the target at 100 yards, a two-minute, two inches, etc. Dots come in different sizes with the larger four-, five- and six-minute dots recommended only for low-power scopes used at comparatively short range, such as in deer hunting. Dots as small as ⅛ minute can be used on twenty-four- to thirty-power scopes, while ¼-minute dots are the smallest suitable for six- and eight-power glasses.

Using a dot that is too small on a low-power scope makes the dot difficult to find, especially for snap shooting and is next to useless. Many scopes now come equipped with a suitable dot if you specify this type of reticle. However, if you plan to have a dot installed, advise the installer regarding your proposed use of the scope and follow his suggestion.

Windage and Elevation Adjustments. Telescope sights, of course, are adjustable for elevation and windage with several hunting scopes having the adjustment mechanisms within the

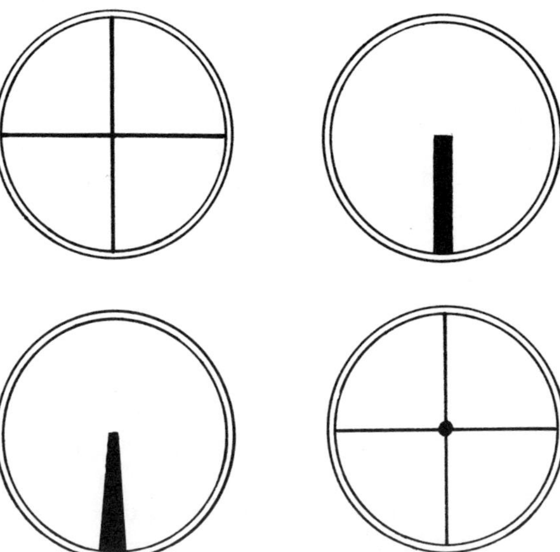

Popular reticles in today's telescope sights: the cross hairs, post, tapered post and the dot, the latter invented by the late T. K. Lee.

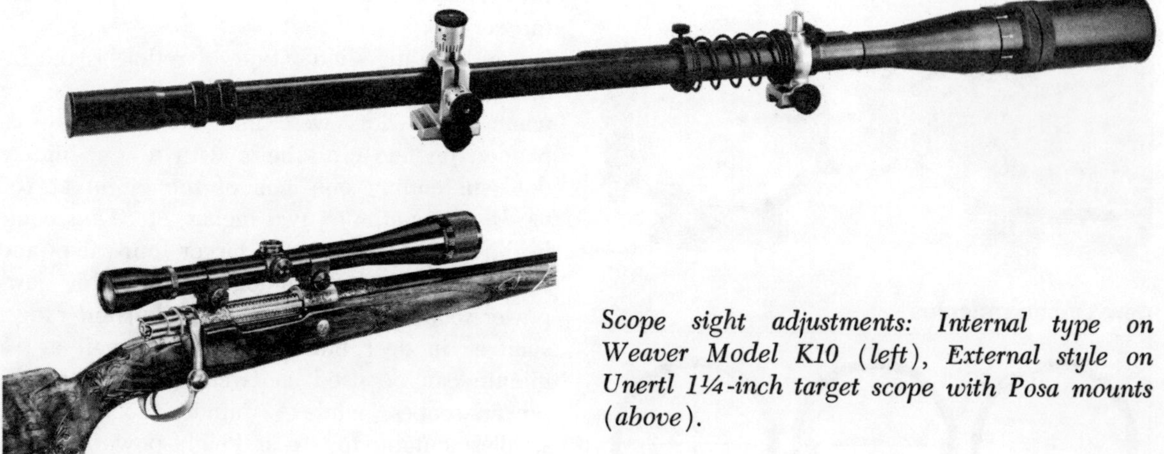

Scope sight adjustments: Internal type on Weaver Model K10 (left), External style on Unertl 1¼-inch target scope with Posa mounts (above).

tube and known as "internal adjustment" scopes. Target scopes have external adjustments, usually an integral part of the scope mounts.

Internal adjustments are made by means of two dials or knurled screws usually located on a "turret," a slight projection on the top or side of the scope tube. Early internal units frequently moved the reticle off center within the scope when extreme adjustments for elevation or windage were made but this problem has now been overcome. While early adjustment units, mostly of the external type, were prone to get "out of zero," present-day scope construction practically guarantees that a scope will hold its zero almost indefinitely. I once carried such a scope for some five years along the Canadian border country in cars, canoes, motorboats, snowmobiles and even dog teams, and never once did the scope lose its zero!

The external adjustment units for target scopes are somewhat more sensitive and considerably more critical since they are used in fine, deliberate shooting which may call for changing the point of impact as little as ¼ minute of angle.

In making adjustments for elevation and windage much the same system is used on scopes as on receiver sights, including clicks or minutes of angle. Low-power hunting scopes usually have ¼- to ½-minute clicks, while scopes in the varminter class, of six to eight power, are generally equipped with ¼-minute click adjustments. Scopes for .22 rifles almost always have ½-minute graduations, either by means of clicks or continuous adjustments.

Parallax. Your rifle scope suffers from parallax when, with the rifle held absolutely still and with your sighting eye moving laterally or vertically across the exit pupil, the target appears to move away from or across the reticle. This is commonly described as "the apparent movement of an object in the field of view in relation to the reticle." An optical explanation of this quirk is likely to be as complex as breaking down Einstein's theory of relativity for laymen's consumption and I'd as soon try one as the other!

The presence of parallax has been overemphasized and few shooters need worry about it. All telescope sights are "guilty" of parallax to some degree since there is only one sighting range for a particular scope at which it is completely free of parallax. Manufacturers assemble a scope to be parallax-free at a certain range, possibly 100 yards in hunting scopes. At all other ranges, some parallax exists but it is so minor that it can't be observed by the scope's user.

In high-power scopes used for target shooting or long-range varmint hunting where fine sighting is critical, parallax becomes a factor with which to contend. On such scopes, adjustment is provided in the objective lens system so that shooters can free their scopes of parallax at all ranges.

Parallax occurs when the reticle becomes loose so that it can move forward or backward slightly, thus throwing off the optical relationship between the reticle, the objective lens and the target or field of view. When this happens, the image transmitted into the scope falls slightly in front, or back, of the reticle so that the scope's image of the target and the latter are not perfectly superimposed. Parallax can also occur in a scope with an exit pupil that is too wide, allowing the sighting eye to move too far laterally or vertically. When the eye is aligned perfectly along the scope's longitudinal axis, parallax cannot occur, which is why quality hunting scopes rarely have an exit pupil greater in diameter than 5 mm. A wider rear lens would allow greater latitude in movement of the sighting eye —and possible parallax.

If, by some chance, your scope *does* develop parallax, don't attempt home repairs. This is work for optical experts. Beg or borrow a replacement while your scope is returned to its manufacturer for realignment. Chances are not one shooter in a thousand ever needs to do this. Parallax problems, like the premature report of Mark Twain's death, are "greatly exaggerated"!

Types of Scope Sights

Generally speaking, scope sights are made for .22 rifles, hunting rifles and for target rifles. Should you wonder why an inexpensive .22 scope can't be used on a big-bore hunting gun, there are two reasons. Firstly, the eye relief of a .22 scope is short—short enough so that recoil could well drive the scope into the shooter's eye. Sec-

Scope sights for .22 rim-fire rifles: Weaver V22 with 3X to 6X variable power, Tasco fixed-power 4X Model 601, Weatherby 4X with dovetail mounts.

Scopes for high-power rifles must withstand recoil and maintain their "zero." Weaver V9 3X to 9X variable-power on Model 70 Winchester, Weatherby Imperial 2¾X to 10X variable-power on a .30/06 Weatherby Vanguard with Buehler mounts, Marlin 800 scope on Marlin Model 336C in 30/30 or .35 Remington.

ondly, the little scopes won't stand the abuse of the heavy recoil of many hunting rifles.

My first .22 scope, purchased for a single-shot rifle, cost less than $10 and was completely serviceable for some twelve years; but I doubt if it would have lasted one day mounted on my .270 or .30/06. Scopes for .22s usually have a ¾- or ⅞-inch diameter tube instead of the standard 1-inch or 26-mm tube used for high-power rifle scopes. Only the better .22 scopes have click adjustments and generally the optics are not as good as those of the higher-priced hunting or target scopes. But that stands to reason—some of today's completely suitable .22 scopes still sell for slightly under $10!

A hunting scope, on the other hand, must not only have sufficient eye relief, a wide field of view for running or snap shots, and the ability to withstand recoil and abuse, but it must also be lightweight, compact and designed to be mounted as low as possible atop the rifle! These requirements make up a big order, but scope designers and makers have filled it well.

Target scopes have fewer limitations, since weight is no object, nor is bulk, some target models being nearly as long as the barrels atop which they perch and having objective lenses as wide as 2 inches in diameter! However, these are precision-like sighting instruments with the finest optics and mechanisms for pin-pointing shots at great distances. They are, as a result, the most expensive of all scope sights.

A fourth classification might be the varminter scope, having the characteristics of both hunting and target models. The good qualities of a varmint scope have already been discussed, but it might be pointed out that besides offering greater magnification and a reasonable field of view, varmint scopes too must be fairly compact and lightweight.

It's obvious then that the scope you may decide to buy must be suited to a particular type of shooting, although some of the variable-power models successfully transgress the lines between hunting-varminter-target shooting. Once you've decided upon the type you want, buy the best you can afford. I won't urge you to go out on a financial limb, but even the best American scopes can be financed. You'll never regret cutting corners to make possible the purchase of a

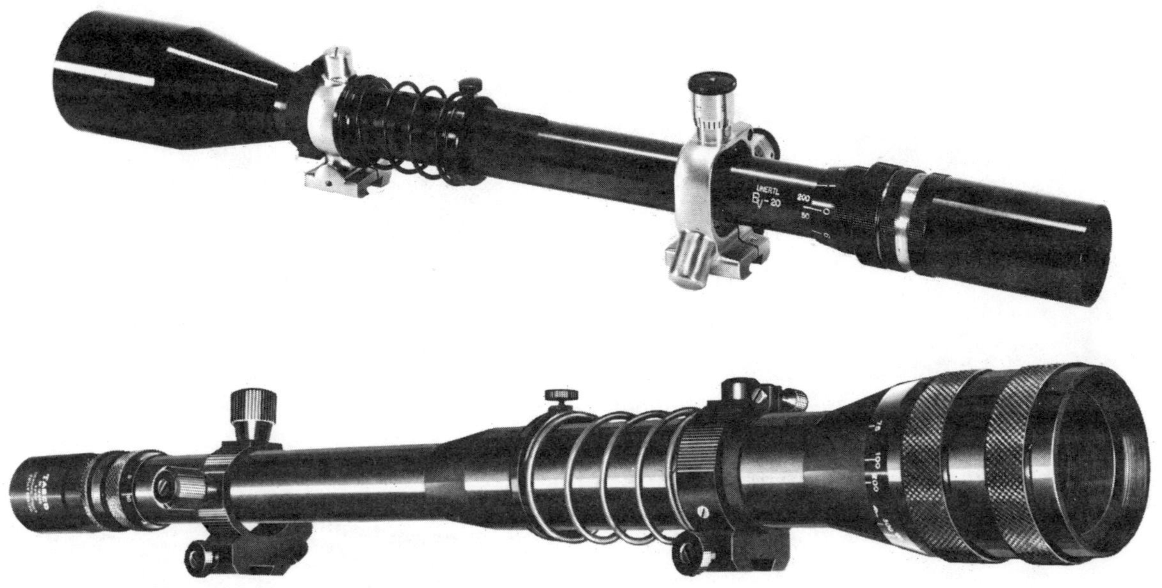

Bench-rest and varminter scopes require great magnification and fine adjustments. These are—the Unertl BV-20X with a 43 mm objective lens, and the Tasco No. 708, also a 20X scope, with a 40 mm objective lens.

high-grade scope. Buy a well-known brand and read the small print in the catalogs—for therein lie some of the secrets you may regret not knowing about until after you've made a disappointing purchase.

Good advice is to stay away from "mongrel" scopes, off-beat brands or so-called military surplus models. Guns in this category can be altered, rechambered, rebarreled, etc., but once you've bought an odd-ball scope, nothing can be done for you except by its manufacturer and chances are ten to one you'll never be able to learn his name!

Japanese scopes today are the subject of many a bull session at gun clubs. Frankly, some are junk; others are excellent. I know of one importer who ordered several hundred and found, when they arrived, that they could not be used on bolt-action rifles unless mounted too high to be practical! On the other hand, there are several reputable importers of Jap scopes who offer high-grade medium-priced scopes. If you can't afford the best domestic scopes, look into the possibility of one of these.

Several firms also offer domestic scopes in the medium-price range and these are probably the best dollar-for-dollar buy—short of the high-grade domestic scopes. Many of these, in fact, sell for only a few dollars more than the Japanese imports, and as experienced shooters will tell you, you can't go far wrong dealing with such names as Redfield, Leupold, Lyman, Weaver, Weatherby, Unertl, and Bausch & Lomb.

Qwik-Point Sight

I have an aversion for the contrived spelling of brand names but the Qwik-Point is unique and rather a wondrous little instrument. The product of W. R. Weaver Co., this is an optical, non-magnifying sight that resembles a 6-inch scope mounted on a see-through base, for use either on a rifle or shotgun.

Essentially the "scope" picks up the target image and transmits it into the viewer in the base. In the center of the viewer is a luminous red dot. As the shooter looks through the sight, the red dot becomes superimposed on the target, but unlike metal sights, the dot does not obliter-

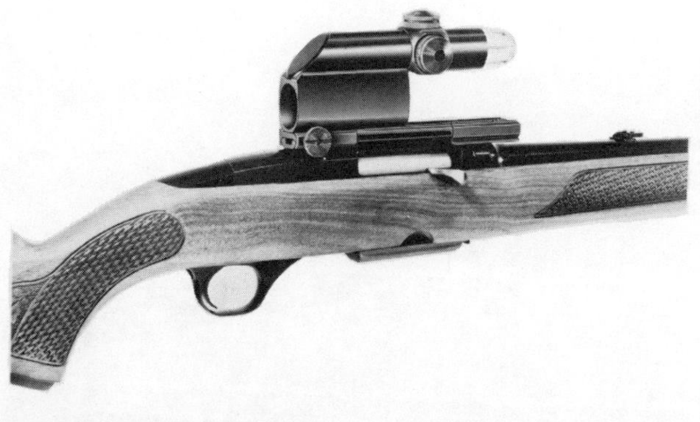

The Weaver "Quik-Point" is a non-magnifying glass sight that superimposes a transparent red dot on the target to speed up sighting of a rifle or shotgun.

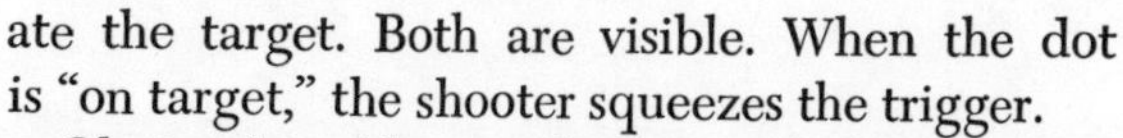

ate the target. Both are visible. When the dot is "on target," the shooter squeezes the trigger.

Obviously such a sight is not for long-range precision work. On a rifle, at short range or in heavy growth, its "Qwik-Point" claim is very valid! On a shotgun it helps a beginner understand "swing," "lead" and "follow through," since he can see flying targets enter the sight's field of view. (And leave it, if he misses!) He has then only to direct the red dot.

The new concept in sighting isn't going to eliminate the need for skillful shooting but in the case of a shotgunner, especially, it will help to correct poor technique.

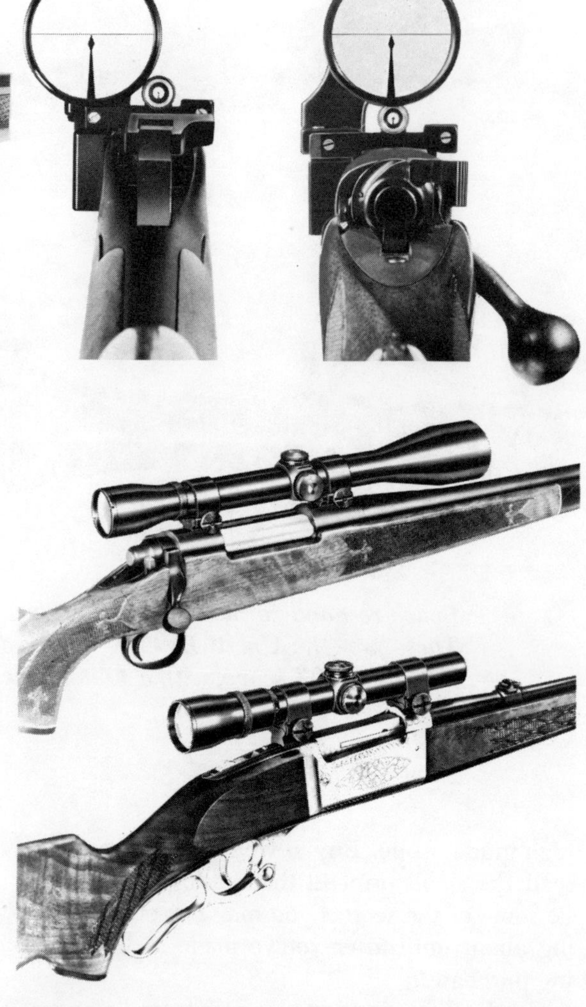

Telescope mounts must provide clearance for shell ejection and be set as low as possible on the receiver. This is accomplished by Williams offset mount on a lever- and on a bolt-action rifle. Weaver bridge-type mounts hold a Weaver K6 scope on a Model 70 Winchester, and a V4.5 scope on a Savage Model 99 lever-action.

Telescope Mounts

Your scope sight will be only as accurate as your scope mounts are stable. Mounts that work loose from their bases, or even bases which may loosen will allow the scope to wobble with resulting wild shots. Most scope mounts can be attached by the shooter himself if he has a rifle of recent vintage, since nearly all of these have their receivers tapped and drilled to standard specifications to which nearly all scope-mount makers have adapted their products. Usually, all that's needed is a small but rugged screwdriver which can apply the necessary pressure to properly tighten the screws for attaching bases to the rifles. If you do the job yourself, be sure to apply this pressure. Have no fear of stripping the screws—they're hardened for this purpose. It's a good plan, too, to check these after shooting the rifle a few times, to make sure they haven't worked loose.

Strangely, there are more different scope mounts on the market than there are scopes! Every scope manufacturer and importer offers mounts that are matched to his scope sights and which will fit any of the modern rifles, in most cases without drilling or tapping. In addition to these, there are several independent mount manufacturers who offer modifications and improvements over "factory" mounts, also adapted to the standard drilling and tapping of new rifles. Only rarely will you have to consult a gunsmith in mounting your scope!

All mount manufacturers—and experienced shooters—agree that two prime qualities govern the design of scope mounts. One of these is ruggedness and precision machining, so that the scope cannot shake loose, no matter how heavy the recoil and so that it will retain its zero, even if detachable mounts are used. The second requirement is that the scope be mounted as low over the receiver as possible so that its axis is as close to that of the rifle bore as is feasible. Shooters today are fortunate in the wide variety of mounts that fully qualify under these requirements.

Telescope sights can be mounted on any type of modern rifle, no matter what its action, whether lever, bolt, pump or automatic, and scope mounts are designed even for rifles that load and eject empties through the top of the receiver.

Most popular today are the "detachable mounts." Before discussing these, let me point out that a scope mount comprises a base, sometimes one, sometimes two pieces, and a pair of rings which encompass the scope tube. The rings are attached to the base by various means. Detachable mounts are designed so that the scope can be removed, usually in a matter of seconds by turning a pair of screws with the edge of a coin or simply by flipping a tiny locking lever. This loosens the rings from the base, the latter remaining on the rifle. Removing a scope in this manner, and returning it to shooting position, *does not change its zero* or point of impact. You won't have to resight the rifle.

Bases used on automatics or pump guns that have solid receivers are usually one-piece, and these are screwed directly to the top of the receiver or to its side. Bases for top-loading or ejecting rifles, such as the bolt-actions and certain lever-actions, are usually two-piece or the "bridge" type. The two-piece bases have one unit screwed to the rear of the receiver opening and one at the front to which the split rings are then attached. The "bridge" mount is much what its name signifies. It is a one-piece base which "bridges" the action opening, yet does not interfere with loading or the ejection of empties. One split ring is then attached to each end of the bridge base.

In the case of rifles which are top-loaded, or which eject shells directly upward, an offset mount may be used. This is screwed to the *side* of the receiver, and the scope may be held directly over the bore, centered as with the bridge or two-piece mounts, or it may be held slightly to one side of axis of the rifle's bore, somewhat off center. This in no way detracts from sighting ease but it does make possible scope sights on certain rifles.

Detachable mounts are useful to a shooter who wants to retain the iron sights that came with his rifle. These mounts are built so that their bases do not interfere with the use of the iron sights once the scope and split ring units are removed. In fact, a number of bases are available which have a built-in peep sight for use when the scope is removed.

Similar in purpose to the detachable mounts, are the "tip-off" or "pivot" mounts. With a simple shove of the hand, some of these allow the telescope to be swung off its center above the bore, freeing the iron sights for use. Tipping the scope back into position, as I pointed out earlier, doesn't change the rifle's zero! Such mounts are handy for the hunter who may find himself in a spot where iron sights may be more suitable than the glassware. He can then switch at a moment's notice.

Williams Sight-Thru mounts on Winchester Model 100 permit use of iron sights without removing scope.

Details of mounts which permit easy removal of a scope sight without affecting zero: Redfield split-ring mount and Bushnell groove-type detachable mounts.

Some of the scope bases have built-in click adjustments for windage and elevation to be used with scopes lacking these adjustments—and some of the finest scopes lack them.

The wonders and ingenuity of modern scope bases and mounts are worthy of a book unto themselves and any explanation of their many features would require one. However, I've pointed out the highlights. Before you buy any scope and mounts for it, I would suggest that you obtain the catalog of every major scope and mount manufacturer and study these, since each has some variation from the other which might affect your purchase decision. Again, in doing this, you'll encounter well known names in the gun and scope field, Weaver, Bushnell, Unertl, Redfield, Buehler, Leupold, Williams, Bausch & Lomb, and Lyman. The shooters of a few years ago had to go overseas for scope mounts. Today, overseas shooters are sending for American catalogs.

Bore Sighters

Sighting in a scope sight requires anywhere from five to thirty shots, and at 30 cents or more per shot for factory-loaded ammunition, it's an expensive process. It's not practical for a shooter to invest in a bore sighter if he has only one rifle, but gun clubs can save their members a small fortune in ammunition by obtaining one for community use.

The bore sighter is an optical instrument that is fitted into the muzzle of a rifle by means of a fixed-diameter or expandable arbor. From the arbor projects an optical tube containing a grid. The shooter merely looks through his scope sight and aligns the cross hairs, or other reticle, with the grid pattern in the bore sighter. Without firing a shot, the scope sight is "sighted in" roughly. In the case of the Bushnell bore sighter, each graduation of the grid is the equivalent of 4 inches at 100 yards.

Knowing the trajectory of your particular load, you can then make corrections for bullet drop. From there, it's only a matter of a few shots to refine the sighting-in job.

Bushnell has adjustable studs that range from .22 to 7 mm; from 7 mm to .35; from .35 to .45 calibers. Also available are single-caliber studs ranging from .22 to .375 caliber.

For use with the Tasco bore sighter, studs are available in sets from .22 to 6.5 mm; from .30 to 7 mm; and from .375 to .45 caliber. Individual bore studs come in calibers ranging from .22 to .45.

Tasco Shot Saver, a bore sight which accomplishes preliminary sighting when inserted into a rifle muzzle.

Chapter VIII

GUNSTOCKS

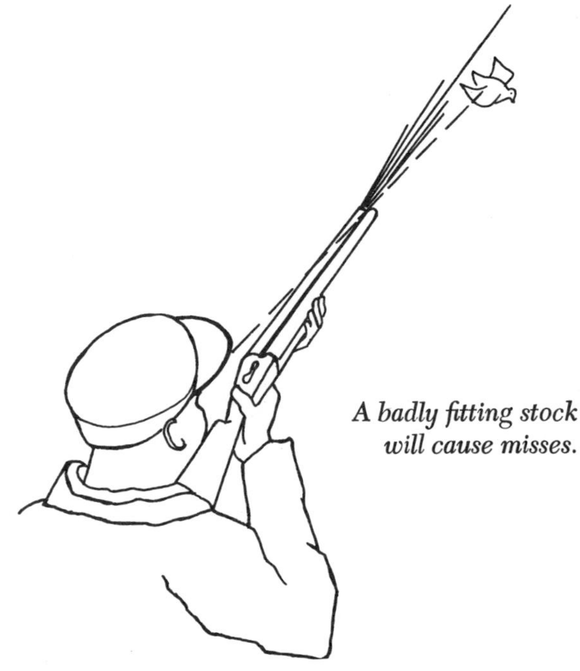

A badly fitting stock will cause misses.

It stands to reason that manufacturers of rifles and shotguns, using mass production methods, can't offer a variety of stock dimensions to fit each individual shooter's preferences. Most sporting arms, and all military pieces, are made with standard stocks to fit an "average" shooter. The result is that such stocks fit a few men quite well, but the rest of us must adapt ourselves to a stock that fits not at all or, at best, fits very badly. This is contrary to the correct premise that a stock *should fit the shooter*—not the other way 'round!

While in training with the U. S. Border Patrol at El Paso some years ago, we were required to qualify with the .30/06 Springfield, as issued by the U. S. Army, by putting ten shots into a 9-inch bull at 200 yards from the prone position. My first three shots were in the black, but so was the side of my face! The Springfield's stock, as hideous a handle for a rifle as I've ever cradled, is much too short and straight for my long arms and neck, especially when I'm shooting in the prone position. The recoil drove the gun into my cheekbone while my fingertips, curled about the straight tang, gouged my chin. I begged off and got permission to shoot in a sitting position. With this stance I was able to qualify without becoming disfigured for life. This was not a case of excessive recoil—the Springfield isn't *that* bad—but rather one of a badly fitting stock. Whether for a rifle or a shotgun, a stock must fit the shooter—for safety, comfort, greater accuracy and increased ease of handling, all of which add up to more hits.

A gunstock is, in fact, more than just a handle with which to carry and point a gun. In the case of a shotgun, it's imperative that the stock fit well in order to put the shooter on target automatically when he brings up the gun. If the stock is too low at the comb, for example, he'll shoot under his target; if too high, the pellets will fly over the bird.

A badly fitting stock that forces a shooter consciously to seek out his line of sight can lead to nothing but misses since there isn't time enough for this procedure in wing shooting. Since scatterguns are always fired in the offhand or standing position, it's possible to custom-build a stock almost to a perfect fit for any one shooter who will use it. A rifle stock, on the other hand, may be used in any one of several positions, sitting, prone, offhand or kneeling, to say nothing of the various awkward stances that are called for in hunting snap shots. Here, a compromise is necessary in the matter of fit and that's what makers of factory stocks seek to achieve. In other words, a factory stock is an attempt to fit possibly thousands of shooters of different builds and sizes shooting in several positions or stances. There just ain't no such animal!

A well-designed stock—one that fits the rifle *and* the shooter—automatically increases accuracy of fire because it "points naturally," imparting to the shooter a feeling of confidence that he won't have to seek out his sights or the target picture by adjusting the position of his shooting eye behind the sights. For example, the same stock cannot be used with equal efficiency on both a scope-sighted and an iron-sighted rifle, without some modification. A high-combed stock will make it impossible for a shooter to get his eye down to the level of the peep or notch of his rear sight, unless he badly crowds the stock with his cheek. Inversely, a low-combed stock will force him to raise his face away from the stock, even craning his neck a little, to see through a telescope sight.

A popular misbelief is that a well-designed stock will cut down recoil. This is true only to the extent that the stock's weight shifts the ratio between the gun's over-all weight and that of the bullet, likely to be a trifling difference. *Apparent* recoil, however, can be cut in half, resulting in less recoil abuse heaped upon the shooter which, in turn, can well eliminate a tendency to flinch. As an example, the so-called California comb is higher at the heel (rear) than at the nose (front) and may even be slightly offset as well as heavier at the heel. When the rifle kicks, the stock is actually pushed *away* from the shooter's face with the brunt of the recoil then absorbed by his shoulder and arms.

Apart from the inflexible mechanical requirements of a good stock, the personal tastes of a shooter enter into the matter. Gunstock manufacturers for mass production rifles can't consider embellishments to suit individuals, except in the case of very high-priced stocks. Factory stocks, as a result, are rarely noted for their beauty or individuality—they're general utility handles! Such personal touches as colorful inlays, engravings or carvings are out of the question.

This isn't to say that factory stocks are of unsuitable quality. Quite the contrary. Many follow today's trend toward lighter weight rifles, and their strength and durability can be attested to by the abuse factory stocks take and still continue to deliver service. They are stable and usually will not warp or "walk," to apply undue pressure against the barrel with subsequent "flyers" or wild shots. It's simply that they do not properly fit *all* shooters.

Take, for example, a hunter with short arms, hunting in a cold area where he must wear a heavy jacket. He may well find that the more or less standard "pull" (the distance between the trigger and the butt plate) of 13¾ inches is too long. In snapping up his rifle, the butt may catch in the armpit of his coat. By way of contrast, a southern hunter, afield in shirt sleeves, might well find the 13¾ inches pull too short. Another hunter, possibly a little fearful of recoil, might wish to add a recoil pad but this will lengthen the gun's pull by ¾ inch to 1 inch, unless he goes to the expense of having the stock cut to compensate for fitting the pad.

Other individual requirements of various shooters which can't be fulfilled in a factory stock include forearm dimensions—some hunters preferring a heavy, beavertail fore-end while another might want the slender European style. Tastes in pistol grips will vary, too, with one shooter wanting a "full handful" while his partner, because of small hands and short fingers, must have a slender grip.

It's obvious, then, that *all* the requirements for a good stock cannot be supplied to *every* shooter by mass production methods.

The answer, then, lies in the custom stock, made for a shooter to his specifications at a substantial price, or by himself from a do-it-yourself wood blank at a substantial saving. Either method can produce the near-perfect stock.

A custom gunstock, fully finished and ready to use, entails craftsmanship whose tolerances are even more critical than those of fine cabinetmaking. Such skill with hand tools is likely to be expensive. The price of a custom stock, however, is not governed only by the quality of work that goes into it but also by the wood that is used. Not just any "lumber" may be used for gunstock making, although trappers and explorers in remote regions have been known to carve replacements for broken stocks from almost all kinds of hardwood. Wood for custom stocks is graded according to availability or rarity; density of grain and its figuring are considered, since the latter frequently lends itself to natural designs of great beauty when brought out by proper finishes; color and weight are also grading factors.

Wood blanks, the uncarved stock, that contain certain small irregularities, sapwood, small knots, checks and other minor defects are likely to be graded into a utility or low-priced blank and these are almost never used for a fully customized stock. Blanks containing a minimum of minor defects but having an attractive coloring or grain structure, will be upgraded into third- or second-class blanks. Woods of close, dense grain without imperfections in grain patterns,

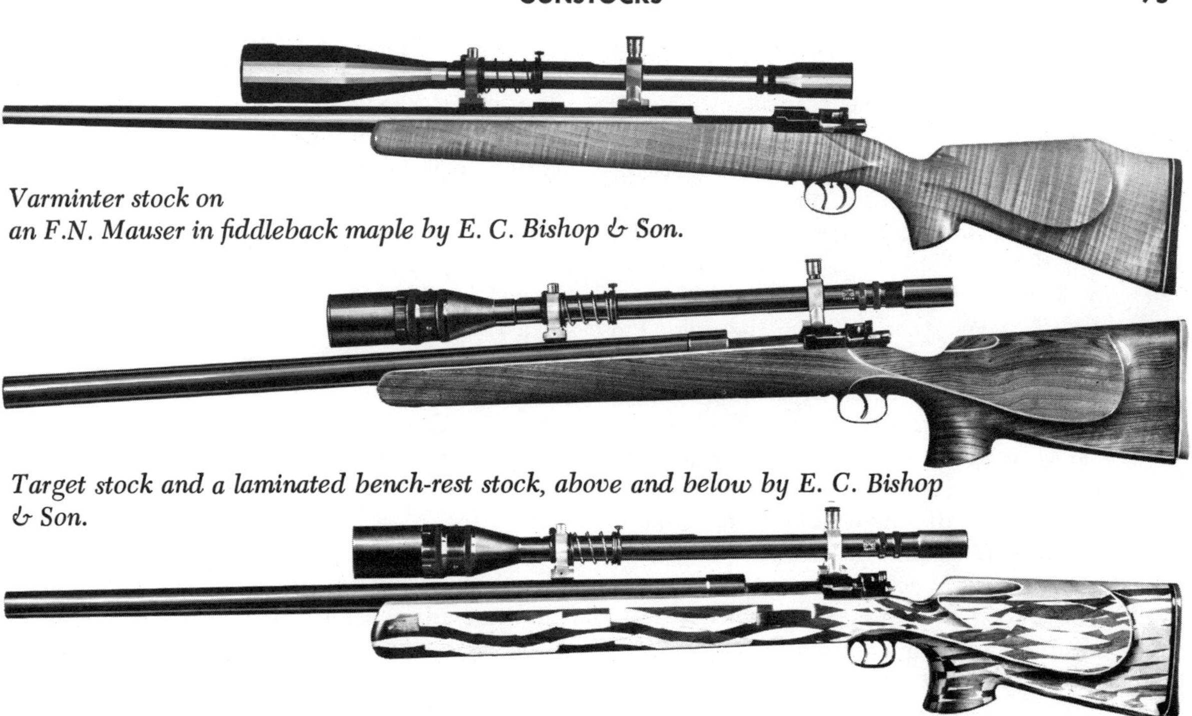

Varminter stock on an F.N. Mauser in fiddleback maple by E. C. Bishop & Son.

Target stock and a laminated bench-rest stock, above and below by E. C. Bishop & Son.

that might produce stocks of unusual beauty and stability, are graded into No. 1 or "super" status. These are the blanks that go into fine custom-made stocks. There are several firms in the United States turning out such stocks and their catalogs are a delight to study. Some will even send a proposed blank of wood to a customer for his approval if he pays the postage. A better arrangement, of course, is to choose a stock maker within driving distance of your home so that you can personally choose a stock blank and so the stock maker can give you personal "fittings."

For a shooter of means, a stock made to his personal specifications will yield a lifetime of shooting joy and pride of ownership long after its price is forgotten. One of the facts of life, however, is that few of us can afford this craftsmanship and so the "semi-inletted" stock was developed—a do-it-yourself blank with most of the difficult and tedious work of barrel and action inletting done on automatic carving machines. The shooter finishes the job himself with a few simple tools at the expense of painstaking but not difficult labor. By doing the job yourself, you can well obtain a truly fine "custom" stock at a saving of $50 to $100. Even with average skill in the use of carving tools, you can turn out a highly satisfactory stock by following directions and exercising patience.

The grading of wood blanks as described for custom stocks applies to blanks used for semi-inletted do-it-yourself blanks also, so that you can, by paying a premium price, obtain the finest blank. However, you shouldn't attempt a "first" with one of the better grades. My first attempt, fortunately on a $6.00 blank, was a complete failure which I had to discard. Make a "trial run" on an inexpensive block for a starter, thus keeping down the costs of your mistakes.

A semi-inletted blank is roughly carved by machine to the exterior conformities of the type of stock you want, with the interior carving also roughed out. It is by no means ready to receive the barrel, action and magazine. Some catalogs may advertise that only a "few hours" are required, but don't take these claims too literally. Fitting the stock to your gun is a matter of carving, trying—and more carving, each application of the carving tool removing only a sliver of wood. Don't try to inlet a stock on a time schedule and don't feel that you're an inadequate workman if you can't complete the job within the catalog's claimed "few hours." Hurrying the process will only hurry the day when you'll have to discard your mistakes and start over. Buy the blank well in advance of the hunting or shooting season and plan to spend several weeks of spare time work on the job. Your craftsmanship may then well match that of the professionals!

The inletting process generally consists of lightly daubing the barrel, action and magazine with Prussian blue or other dye, then fitting the rifle into the stock as far as it will go before lodging. Don't force the gun in making this insertion. When you then lift out the rifle, the stock's "high spots" are stained with Prussian blue. These are then carefully whittled down *only to the depth of the stain,* until the interior of the stock is again clean. Another fitting with Prussian blue then follows. You can probably count on several dozen, possibly well over a hundred, individual fittings before the job is done.

The greatest danger lies in being too enthusiastic with the carving tools, which is what happened during my first attempt. Carve away only thin slivers, never gouging deeply. You can always cut away more wood but you can't replace it once it's cut out.

As work progresses, the action and barrel fit deeper and deeper into the stock. For accurate fitting, you'll need a pair of guide screws which will properly center the rifle into the stock. These are tapped to fit the screw holes into which normally go the receiver guard screws. You can use these regular screws, but several fittings may lead to marring them and there's always the chance of a screwdriver slipping and gouging the unfinished stock. Guide screws can be obtained from most stock makers for a few cents.

Care should be taken, too, that the stock's recoil shoulder is not shortened so that the recoil lug, a solid steel projection beneath the receiver, does not fit snugly. If this happens, recoil could well split the stock. Probably as critical is the process of bedding the rifle barrel in the forearm. Probably a majority of stocksmiths and shooters believe in the "floating barrel," one that does not touch the stock firmly forward of the front tang screw. The reason for this is that a barrel, when fired, is not unlike a harp string that has been plucked in that it vibrates. Undue pressure from either side of the barrel or against the bottom of it, by the stock, causes wild shots and loss of accuracy. Fitting the forearm then calls for the most painstaking work which cannot be hurried. Slivers removed with the barrel bedding gouge should indeed be slivers—very thin ones.

Stock makers of the old school, skilled artisans with delicate carving tools, are likely to sneer at the process, but the use of Fiberglas or plastics for a firm bedding of a rifle barrel has gained considerable favor. It makes the bedding of a barrel a simple job, one which the rawest amateur stocksmith can perform easily. The stock's barrel groove is gouged slightly oversize and the plastic or soft Fiberglas is then lined in the groove. Into this is pressed the barrel itself which then molds its own perfect conformity. When the plastic or Fiberglas has hardened, you have a perfectly fitting groove. Because forearm pressure against the barrel is then equal on all sides, advocates of this method claim equal, or even greater accuracy than is possible with the free-floating barrel.

Exterior Fitting

Under no circumstances should you attempt to finish the exterior of your stock until the rifle or shutgun itself has been fully and perfectly inletted into the stock. You may be tempted to "see what it'll look like," before the inletting work is finished. However, the gun must be perfectly fitted into the stock before you can obtain perfect outside dimensions.

The best way to estimate these dimensions is to try the gun to your shoulder after the inletting is completed, preferably while wearing your usual shooting clothing. Blanks come with ample dimensions, the stock maker knowing well that some of his customers may like an oversized stock. Check the pull, the distance between the trigger and the butt plate, remembering that adding the latter will lengthen the pull by ¼ to ⅜ of an inch. If you plan to use a recoil pad, this will add ¾ to 1 inch. You can then saw off excess lumber accordingly.

Check the thickness and height of the comb if your stock has one. Does your shooting eye fall directly in line with the scope's sighting axis, or in line with the iron sights? This involves bringing up the gun to the shoulder in a smooth, easy manner, entailing no conscious effort to align it. It should come up comfortably and naturally. If you find that your eye does not center easily behind the sights, you may have to remove some of the comb's thickness or height. This, like the inletting, is a matter of whittling, trying, and then more whittling, though of course, you'll no longer need the Prussian blue stain.

The fit of the comb is critical, but don't carve the face side so that it is concave in the belief that your cheekbone will fit more accurately, especially if the gun is a heavy-bore. This will direct much of the recoil effect against your face with bone-cracking results. If yours is a bolt-action rifle, be sure, too, the bolt comes back freely without striking or gouging the comb, keeping in mind that a drawn bolt has some free play or wobble.

The thickness and pitch of the pistol grip, if there is one, are also determined by fitting and whittling. Remove only thin layers, then try it in your hand for fit until you obtain a comfortable grasp. The thumb rest, too, should afford the thumb a natural and comfortable position. The forearm is likewise fitted until your hand can grasp it firmly, for this will not only aid in bringing up the gun and sighting, but it will help to cut down *apparent* recoil.

While these instructions may seem very basic, instruction manuals accompanying semi-inletted stocks frequently assume that the buyer has some knowledge of gunstock making and such details are sometimes not pointed out. The first stock I attempted—the one I ruined—came completely without instructions, but few stock makers today are that independent of their customers' needs!

Removal of excess wood from the stock's exterior is best accomplished with a gunsmith's rasp, which will wear off thin layers and still conform to the stock's shape. This form can be changed to suit your specifications by application of additional pressure with the rasp on areas that are to be cut down. Use a carving tool on the exterior only at those points which are difficult to work with the rasp. The latter will leave a corrugated effect on the surface of the wood but don't be alarmed about this, for there's much sandpapering to follow before you reach the smoothness you're seeking.

Carving in the inletting areas or interior of the stock is done with simple and inexpensive carving tools, which come in sets of five or six different-shaped blades and which are obtainable from most stock manufacturers. A jackknife is a handy addition, if you've acquired some skill in its use.

When you've made your final try or fitting and you're satisfied with the contour and thickness of all parts of the stock, you're ready for the finishing work. The first step is with a coarse grade of sandpaper, always sanding *with* the grain. This is done until all signs of the rasp's work is erased, but don't overdo it, lest you thin out parts of the stock too much. The process is then repeated with a finer grade of garnet paper until a smooth finish is obtained.

For a really smooth finish, wet the outside of the stock lightly with a wet cloth. This will raise the grain ends or "whiskers." Dry these completely and quickly, over a radiator or open flame, being careful not to scorch edges or corners. When thoroughly dried, sand again with fine garnet paper. Repeat the process several times until you fail to raise any grain ends or whiskers. You are now ready to apply the finishing coat.

If you want to alter the color of the wood, a stain must be applied. This is best applied in thin coatings so that you won't end up with a stock darker than you want. Keep in mind that an oil or varnish finish will darken this stain somewhat. Allow the stain to dry perfectly before any final application of finish.

Outside finishes vary considerably according to stock makers' opinions of what they believe to be best. The prime requisite, however, is that it be moisture-proof. Improperly finished, a well-seasoned stock may well absorb considerable moisture, resulting in warpage and subsequent loss of accuracy. *Be sure to finish the inletted areas* or interior, as well as the exterior surfaces. Most of the finishes supplied by stock makers are of the varnish type, although the chemicals may have been given a trade name with the word "varnish" minimized.

At least one stock maker discourages amateur stock makers from using the so-called London oil finish but I suspect that this is an attempt to substitute his own product which, incidentally, I found unsatisfactory. The London oil finish is a process of repeated rubbings with linseed oil, a lengthy and tedious chore and one which will require the utmost in patience and perseverance. Some stock makers offer suitable oils for this process but most finishes are varnish, applied with a brush or sprayed over a hand rubbing of linseed oil. If you use a varnish of your own choosing, be sure it is a spar or waterproof grade.

Checkering

Checkering consists of surface corrugation, either simple crisscross lines with a border or attractively engraved designs on the forearm and pistol grip of rifles and shotguns. Checkering is also common on handgun grips. There is some belief that these are strictly ornamental but in hot weather, when hands perspire or in cold climates where gloves are worn while shooting, checkering probably affords a firmer hold on the stock than is possible with a highly polished, smooth surface.

Inexpensive and easy-to-use tools are available with which to checker a stock and, with care, the job can be done by amateur stock makers. It should be performed before the final finish is applied, however.

Inlays

Fundamentally ornamental, inlays also serve to cover minor defects such as knots or unsightly burls. Available from stock makers, these may be of plastic material or one of the rare woods such as vermilion, purple heart, holly, burl maple, myrtle or ebony in shapes that include square, rectangular, diamond, teardrop, round, kite and oval. These may run up to three inches in length or diameter. Inlays, if too numerous, will give a rifle or shotgun a rather over-ornate appearance but if used with discretion, they will dress up an otherwise mediocre stock. Multiple inlays, one within another, can give an unusual or distinctive appearance, once again if not overdone.

Inlays require fine craftsmanship, but an amateur stocksmith, using care, can successfully apply them. They require that an area be cut to the exact shape and size of the inlay and to the proper depth for a flush fit. Full instructions usually accompany inlays or the simple tools required for installing them.

Caps and Tips

These may be of hard rubber, bakelite or Tenite, or other similar plastic material and they serve a utilitarian purpose as well as being ornamental. They seal the raw ends of the wood, notably at the foot of the pistol grip and at the butt. An otherwise plain stock can be embellished in appearance by such caps and tips, which are usually black. Ivory-colored spacers may be used between the wood surface and the caps or tips and these, too, add somewhat to appearance. Attaching is done with cement, reinforced by wood screws. While pistol grip caps or forearm tips are not a necessity, a butt plate is a must for the protection of the stock against moisture and marring. These are attached in the same manner.

The use of butt plates or caps having such built-in gadgets as a compass or waterproof matchbox is rarely worth the effort. The match safe requires that you drill the stock, which could well weaken it, exposing it to the possibility of splitting. It's better to carry your matches in a pocket waterproof matchbox. As for the compass, these are usually so small as to be of dubious value, especially when located so close to the steel in the gun itself.

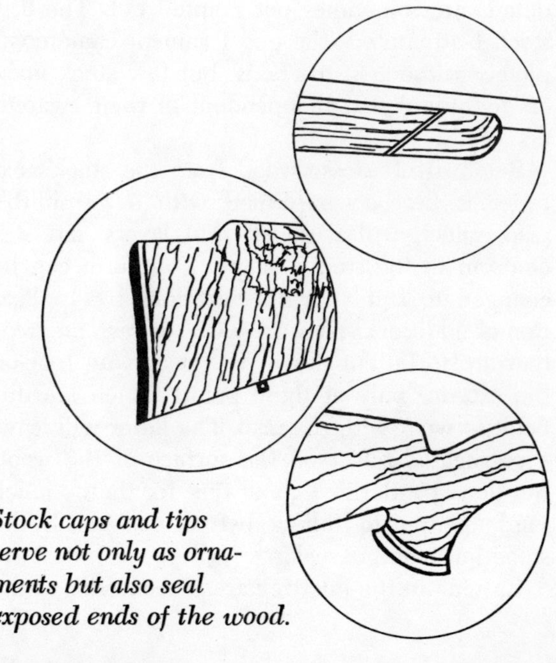

Stock caps and tips serve not only as ornaments but also seal exposed ends of the wood.

Swivels

Sling swivels are installed in the same manner as in the case of a factory stock. The butt swivel screws into the bottom of the butt, preferably 1½ to 2 inches from its back edge. It is best to drill the screw hole to avoid possible splitting of the wood. The forearm swivel is attached by means of a short bolt, with its head countersunk within the barrel groove. Be sure that it is sufficiently countersunk so that it does not touch the rifle barrel. Swivels are best attached after the stock is finished, care being used not to mar the surrounding wood surfaces.

Available Do-It-Yourself Stocks

You can buy semi-inletted stocks in various grades for nearly all American-made and most of the better imported sporting rifles and shotguns. Catalogs list all of the standard models for which stocks are available. Semi-inletted stocks may also be purchased for military arms, including a wide variety of foreign rifles, which are favorites among those who convert these to sporting or hunting guns. One or another of this country's stock makers has semi-inletted stocks for the following military rifles:

1903 Springfield
1903–A3 Springfield
1917 Enfield
U.S. Krag 30/40
U.S. M-1 Garand
U.S. M-1 Carbine
M88 Mauser
Russian 7.62 Moisin
1911 Swiss Army 7.5
M95 Austrian Mannlicher
M93 Spanish Mauser
Brevex Mauser
Czech VX 24 Mauser
M96 Mexican Mauser
Polish 98 or 29 Large Ring Mauser
Czech G33/40 Small Ring Mauser
1891 Italian Carcano
M38 Italian Terni
7.7 Jap. Arisaka
6.5 Jap. Arisaka
1917 Eddystone
Norwegian Krag
G98 Mauser
German G-43
M91 Argentine Mauser 7.65
M95 Dutch Steyr Mannlicher
M94 Swedish Mauser
1924 Jugoslav Mauser
89 Belgian Mauser
1909 Argentine Mauser
Yugoslav Puska M24
98 German "Karabinier" 33/40

If the rifle for which you want a new stock isn't listed here, check with stock makers' catalogs, as frequent additions are made to their lines.

Pushing the pin on these swivels releases a sling from the studs without need for unlacing the strap. (WILLIAMS GUN SIGHT CO.)

Gunstock Woods

Required characteristics for woods suitable for gunstocks include strength, durability, stability, lightness and close grain. Availability generally governs the price. The wood must have great strength, especially when you consider how little of it remains on each side of a box magazine in the forearm. Also, the sweep of a pistol grip is often quite abrupt for hand comfort and beauty of line, and may result in the weakest point in a gunstock.

Wood must be hard to resist marring. A dent or scratch doesn't affect "shootability" but it does detract from appearance and can well put a dent in a shooter's pride in his guns. At the same time, however, wood must not be so hard as to be difficult to carve.

Stability of the wood used in a stock is important to a rifle's accuracy. This is the ability of wood to resist warping, shrinking or expanding. Should any of these occur, especially in the forearm, undue pressure will be applied to the barrel, resulting in erratic shooting.

Lightness seems to be of growing importance, although I believe too much stress is being laid on this quality. A popular soliloquy nowadays among gun writers is that a hunter toting a 6¾-pound rifle comes into camp at night plumb tuckered out, while his partner carrying a 6¼-pound rifle is fresh as a daisy. Weight of a rifle, and especially the weight of a gunstock, just isn't *that* important! The difference in weight among several similar gunstocks of different woods is likely to be no more than a few ounces!

Wood Characteristics

Walnut, American or black, is the most popular gunstock wood and is used in factory stocks. It has most of the favorable characteristics although it may vary in quality depending upon its origin. If grown in a favorable climate it is often softer and coarser-grained than trees in a harsh climate which toughens it and results in curly, crotched and "fiddleback" patterns.

Walnut, Claro, a California species said to be of French origin and considered superior to black or American walnut. Usually has more color, even light streaks and more frequently a fiddle-back grain structure.

Walnut, English, which, along with French, Spanish, Italian and Circassian walnuts, is considered excellent, particularly due to its stability.

Myrtlewood. Quite rare, it grows only in a small section of the Oregon and northern California coast with comparatively few trees remaining. It is close-grained and yields stocks of great beauty, no two of which are ever alike in grain pattern, which may run to burls, curly or fiddleback. It varies considerably in color from reddish through brown, gray, black, silvery and even yellow tones. One of the finer stock woods.

Maple, western, is the big-leafed maple, one of the lightest woods used for gunstocks. Tough and stable with a variety of grain patterns, it can be "flamed" by scorching to accent the patterns. A "blond" or light-colored species.

Maple, eastern, is the rock or hard maple with similar characteristics of the western variety. Bird's-eye and tiger-stripe patterns are obtained from this wood. Since only an occasional log is suitable, it is not always available.

Mesquite. Easterners think of mesquite as a southwestern bush of little value. However, an *occasional* mesquite blank offers superb possibilities. It's a heavy wood (some drill out the butt to lighten a stock) of light color with splashy grain patterns. Good blanks are difficult to come by and a poor blank may be highly porous and never "settle down," continually warping so that frequent resighting might be necessary. Get the advice of a friendly stock maker on a particular piece of mesquite. It may be an outstanding blank—or suitable only for firewood.

Wild Cherry. An indication of this wood's stability is that it was used for mounting carpenter's levels until the advent of aluminum models. It is also used for mounting printers' engravings. Somewhat lighter than walnut, it is easy to work, has an even and consistent grain and a distinctive and naturally red coloring.

Purple Heart (amaranth), a South American species is much harder than walnut and of great strength. The color is purplish and may be finished with unusual effects, often classified as exotic.

Yama, Japanese. A light-colored, almost white wood of suitable strength, fine grain and hardness and somewhat lighter than walnut. Grain pattern may vary considerably, and despite its light color, Yama stains well. It is also considered exotic.

Blackwood, New Zealand. One of the finest of gunstock woods. Easy to work, dense grained, slightly harder than walnut, well known for its stability. Not really black as its name implies, but characterized by streaks of dark and light brown which can be brought out beautifully in finishing.

Mahogany, African. At least one stock maker rates mahogany as an excellent stock wood, but most disagree because of the wood's softness and susceptibility to marring. This softness also makes checkering difficult. However, an occasional mahogany blank may be found suitable.

Maple, Queensland. An Australian species, lightweight and tough with suitable strength. Not a true maple, its color is a very light brown, lacking somewhat in hardness.

Laminates. These are man-made blanks of layers of ⅛- to $^3/_{16}$-inch sheets of walnut and maple or alternating shades of walnut. Such stocks are noted for their great stability and rather bizarre beauty, with the alternating layers of woods creating a tiger-stripe effect.

Chapter IX

SIGHTING AND SHOOTING RIFLES

Sighting-In

Sighting-in a rifle consists of trial shooting to see "if it shoots where it points" and making sight adjustments to compensate for any straying of the bullets from the point of aim. No one else can properly sight a rifle for you. Strange as it may seem, a rifle will rarely have exactly the same point of impact with two—or three—different shooters, even without a shift in sights or a change in ammunition. This is because no two shooters see the target picture alike in the sights nor do any two shooters hold a rifle exactly alike. One shooter may take a "full sight" (holding the front sight high on the target) while another will take a "fine sight" (holding low), while a third may cant or tilt the rifle slightly. Guns *are* sighted in the factory and they *will* make a reasonably close group in the hands of several shooters, but for the ultimate in accuracy, only *you* can sight *your* rifle.

When should a rifle be sighted-in? Certainly when you receive it from the dealer and with the ammunition you intend using regularly. As time goes on, you may discover that your particular gun changes its point of impact slightly which means additional sighting-in if you want to pin-point your shots. Resighting is also necessary each time you change bullet weights or brand of ammunition unless you keep a record of the behavior of various loads in your rifle. It then becomes simply a matter of sight adjustment with possibly a few checking shots.

One of the mistakes made by some hunters in sighting-in rifles is to lay the forearm of the gun on a sturdy rest—too sturdy, in fact. Such firm supports as posts, fence rails, logs, rocks and other solid inflexible objects should not be used for a forearm rest without a soft padding, which may be a rolled sleeping bag or shooting coat. A solid rest causes a rifle to shoot high and consequently, when *you* hold the rifle without a rest, it may well shoot too low. Sighting-in should be done from the prone position or while seated solidly at a heavy bench or table.

If you have access to a target range, this is the place for sighting-in, since you'll have measured distances to the targets. Too many shooters estimate ranges, in someone's field or pasture, with the result that sighting-in is, to a greater degree than they realize, guesswork. It's important to use a fairly accurately measured range especially when sighting-in long-range rifles.

As for correct range at which to sight-in a rifle, this depends upon the ballistics possibilities of your caliber and load, and the ranges at which you expect to use it. For example, it would be unsuitable to sight in a .30/30 Winchester for 300 yards, since its mid-range trajectory of 13 inches would easily cause you to miss a deer at 150 yards, by shooting over it. It would be doubly futile to sight in at this range also, if your hunting will be for white-tails, invariably found in heavy cover and shot at short ranges. Sighted in at 100 yards, your .30/30 bullet would be only 0.4 inches high at 50 yards and 8.3 inches low at 200. A 100-yard sighting, then, would not be unreasonable for woods hunting.

On the other hand, such a caliber as the .264 Winchester Magnum sighted-in at 200 yards would not be taking advantage of that load's long-range potential, because its mid-range trajectory at 300 yards is only 4.2 inches! This would be point-blank on an animal the size of an antelope or deer.

There are several systems of sighting-in a rifle, each devised to simplify the process or to save ammunition. To illustrate one of the simpler methods let's assume that you've just purchased a rifle shooting the popular and, now old reliable, .270, and that you've decided upon the 130-grain bullet. You checked the ballistic table and found that, if sighted-in at 200 yards, your bullet will be 1.6 inches high at 100 yards, on zero at 200, and 7 inches low at 300 yards.

Let's assume further that you've equipped your rifle with a 4X hunting scope, compatible with 200-yard shooting where iron sights might fail you. Set up a target, in a safe area, preferably with the sun at your back. Almost any type of target will do but a new type of sighting-in target with a white square within the black bull's-eye makes it easier to sight.

Try your first three shots from 25 yards. This may seem strange, in view of your plans for 200-yard sighting, but in mounting the scope, perfect alignment may not have been achieved, with the result that your shots will be wild. At 25 yards, you can't help hitting the target *somewhere*. After firing the three shots, walk to the target and examine your "group."

In sighting-in, think in terms of "groups" rather than bull's-eyes. The latter is simply a reference point. If the cluster of three shots is reasonably small and in the center of the bull, then move back to the 100-yard line and fire three more shots. With these in the black, you can then move back to the 200-yard line for a final three-shot checking group. If these are satisfactorily centered to coincide with your point of aim, your rifle is sighted-in for your purposes.

This, however, has been a sighting-in session where everything has gone well—and it's a rare one! Suppose, though, your initial three shots are well in the black and well grouped and you try three shots at 100 yards and find these to be well grouped, but in the eight ring of the target at 2 o'clock. They are, then, about 2 inches high and 3½ inches too far right. Your task now is to bring that group into the center of the bull's-eye to coincide with your point of aim.

You will recall, in reading the chapter on sights, the term "minute of angle," with reference to micrometer click adjustments. A minute of angle, you will also recall, is equal to one inch at 100 yards. Assuming that your scope sight is equipped with click adjustments, each click equal to ½ minute of angle, you will have to make *four* click adjustments to lower the elevation by 2 inches at 100 yards. At the same time, you will have to make *seven* click turns, on the windage dial, to bring in the group from its 3½-inch-wide position. The direction in which you must turn the dials on your scope will be indicated by the letters *L* or *R*, for left or right. If the point of impact, as in this case, was to the right, you will have to compensate by turning the dial to left. The elevation dial may be marked + or —, plus being up, and minus being down. Since your shots were high and will have to be lowered, the elevation dial must be turned toward the minus.

Once these adjustments are made, try three more shots and you should find these reasonably clustered in the black. If not, make further adjustments accordingly. Occasionally you may have a "flyer" in the group, which is a shot which apparently went slightly wild. This is probably due to your shooting rather than the scope or rifle. Don't make compensations for such flyers. Always compensate for the distance between the center of your group, ignoring wild shots, and your point of aim.

Once you're satisfied with the 100-yard groups and their point of impact, move back to the 200-yard line for the final check shots. Fire three, holding on the target exactly as you did at 100 yards. Quite like your windage adjustment, if suitable at 100 yards will be satisfactory at 200, but you are liable to find that your group is low. You will then have to raise the elevation slightly. Assuming that a group is 2 inches low, you will have to raise the elevation clicks only *two* notches. This is because, if each click changes the point of impact ½ inch at 100 yards, it will shift this *one* inch at 200 yards. Two "clicks," then, will bring your group up two inches into the bull's-eye's center. If lateral or windage adjustments are necessary, the same click ratio applies: ½ inch at 100 yards and one inch at 200.

Use great care in sighting your scope—or iron sights—during this process, shooting as if each shot meant life or death. Sloppy shooting makes proper sighting-in impossible and, worse yet, it's expensive in terms of ammunition used. I've known shooters to fire two boxes and still remain unacquainted with what their rifles were capable of, while others can part a woodchuck's hair at 200 yards after test firing a half-dozen shots!

Aiming

During World War II, civilians learned a new term, "near miss." It referred mostly to bombs dropped from planes which missed their targets but struck close enough to inflict some damage. In rifle shooting, a near miss is as good as a mile, for cutting a few hairs from the top of a buck's neck won't bring him down! Direct hits are needed. The difference between a near miss and a direct hit lies in the co-ordination between aiming and pulling the trigger.

If, by some magic, your line of sight were transformed into a long thin pencil, its point would trace an erratic path, back and forth across the bull's-eye, looking not unlike a child's scrawling on the living-room wallpaper. No shooter, unless he's using a solid rest, can avoid this weaving, which is the result of body sway, heartbeat and natural body tremors. The trick is to co-ordinate the trigger pull with the rifle's weaving motion so that the gun fires just as it's on target. That takes practice.

This weaving across the target is very apparent seen through a scope sight, but since the reticle appears to be on the same plane as the target, it is less disturbing. If you're shooting with iron sights you will be concerned with aligning three points simultaneously, the target, front sight and the rear sight.

The front sight will give you the most trouble whether you're using a receiver peep or open "sporting" middle sight. The front post may appear as a tiny tip or a "full sight" in the rear notch or peep, hiding part or all of the target, if the latter is small enough. The correct sighting technique is to have the top of the front sight even with the top of the notch in the rear open sight, or centered in the aperture of a peep sight. In turn, the post should be aligned at 6 o'clock at the *bottom* of the bull's-eye in target shooting or immediately below the expected point of impact on a game animal. Raising the post any higher than this will hide some of the target area—or even all of it! How can you hit what you can't see?

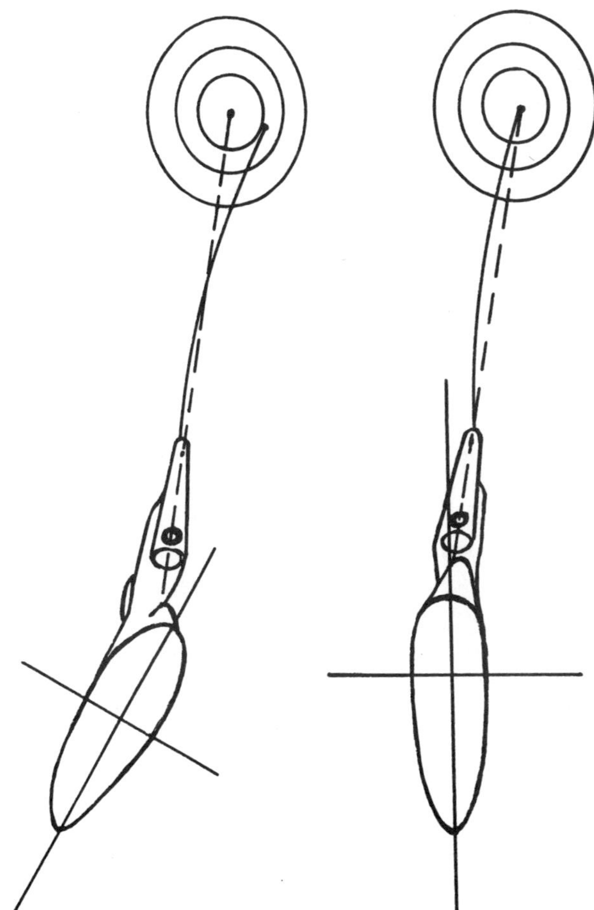

"Canting" or tipping a rifle to one side will cause groups to stray from the point of aim.

There's more to aiming, however, than just looking through the sights at the target. It's important that you hold your rifle in exactly the same manner, with the same firmness of grip for every shot. Shooters under tension may hold a rifle too tightly. The grip on the forearm should be firm, of course, as should the hold on the pistol grip with the three lower fingers, but not so firm that the knuckles turn white! Too tight a grip will actually create additional body tremors and every experienced shooter knows he has enough of these!

The rifle butt should set well into the shoulder and your cheek should rest firmly against the comb of stock so that your eye is *comfortably* centered back of the sights or scope.

As your sights weave about on the target,

breathe normally. Don't try to steady yourself through deep breathing. It doesn't work! However, as the front sight, or scope reticle begins to "settle down," exhale gently, and then hold your breath while you continue sighting. At the same time, apply a steady pressure against the trigger. As the sight wanders away from the bull's-eye, cease applying further trigger pressure but don't give up what you've already applied. Then, as the sight weaves back on target, resume pressure. It's difficult for a beginner to understand, but a skilled rifleman doesn't know *exactly* when his gun will fire! As trigger pressure increases, the sight's weaving should diminish somewhat, and if you've co-ordinated well, the gun will suddenly fire just as the front sight pauses at the critical point. This takes practice, hour upon hour. Entire books have been written on the subject, but what I've just described are the basic essentials which, when coupled with practice, will produce your share of hits.

Regarding "trigger squeeze," this is a misnomer and new shooters, hearing the expression think in terms of "squeeze" rather than "pull," which is incorrect. Some even squeeze the entire pistol grip, even until knuckles whiten! The grip on the gun should not be tightened, although nervous tension may induce this somewhat. The pressure on the trigger is a pull, directly backwards, by the *first joint* of the trigger finger.

Shooters who are new at the game, when confronted by a weaving set of sights, are often tempted to "touch 'er off" prematurely by a quick pull or jerk, as if they're anxious to get rid of the shot. Don't! This is "pulling" and results almost inevitably in a miss or "flyer." Practice coordinating the trigger *pull* with the sight's movements across the face of the bull's-eye but don't ever try to hurry a shot.

If tension becomes too great or holding your breath more than ten to fifteen seconds is necessary, relax your pull on the trigger, slip on the safety and lower the rifle for a few seconds' rest. Then try again.

Shooting Stances

There are a number of formal shooting positions or stances used on the rifle range, including the prone, sitting, kneeling, standing or offhand.

In conjunction with the kneeling and sitting positions, and frequently in the prone stance, the sling comes into play. Except among experienced target shooters, and the military, the sling is the most misunderstood of all shooting accessories.

There are a number of types of slings, with the two-piece military style the most common. Made up of two sections, a sling, properly adjusted, forms a loop through which the left arm (in the case of a right-handed shooter) is projected, until the loop grasps the arm *above the elbow.* The left arm, at the same time that it holds up the forearm of the rifle, applies a side pressure on the sling with a firm but comfortable tension. If the arm cannot be raised to proper shooting position, the sling should be lengthened slightly, but not so long that the arm cannot easily apply tension to the loop. For long-range shooting in hunting, a sling is almost an absolute necessity unless you want to depend upon natural rests such as logs or rocks. For target shooting, it is indispensable.

For woods hunting, where snap shots are the order of the day, the sling is of little value except for carrying the rifle. A fine sling of this type is the one-piece Williams Guide Strap, which may be used for toting the gun or as a simple sling without a loop.

Much has been written regarding shooting positions, especially with reference to target and military shooting. For hunting or sport shooting, however, you need not follow exactly the somewhat strict requirements of correct form. It's silly, for example, for a hunter to hold his right elbow at the horizontal, in a somewhat stiff and

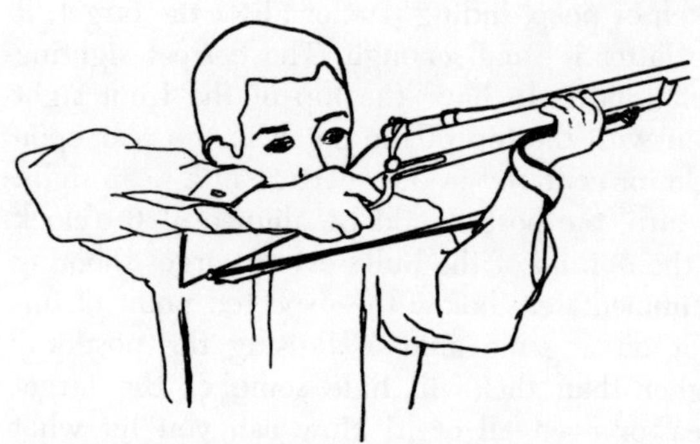

Correct offhand shooting position with sling.

miserable stance, while trying to pin down a running buck at 100 yards! This may seem like heresy to many, but it's better to undergo constant practice, even using a reasonably comfortable shooting position, than it is to be aware of the requirements for perfect form and shooting only occasionally. I've known crack shot hunters who haven't the slightest notion about good form but I'd hate to get into a gun duel with any of them! On the other hand, if you want to become an expert rifleman, afield as well as on the target range, you'll have to conform to proper stance requirements.

The prone position is the steadiest, and for most shooters, the easiest one. A sling may be used. Lie on your stomach at about a 45-degree angle from your line of sight, with your feet comfortably spread apart. As you raise your rifle, it should point naturally at the target. If you must crane or shift your shoulders to align the sights on the bull's-eye, your position is wrong. Shift your body one way or the other, until the gun points easily at the target. Your two elbows and chest should form a tripod, with your elbows firmly but comfortably apart. As in most positions (there are certain exceptions) the forearm should rest in the palm of your hand. Don't hold the gun up by your fingertips.

The sitting position calls for more shooting skill if you're seeking consistent bull's-eyes since, naturally, it isn't as steady as the prone. Sit facing the target at about the same angle used in the prone stance, feet well apart and, if you like, with your heels dug in slightly but not with your toes pointed skyward! Let your feet extend themselves naturally so that there is no strain or tension in the arch. Don't place your elbows directly on your knees, as many are prone to do, since this is not only difficult but will cause excessive body wobble. Instead, allow your elbows to slide down along the inside of your knees and arch your back forward until your shooting eye is in line with the sights. No two shooters hold this stance exactly alike since no two persons have exactly the same build or body flexibility. Vary it slightly to fit *your* physique. If any part of the body feels strained uncomfortably, relax the stance slightly. Weight should be pretty well on your fanny with the feet used as braces.

Another version of the sitting position calls for crossing the legs just above the ankles, but this tends to cause the body to sway until you've mastered it.

The kneeling position, from the standpoint of steadiness, is probably the least desirable of all, especially since it's hard on the right ankle. Again, face about 45 degrees to the right of the target with the right leg folded under the body so that you sit on the heel of the right foot. The latter should be upright with the toes turned up and flat on the ground. Some shooters prefer to sit on the inside of the right foot but this is difficult for all but the limberest of riflemen. The left knee is then used as a rest for the left arm and should point pretty much along the line of fire. Here again, don't rest the elbow directly on the knee, but rather, slide your arm down slightly so that the elbow is beyond the kneecap. The right elbow is not rested and should be held out away from the body which leans forward until good balance is attained.

The offhand or standing position calls for the body to be poised at almost right angles from the target, facing 3 o'clock. Personally I prefer to face a little closer to the target, almost at 2 o'clock. Hold the forearm at comfortable length and the right arm away from the body, the latter nearly horizontal with the right elbow pointed directly away from the body. The feet should be spread, the distance depending upon the length of your legs and the comfort you attain. In this position, you will be most conscious of the weight of your rifle and you may correctly tend to lean backwards from the waist slightly to compensate for this. As in all positions, the cheek should be set firmly against the comb or stock and no part of the body should be so rigid that tension and tremors result. Use your bone structure to "hold you up" and the muscles of your body to balance and control its stance. Relax as much as you possibly can without defaulting any part of the position I've described. Offhand shooting is the most difficult of all and don't be surprised—or discouraged—if your first few attempts end in low target scores. It takes practice to become an expert in any position, but especially in the offhand stance!

Variations of the offhand position include the "Schutzen," whereby the shooter may have a projecting knob under the forearm which he grips while his left elbow rests against his body or hip. One of the NRA positions also allows the left elbow to rest in this manner, while the forearm is held in the palm, on the fingertips or even on the knuckles of the left hand.

Hunting Stances

For hunting above timberline or on the open prairie, the prone position is almost essential to long shots. Often, too, a hunter has spotted his game in advance and has had time to work within shooting range for the best possible first shot. This usually includes sufficient time to "climb into" a suitable position. There are exceptions, of course. For example, while buffalo hunting in the Dakotas, we were not able to shoot in the prone position because prairie grass in some areas interfered with sighting. We shot in the next best position—sitting.

An expert hunter, however well trained in all of the standard shooting positions, will use a natural rest along with one of the stances if possible. Climbing in the mountains will cause rapid heartbeat and heavy breathing, to say nothing of the tension created by the excitement of the hunt. It's not uncommon then for a hunter, under these conditions, to rest the forearm of his rifle, well padded by his own hand or wrist, on a log or rock outcropping. I've even known a hunter to use his guide's shoulder for a shooting rest.

A varmint shooter, too, often shoots prone, but if possible, he'll use a fence rail or stone wall for additional steadying of his rifle. In the kneeling position, he might even use the crotch of a bush or small tree, and in Europe many hunters carry a man-made crotch in which the forearm is rested for steadier aiming. All of which adds up to: Use every natural or artificial aid you can for steady shooting.

The shooter who gets the least help, though, is the deer hunter, prowling in thick growth for white-tails and, in some cases, mule deer. Here, offhand shots are a must, since few deer will wait for a hunter to climb into a sling and adopt one of the standard shooting stances.

A hunter "on stand"—posted on a deer run or in front of a deer drive—has an advantage in that he can post himself in any position he chooses and be more or less "at ready" when a deer appears. He's less likely to be taken by surprise since he's probably already facing the direction from which a deer will appear. He has only to bring up his rifle cautiously, aim and shoot. Hunters on stand usually stand or, if a long wait is expected, they'll often sit, either position making possible a quick shot if necessary. Even under these favorable circumstances, a hunter will subconsciously omit some of the refinements of correct shooting stances.

Deer habits being what they are, however, can make exceptions to rules. Another hunter and I once came upon a fat doe feeding along a logging road near Cocaumgomoc Lake in Maine. Even as we approached within 30 yards, the deer kept on feeding, pausing only a moment to glance at us before resuming her grass diet. We discussed for at least two minutes whether or not we should shoot the deer. It was too far to the car to drag her, we thought, but then it occurred to us that we could hang up the carcass and have the tote team take it out the next day on its regular trip "outside." I shot her, and later enjoyed the finest venison I ever ate. It's a rare occasion, though, when you'll be able to debate with yourself whether or not to shoot a deer and have the animal wait while you make the decision!

A much more probable situation occurs when a hunter suddenly "jumps" a deer, each as startled as the other. If the deer bounds away in front of the hunter, all he has to do is bring up his rifle, sight quickly and pull the trigger. A hunter isn't always that lucky.

White-tail deer have a habit of skulking behind heavy brush while a hunter passes by, or once in a while, a deer will quietly work its way around a hunter. If something startles the deer, however, such as a sudden move by the hunter, it may well send the deer bounding away. This may happen to one side or the other of the hunter, or in back of him. He hears the deer run, of course, and turns to shoot but invariably he's caught off balance and considers himself lucky to get off one quick—and badly sighted—shot.

There are tricks which effect a quick turn and greater sighting time, however. Jumping a deer that suddenly bounds away on your left or even in back of you calls for a quick turn. Don't try to make the turn with your feet, however. Instead, twist your body from the hips and waist without moving your feet as you bring up your rifle, turning your shoulders and head toward the running deer. This can be called an over-the-shoulder shot, actually and it amazingly puts you in a fairly comfortable and steady shooting position.

For a right-hander to shoot over his right shoulder, though, is quite impossible. A quick shot to the right or right-rear can be effected by buckling the knees as you turn to the right and spinning on the balls of your feet, just as is done in a military about-face but with the feet farther apart. Don't try to move the feet. This crouching about-face will put you into a slightly crouching position or even into a kneeling stance at amazing speed. As you spin about, you'll find your rifle coming up to your shoulder in a smooth and natural manner. Whether or not you connect will depend upon how quickly you can then get the sights "on target." For a left-handed shooter the motions are simply reversed.

In the excitement of the hunt, 97 per cent of the hunters forget all about proper trigger pull. Shooting at a deer at 20 yards, it will make little difference, although a miss at this range occurs more often than hunters like to admit! Jerking or pulling the trigger sharply will cause flyers in hunting as well as in target shooting. It's difficult to keep completely calm at the snort of a big buck as he bounds along in front of you, but if you take an extra fraction of a second to pull that trigger smoothly, instead of jerking it, your chances of collecting that buck are increased tremendously. Good shooting habits count in the woods as well as on the target range!

Chapter X

HANDGUNS AND THEIR LOADS

Despite the growing popularity of handguns, there is still some misunderstanding as to which is a pistol, a revolver or an automatic. Generally speaking, a pistol is any handgun, single-shot, revolver or automatic, but the term is applied by many only to the latter. The term "revolver" is more specific, applying only to handguns having a revolving cylinder magazine which rotates automatically as the gun is fired.

Revolvers may be either "single-action," "double-action" or both. A single-action revolver is one whose hammer must be drawn back or cocked before it can be fired and the most noted example of this type is the famed Colt Army Single Action Peacemaker. A double-action revolver is one which cocks itself when the trigger is pulled and most modern revolvers are of this type, although they may. also be fired single-action.

The loading and extracting of cartridges from revolvers depend upon the type of cylinder mechanism with five different types being used in present-day revolvers. The most popular is the "swing-out" cylinder which pivots out of the frame. A push rod, running through the cylinder and acting as its axle, pushes the empty cases out simultaneously. A "snap-out" cylinder is also used, in which the cylinder and its axle pin are held in place within the frame by a friction spring and may be removed as a unit for loading and unloading by snapping out the cylinder to the side so that it is completely free of the gun. Another type, used in less expensive revolvers, calls for pulling out the axle pin which then frees the cylinder from the frame. The pin is then used as a push rod with which to remove the empties individually. Some revolvers are of the break-open type, much like the double-barrel shotgun. Opening the revolver activates the extractor which pushes the empties out of the revolver as the barrel and cylinder are tilted out of the frame alignment. Replicas of old-time revolvers do not have removal cylinders, loading and unloading is done through a side port.

Shot capacity of revolver cylinders ranges up to nine shots in the case of .22 rim-fires, while center-fire revolvers are generally limited to six shots—hence the term "six-shooter"—because of the larger diameter of cartridges and the additional size of the cylinders to contain pressures created by such loads. Within the center-fire group are regular and Magnum loads.

The automatic is, of course, really the semi-automatic, as explained in the rifle section, firing one shot with each pull of the trigger and automatically ejecting the empty and loading a fresh cartridge along with cocking the gun. The automatic offers the advantage of a rapid rate of fire and additional magazine capacity. Automatics have no cylinders but rather a clip-type magazine that feeds shells from within the pistol's hand grip. A further advantage is that a freshly loaded clip magazine can be slipped into firing position in a matter of a few seconds, as opposed to the individual loading of each cylinder chamber required in a revolver. Automatics are made in .22 and center-fire calibers but none handle the Magnum loads which are confined to revolvers. Magazine capacity in .22 caliber ranges up to ten shots with the center-fire loadings limited to nine, although Browning has a thirteen-shot capacity in its 9 mm auto.

One point to consider when buying that "first handgun" is the safety factor. For informal target shooting, plinking, or as a sidearm on fishing or camping trips, the revolver is a better choice. If you've had little experience with handguns, it's comforting that when a revolver is cocked and ready to fire, *this fact is obvious* since the hammer is raised and poised. With an automatic, the gun may be cocked, but this is less apparent except in the case of certain .38s and .45s which have visible hammers. I don't mean to run down automatics. Thousands are in safe use daily in the hands of careful shooters and most of them are a joy to shoot, but *they do require extra care in handling.*

Most handguns, especially the .22s, are bought for plinking, informal target shooting and even for shooting some pests such as red squirrels and rats. For many years, I carried a .22 revolver on fishing trips, not for protection, but for the fun the little gun afforded when fishing slowed or after the supper dishes were done. This kind of shooting appeals to all members of the family, and with a .22 which has no noticeable recoil, women and children can enjoy shooting. Women especially, who may have been aghast at the first sight of a pistol, often become ardent and skilled shooters once they've tried it.

Another feature of the .22 handgun is its lack of a loud report. With a safe backstop, it can be used anywhere—even indoors—without annoying the neighbors. Its initial cost is low and its appetite for ammunition is not an expensive one to satisfy. For those who prefer the center-fire loads, reloading will cut the cost of shooting considerably, but their use is more limited because of greater recoil, louder report and more extended range.

Many states allow small-game hunting with a handgun and this develops shooting and stalking skill as well as affording hunting thrills. For many years, I hunted ruffed grouse in northern Maine with a .38 revolver. Grouse in the wilderness are comparatively tame and will stand for several shots. We concentrated on head shots, which usually meant a dead bird with no spoiled meat, or a clean miss. Needless to say, there were more of the latter! At my summer camp, shooting red squirrels with a pistol is not only good shooting fun but it keeps the little red devils from invading the building during the winter

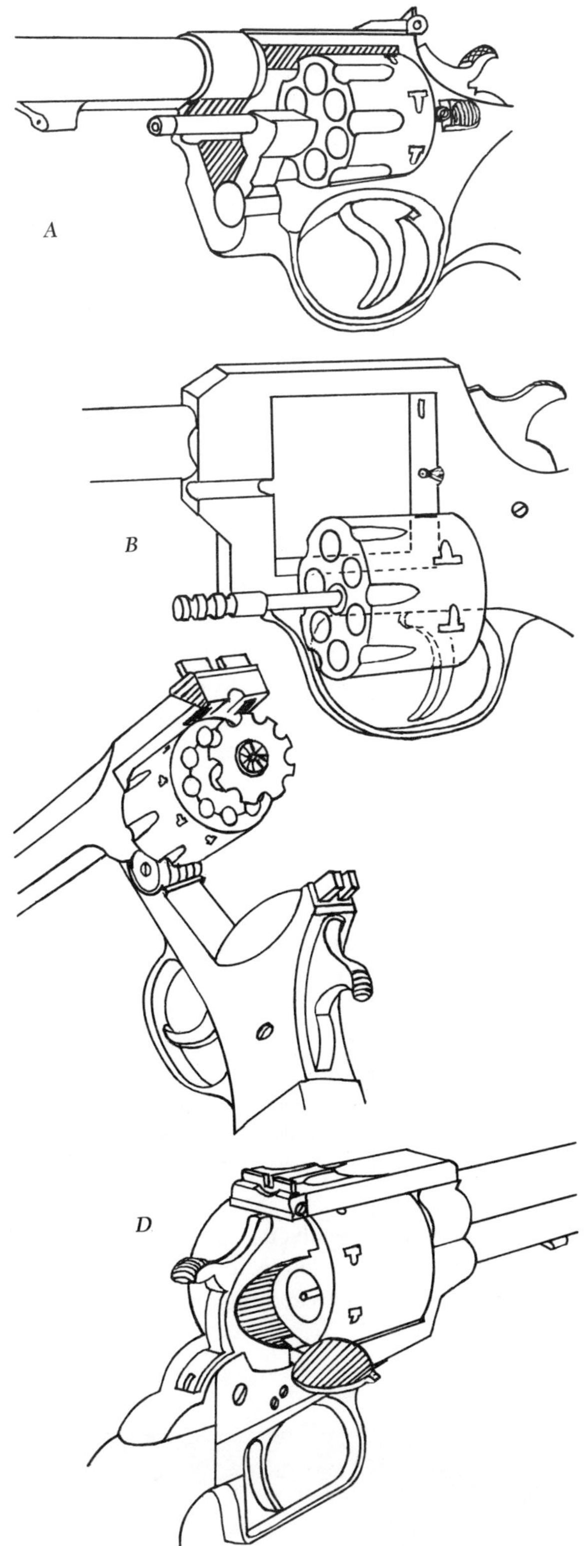

(A) The "swing-out" cylinder is most convenient and, hence, most popular. Frequently used, however, are (B) the "snap-out" cylinder, (C) the "break-open" type and (D) the western-style non-removable cylinder which is loaded and emptied through a side port.

and chewing up mattresses, snowshoe webbing, books and other squirrel edibles.

Deer hunting with handguns is also legal in several states, but this calls for using one of the few big bores such as the .44 Magnum, with a fairly long barrel for suitable sighting radius, to say nothing of considerable stalking skill and marksmanship. This is not sport for the once-a-year deer hunter but rather for the handgun shooter who is master of his weapon and who knows the ways of deer.

Target pistols are confined to the .22, .38 and .45 calibers, and these may be equipped with simple fixed sights in the cheaper models, while at the other extreme, target pistols may be precision hand-operated shooting machines. Automatics are much favored in timed and rapid-fire events and these are available with muzzle brakes, weighted barrels, micrometer rear sights, and adjustable trigger pulls. Pistols for .22 events are most likely to have such features, while the .38 and .45 handguns concentrate on finely machined mechanisms.

Standard-grade American automatic pistols, however lacking in such embellishments, are far more accurate than the average shooter's ability to shoot them. By this, I mean that few can shoot with the accuracy that is possible with the so-called standard models.

There's no way of estimating the number of handguns lying in bedside night table and business desk drawers, awaiting use as protection weapons. In choosing a gun for this purpose, take a cue from the police plain-clothes man. His gun is usually a .38 caliber with a 2- or 3-inch barrel, ideal for close-up work. Some of these, even though they are revolvers, are made without visible hammers, to allow a quick draw without fear of the weapon's catching in clothing. The sights on this type of gun are a mere notch in the frame at the rear and a rounded blade up front. Naturally, in a pinch, any type of pistol will do the job, but if you're planning to buy a gun strictly for protection, why not follow the example of the professional? Police-type weapons are best.

Remington XP-100, an imaginative departure in modern handgun design, is a bolt-action single-shot long-range weapon that handles the .221 Remington Fireball.

The Single-Shot Pistol

During the mid-1960s at least three American firms turned out single-shot handguns. Only one remains—the Remington Model XP-100. This is a bolt-action, target-type pistol chambered for the hot Remington .221 Fireball center-fire. Its 50-grain soft-point bullet leaves the muzzle at 2650 foot seconds, outrunning all other handgun loads and many rifle calibers. As for energy, it strikes with a 505 foot pound blow at 100 yards, on a par with the famed .357 Magnum! Sighted for 100 yards, its mid-range trajectory is less than 1 inch (0.8 inch).

The gun itself is interesting too. The grip is designed to fit either the right or left hand, and the entire stock is made of a Du Pont synthetic. There are cavities in the forearm into which weights can be inserted for a steadier aim. The receiver is tapped and drilled for a scope sight, not a bad idea for handgun varmint shooting.

The Derringer

Although not a sportsman's gun, interest in the Derringer persists. Remington made it as a .41-caliber sleeve gun during the heyday of the Mississippi river boat and the wild West. Many a gambler, confronted while holding five aces, used the Derringer as a way out. Western gunmen often carried a Derringer as a "back-up" weapon.

Today, it is largely outmoded, now looked upon as a novelty, except by a few persons who want a small, defensive weapon. The Derringer is an ideal ladies' protective arm. Society now frowns on the carrying of weapons, even for protection, but many women would be alive and well today had they carried a Derringer in their purses.

The Derringer—at least today's version—is a single-shot, break-open gun, chambered for the .22 Short, Long, Long Rifle or .22 Magnum. Only

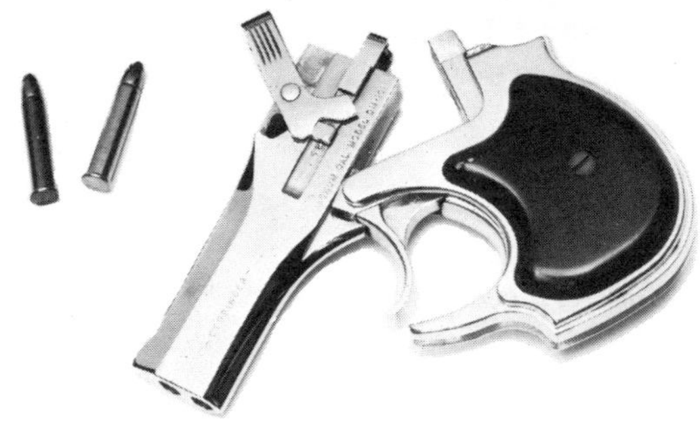

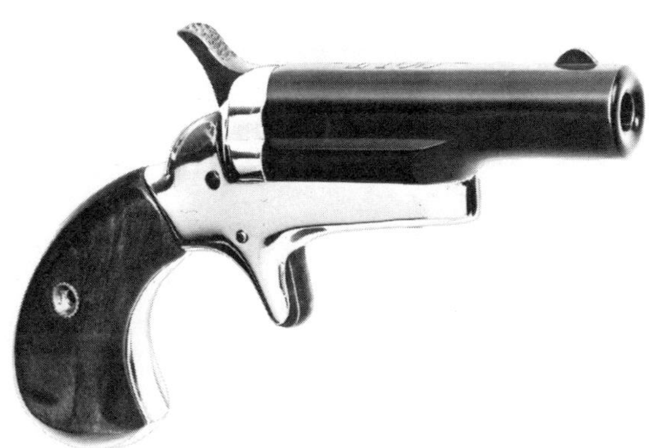

Modern Derringers: High Standard two-shot model available in either .22 standard or 122 Magnum, Colt's "Lord Derringer," a single-shot .22, and its companion, "Lady Derringer."

two American firms make it—Colt and High Standard. Barely 5 inches long, and weighing well under ¾ of a pound, Derringers are easily concealed. This does not imply that they are ideal for bank holdups or other robberies! No thug is going to arm himself with a single-shot .22. Derringers are strictly close-up defensive weapons, or interesting wall ornaments.

"Western" .22 Revolvers

There are so many modern replicas and semi-replicas of old-time "western-type" .22 revolvers that they deserve a separate evaluation here. Except for the use of modern metals and alloys, these are generally quite faithful reproductions, even to including what are, today, minor shortcomings. The .22 was *not* a gun of the early West but the popularity of the little shell has caused its chambering in modern guns reminiscent of the wild and woolly West.

The more authentic models are single action, but this is a minor drawback since double-action firing is extremely inaccurate. Old-time guns did not have a swing-out cylinder, loading and unloading being accomplished through a side port at the rear of the cylinder; and today's replicas are similarly designed. Naturally, this is a slower process, since the cylinder must be rotated by hand and each empty pushed out through the port, and new cartridges inserted in the same manner. For rapid reloading, this is not a suitable action.

The "Old West" in .22 caliber: the famed Colt "hogleg" Peacemaker, the Harrington & Richardson Model 949, the Ruger Single-Six.

Some manufacturers, realizing the popularity of the swing-out cylinder, have incorporated this in semi-replicas, along with double-action mechanisms. These guns are not, of course, "authentic," but they're easier and quicker to load. Catalog descriptions should be checked carefully if you prefer a modernized version or an authentic hogleg!

Handgrips in the .22 western-style handguns are likely to be small and if you have a large hand and long fingers, shooting such a weapon may be difficult. This is not true of *all* models, but the heftier .22s are few. Again, it's a case of checking specifications closely before buying. Characteristic of the old-timers was a handgrip the top of which butted into the frame on a level with the bottom of the cylinder, so that the gun was held high in the hand. This allowed the thumb plenty of room for cocking the long hammer. Modern revolvers, with their shorter hammer falls, snuggle deeper into a shooter's hand because the grip slopes up to a point approximating the cylinder axis pin.

Most "western" revolvers have rounded blade-front sights, designed to slip easily out of a holster since many of these replicas are used by "quick-draw" fans. Rear sights vary from simple frame grooves to more elaborate adjustable types.

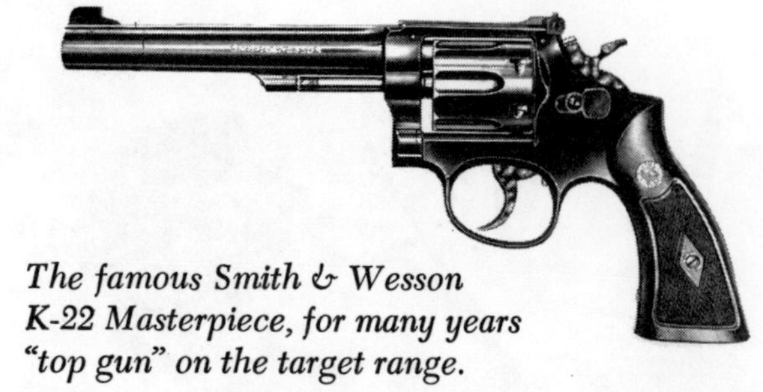

The famous Smith & Wesson K-22 Masterpiece, for many years "top gun" on the target range.

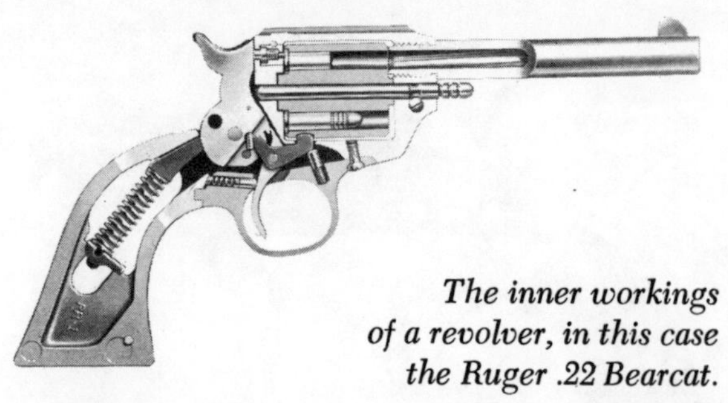

The inner workings of a revolver, in this case the Ruger .22 Bearcat.

Modern .22 Revolvers

The first .22 revolver I ever owned was an inexpensive Iver-Johnson which at that time sold for about $10. Shortly after I obtained the gun, I applied for a position with the U. S. Border Patrol, probably the most gun-conscious police organization in the country and the contributor of several national pistol champions. I was not called up for several weeks and, in the meantime, I practiced in the basement of my home with the little Iver-Johnson .22, firing fifty shots per day. When I was finally ordered to the training school at El Paso, Texas, I managed to place first among the sixty men in my class with the .22 revolver supplied by the school. This was not necessarily an indication of my shooting skill. It was simply the result of practice with a $10 handgun which paid off when I was issued a weapon costing six times that price!

Which is by the way of saying that, if you can afford the best in handguns, by all means, buy it. However, don't fret about being confined to using one of the less expensive models. Most of the marksmanship comes out of the shooter—not the gun.

All modern-type .22 revolvers can be fired either single- or double-action. Whether or not they have swing-out cylinders depends upon the price range. Adjustable sights usually come only on the better-grade revolvers, but there's nothing seriously wrong with fixed sights for all shooting but target-range competition. Those with adjustable sights may have this feature for windage or elevation, sometimes both. The size and shape of handgrips will, of course, vary and I regret that most of them, including those on better guns, tend to be too slender and too short. Barrel lengths vary greatly, too, from as little as 2½ inches up to close to 14 inches. The longer the barrel, the more accurate your sighting will be, due to the longer sighting radius, but long-barreled revolvers are unhandy when carried in a holster. For a field gun, to be carried as a side-arm, or to be used for general shooting fun, a shorter barrel is generally preferable, probably in the 5- to 8-inch range. Weight is not a vital

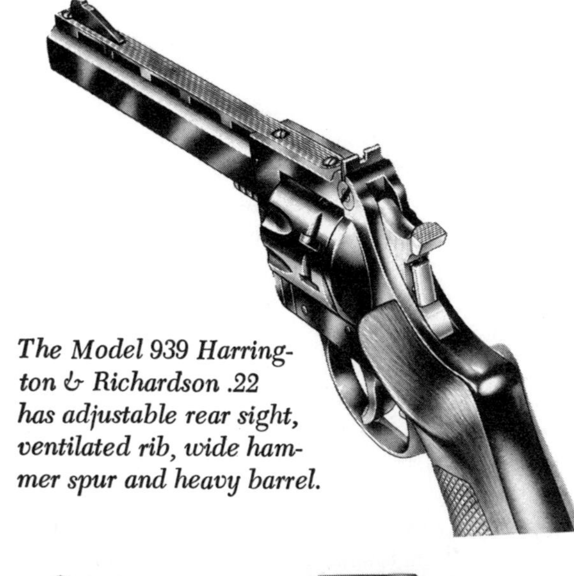

The Model 939 Harrington & Richardson .22 has adjustable rear sight, ventilated rib, wide hammer spur and heavy barrel.

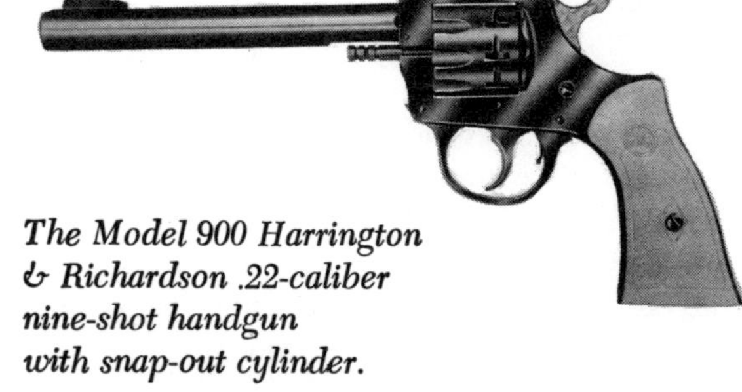

The Model 900 Harrington & Richardson .22-caliber nine-shot handgun with snap-out cylinder.

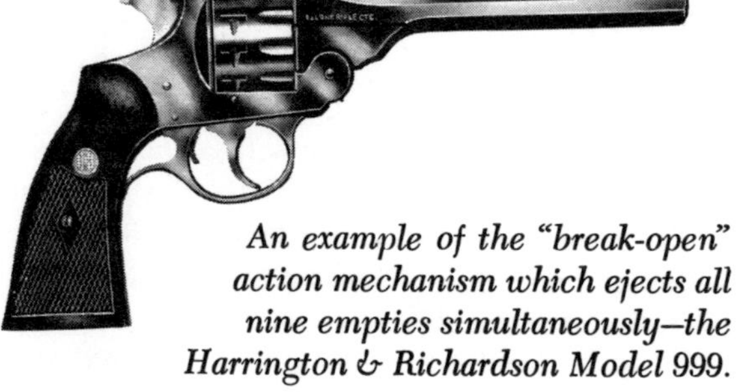

An example of the "break-open" action mechanism which ejects all nine empties simultaneously—the Harrington & Richardson Model 999.

factor except that it's governed by the over-all size of the handgun. Tiny .22s which almost fit in the palm of the hand are of little value for anything but a second-rate protection weapon. You'll do better shooting with a hand-filling model, the additional weight actually serving to steady your aim. The heaviest of domestic .22 revolvers weighs only 43 ounces—hardly an unbearable burden!

The .22 Automatics

Although my enthusiasm for automatics, so far as beginners are concerned, isn't great, these little rapid-shooting handguns probably offer the greatest amount of sport per hour of any pistol. Although averaging a little heavier than .22 revolvers, they're more compact and are more easily carried at the belt or in a pack. For the small-game hunter who has developed sufficient skill there's no finer handgun for exciting sport. The ten-shot magazine capacity and the pull-of-the-trigger shooting speed can keep a running jack rabbit in high gear.

The automatics are in the same price class with the better cylinder guns. They'll use up more ammunition, of course, because of their ease of loading, and rapidity of fire, but in turn they'll supply more shooting per hour. A few models, including some very fine target guns, will handle the thrifty .22 Short for outdoor use or for indoor target practice. Rainy or cold weather, then, won't stop you from shooting. Many have interchangeable barrels so that you can use a 4½-inch barrel for field use or as a belt gun, or a 10-inch barrel for serious competition. Most models lock open when the last shot has been fired and all are easily taken down for cleaning and oiling. The automatics are available as "stripped down" models with basic fixed sights, or as deluxe target jobs with the finest of adjustable sighting equipment. As for efficiency, I recall a cold November afternoon when a friend and I poured some five hundred shots through a standard automatic without a single jam. Complaints against early models of frequent jamming are no longer justified.

Loading an automatic is simply a case of slipping a full clip into the grip and then pulling the slide back once to cock the gun for the first shot. Thereafter, cocking is automatic as is ejection of the empty shells. A small lever or cross bolt locks the slide when the gun is on safety, securing it positively against accidental firing. Keep your eye on this safety and you'll find a .22 automatic a worthwhile field companion.

The American-made .22 automatic is a superlative in gun design which no foreign maker has been able to match, as evidenced by the fact that nearly all sport shooting .22 automatics sold in this country today are domestic guns.

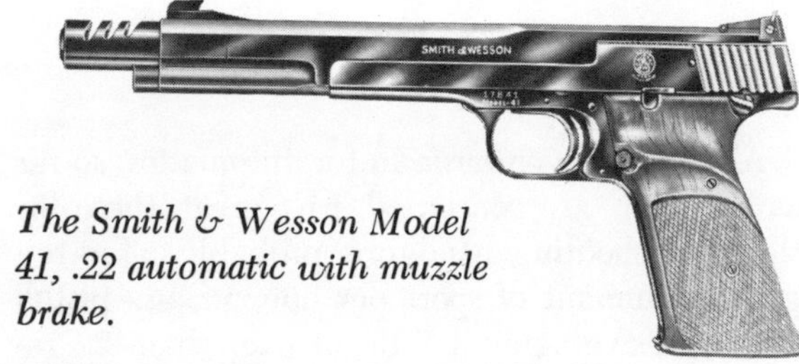

The Smith & Wesson Model 41, .22 automatic with muzzle brake.

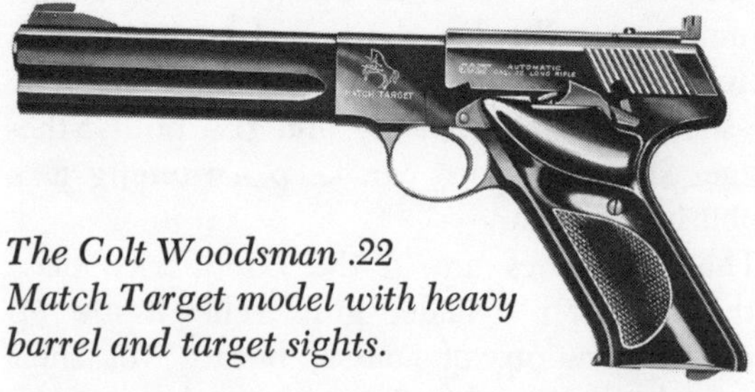

The Colt Woodsman .22 Match Target model with heavy barrel and target sights.

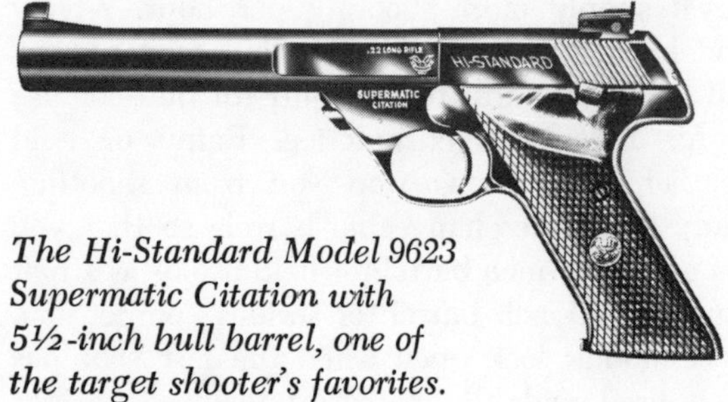

The Hi-Standard Model 9623 Supermatic Citation with 5½-inch bull barrel, one of the target shooter's favorites.

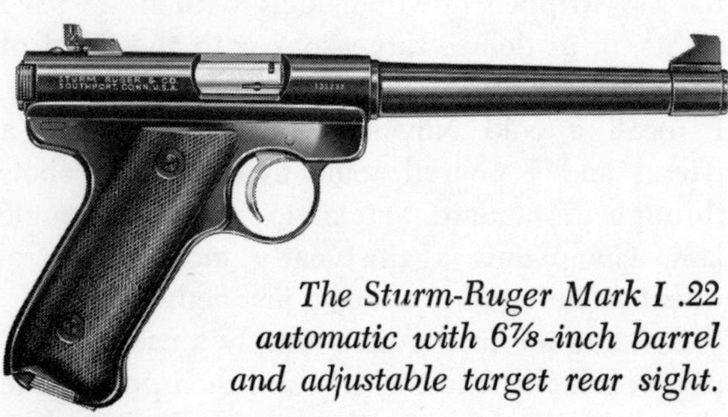

The Sturm-Ruger Mark I .22 automatic with 6⅞-inch barrel and adjustable target rear sight.

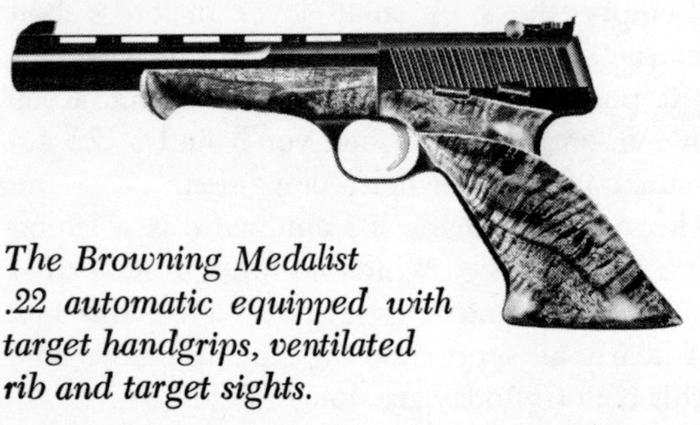

The Browning Medalist .22 automatic equipped with target handgrips, ventilated rib and target sights.

Center-Fire Revolvers

Choosing a center-fire revolver is pretty much matter of personal taste. There are, in fact, no fewer than thirty-two standard pistol loadings offered over the counter and probably three times that number of different handguns, from the anemic .32 up to the overpowering .44 Magnum. Somewhere within this range there's a handgun to please every would-be shooter.

There was an era when many Americans felt that their homes should be protected by a pistol and invariably chosen was a nickel-plated .32 revolver, which too often ended up in a bureau drawer beneath its owner's underwear, there to remain. In a few cases, the owners learned to shoot and to enjoy the guns, despite the fact that they had awkward undersized handgrips and a trigger pull that whitened knuckles. There's little excuse for the continued existence of the .32, especially as a protection gun. Compared to the more powerful and popular .38 Special loadings, the .32 is a feeble weapon. Some small-town police forces still issue it to their officers, because it is cheaper to buy than the .38 and ammunition for it is less expensive. For these customers, both Smith & Wesson and Colt continue its production. As a sportsman's gun, however, it is practically ignored.

Another type of center-fire revolver is one carried by plain-clothes police, bank messengers, payroll employees and others authorized to carry concealed weapons. This is the "belly gun," invariably a .38 Special caliber with a short barrel, rounded butt, and frequently without a hammer spur so that it can be drawn quickly without its snagging clothing. As the name "belly gun" implies, it's strictly a defensive weapon for close-up work, to be fired double-action, usually without the use of sights.

Similar guns, more likely to be carried in a belt or shoulder holster, have the usual hammer spur for hand cocking and more accurate fire. Occasionally assigned to undercover work with the U. S. Border Patrol, I used to tote a .44 S & W snub-nosed English revolver which I'd grown to like and which I could almost conceal in one hand. Despite its small size, however, its big snout could speak with authority. While on an assignment in an eastern slum district one night, I met a local police officer as I entered a dark alley. He'd helped me on previous details, and

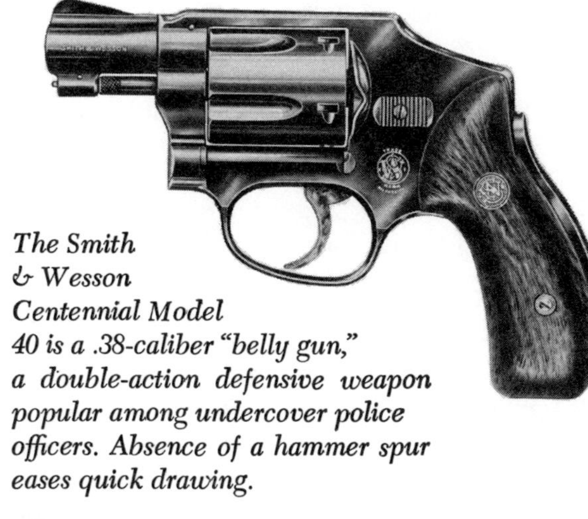

The Smith & Wesson Centennial Model 40 is a .38-caliber "belly gun," a double-action defensive weapon popular among undercover police officers. Absence of a hammer spur eases quick drawing.

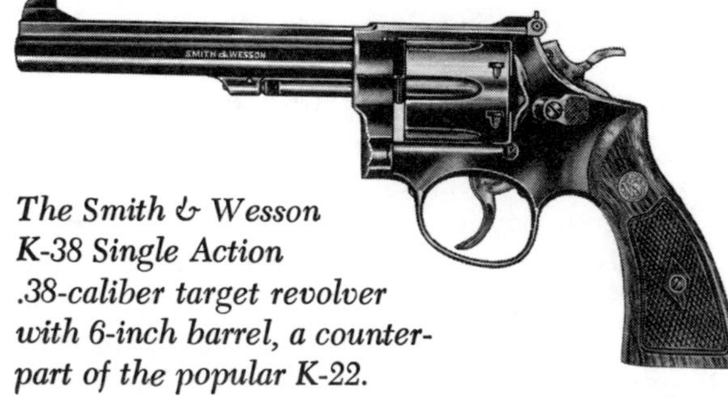

The Smith & Wesson K-38 Single Action .38-caliber target revolver with 6-inch barrel, a counterpart of the popular K-22.

The "big gun," a .45-caliber revolver produced by Smith & Wesson for heavy-bore target shooters.

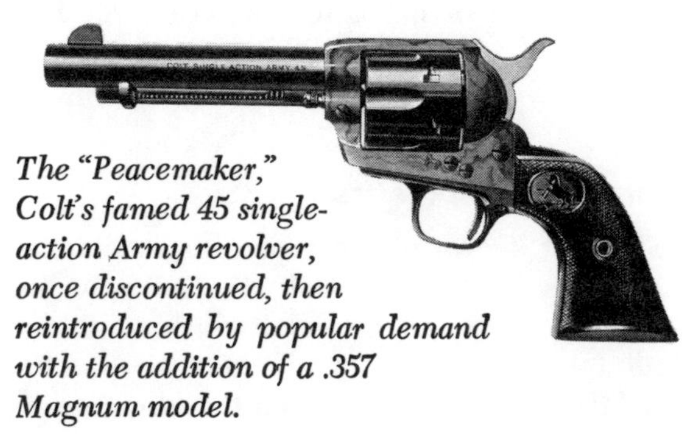

The "Peacemaker," Colt's famed 45 single-action Army revolver, once discontinued, then reintroduced by popular demand with the addition of a .357 Magnum model.

thinking I might be unarmed since I was in plain clothes, he insisted that I take his service revolver, a .32 belt gun. I refused the gun and also refused his offer that he accompany me, for fear his uniform would give me away. When he persisted with offers of help I finally showed him my .44. Looking into its muzzle, the officer muttered, "Well, you can always crawl up into it and hide!"

The heavier field-grade revolvers in .38 caliber with longer barrels, better sights and larger grips are far superior to the belly guns for sport shooting. Many of these are made to target-gun specifications including adjustable sights, target grips, crisp trigger pull and even swaged or widened triggers for steadier firing. The greatest boon to present-day shooters of this class of revolver is the mid-range load, a target-type wadcutter bullet fired by a light powder charge for lower velocity, greater accuracy and light recoil. Even women enjoy shooting these.

With full velocity loads, these weapons are popular with professional outdoorsmen who like to carry a handgun in place of a rifle. They are also the type of gun issued to uniformed police, highway patrols and sheriff's departments.

For anything heavier than the .38s, look to Colt, Smith & Wesson, and Ruger. Smith & Wesson's Model 58 Military and Police is chambered for the .41; its Model No. 25 Target gun, the .45 A.C.P. (Automatic Colt Pistol). The most famous of all Colts, of course, is the Single Action Army "Peacemaker," now chambered in the .357 Magnum as well as the .45 Colt. The Buntline Special also handles the .45, as does the New Frontier version of the Single Action Army. The latter also is chambered for the .357 Magnum. The Ruger Blackhawk, too, is chambered for the .45 Colt, and an accessory cylinder is available for shooting the A.C.P. in the same gun.

Although not in the .40-caliber classification, another version of the Blackhawk by Ruger handles the .30 U.S. Carbine shell which develops 600 foot pounds energy at the muzzle.

Hand loaders can have a field day with the .44s and .45s. Keep in mind, however, that recoil increases with power and with increased recoil comes louder report. Guns in this class are not generally considered plinkers.

Going a step further, we encounter the two famed Magnums, the .357 and the .44. These

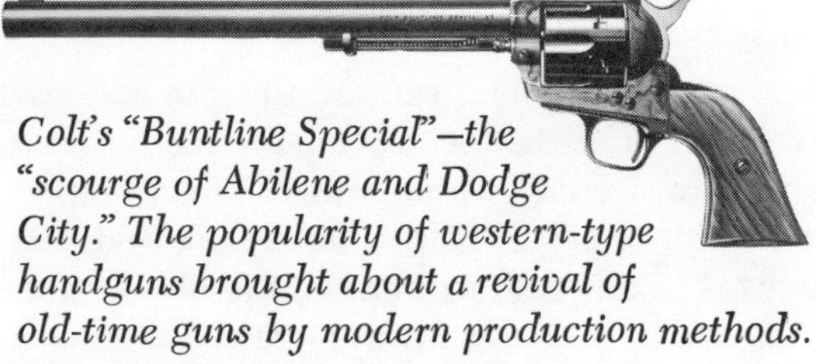

Colt's "Buntline Special"—the "scourge of Abilene and Dodge City." The popularity of western-type handguns brought about a revival of old-time guns by modern production methods.

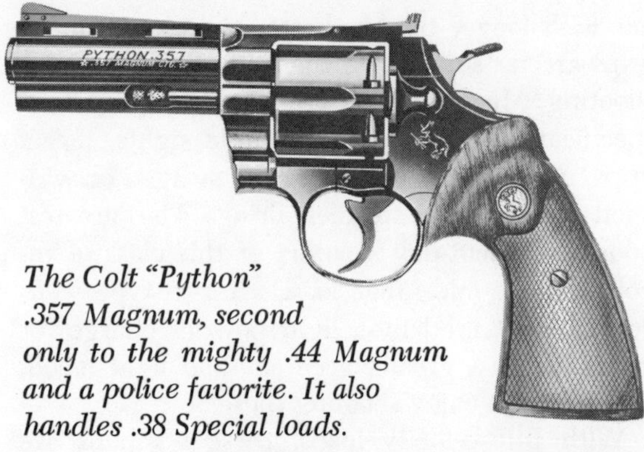

The Colt "Python" .357 Magnum, second only to the mighty .44 Magnum and a police favorite. It also handles .38 Special loads.

The Sturm-Ruger Blackhawk, a compact .357 Magnum with a 4⅝-inch barrel, is also available with a 6½-inch barrel.

The Sturm-Ruger Blackhawk, chambered for the awesome .44 Magnum, is suitable for big game in the hands of an expert.

Smith & Wesson's .44 Magnum revolver, the Model 29, packs more wallop than many deer rifles.

souped-up giants outclass many a center-fire rifle. The .357, with its 1550 foot seconds muzzle velocity and 845 foot pounds muzzle energy, was tops in the handgun power field until the advent of the .44 Magnum. Current handguns chambered for the .357 include the Smith & Wesson Models 27, 28 and 19; the famed Colt Peacemaker, and Python, along with the Ruger Blackhawk. Revolvers for the .357 are somewhat heavier than those for the .38, but an advantage of these is that .38 Special ammunition, including the mild mid-range loads, can be fired in the .357 Magnum guns, thus allowing the use of comparatively inexpensive ammunition in circumstances where the .357 might be too much gun.

The .44 Magnum, handled by the Ruger Blackhawk and the Smith & Wesson Model 29, is pretty much in a class by itself. This giant will hold its own against all comers, especially when you consider its 240-grain bullet leaving the muzzle at 1470 foot seconds, and packing a wallop of 670 foot pounds, at 100 yards! This is a *big* gun, in every sense of the word, having proved effective on large game at ranges up to 50 and 60 yards. Although designed as a handgun load, Ruger saw the possibilities of this cartridge for brush hunting and produced a .44 Magnum semiautomatic carbine for hunters. The .44 Special load can be handled by the .44 Magnum handgun. However, as is true of the .38 and the .357, the reverse is not possible.

If you can't afford a new gun, check with a local dealer to see what he has available among guns he has taken in trade. Examine the cylinder by trying to rock it while the gun is cocked. If it moves appreciably, discard it. It's worn. If there's a line of wear (finish worn off) where the latch rotates the cylinder, discard this too. If the ejector rod, which pushes through the cylinder to operate the ejector lugs, is worn or scratched noticeably, the gun has seen its better days. Check also the barrel for wear or corrosion.

Center-Fire Automatics

The best known of the center-fire automatics is, of course, the famous Colt .45, known for its tremendous stopping power, its kick, and best of all, for its reliability as a military weapon for over fifty years. Its accuracy on the target range is just as well known. You can't ask much more of any gun that was originated more than half a century ago!

Several civilian versions from Colt are available. The Government Model MK IV Series '70 is chambered for the .45 A.C.P., .38 Super Auto and 9 mm Luger. Especially in the .45 version, this is not a weapon for the timid shooter. It takes a strong arm to handle the recoil but its power and accuracy offset its orneriness. Other versions include the Combat Commander and the lighter and shorter Commander. For target shooters Colt has its Gold Cup MK IV National Match Model in .45 mid-range, .45 A.C.P. and .38 Super Auto.

Harrington & Richardson has a .380 version, the Model HK-4, with an optional conversion kit which provides a .22-caliber barrel for use on the .380 action. Thus, with one handgun—and two barrels—you can shoot either .22s or .380s.

Smith & Wesson entered the .38 automatic field recently with its new Model 52, chambered for mid-range loads only, being primarily a target model. Empty, the gun weighs 41 ounces and is 8⅝ inches long over-all. Magazine capacity is five shots and it will accept only cartridges whose bullets are seated within the mouth of the shell, as are the wad-cutter-type bullets in target loads. Developed from Smith & Wesson's Model 39 (chambered in 9 mm), the gun is unusually attractive for an automatic. Its sights are excellent, the rear being adjustable for windage and elevation, and they can be locked, after adjustment, by a coin edge.

The only other center-fire automatics worth serious attention are Browning products, a 9 mm Parabellum model with a thirteen-shot magazine, and the Browning .380.

The 9 mm great magazine capacity is made possible by a double-row loading of the shells within the grip. Before loading, the gun weighs 2 pounds. The 9 mm Parabellum is the official sidearm load of the North American Treaty Organization (NATO).

The .380, although originated by Colt, has lost favor in this country, Browning and Harrington & Richardson being the only suppliers of autos that handle it.

There seems to persist some demand for the .25-caliber automatic, packing somewhat more power than the .22s, yet falling far short of the

Designed as a war weapon, the Colt Government .45 Automatic has become a target shooter's favorite, now also available in .38 and 9 mm calibers.

The Smith & Wesson Model 52, a target automatic designed for mid-range .38 Special "wad-cutter" loads.

The Colt Commander, a lightweight version of the Colt Government .45, also supplied in .38 or 9 mm calibers.

The Browning 9 mm automatic pistol.

.38s. I suppose, for a personal protection weapon, the .25 has its place. Which is probably why Colt continues to produce it. Slightly over 4 inches long and weighing only about 12 ounces, it's a handy and effective gun at close range.

But for real stopping power, or for target shooting with an automatic, I would consider only the .38, .380, .45 and 9 mm Parabellum.

The Hutson scope mounted on this Ruger Single Six weighs a mere 3 ounces. (HUTSON CORP.)

Scope Sights for Handguns

The use of scope sights on pistols has come about among a small group of six-gun shooters who want to take advantage of the long-range potential of such loads as the .357 Magnum, .44 Magnum, even the .22 Winchester Magnum. These loads, with their flat trajectory, cannot be used to best advantage with iron sights unless, of course, a bench rest is utilized—not a practical accessory for handgun hunters. Few shooters can use a handgun accurately enough to hold on a woodchuck at 60 yards. The scope makes such shots possible—and even beyond.

Smith & Wesson .22 Colt Python .357 Magnum and Sturm-Ruger Blackhawk .357 Magnum, all equipped with Buehler mounts for scope shooting. (MAYNARD P. BUEHLER, INC.)

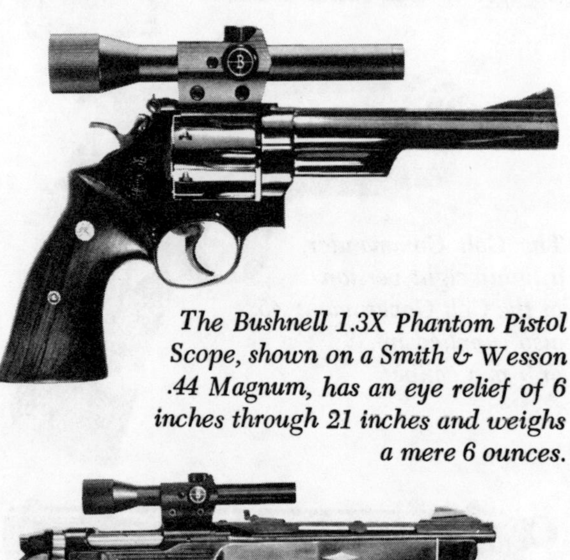

The Bushnell 1.3X Phantom Pistol Scope, shown on a Smith & Wesson .44 Magnum, has an eye relief of 6 inches through 21 inches and weighs a mere 6 ounces.

Ideal long-range handgun-scope combinations include the Bushnell 1.3X Phantom scope mounted on the Remington XP-100 chambered for the Remington .221 Fireball.

Handgun scopes and mounts are relatively few. One is the Bushnell 1.3X with a 6- to 21-inch eye relief. Another very interesting scope is the Hutson 1.7X with arm's-length eye relief which weighs only 3 ounces. Notice that both are low-power scopes. Any scope with greater power would be virtually impossible to see through at arm's length!

When first introduced some dozen years ago, scope-sighted handgun shooting was believed to be the "coming thing." Its popularity outstripped that of the hula hoop, but not by much! During field trips covering hundreds of miles afoot within the past years, I've never met a scope-sighted handgun hunter!

Shooting with a scope-equipped handgun is best done, of course, from a rest, since the scope will also magnify body tremors, likely to be at their worst in normal pistol shooting stances.

(A) Sitting position for shooting scope-mounted pistol is not unlike regular seated stance for shooting any handgun.
(B) The cross-arm position for shooting a scope-equipped handgun, in this case a Colt .357 Magnum Python with Buehler scope mounts.
(MAYNARD P. BUEHLER, INC.)

Iron Sights

Most commonly supplied with low- and medium-priced handguns are simple blade-front sights and rear sights that consist of a longitudinal groove cut into the gun's upper frame surface. For most instances of plinking and informal shooting, these sights are usually more than adequate. You should, however, try the gun from a bench rest to learn exactly where it will shoot for *you*. If the gun shoots high, there's little you can do except to compensate by shifting your hold on the bull's-eye accordingly, or replacing the front sight with a higher one. This is not a frequent need, however, as most sights of the fixed type are surprisingly accurate.

If the gun shoots too low, you can file or cut down the front sight to raise the point of impact. Another alternative, naturally, is to take "a full sight" when shooting. This problem is not likely to arise very often, however.

Many of the better revolvers and automatics come from the factory equipped with adjustable rear sights and some even have micrometer adjustments for windage and elevation which operate much like those described for use on rifles.

Holsters

Sticking a handgun into your trouser belt, in the manner of too many Hollywood and TV gunmen, is asking to be gut-shot, a rather unpleasant experience. Carrying a handgun loose in a car's glove compartment, or packed among camping gear often leads to damage or an accidental discharge. A suitable holster is practically a necessity.

For a light handgun, a simple leather pouch-type holster, with or without flap, and which can be slipped onto a trouser belt is fully adequate. The flap is a matter of choice, though it will protect the gun against rain or snow and keep it from falling out of a loose-fitting holster. If you decide against the flap, be sure the gun fits snugly in the pouch or that the holster has a safety strap that can be snapped across the underside of the hammer spur. For heavier guns, the combination belt and holster is best, with the belt most comfortable if it is two to three inches wide. Wear the rig high for greater comfort—not so that it looks like a gunfighter's outfit

Western-type holster for Sturm-Ruger .44 Magnum and similar heavy revolvers. (GEORGE LAWRENCE CO.)

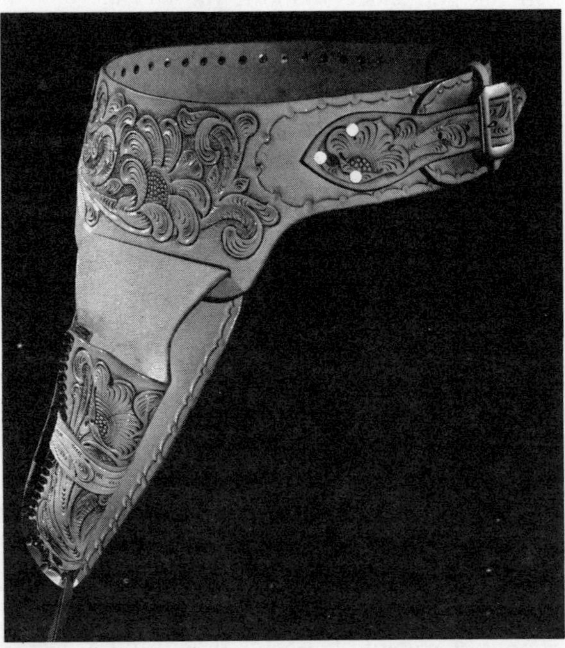

A "do-it-yourself" gunbelt and holster, assembled from pre-cut parts. (TANDY LEATHER CO.)

The "Buscadero" belt and holsters, for the "two-gun" shooter, is a handsome accessory. (GEORGE LAWRENCE CO.)

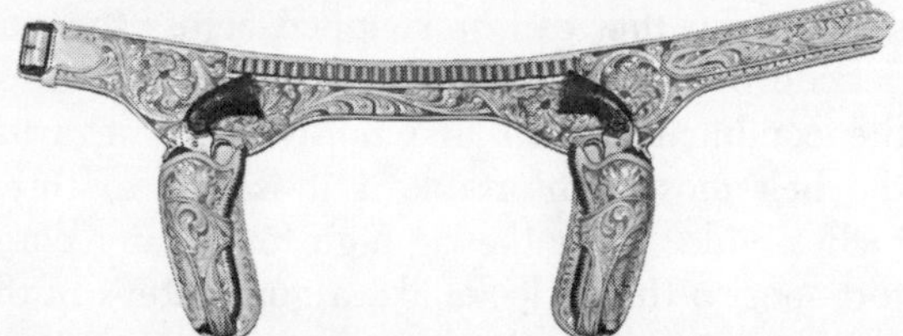

—a miserable one in which to walk. The higher on your hip the more comfortable.

Fine-quality holsters are metal-reinforced to hold their shape. Some have spring clips that grasp and hold the gun firmly yet allow a quick draw. If your handgun has target sights, the holster should have a sight protector, a heavy leather insert which keeps the rear sight from rubbing against the holster itself. Otherwise, constant chafing may damage the holster and it may also disturb the sight settings. If you're likely to wear the holster in a car, there's a swivel type which swings "fore-and-aft," so that the gun butt won't gouge your ribs.

A utility holster and gun belt is simple in design and looks much more businesslike than the highly polished, carved and metal-studded "Buscadero" belts which tote along a couple dozen shells in loops and make the wearer look as if he expected a "shoot-out" at any moment. If your tastes run to ornate "gunslinger" leathercraft, however, there are plenty of these on the market at prices that match the guns that go into them.

The best holsters are made of top-grain heavy steer hides which need only an occasional application of saddle soap. In time, such leather takes on a natural high gloss and a warm rich shade of brown or black. Oiling a holster is likely to soften the leather, cutting down on gun protection and ease of draw.

One of my early holsters was a hand-me-down which had been used to house a .32 revolver and which I adapted to my .22 Iver-Johnson. I soaked the old holster in water until thoroughly saturated. Then, after greasing and oiling my handgun thoroughly, I slipped it into the wet holster and placed it in the sun to dry. The leather shrank, of course, and molded a perfect fit about the handgun. A few rubbings with saddle soap restored the luster to the leather. Don't do this to a holster containing metal, however, for fear of rust. Neither should it be done to a quality holster. It's strictly a salvage operation.

Handgun Ammunition

.22 Short. While this is the ideal cartridge for handgun plinking it is also a sound choice for target shooting, especially since a number of fine automatics have been adapted to handle it. It

can be used indoors with a minimum of noise and danger since any bullet trap will stop it safely.

.22 Long. As I pointed out earlier, I can think of no reason for the continued existence of this load. It's not as accurate as the .22 Short and lacks the punch of the .22 Long Rifle.

.22 Long Rifle. Available in high-velocity and standard loadings. The high-speed hollow-point bullet makes an excellent small-game hunting load while the lower velocity shells, especially in the match loadings, are superbly accurate for target work.

.22 Winchester Rim-Fire Magnum. This is the "hottest" of the .22 rim-fires, making the standard .22 rim-fires look like Halloween peashooters! Colt, Ruger and Smith & Wesson have succumbed to its wiles and produced a variety of handguns for it, along with High Standard.

.221 Remington Fireball. Walking into a gunsmith's shop, only a few days before this writing, I encountered a sign which read "Rem. .221 Fireball—World's Most Powerful Load." The sign, of course, referred only to handgun loads, but I still questioned the gunsmith pointing out the .44 Magnum's potency. "It's got the most penetration," replied the gunsmith and he handed me the quarter-inch steel plate which I mentioned earlier—neatly drilled by a .221. Whether or not the gunsmith is right in his claim, the .221 will nudge aside many other calibers in the field of flat trajectory and power. It, too, will prove popular among handgun varmint hunters who, for the time being at least, can shoot this potent load in the new, and handsome, Remington XP-100 single-shot handgun.

.25 Automatic. With its mere 73 foot pounds muzzle energy, this is a weak load, suitable only for tiny pocket automatics, many of which come out of Spain. They're hardly man-stoppers!

.30 Luger. For use in automatic weapons, its comparatively high velocity makes it appear to be a powerful cartridge. However, due to its fully jacketed bullet and the latter's lack of expansion, it's a poor game killer.

.32 Automatic. Has twice the punch of the .25 auto but is still a mediocre load, although it's popular in small automatics. Muzzle energy is about equal to that of the .22 Long Rifle high-velocity load.

.32 Smith & Wesson. A rather obsolete load, so far as power is concerned, although there are still thousands of revolvers that handle it. Muzzle energy is only 94 foot pounds.

32 Smith & Wesson Long. Somewhat more powerful than the .32 S & W with its 114 foot pounds energy, but it still compares unfavorably with more modern loads.

.32 Colt. Available in Long and Short and designed for old-time Colt revolvers. Cannot be used in modern .32 revolvers and can well be considered obsolete although still available.

.32-20 Winchester. A rifle as well as a handgun load, although only the standard velocity cartridge should be used in a handgun. The 100-grain bullet builds up 271 foot pounds energy at the muzzle, making it the most powerful of the .32s in a pistol.

.357 Magnum. Outdone by only the .44 Magnum, this is the second most powerful handgun load, popular with police because of its tremendous stopping power. Suitable as a game cartridge where pistol hunting is permitted, it develops 690 foot pounds energy at the muzzle. .38 Special ammunition can be fired in revolvers that are chambered for the .357, but not the reverse. These include models by Colt, Ruger and Smith & Wesson. No automatics handle the .357.

9 mm Luger. A load of international popularity for automatics, it is one of the most potent of handgun loads, rated at 330 foot pounds muzzle energy. It's accurate and quite flat shooting. This bullet, however, is metal-cased and a poor game stopper.

.38 S & W Special. Certainly the most popular of the center-fire handgun loads, well proven on the target range and as a police cartridge. A favorite with reloaders. The 148-grain mid-range wad-cutter bullets and loadings produce light recoil and fine target accuracy, while the heavier 158- and 200-grain bullets, are excellent protection gun loads, as well as field loads.

.38 Colt. These are made in Long and Short and may be fired in revolvers chambered for the .38 Special but their performance can hardly match the latter. To all practical purposes obsolete.

.38 Super Automatic. Loaded with its 130-grain metal-cased bullet, this load develops 469 foot pounds muzzle energy, potentially the third best man-stopper in the handgun field. However, the metal-case bullet lacks expansion qual-

ities needed in a game bullet. It's a popular load with police who prefer to carry the Colt automatics.

.380 Automatic. This is the heaviest load possible in small pocket automatics, developing 192 foot pounds muzzle energy. Far better than the .32s but still quite short of the power of the .38 Special.

.38 Automatic. For use in all .38 automatics, whereas the .38 Super Automatic is limited to two guns. Not as powerful a load, but still ample for those who prefer automatics as protection guns.

.38 Smith & Wesson. Not to be confused with the more potent .38 Smith & Wesson Special. Quite a good cartridge, however, for use in lightweight, short-barreled "belly guns."

.38-40 Winchester. This, like the .32-20, is also a combination pistol and rifle load. No handguns are made today to handle the cartridge although it's still popular as a brush or woods load among shooters of the older .38-40 rifles.

.41 Magnum. Smith & Wesson's Model 57 handles this load with a muzzle velocity close to that of the .44 Magnum. Its muzzle energy runs from 1050 to 1500 foot pounds, depending upon the loading. The more popular Magnum overshadows this excellent load.

.44 Magnum. This is the "H-Bomb" of the handgun loadings and it has been successfully adapted to a carbine by Ruger. Smith & Wesson, Colt and Ruger make revolvers only to handle its tremendous power. With muzzle velocities of 1470 foot seconds, it develops 1150 foot pounds energy, by far our most potent handgun load. Fast growing in popularity among big-game hunters who like its 240-grain flat-nosed bullet. Heavy recoil and report confine its use to areas of wide open spaces by shooters accustomed to handling heavy weapons. The .44 Special and .44 Russian (the latter now discontinued) cartridges may be fired in a handgun chambered for the .44 Magnum, but not the reverse.

.44 S & W Special. A slow-moving (755 foot seconds at muzzle) load firing a 246-grain lead bullet with a muzzle energy of 310 foot pounds. Can be hand loaded to greater velocities. Designed originally as a target load, hence its low velocity for accuracy's sake.

.44-40 Winchester. While not in a class with the .44 Magnum, this is still an excellent game load for handguns, driving its 200-grain soft-point bullet at 975 foot seconds and developing 420 foot pounds at the muzzle. It is a rifle-pistol cartridge but the high-velocity loadings should be confined to rifle use.

.45 Colt. This is the powerful fodder handled by the famed Colt Single Action Army Peacemaker and several other revolvers. Its 250-grain lead bullet is among the best man-stoppers and a good game load to boot, developing over 400 foot pounds muzzle energy.

.45 Colt ACP. The ACP stands for Automatic Colt Pistol. This is the U. S. Army Colt .45, famous all over the world where our fighting men have gone and it's equally famous on the target range. Unfortunately, factory loadings are all with full metal casings, eliminating these loads for game use. It develops 850 foot seconds and 370 foot pounds energy at the muzzle. Available with match loads at reduced velocity for target work.

Ballistics Tables Winchester-Western Center-Fire Handgun Ammunition

Explanation of bullet-style abbreviations: M.Pi., Metal Piercing; F.M.C., Full Metal Case; S.P., Soft Point; L., Lead; M.Pt., Metal Point; O.P.E., Open Point Expanding; H.P., Hollow Point.

Cartridge	Bullet Wt. (grs.)	Bullet Style	Barrel Length (inches)	Muzzle Velocity (ft. sec.)	Muzzle Energy (ft. lbs.)
.25 Automatic	50	F.M.C.	2	810	73
.256 Winchester	60	O.P.E.	8½	2350	735
.30 Luger	93	F.M.C.	4½	1220	305
.32 Automatic	71	F.M.C.	4	960	145
.32 Smith & Wesson	85	L.	3	680	90
.32 S & W Long	98	L.	4	705	115
.32 Short Colt	80		4	745	100
.32 Long Colt	82		4	755	105
.32 Colt New Police	98	L.	4	680	100
.32–20 Winchester	100	L.	6	1030	235
.32–20 Winchester	100	S.P.	6	1030	235
.357 Magnum	158		8⅜	1410	695
.357 Magnum	158	M.Pi.	8⅜	1410	695
9 mm Luger	115	F.M.C.	4	1140	330
9 mm Luger	100		4	1325	390
.38 Smith & Wesson	145	L.	4	685	150
.38 Special	158	L.	6	855	255
.38 Special	158	M.Pt.	6	855	255
.38 Special Police	158	L.,H.P.	6	1060	295
.38 Special Super Police	200	L.	6	730	235
.38 Special	150		6	1060	375
.38 Special	150	M.Pi.	6	1060	375
.38 Special Match	148	L.	6	770	195
.38 Special Match	158	L.	6	855	255
.38 Short Colt	130		6	730	150
.38 Long Colt	150		6	730	175
.38 Automatic	130	F.M.C.	5	1280	475
.38 Automatic	130	F.M.C.	4½	1040	310
.380 Automatic	95	F.M.C.	3¾	955	190
.38–40 Winchester	180	S.P.	5	975	380
.44 Smith & Wesson	246	L.	6½	755	310
.44 Magnum	240		6½	1470	1150
.44–40 Winchester	200	S.P.	7½	975	420
.45 Colt	255	L.	5½	880	410
.45 Automatic	230	F.M.C.	5	850	370
.45 Automatic Match	210	L.	5	710	235
.45 Automatic Match	185	F.M.C.	5	775	245

Ballistics Tables Remington-Peters Center-Fire Handgun Ammunition

Explanation of bullet-style abbreviations: L., Lead; W.C., Wad-Cutter; M.C., Metal Case; M.P., Metal Point; S.J.H.P., Semi-Jacketed Hollow Point; S.P., Soft Point; P.S.P., Pointed Soft Point

Cartridge	*Bullet* Wt. (grs.)	*Bullet* Style	*Barrel Length (inches)*	*Muzzle Velocity (ft. sec.)*	*Muzzle Energy (ft. lbs.)*
.22 Rem. Jet Magnum	40	S.P.	8⅜	2100	390
.221 Rem. Fireball	50	P.S.P.	10½	2650	780
.25 Automatic	50	M.C.	2	810	73
.30 Luger	93	M.C.	4½	1220	305
.32 Short Colt	80	L.	4	745	100
.32 Long Colt	82	L.	4	755	100
.32 Colt New Police	100	L.	4	680	100
.32 Automatic	71	M.C.	4	960	145
.32 Smith & Wesson	88	L.	3	680	90
.32 S & W Long	98	L.	4	705	115
.32–20 Winchester	100	L.	6	1030	271
.357 Magnum	158	S.P.	8⅜	1550	845
.357 Magnum	158	M.P.	8⅜	1410	695
.357 Magnum	158	L.	8⅜	1410	695
.357 Magnum	158	S.J.H.P.	8⅜	1550	845
9 mm Luger	115	S.J.H.P.	4	1160	345
9 mm Luger	124	M.C.	4	1120	345
.38 Smith & Wesson	146	L.	4	685	150
.38 Special	125	S.J.H.P.	6	1370	520
.38 Special	148	L., W.C.	6	770	195
.38 Special Target	158	L.	6	855	255
.38 Special	158	M.P.	6	855	255
.38 Special	158	L. (High Speed)	6	1090	415
.38 Special	158	S.J.H.P.	6	1150	465
.38 Special	200	L.	6	730	235
.38 Short Colt	125	L.	6	730	150
.38 Long Colt	150	L.	6	730	175
.38–40 Winchester	180	S.P.	5	975	380
.38 Super Auto Colt	130	M.C.	5	1280	475
.38 Automatic Colt	130	M.C.	4½	1040	310
.380 Automatic	95	M.C.	3¾	955	190
.41 Magnum	210	L.	8⅜	1050	515
.41 Magnum	210	S.P.	8⅜	1500	1050
.44 S & W Special	246	L.	6½	755	310
.44 Rem. Magnum	240	L.	6½	1470	1150
.44 Rem. Magnum	240	S.P.	6½	1470	1150
.44 Rem. Magnum	240	S.J.H.P.	6½	1470	1150
.44–40 Winchester	200	S.P.	7½	975	420
.45 Colt	250	L.	5½	860	410
.45 Automatic	185	M.C., W.C.	5	775	245
.45 Automatic	230	M.C.	5	850	370
.45 Automatic Rim	230	L.	5½	810	335

Ballistics Tables Norma Center-Fire Handgun Ammunition

Explanation of bullet-style abbreviations: F.J., Full Jacket; L., Lead; A.P., Armor Piercing; H.P., Hollow Point; F.J.S.W., Full Jacket Semi-Wad-Cutter; L.W., Lead Wad-Cutter; S.P., Soft Point.

Cartridge	*Wt. (grs.)*	*Style*	*Barrel Length (inches)*	*Muzzle Velocity (ft. sec.)*	*Muzzle Energy (ft. lbs.)*
.25 Automatic Colt	50	F.J.	2	810	100
.30 Luger	93	F.J.	4.7	1230	312
.32 Automatic Colt	77	F.J.	4	900	139
.32 Smith & Wesson	85	L.	3	680	87
.32 S & W Long	98	L.	4	705	108
7.5 Nagant	104	L.	4.5	722	123
9 mm Luger	104	A.P.	4.7	1260	367
9 mm Luger	115	H.P.	4.7	1165	350
9 mm Luger	116	F.J.	4.7	1165	350
.357 Magnum	158	S.P., F.J., H.P.	8⅜	1450	735
.380 Automatic Colt	95	F.J.	3¾	955	190
.38 Special	110	H.P.	6	1542	580
.38 Special	148	L.W.	6	800	210
.38 Special	158	H.P.	6	900	285
.38 Special	158	F.J.S.W.	6	900	285
.38 Special	158	L.	6	870	266
.380 MK II	180	F.J.	5	620	153
.38 Smith & Wesson	146	L.	4	730	173
.44 Magnum	236	H.P.	18.5	1675	1476
.44 Magnum	240	S.P.	18.5	1675	1496
.45 Automatic Colt	230	F.J., H.P.	5	850	370

Chapter XI

SHOOTING THE HANDGUN

At first glance target shooting with a handgun may seem a pretty dull sport—especially from the viewpoint of a spectator. As a participant, however, you'll find it quite exciting. What's more, you can never become a consistently good shot without target-shooting techniques well learned and applied. At the Border Patrol training school we were made to shoot hundreds of rounds with the .22 and .38 at paper targets before we got into the more exciting quick-draw, running-target and double-action shooting. This approach in training is standard in nearly all military and police shooting courses, because the fundamentals of *all* sound handgun habits lie within the standard practices of the target range.

There are dozens of interesting shooting possibilities in any one day afield with a handgun, but to take best advantage of them, you'll need target-shooting background. Such shooting need not be done on an organized range or at a shooting club. After graduation from the Border Patrol school, I spent many more hours shooting in gravel pits than on measured ranges! Not far from my station in northern Maine, we had a favorite check point where we inspected incoming car traffic. Automobiles were few, though, sometimes fewer than a dozen per day and we whiled away the time practicing with our service revolvers, shooting mid-range wad-cutters, at a target nailed to a tree. We cut down a 10-inch spruce during one two-week period!

Stance

The proper shooting position for handgun shooting is not unlike that for offhand rifle shooting—facing about 45 degrees from the target, except that you should face *to the left* of the target instead of to the right. With the feet well apart for steadiness, the spine straight, shoulders level, head erect, raise your gun and point it at the target. Then close your eyes for ten to fifteen seconds. When you reopen them and you find your gun still pointed at the target, your angle of stance is correct. If, however, your gun has drifted right or left slightly, you should shift your position accordingly. Shift your feet but don't twist your body, until the gun points naturally and easily at the target.

The military stance, in which a shooter sights and fires with his body at a full right angle to the target is unnatural and allows body swaying, causes muscle strain in the arm, neck and back, and is tiring on the eyes. Military officials are realizing this and the trend is now toward a more comfortable position.

Many shooters don't raise the handgun high enough, so that they must lower or cant their heads to align the sights. This is incorrect. Raise the gun to eye level with the head erect. The shooting arm should be straight but not so rigid that it causes discomfort in the elbow or tremors of the hand. Bending the elbow excessively brings arm muscles into play unnecessarily. In fact, the gun barrel should be aligned with the arm almost perfectly. All body muscles should be working as little as possible, for a relaxed stance is the secret to a steady hold. The knees, though, need to be slightly rigid with the weight evenly distributed on both feet. Some shooters are inclined to lean backwards from the waist, as if to compensate for the weight of the gun, but no handgun is that heavy! Leaning backwards will cause back pains and tired muscles. It's preferable to lean forward slightly so that you become conscious of weight or pressure on the balls of your feet, with this weight evenly distributed between the two. Good shooting stance can be boiled down to a relaxed position that follows the natural structure of the body's bones with muscles under minimum tension.

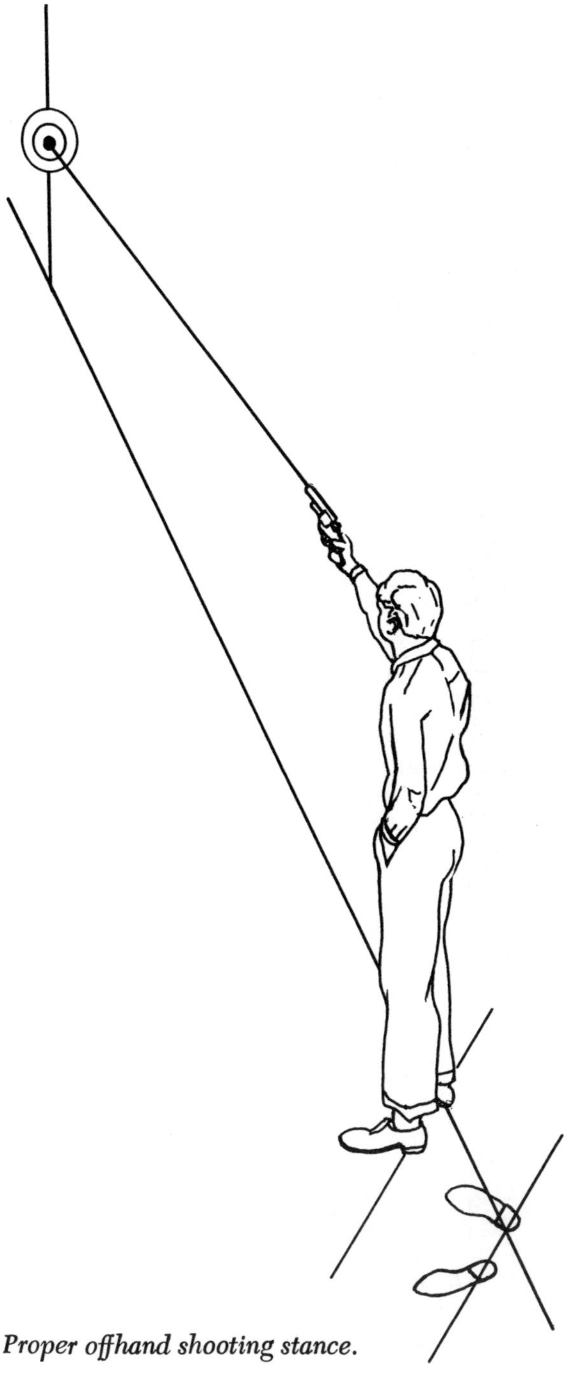

Muscles in the shooting arm will, of course, be under some tension, but this should be only enough to hold the pistol and to keep the arm extended outward in a straight line toward the target. Hand muscles, too, will get somewhat of a workout and these should be developed through the use of grip exercisers or through "dry shooting." The latter is nothing more than aiming and shooting an empty gun—a chore which I used to perform fifteen minutes per day, "shooting" at doorknobs in my living room!

Proper offhand shooting stance.

Grip

The manner in which a handgun is held can make the difference between hits and misses, even at short ranges and on big targets. In time, you'll adjust your hand to your handgun instinctively, giving no thought to the process, but until you acquire this knack make a conscious effort to get a correct grip. Spread your hand out to form a *V*, with your thumb on one side and the palm and four fingers on the other. With your other hand, lodge the gun solidly into this *V*, then close your fingers about it. The trigger finger should enter the trigger guard comfortably with the *first joint* of the finger resting on the trigger. The thumb should be applied against the side of the frame on the opposite side, either on a level with the trigger finger or slanted slightly downward. The lower three fingers should be wrapped firmly about the butt.

With a .22 handgun, the shooting hand may be slightly offset but when you graduate to .38s, .45s or one of the Magnums, you'll want the *V* joint at the base of the thumb, directly back of the butt and line of sight. This will permit you to absorb recoil into the arm and shoulder instead of into the sensitive and comparatively weak wrist joint. Recoil control is easier with this grip, and as a result, you can get your heavy gun back on target more quickly after firing a shot.

The grip on the gun should be high enough so that you have firm control and so the revolver, especially, doesn't feel top-heavy. At the same time the thumb should have room enough for full freedom to cock the hammer easily and quickly. Be sure, also, that the handgun is not canted to one side or the other as this will cause

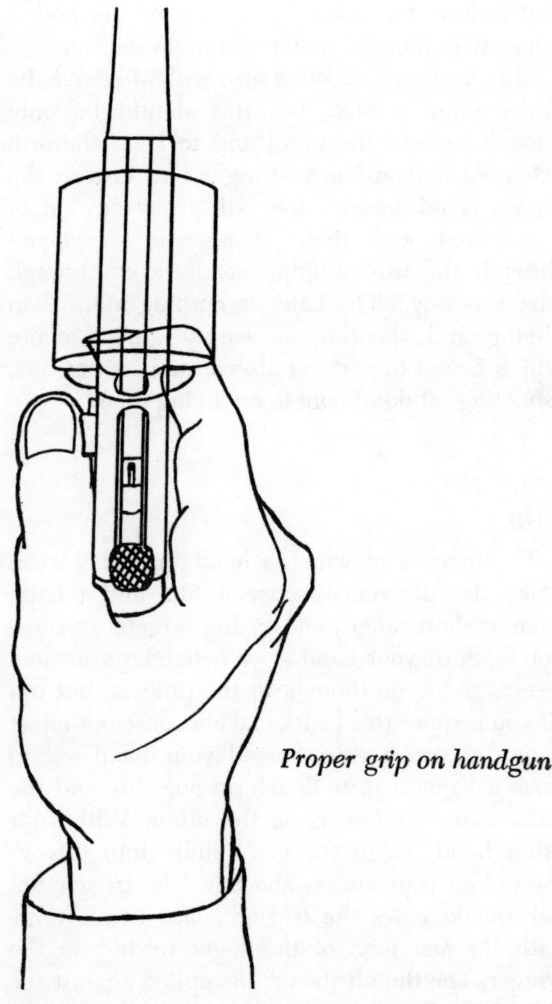

Proper grip on handgun.

shots to center low and to the side of the bull's-eye. No matter how long your trigger finger may be, don't crowd the trigger. This finger should be arched horizontally so that the sensitive first joint is free to pull the trigger directly backward. Don't apply any side pressure.

What to do with the idle hand? Put it in your trouser pocket or let it hang loosely at your side but don't hook your thumb in your belt as I've seen shooters do. This raises the left shoulder and creates tension of the upper back and neck muscles.

Sighting and Shooting

Sighting and pulling the trigger of a handgun requires exactly the same co-ordination described for rifle shooting. You'll be confronted with the same wavering of the front sight and the same body tremors, but these will be more pronounced since your gun is being held at arm's length. Perfect co-ordination will be tougher to attain.

As your sights line up on the 6 o'clock point at the bottom of the bull's-eye, start your trigger pull, slowly and deliberately. If the front sight moves away from the target, hold the trigger pressure but don't release any. As the sights return on target, reapply trigger pressure. As with rifle shooting, you shouldn't know exactly when the gun will fire. Breathing in pistol shooting is much like that in fine rifle shooting. Hold your breath while pulling the trigger, but no longer than ten to fifteen seconds. If you haven't fired by that time, put down the gun a few seconds to rest.

There's no point to my going into further detail regarding sighting and shooting the pistol or revolver. As I've pointed out, the technique described for rifle shooting is much the same as that for handguns.

However, as the shot goes off, call it, according to where you think it will hit on the target, such as "3 o'clock, seven ring." When you can call your shots fairly accurately—and they need not be bull's-eyes—you're well on the road to understanding proper sighting and trigger pull. A skilled shooter can sense where his shot will hit, even though he didn't know just when his gun would fire.

As your slow-fire technique improves, the sighting and squeezing—or pulling—of the trigger will become second nature to you and you'll be ready for timed and rapid-fire shooting. Timed fire calls for five shots in twenty seconds; rapid fire, five shots in ten seconds.

In these events, beginners are inclined to get off their shots too quickly, using much less than

Proper sight alignment results from aligning front sight at six-o'clock position on bull's-eye and centered within notch of rear sight.

the allotted time. Five shots in ten seconds is an easy accomplishment—*aiming* those five shots is the tough part of the job. Ed McGivern, probably the all-time rapid-fire champion fast-draw shooter, once placed five shots from a double action .38 into a target the size of a playing card in two fifths of a second. This was trick shooting, of course, but it was *practical* in that McGivern hit what he aimed at!

Despite the time element involved in timed- and rapid-fire courses, make each shot a deliberate one, concentrating on hitting the bull rather than on getting all five shots off in sufficient time. Naturally, there's no time to be wasted, but four hits within a time limit will give you a better score than five misses!

I used to practice timed- and rapid-fire events by dry-firing with a watch, having a sweep hand, propped up in front of me. I didn't look at the watch while firing of course, but it's amazing how quickly you can learn to estimate a ten- or twenty-second interval, in relation to the motions necessary to aim, and fire five shots within those time limits. This is one of the best methods I know to overcome the tendency to try to "beat the clock" rather than to try for accuracy. Once you get the feel of the ten- or twenty-second time periods, much of the tense urgency disappears.

A common difficulty of beginners is "flinch," the tendency to blink or even to jerk the head and arm aside at the moment the gun is expected to go off. This causes the shooter to pull or jerk the trigger, and since he then knows just when the gun will fire, the tendency to flinch is increased. It's a vicious circle.

Proper technique which eliminates knowing *exactly* when the gun will fire diminishes the flinching tendency. However, if it continues, have a friend load two to four shells in a revolver, leaving at least two chambers empty but so that you don't know which is loaded and which is not. Fire the five-shot course. Since the gun won't jump when you fire an empty cylinder chamber, you'll be made aware of your flinch. As a matter of fact, you'll probably feel quite sheepish about flinching at the sound of a click. Possibly expecting another click on your next shot, you'll fire, quite likely, without flinching. A few sessions at this type of shooting will soon cure the flinching habit. Incidentally, don't be embarrassed about flinch. It's a common ailment and, fortunately, one that's easily overcome.

This is by no means intended to be a complete course in target shooting. I've merely pointed out certain fundamentals. As you progress with the handgun, you'll pick up fine points that will upgrade your marksmanship. You'll acquire these finishing touches to your technique quickly by shooting as often as possible alongside experts. Don't be shy about asking for suggestions or advice. They've been through the mill and will be willing to help you. I've never known a man yet who was not flattered to be asked for advice on shooting—or any other subject!

Double-Action Shooting

Double-action shooting consists of firing the revolver *but not cocking it manually;* the double-action revolver cocks itself when the trigger is pulled. Fast defensive shooting is invariably double-action, and although police shooting techniques won't be discussed here, there's fun to be had in getting off five shots in rapid succession and hitting the target.

Double-action firing is done from the hip "wild West style" or at eye level. Stance is important in fast shooting, too, but it's a stance quite unlike that of the target shooter. Face the target squarely, one foot a little in front of the other and with the knees bent so that you stand in a slight crouch. This isn't for "gunslinger" effect but rather for steadiness. Grip the gun firmly with the arm and wrist muscles quite taut. Hold the gun so that it is an extension of your arm and wrist; these should be about parallel to the ground. Don't jerk the trigger! Instead acquire a smooth, though quick, backward pull to avoid "pulling" your shots. Don't look at the gun—the sights are not used in hip shooting—but rather keep your eyes on the target. Great speed shouldn't be your immediate goal. Hits are more important but speed will come naturally with practice.

Shooting double-action at eye level requires much the same technique, although your eyes will be conscious of the gun barrel and, roughly, the sights; but they should be kept on the target. Double-action shooting is a case of acquiring an accurate sense of pointing the handgun rather than sighting it. It's not unlike the principle of a pitcher's throwing to a batter. He doesn't see his pitching hand or the ball during his windup and throw. His eyes are on the plate where he manages to point his throw.

For practice, a man-sized silhouette target is excellent and your early attempts should be confined to 8 or 10 yards. As you acquire some degree of skill, move back to 15 yards. Eye-level double-action shooting produces greater accuracy at longer ranges but double-action shooting can rarely be done accurately at much over 20 to 25 yards. Four out of five misses during early stages of practice are not uncommon so don't get discouraged! When you can hit a man-size silhouette three out of five shots at 15 yards you're moving up into the expert class!

Fast-Draw Shooting

Fast-draw shooting can hardly be called practical in our present-day society since the chance of a surprise "shoot-out" is a remote possibility, indeed. It's strictly a game. It can be enjoyed out-of-doors with live ammunition or indoors with an empty gun.

Incidentally, were any of the old-time gunfighters to come up against some of our present-day fast-draw artists, they'd likely come off second best. Not because they were slow, by any means. Their equipment was far inferior to the rigs used nowadays. Their holsters, for example, were often of soft leather which had been thoroughly oiled, making them flabby. Also, they wore these quite high, so that an 1885 fast draw meant pulling a gun up almost to the shooter's armpit before he could level it off for a shot. Today's gunfighter rigs are worn low (though not as low as is often seen on TV) and the holsters are stiffer, with metal liners or reinforcement, which make slipping the gun out much more rapid. Of course, comparing one of the original gunfighters with one of today's gunslingers is like conversationally matching Joe Louis and Jack Dempsey in a hypothetical fifteen-rounder. The actual results can never be known!

Fast-draw experts advise beginners to practice in front of a full-length mirror, not in an attempt to beat yourself to the draw, certainly, but rather to give yourself some one to race against. You'll never win, but the incentive to try is there.

Like any other form of shooting, constant practice makes the expert, but there are also techniques to be learned. As you reach for your holstered shootin' iron, your thumb is the first part of your hand to touch the gun and this should be on the hammer spur. The gun is then cocked while it's still in the holster and on its way out. This doesn't mean that you cock the gun and then draw it. Cock it as you draw, clasping your three lower fingers into position. When the gun is finally cleared of the holster and aimed—or pointed—at your target, you should be ready to pull the trigger. This takes a fine sense of co-ordination.

Ever since fast-draw shooting went from Hollywood into the homes of American shooters, there's been a rash of blown-off toes, decapped knees and powder-burned legs, the inevitable results of practice with loaded guns, a sport only once removed from Russian roulette. Don't load your revolver for fast-draw practice until you've learned a near-perfect draw consistently performed without accidental firing. Accidents will happen but if the gun is empty they merely add to your experience and, eventually, to your skill. When you've acquired this skill, you can then load with inexpensive wax bullets motivated by mild powder loads.

Most fast-draw revolvers are of the western, single-action type, but these guns usually require a little tinkering before they're completely suitable. Most factory hammer springs are too stiff for easy cocking. Have a gunsmith weaken the spring so that it cocks easily, yet will hold the hammer to full cock safely until you pull the trigger. Since sights are of little value, you may want to file down the front blade to facilitate drawing, but this will make the gun nearly useless for other types of shooting. If you want to use the gun for other sport you'll have to be satisfied with a slightly slower draw with your six-shooter. Most single-action guns are equipped with a rounded blade-front sight, anyway, which offers a minimum of holster resistance.

Fast-draw shooting is a widespread sport today but police officers have been practicing it for years. By removing the shoulder strap from our Border Patrol Sam Browne belts, we could drop our holsters to a suitable height for fast-draw practice. The Border Patrol holster, incidentally, was designed by the late Sam Myres of El Paso with the fast draw in mind. It's an open holster that tilts the gun butt forward with the entire grip and trigger guard exposed. Placing a penny on the back of his hand, a patrolman would go for his gun. If he fired before the coin struck the ground, he was considered to be doing well, but if he managed to puncture the man-size silhouette, ten yards in front of him as well, we classed him as an expert. Few of us attained that status.

There are a variety of gunslinger belts and holsters on the market, including an open-front or slit holster which holds the gun by means of a spring clip and allows a fast draw through the front slit, eliminating the upward motion required when using a pouch-type holster. Another model is the "clamshell," which springs open at the touch of a button on its side. Most experts, however, shy away from trick holsters and use the modern versions of the old-time western pouch holsters, hung low on the thigh.

Hunting with the Handgun

In the cause of humane and sportsmanlike kills, hunting with the handgun should be limited to the elite among shooters—those who can consistently puncture an 8-inch bull's-eye at 50 yards. If you're not capable of this kind of shooting, confine your handgun shots at game to those which can be made from some kind of a rest. A squirrel at 25 yards is a small target, indeed, and the vital area of a deer at 50 yards shrinks disconcertingly over the sights of a handgun. A poor shot with a handgun has no business hunting, since he'll wound and lose more game than he will collect.

Some thirty states prohibit the use of handguns on deer-sized animals and a few even prohibit handgun hunting altogether. It's wise, consequently, to check the law in your state before going afield to fill the pot with a revolver or automatic.

Regarding state hunting laws, it's beyond my powers to understand why some which prohibit handgun hunting allow hunting of deer with archery equipment. Fortunately, archers hit very few animals but when they do, the result is not a pretty picture. Arrows kill through bloodletting, since they lack the shocking power of bullets. A deer, hit by an arrow, may run great distances, especially if a greenhorn hunter anxiously pursues it. Eventually, if the wound is serious enough, the animal dies of loss of blood. This is permitted in states where a hunter may not use a .44 Magnum revolver, for example, with its killing power in excess of that of the .30/30!

For small game, such as squirrels, the .22 rimfire is ideal while the new .22 Winchester Rimfire Magnum, interchangeable in *some* handguns, makes available suitable power for slightly larger game, such as fox, wildcat, coyote and other critters of this size.

The .44 Remington Magnum, of course, is the ultimate in handgun loads for game up to the size of deer. In fact some writers insist that this is the *only* suitable load, a stand with which I disagree. My first "handgun deer" fell to a .38 Special 158-grain lead bullet. I'd come into an abandoned lumber camp yard late one afternoon, intending to spend the night in the empty office shack. Behind the bunkhouse I spotted a spikehorn buck and a small doe feeding on raspberry tips. Slipping around the bunkhouse quietly, I rested the .38 on one of the projecting logs of the building and sighted carefully on the spike's shoulder at some 35 yards. At the gun's loud *boom* in the quiet woods setting, the deer fell—dead before I was able to approach. Later, I discovered that the bullet had broken its spine just back of the shoulder. On that same trip, I saw a lumberjack "walkin' boss," drop a similar spikehorn with a neat heart shot at 30 yards from a P-38 Walthers 9 mm automatic. I've known other woodsmen who have taken deer with handguns of this power range.

Therefore, I'd like to propose that handguns in the .38 Special class, as well as the .357 and .44 Magnums, may well be considered suitable on deer. At no time, though, should a hunter feel that he can substitute power for shooting skill and care in sighting. Handgun hunting is for the sportsman who's willing to take a little extra care. He is, in fact, one of the elite.

The techniques of holding, sighting and trigger pull used on the target range still apply in hunting country, but correct stance isn't always possible. Shooting offhand, for example, shouldn't be attempted for there's an element of excitement in hunting that will produce body tremors which make those on the target range seem like the Rock of Gibraltar! To shoot from a standing position, place your shooting arm against a tree to steady it, using your left hand for added stability. Another trick is to wrap your left arm *around* a small tree in a "scissor hold" on the trunk. If there's a branch or fork at the right height, rest your shooting hand in this. Don't place the barrel directly against anything solid, however. This can well result in a wild shot.

Unheard of on the pistol target range, a smart handgun hunter will use the tricks of the rifleman. If no suitable artificial aid for a standing shot is at hand, drop quickly to a sitting position. Rest your back against a tree, rock or log, and with knees drawn up rest your arms on the latter, holding the gun in both hands while you sight. Place your feet somewhat widely apart and hold the gun at eye level. Getting into this position and touching off a shot actually takes less time than it has taken you to read this paragraph!

Even faster is the kneeling stance, though it's not as steady. Drop your right knee to the ground, place your left elbow against your left thigh which will be approximately horizontal, and raise the gun to eye level. Grasp the buttstock and your right hand in your left, sight—and pull! It's that fast, and whether or not you will connect will depend somewhat upon how often you've practiced this maneuver.

Shooting a handgun in the prone position is effective providing no grass or low brush interferes with sighting vision. The stance is not unlike the rifleman's, slightly angled and with the chest and two elbows forming a tripod.

One point to remember if you're shooting a revolver is that you should not grasp the gun with your left hand touching any part of the cylinder. Revolvers have a habit of spitting burnt powder and even slivers of lead out to the side between the cylinder chamber and the barrel throat. These can be painful. Use your left hand to steady the right by grasping the latter at the wrist or under the buttstock.

Chapter XII

RELOADING CENTER-FIRE AMMUNITION

The most commonly advanced reason for reloading ammunition is that it saves money. This, in a sense, is misleading. Your price per shot will be cut considerably but the over-all cost of your sport will go up because *you'll shoot more than ever.* As far as I'm concerned, that's a good reason for reloading.

Manufacturers of reloading equipment are, of course, quick to point out the savings and according to the comparison which follows, their claims are justified.

*Savings That Can Be Realized by Reloading**

RIFLE:	
20 factory-loaded .30/06 cartridges	$6.20
Component costs:	
primers, powder, bullets	$1.80
Savings per box of 20 shells	4.40
PISTOL:	
50 factory-loaded .38 Special cartridges	$6.00
Component costs:	
primers, powder, bullets	2.11
Savings per box of 50 shells	3.89

* NOTE: The cost of cases or cartridge shells has not been included since it is assumed the reloader has saved his fired factory ammunition cases. Otherwise, unused cartridge cases are available for reloading, either primed or unprimed. These can be reloaded repeatedly.

These costs may vary slightly according to quantities purchased, and even taking into account the year-to-year price fluctuations, the comparison is accurate.

On the other hand, they don't take into consideration the initial outlay for reloading equipment nor the labor involved. Depreciation on equipment, fortunately, is very slow and can be discounted if you do at least a moderate amount of loading. Naturally, the more you reload, the less your cost per shot will be. As for labor, this can be charged to an interesting hobby.

Apart from economy there are other good reasons for "rolling your own." Factory ammunition is extremely accurate as a whole, but cartridge cases are made to minimum dimensions so that they'll fit all rifles and handguns of a given caliber. Some fit snugly into firing chambers, others loosely. When you fire such a cartridge in your gun pressure expands the shell to fit *your* rifle perfectly, resulting in greater accuracy in any future handload in that case. This is known as "fire forming." Accuracy will be further enhanced by matching bullet weight and type to proper powder loads. Since ammunition does not perform exactly alike in all guns, you'll soon discover a handloaded combination which delivers the ultimate accuracy in your particular rifle or pistol. This is the reason many target and bench-rest shooters handload their own fodder.

Still another reason is the greater variety of loads that are available to reloaders. Naturally, commercial loaders can't offer every possible combination of bullet and powder load. The handloader, however, can concoct just exactly what suits him best—quite probably a load he can't buy over the counter.

After you've fired a cartridge, all that remains of any value is the shell, the most expensive component. The primer must be replaced, the powder has been burned and the bullet is in or near the target. Since these components can be purchased separately and factory shells can be reloaded time and time again, handloading is possible for anyone—even a beginner.

The Tools

The basic need is for a reloading press. One of the better types is the C-tool, a heavy-duty machine weighing 15 to 25 pounds and designed to be bolted to a rugged workbench. Smaller presses, weighing six to eight pounds, are suitable only for pistol and small rifle cartridges. Another is the H-type press which operates on two steel vertical shafts and which can withstand the great pressures that are applied in loading larger rifle cases. The C-tool makes finger access to the shell easier, but this is a minor advantage.

A more complex tool is the turret press which turns out a completed cartridge with each stroke of the lever. Such presses are reportedly capable of 600 cartridges per hour, once a miniature "assembly line" is set up. They are designed to handle the five basic steps of reloading progressively so that while one part of the machine is punching out a primer and resizing the shell, another section is loading powder while still another station is seating a fresh bullet. Such machines are, naturally, somewhat expensive, but their cost is soon written off by shooting clubs or police departments that do a great deal of shooting and reloading.

The C-tool is the most popular and the least expensive. Such a tool operates by means of a lever to drive a ram into a die station at the top of the *C*. Some work with a downstroke of the handle, which I prefer because it's an easier motion and less likely to lift or tilt a workbench. Upward-stroke models, however, are also popular. Some C-tools offer a choice of up or down handles. A few models have available a steel bar which closes the mouth of the *C*, thus reinforcing it against abnormal pressures that may arise in resizing rifle shells or in swaging bullets. Other models feature automatic primer feeds.

Besides the press, you'll need a set of dies which can be purchased from toolmakers at prices that range all the way from $5.00 to $20. These dies resize shell, decap primer, expand neck of shell to receive bullet and seat a fresh bullet. Some dies combine sizing and decapping

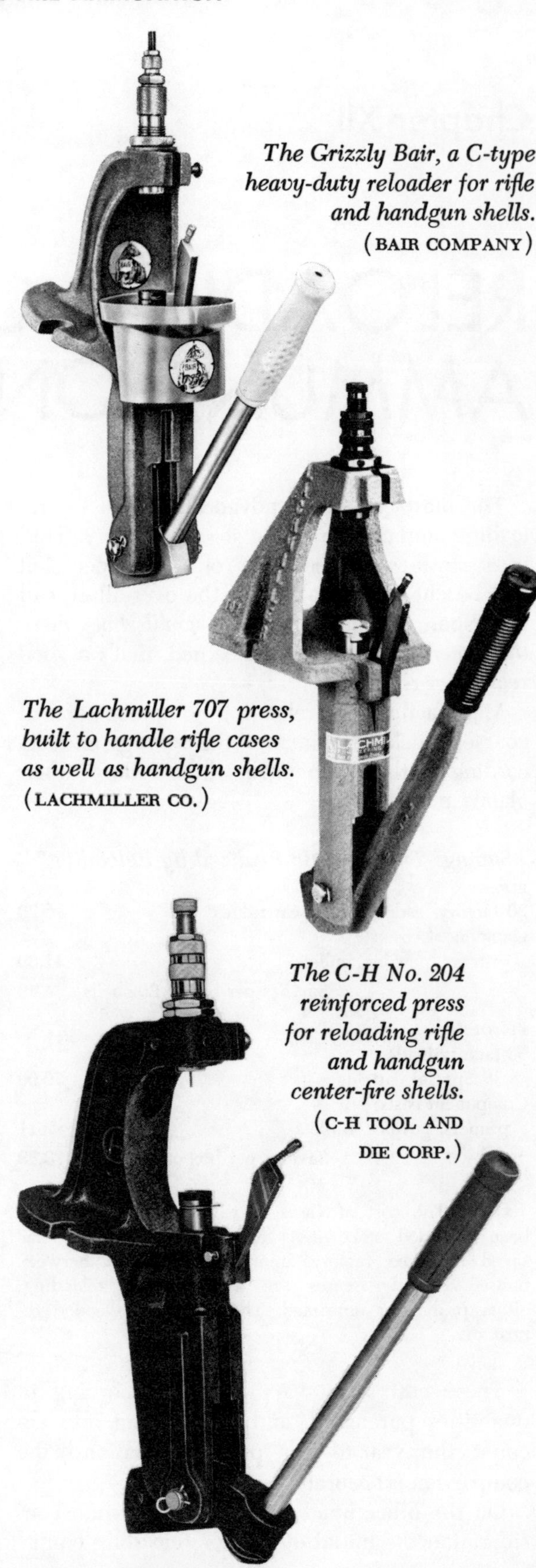

The Grizzly Bair, a C-type heavy-duty reloader for rifle and handgun shells. (BAIR COMPANY)

The Lachmiller 707 press, built to handle rifle cases as well as handgun shells. (LACHMILLER CO.)

The C-H No. 204 reinforced press for reloading rifle and handgun center-fire shells. (C-H TOOL AND DIE CORP.)

in one operation. Another necessity is a shell holder which fits at the top of the ram and is used, as the name implies, to hold the empty shell being reloaded. Shell holders are machined to hold any one caliber, but since many rifle and pistol cartridges have the same base dimensions, one shell holder may serve to hold several calibers. As an example, the same shell holder may be used for the .30/06, .270, .244 Remington, .280 Remington, .250 Savage, .300 Savage, .35 Remington, .45 ACP, and the 7 mm. However, not *all* calibers are interchangeable and manufacturer's catalogs will advise you concerning those that are.

A further necessity is a powder scale which will help guarantee accurate powder charges. Powder, as previously pointed out, is measured in grains and since there are 7000 grains to the pound, the need for accuracy becomes obvious. Most powder scales will give you $\frac{1}{10}$-grain accuracy if used carefully. Certain types have an oil reservoir in which a vane, attached to the beam, produces resistance to swing for a faster

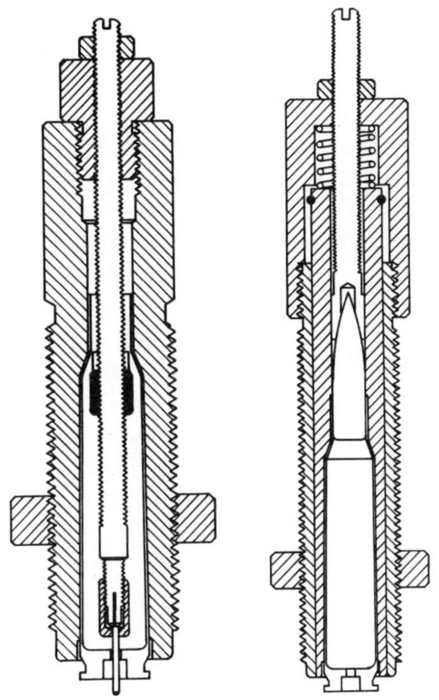

Interior view of rifle die, showing position of decapping pin and shell being resized, and bullet being seated into cartridge. (BONANZA SPORTS CO.)

Three-die set decaps, sizes and seats bullet. (BONANZA SPORTS CO.)

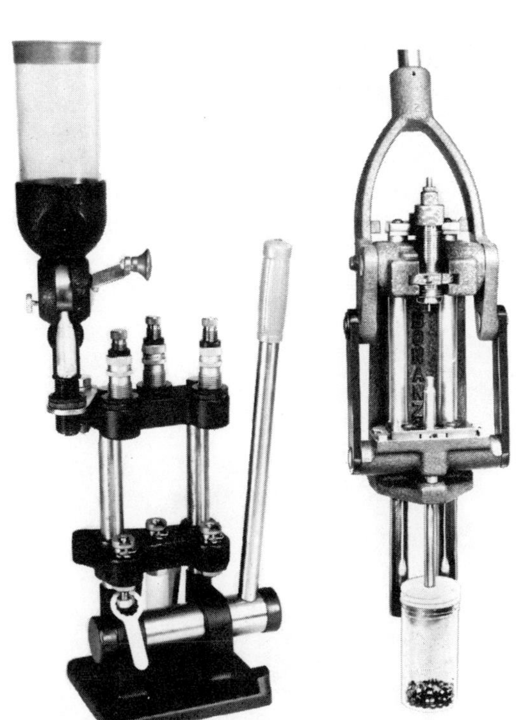

Left, the three-die C-H "H" tool which reloads progressively, decapping, sizing, charging, priming, seating—all without changing dies. (C-H TOOL AND DIE CORP.)

Co-Ax type press showing rifle shell about to be decapped and resized. Downstroke of handle will raise shell into the die. (BONANZA SPORTS CO.)

weight reading. Some doubt the value of this unit but it's popular nonetheless.

Not a necessity, though a great convenience, is the powder measure. This differs from the scale in that it measures powder in bulk. It's made up of a plastic hopper mounted on a cast-iron or steel base, with an adjustable arm which "throws" a pre-measured amount of powder through a drop-tube into the empty shell. Most measures will throw loads that are accurate within a half-grain, sufficiently accurate for all loadings except those involving ultra-maximum powder charges which should be weighed. Don't buy a powder measure as a substitute for a scale, however, since an accidental misalignment of the powder measure might produce disappointing loads or extremely dangerous charges. Such a measure should be checked occasionally by weighing one of its charges.

If your reloading will be done entirely with a powder scale, you'll need a small plastic funnel through which the powder is poured from the scale's pan into the shell.

Other conveniences include a bullet puller, used to remove a bullet from a shell when it has been seated improperly. A primer pocket reamer or cleaner aids in cleaning primer pockets and a deburring tool, sometimes called a burring tool, will remove dents or burrs which may have occurred about the mouth of the shell. None of these are absolute necessities, though.

Your final need, and an absolute necessity, is a reloading manual. This will tell you what powders to use, the correct amounts, and it will indicate by means of charts and tables the velocities you can expect. Until you become proficient at reloading and have acquired a thorough knowledge of powders, it's a must for you to stick to recommended loadings. Experimenting "with just a few extra grains" could well lead to critical pressures and possibly a blown gun and even serious injury! Loads prescribed in these manuals have been tried by experts and found safe and practical. Accurate loads are generally those of lower velocities and it has been proven repeatedly that increased powder loads rarely,

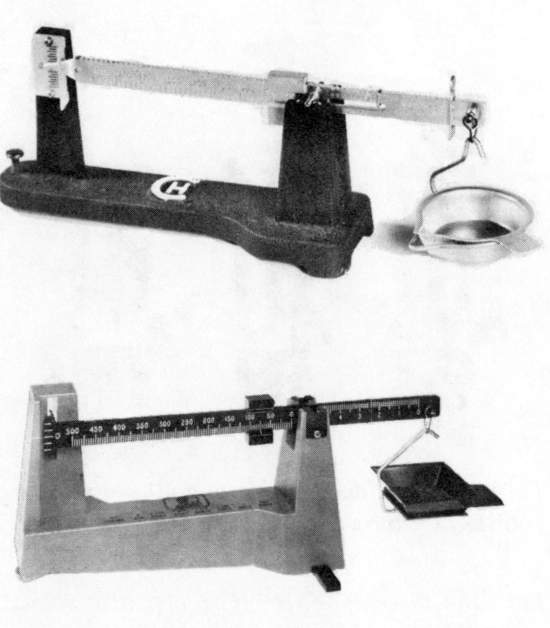

Scale for weighing powder, accurate up to 1/10th grain. (C-H TOOL AND DIE CORP.)

Another powder scale, with "dampening" device that speeds weighing. (BONANZA SPORTS CO.)

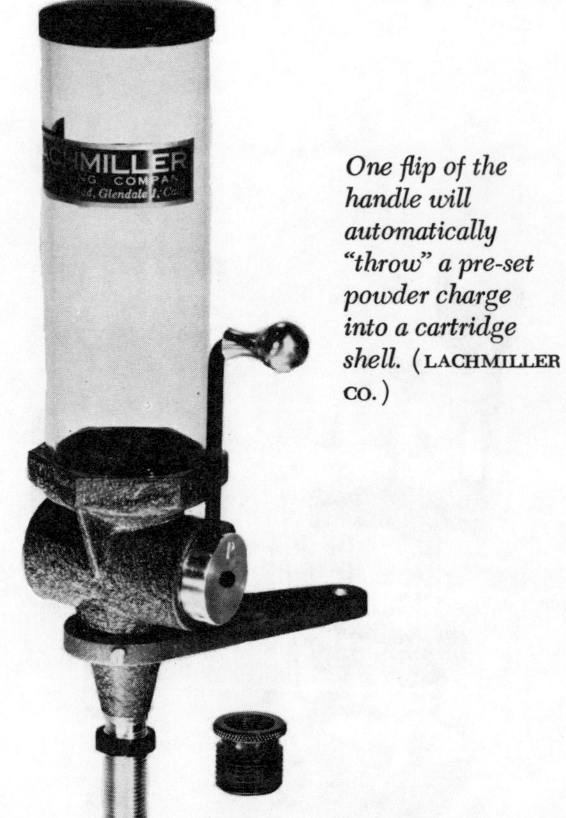

One flip of the handle will automatically "throw" a pre-set powder charge into a cartridge shell. (LACHMILLER CO.)

if ever, increase velocity satisfactorily. Accuracy usually suffers with high velocities. Reloading manuals are available from the Lyman Gun Sight Corp., Middlefield, Connecticut; Speer Products Co., Lewiston, Idaho; the Pacific Tool Company, Lincoln, Nebraska; and Sierra Bullets, Santa Fe Springs, California.

How to Reload—a Thumb-Nail Sketch

The reloading process starts with an inspection of the empty cases or hulls. Look for bulges anywhere on their surfaces which can be detected by rotating the shell horizontally at eye level in good light. Look, too, for cracks in the extractor groove and splits in the neck or along the body. The latter often appear as thin dark lines running in an erratic, jagged manner. A magnifying glass will help. Any shell showing symptoms should be discarded.

The actual reloading process starts with mounting the sizing die by screwing it into the station at the top of the tool. Since it is the simplest to use, and the most popular, I'll describe the loading process as it is accomplished with a basic C-tool. After inserting the die, attach the shell holder to the top of the ram. This may vary with different tools but, generally, it is screwed into the ram's head. The shell is then inserted into the holder, the rimmed base fitting snugly into parallel slots in the shell holder. The stroke of the tool's handle will now raise the ram, driving the shell, under some pressure, in the die. A decapping pin, centered within the die, punches out the used primer. At the same time, the constricting effect created by driving the shell into the die, resizes or constricts the shell to correct dimensions.

Before dropping the ram, a fresh primer is placed in the cup atop a primer arm and this is pushed into a slot in the side of the ram. This places the new primer directly under the shell's primer pocket and the downward stroke of the ram forces the primer into this pocket, wedging it in solidly. Your shell is now reprimed and the primer arm is allowed to swing out away from the ram.

The ram now continues its downward course and an "expander nipple" located just above the decapping pin, expands the mouth of the shell slightly so that a new bullet can later be inserted.

Dies are made for either neck or full-length resizing. This resizing is necessary, as explained earlier, because gas pressures have expanded the case somewhat. Neck-sizing is always necessary, but if the shell was fired in your own bolt-action rifle and will again be used in that same rifle, full-length sizing will not be needed. If it has been fired in another bolt-action rifle, or in a lever, pump or automatic rifle, full-length sizing is necessary, and the shell will have to be run through a full-length sizing die.

The die interior is simply a female mold, shaped to the contours and dimensions of the particular caliber for which it was made. Because of the flexibility of shell brass, the case can be remolded under die pressure. A light coating of lubricant should be applied to the shell's exterior to prevent its "freezing" or wedging too tightly within the die. Lubricants include lanolin, soap and graphite, as well as a number of patented lubricants put out by reloading suppliers. While graphite is effective, it is messy.

At this point your cartridge is ready for a powder charge. However, it's not practical to decap, prime and expand a single case, then reload the powder and seat a fresh bullet as consecutive steps, because this would require that the sizing die be removed from the tool after each shell has been decapped and sized. You would then have to screw in the bullet-seating die. Needless to say, you'll save time by repriming and resizing *all* of your empty cases at one session, without having to swap from the sizing die to the seating die after each shell. After each case is resized and primed, place them *upside down* in a reloading block or shell box to indicate that they do not yet contain powder.

Now, double-check your powder measure if you're using one, to make sure it's throwing correct charges and make sure, too, that you have the recommended powder—and no other—on the bench.

Here, good loading habits should be cultivated, for safety reasons as well as for the sake of accurate loads. Smoking, of course, is asking for trouble! If you're loading with a scale, pour the measured charge through the plastic funnel into the case and set the latter to one side *right side up,* indicating that it has been charged. The procedure with a powder measure is the same, except for use of the drop-tube in place of the funnel. Sometimes, however, both may be used. Be careful not to mix shells that have received powder charges and those which have not. Most rifle cases won't accept a double charge, but should you accidentally try, you'll have to empty the case and start over. Some pistol cases, however, are large enough to hold two charges of pistol powder and this could result in an exploding handgun with consequent injury.

Once all of the shells have received their powder loads, you are ready to seat new bullets in them. Remove the sizing die from the loading press and replace it with the bullet-seating die. The bullet-seating stem, within the die, will have to set at the correct height for proper bullet seating, and manufacturer's directions will give you the needed adjustments. Such directions also accompany the sizing die, with details regarding the decapping pin and expander nipple. These vary according to different manufacturers so that no attempt to give them here can be made. They are generally quite simple adjustments.

Place the shell in the holder again, with the ram fully depressed. Insert a bullet into the mouth of the shell with just enough finger pressure so that it stays in place. Raise the ram, thus driving the cartridge and bullet into the die. When the bullet comes in contact with the seating cone within the die, the cone will drive the bullet into the shell mouth to its correct depth. At the same time, the edges of the case mouth will be crimped slightly or constricted, locking the bullet into position. Your reloaded cartridge is now ready for firing.

These are the simple basic steps to reloading. Mechanical procedures may vary a little with tools put out by different makers, but these steps are followed in the same order.

"Tong" tools may also be used for reloading, eliminating the need for a heavy tool bolted to a bench. The tong roughly resembles a heavy pair of pliers or a nutcracker, which it is sometimes called. These simpler tools will perform exactly the same functions of the heavier bench tools, but it will take you longer to carry them out. Reloading with a tong tool is, in fact, rather a tedious task. For the few occasions when you may want to reload in the field, the tong is advantageous, of course, due to its light weight and lack of bulk.

The steps which I've described in reloading are routine procedures, with no problems presenting themselves. Problems, however, do arise. A shell may freeze in the die, a bullet may be seated too deeply, or not deeply enough, a primer may protrude excessively or may have been damaged during insertion. Most such problems can be attributed to improperly adjusted tools and dies. The solution is to reread the manufacturer's directions and to follow them exactly. In fact, you should not attempt to reload a shell until you've read thoroughly these directions and understand them fully. Many excellent books and hundreds of magazine articles have been written on the subject of reloading, but regrettably, most of these are written over the heads of beginners, the writer too often assuming that the reader is already well posted on the subject. In my own case, I would have started loading many years sooner had I realized how simple the process *really* is. The maze of technical terms and the discussions of reloading problems, however, scared me off. The best source of initial information lies in the instruction booklets and catalogs of tool manufacturers. Once you've absorbed these, you can assail the more technical and advanced publications with ease.

When you've finished reloading a batch of cartridges, place them in a separate box, being careful not to mix them with shells of other loadings. Several excellent plastic ammunition boxes are on the market, along with gummed labels for recording loading data applicable to any set of loads. There's space for the date, caliber, type of case, primer number and make, powder number, grains used, and bullet weight as well as type and maker. Keeping such records accurately will help you evolve a super-accurate load for any gun.

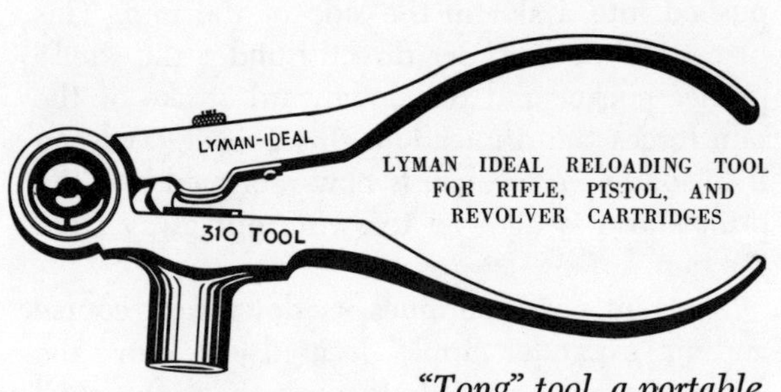

"Tong" tool, a portable reloading tool. (LYMAN GUN SIGHT CO.)

Test Firing Your Loads

In trying out your own loadings, fire at least five shots—ten if the batch is a large one, from a bench rest or similarly steady shooting rest. Don't try to shoot for accuracy without a steady rest. Remember, too, that in test firing, you're not necessarily seeking bull's-eyes. Shoot for groups, seeking to obtain the smallest possible groups, of course. Even if the group appears some distance from the bull's-eye on the target, you can always "bring it back in" through sight adjustments.

Note the size of the groups, measuring them with a rule, taking into consideration the widest diameter between the two shots farthest outside the group. Don't, however, include an occasional flyer or wild shot. These are usually the result of poor sighting or pulling. Make a note of the size of the groups on the data label or in a notebook. If the groups are unsatisfactory—riflemen usually dream of one-inch groups at one hundred yards, a difficult accomplishment—cut back the powder load slightly in your next batch, or change to another powder, according to recommendations in the reloading manual. As I've pointed out, no two rifles shoot alike and a load that may drive tacks in one gun may spray the target in another. Only through accurate test firing and the keeping of records can you determine the load for your gun.

Danger Signs

In reloading ammunition you'll be dealing with pressures which are to be respected. Pressure is necessary—that's what fires your bullet; but if it becomes excessive you may be in for a damaged gun and possible injury. Excessive pressures are due to overloading powder or using the wrong powder. A slow-burning powder is required for rifle cartridges, while pistol loads, because of the short barrel, need a rapid-burning powder. Powders also vary according to the bullet weights involved. Interchanging some of these powders can be disastrous. The first signs of such impending disasters are clearly legible on the surface of shells once they've been fired.

Fired primers that are bulged, especially if this bulge forms a tiny ring around the firing-pin indentation, are danger signs. This could also be a sign of an oversized firing-pin hole or a soft primer metal, but if it persists only in ammunition of your own loading, chances are you're building up excess pressure.

Dark smudges at the edge of the primer, whether in a circle or only in one spot, are also signs of overly great pressure. Primers that are blown out of the pocket altogether and found in the gun's action are *extreme* danger signs and if you haven't been injured, you can thank the maker of your gun! Primers that punch out easily often indicate an enlarged primer pocket, also pointing to excess pressure.

Shells which persistently stick in the firing chamber and are difficult to extract have usually been under extreme pressure and this is often true of those which display cracked necks or crushed extractor grooves. Throw these away and cut back your powder load.

Bullets

Swaging, full-jacketed, gas check, controlled expansion, cannelure—these are all terms appearing frequently in reloading literature. Too often, though, the writers ignore the beginner and fail to explain these.

Bullets are roughly classified into two types, lead and jacketed. Lead bullets are just what their name implies, molded lead with no covering of other metal. Jacketed bullets have a lead core that is either partially or entirely covered with an alloy usually containing copper. Full-jacketed bullets, which includes those fully covered by such an alloy, will not expand suitably on impact and are generally unsatisfactory as game bullets. They are usually military or police-type loads, some of them designed to penetrate automobile bodies in the case of police bullets. Certain full-jacketed bullets, because of their accuracy, are well suited to target shooting.

Bullets designed for hunting are semi-jacketed, or only partially covered by an alloy casing. This alloy jacket is thinner near the point of the bullet than at its base so that, upon striking flesh, the jacket will peel back—not unlike a banana peel—and allow the lead core to expand or mushroom for greater shocking power and tissue destruction. If a bullet of high velocity had no jacket, it could well expand too rapidly on big game, expending its energy before full penetration had been accomplished and likely resulting in a serious surface wound which would allow a game animal to escape momentarily but to die a lingering death later. On the other hand, a full-jacketed bullet would penetrate completely through in many instances, without expanding, causing a deep wound, but one which would not kill quickly. Semi-jacketed bullets, then, are designed to penetrate into a vital area within a game animal's body before full expansion takes place, so that the shocking power and tissue damage are directed into such an area. In other words, jacketed bullets deliver the peak of their power *within* a game animal. Ammunition manufacturers refer to this characteristic of a game bullet as "controlled expansion." Hunting bullets, such as the Peters "Inner Belted" and the Winchester-Western "Silvertip" and "Power Point" are such bullets. Commercial loadings all have their own variations of bullet-jacketing design to accomplish quick, clean kills on game, but the principle is much the same.

Lead bullets are generally used only in low-velocity ammunition, while jacketed and semi-jacketed bullets are likely to be of higher velocity. Lead bullets cannot be driven through a rifle barrel at high speed without some distortion. Slivers and bits of lead would be shaved off and left in the bore and hot powder gases destroy the shape of the bullet's base, both contributing to poor accuracy. For this reason, even low-velocity lead bullets are used with "gas checks." These are simply metal caps that are fitted snugly over the base of the lead bullet as it is being seated into the shell. The gas check serves to prevent the distortion described above, thus increasing accuracy and leaving a cleaner rifle barrel after firing.

The Nosler Partition bullet, manufactured for reloaders, has a unique construction which results in effective "mushrooming" upon impact. (NOSLER BULLET CO.)

The Nosler Partition bullet is a unique variation from the conventional bullet and is sold primarily to reloaders. It is made up of a two-piece lead core, the rear one cylindrical and the forward unit semi-conical, with a gilding metal jacket covering all but the exposed point and filling in a small area between the two lead cores. The jacket, upon impact, peels back only to the center partition of gilding metal so that, according to the manufacturer, two thirds of the bullet's weight remains intact to mushroom for a killing effect.

Bullet Shapes

Basically there are five bullet shapes, the spire, Spitzer, hollow-point, round-nose and flat-nose. Several variations are made for handloaders but they generally encompass the features of two or more of the basic types.

The spire bullet has a nose not unlike the point of a sharpened wood pencil, a popular shape for target shooting and hunting. The Spitzer could well be termed a "rounded spire" since the pitch or contour of the nose is rounded slightly from the bullet's full diameter to the point. It is probably the most commonly used bullet suitable for target shooting and hunting. The hollow-point type is usually a lightweight bullet for smaller calibers of high velocity and has a semi-rounded nose into which is drilled a hole; hence the term "hollow-point." This is done for greater explosive and expansion effect, and is thus a game bullet primarily. The round-nose bullet is generally a heavy missile, used extensively in today's high-velocity big-bores for big-game hunting. Flat-nose bullets look as if the point had been sawed off and are also considered game bullets.

The wad-cutter, a handgun bullet, is a flat-nose type and as its name indicates, "cuts wads" out of paper targets, resulting in neat round holes. Usually it's loaded at low velocities for competitive pistol target shooting.

Another bullet frequently mentioned is the "boat tail," not unlike the Spitzer up forward but having a tapered heel and presenting a well-streamlined appearance. In the midst of controversy, this bullet is described by many shooters as primarily a military missile of little value in sporting arms. On the other hand, there are sport shooters who swear by it, especially for long-range target shooting.

Bullets used for reloading of rifle and handgun cartridges may be purchased from any one of several bullet makers specializing in the reloading field and from the major ammunition makers —Winchester/Western, Remington/Peters, and Norma. Other components, including primers and shell cases, are also available. Powder is most easily available from sporting goods and gun shops which sell reloading equipment.

The handgun reloader has a further advantage, for in addition to the many ready-made pistol bullets, he may cast his own or he may make them through a process known as swaging.

Cast Bullets

Another way of making bullets is casting them from alloys of molten lead and varying parts of antimony and tin. Molds are available for casting up to ten bullets simultaneously for more than 150 calibers and weights. These are all "cannelured" bullets, the cannelures being grooves that ring the bullet and into which the edge of the shell mouth may be crimped to prevent these comparatively soft bullets from being forced too far into the case. The cannelures also serve to hold the lubricant which must be used. For cast bullets which may be used in higher velocity loads, gas checks are available to protect the bullet from hot gases while the lubricant serves to protect both the bore and the bullet.

Besides the bullet mold, youll need a sizer which shaves the castings to exact dimensions and smooths the surface of rough spots which are inevitable in casting. Beyond this a melting pot and a dipper are required. Needless to say that while bullet casting is an economical process, you must do at least a moderate amount of shooting to make the outlay for equipment and labor involved worthwhile.

Alloys for this type of bullet molding range in combinations from one part of tin to forty parts of lead up to one part tin and ten parts lead. The less tin used (or antimony), the softer your bullets will be and, naturally, the tips will be more subject to distortion, especially when used in tubular magazines. When melting lead

Cast bullets available to reloaders. (MARKELL, INC.)

for bullets, drop a small piece of beeswax or tallow into the molten metal as you stir in the tin or antimony. This will cause impurities to rise to the surface where they can be skimmed off.

Bullet Swaging

Swaging is simply a process whereby pieces of lead wire or cylindrically formed slugs are compressed at high pressure within a special die to exact bullet size and shape. There is no metal heating involved since the lead is fed into the die in cold form, nor is it necessary to size a swaged bullet. The swaging die does this automatically.

Some reloading tool firms put out special presses for swaging while others offer dies and accessories which may be used in regular heavy-duty loading presses. Swaging is not possible in lightweight presses since considerable mechanical pressure is needed to cold-form the bullets. Some C-tools have a reinforcing steel bar which closes the mouth of the *C* and prevents this pressure from springing the tool.

Pure lead blanks are used for swaging without the addition of tin or antimony for hardening, although this can be done. However, it will somewhat impair perfect forming. Since pure lead is used, and keeping in mind lead's tendency to deform at high velocities in a gun barrel, copper base cups or semi-jackets are attached to the base of swaged bullets. These jackets are somewhat lighter than those used on factory ammunition but they serve the purpose well. Lubrication of swaged bullets is not necessary. In fact it's not advisable. Lubricant will tend to form pockets in the swaging die, resulting in imperfect bullets.

A B C D E F

A few types of bullets which can be swaged: (A) *Round Nose;* (B) *Spire Point;* (C) *Semi-Wad-Cutter;* (D) *Wad-Cutter;* (E) *Cup Point;* (F) *Hollow Point Semi-Wad-Cutter.*

Similarly, air is often trapped within the die and the bullet must be "backed off" momentarily to allow its escape. A second stroke of the tool handle then forms the perfect bullet. Nose formation is done by means of a nose punch which compresses the bullet's forward end to a pre-selected shape. Removing the new bullet from the die is accomplished by tapping an ejector punch lightly, although at least one swaging tool has a mechanical ejector. Manufacturers of swaging tools claim bullet weight accuracy to within one-tenth grain although some NRA tests have done no better than .5 to .8 grains.

At this writing swaged bullets are being used only in handguns and in certain rifles of low velocity.

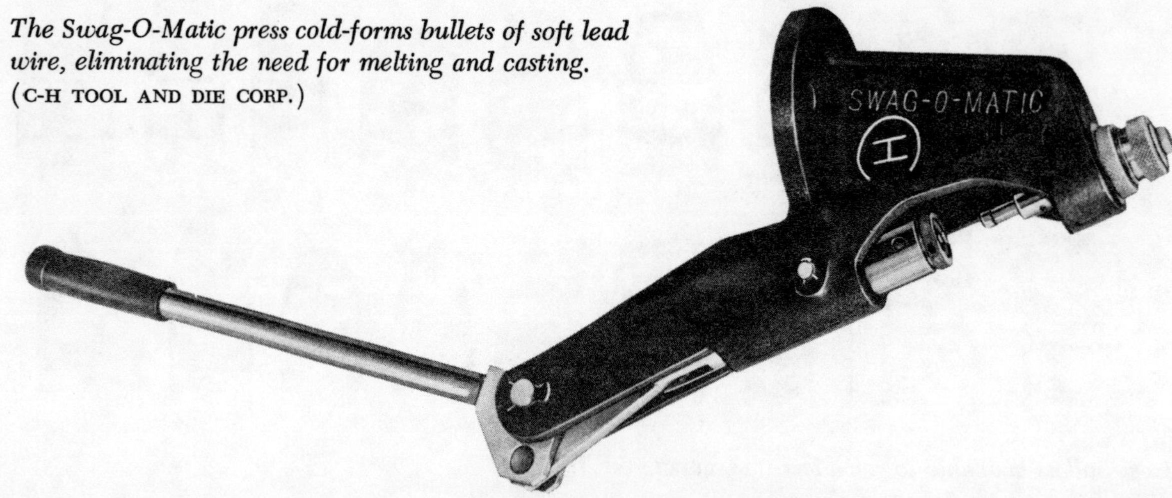

The Swag-O-Matic press cold-forms bullets of soft lead wire, eliminating the need for melting and casting. (C-H TOOL AND DIE CORP.)

Primer Table

Brand	*Large Rifle .210″*	*Small Rifle .175″*	*Large Magnum Rifle .210″*	*Large Pistol .210″*	*Small Pistol .175″*
Alcan	Max-Fire	Max-Fire		Max-Fire	Max-Fire
Cascade	200	400		300	500
Federal	210	200	215	150	100
Norma	LR	SR		LP	SP
Remington	9½	6½–7½	9½M	2½	1½
Peters	9½	6½		2½	1½
RWS	1973	7½		5337	4031
Winchester	120	116		111	108
Western	8½	6½		7	1½

Primers

Boxer and Berdan primers, the former American and the latter European, *are not interchangeable.* All American and some European ammunition made for the American and Canadian markets is designed with cases using the Boxer-type primer which fires a shell through a single flash-hole in the center of primer pocket. Berdan-type primers use twin flash-holes.

Primers are made in four sizes, Large Rifle, .210 inches in diameter; Small Rifle, .175 inches; Large Pistol, .210 inches; and Small Pistol, .175 inches. Although Large Rifle and Large Pistol primers are of the same size they may not be interchanged, nor should the Small Rifle and Small Pistol. As their names indicate, each is suitable for one group of rifle and one group of pistol loads.

Primers are available from several firms, most of them designating their products differently, allotting numbers to them that bear little or no relationship to size or use, a practice that baffles beginners. See table above.

Experienced reloaders have no trouble with this numbering system but beginners should check carefully when buying primers that they order the correct type and size. Reloading manuals will advise you concerning this, specifying either the brand and number or the more general designation. I can well understand that ammunition manufacturers want to give their products individuality, but this is one phase of the gun business that could well be standardized to the advantage of all.

Powder

Chances are the first time you bring a can of gunpowder into your home, your family will be horrified with visions of the house disintegrating into a mass of flying debris. Hollywood and TV have done their work well! You can assure the members of your family that gunpowder is safer to have about than gasoline in your power mower. Reloaders rarely have enough on hand to create a safe storage problem. Reloading powder is sold mostly in small canisters. These containers are not capable of withstanding sufficient gas pressures to cause an explosion should the powder ignite. The greatest danger is from fire, of course, and powder not held in a rugged container will burn, not explode. Common-sense safety rules should be observed, of course, such as allowing no smoking in the room where reloading is done.

Several different types of powder are available for reloading, *each designed for a specific phase of reloading.* In some cases, two or three powders might be interchangeable, usually by increasing or decreasing the suggested powder charge. This is *extremely dangerous* unless you are an experienced reloader with a thorough knowledge of powders and their characteristics. Until you have acquired this experience and knowledge, *never* deviate from the recommended loads found in reloading manuals. Such experimenting might well result in a blown-up gun action and serious injury!

The reason for this lies in the varying speeds with which powders burn and the pressures which they create. Some powders, for example, burn very rapidly because they were designed for use in a short-barrel handgun, in which case the powder charge must be completely consumed before the bullet has left the barrel. Inversely, some powders are made to burn more slowly and to build up pressures more gradually, for use in driving bullets from the longer barrels of rifles and carbines. To interchange these powders in any one gun can lead to nothing but trouble unless you have a full knowledge of powder characteristics. In some cases, you'll be dealing with pressures, in handguns, of 40,000 pounds per square inch! In rifles, this may well rise to over 60,000. These are pressures which, when misapplied, can scatter the parts of a gun over a half-acre field! No admonition regarding recommended powder uses can be too strong. Heed the advice of experts!

Powders Available for Reloading

Du Pont No. 4227. A fast-burning powder for use in small-capacity rifle shells.

Du Pont No. 4198. For use in medium-capacity shells and for reduced loads in larger cases. For rifles.

Du Pont No. 3031. For medium-capacity shells and for reduced or mid-range loads in rifle cases.

Du Pont No. 4064. For use in large-capacity rifle cases.

Du Pont No. 4320. Primarily a powder for high-velocity rifle loadings, although also intended for military loadings.

Du Pont No. 4350. This is a powder for the big Magnum rifle shells.

Hercules Bullseye. A fast-burning powder designed for use in pistol and revolver ammunition.

Hercules No. 2400. A fine-grained powder intended for small-capacity rifle cartridges or for light loads in larger rifle cases. May also be used in some high-velocity revolver loads according to recommendations.

Hercules Unique. A powder which may be used in large-caliber handgun loads and for very light loading of some rifle cartridges.

Hodgdon H4227. Suited to some .222 loads and for the .357 and .44 Magnum handgun ammunition.

Hodgdon H335. For medium-capacity cases. Good results in .222 and .308 Winchester loadings.

Hodgdon 4895. An all-round powder for rifle loads in virtually all calibers. Center-fire.

Hodgdon H570. A slow-burning powder for oversized Magnum loads with heavy bullets.

Hodgdon 450. Well suited for use in maximum loads, especially in the .30/06.

NOTE: The above powders have been cited simply to indicate the great variety of powders that are available. And these are but a sampling. Before choosing a powder for a particular load, talk with experienced reloaders. Then investigate the catalog listings of Du Pont, Hercules, Hodgdon, Norma, Winchester/Western, and Alcan.

Hercules Bullseye, a fast-burning powder for handgun ammunition, magnified four times.

Powder for heavy handgun and light rifle loads, magnified four times.

Hercules X2400, a progressive-burning powder for rifle charges, magnified four times.

Chapter XIII

THE SHOTGUN

The Shotgun Shell

The basic structure of a shotgun shell is similar to that of the rifle and pistol cartridge in that it comprises a shell or case, a primer, powder, and projectile(s). The structural similarity ends there, however. Although shotgun shells were once made almost exclusively of brass, today's are laminated paper or polyethylene plastic which is attached to a brass base or cup to form the shell. Magnum and heavy loads use a "high brass" cup while lighter loads utilize a "low brass" base. If you will compare one of each type of shell, you'll see that the brass cup on the heavy load has a wider metal band than does the field or regular load.

The primer of a shotgun shell extends into the base itself rather than being seated in an exterior primer pocket as is the case with rifle or handgun shells. Surrounding the primer, and some 9/16 inches thick is a "base wad," usually of compressed paper which acts as a gas seal and absorbs some of the back pressure from the burning powder loaded just ahead of this wad. Above the powder is inserted a powder wad which seals gas from "blowing by" and scattering the shot prematurely and erratically. Ahead of the powder wad are placed filler wads, the thickness of these depending upon the amount of shot to be loaded, the latter held in place by crimping the edge of the shell mouth so that its top surface looks not unlike a miniature pie marked for cutting.

Plastic wads with sleeves to contain shot are now a part of shot-shell reloading. After being primed and charged, the wad/sleeve is inserted with shot, the shell crimped. It is then ready for firing. (WINCHESTER/WESTERN)

Reactions set up by firing a shotgun shell are similar to those which occur in a center-fire rifle or handgun cartridge. The firing pin activates the primer which flashes through its flash-hole to ignite the powder. Gas pressures, developed by the burning powder, push the center wads forward and these in turn drive the shot so that it "un-crimps" the shell and escapes.

Winchester/Western has recently come up with a "compression-formed" one-piece plastic shot shell which is virtually impervious to weather but, better still, is supposed to withstand 300 per cent more reloads. So durable is this shell that one gun writer criticized it for being non-biodegradable. He feels that shotgunners will leave these shells by the thousands in the uplands, forever to litter the landscape. Ridiculous. Those upland hunters who do not reload are not likely to blanket the countryside with empty shells! And those who reload will pick up their empties.

Although not an exclusive with Winchester/Western, the new shot shell incorporates a plastic shot cup or sleeve which protects the shot from distortion as it travels through the barrel. This minimizes "flyers" or erratic shot patterns. Although I've cited Winchester/Western—mostly because of greater experience with these—similar features are found in Remington/Peters and in Federal shells.

Shotgun barrels, like rifle barrels, are chambered to conform to the length of the shell, so that shotguns are usually designated for 2¾-inch or for 3-inch shells. This shell length does not refer to the length of the shell as you get it from the sporting goods store, but rather *to its length with the crimp unrolled or opened.* The unfired shell's length may be almost a half-inch shorter than its designation. The chamber of a shotgun is reamed so that, when the shell is fired, the unrolled crimp fits flush within the barrel. Therefore, a 3-inch shell should not be fired in a gun that is chambered for 2¾-inch shells, although the shorter shells may be used in the 3-inch chamber.

Gauge

Gauge in a shotgun corresponds to caliber in a rifle or handgun but is indicated differently, actually by an antiquated method. Whereas rifle barrel calibers are designated in hundredths or thousandths of an inch, a shotgun gauge is indicated by the number of lead balls fitting the barrel and which would weigh one pound. In other words, a 12 gauge shotgun has a bore equal in diameter to a lead ball, 12 of which would weigh one pound. The same proportional designations apply to 10, 16, 20 and 28 gauge. The .410 is an exception, its diameter or bore being given in thousandths of an inch.

One would think that these gauge designations would be standard—and they are—but not to the degree you might imagine. The same gauge in shotguns of different manufacture may vary as much as .025 inches. This is a minor discrepancy, of course, but it does exist nevertheless, as shown by the variance in specifications given below by three different authorities:

Bore Diameters

	12 Gauge	*16 Gauge*	*20 Gauge*
No. 1	.729″	.662″	.615″
No. 2	.729	.666	.613
No. 3	.745	.684	.632

The most popular gauge in America, by far, is the 12, a combination of power, range, a recoil that can be absorbed without undue punishment, and a wide choice of guns. Magnum and heavy loads make it a fine duck and goose load, medium loads immediately convert it to upland shooting, and light loads make it more than suitable for skeet and trapshooting.

The upland shooter is likely to favor the 16 gauge. Its recoil is lighter than that of the 12 and it's also fully adequate for waterfowl with heavier loads.

The 20 gauge is the favorite of the upland hunter who likes to carry a lightweight gun as he roams over hill and dale in search of quail or grouse. As such it's also popular among women shooters who might otherwise shrink from the recoil of the 16 and 12.

The 28 gauge and the .410 have been neglected by ammunition manufacturers so that only light loads are available for them. The most powerful load for the 28, for example, carries only three fourths the pellets loaded into a regular 20 gauge shell. Range, too, is limited, with 30 yards on small game considered pretty much its limit.

A popular misconception sets up the .410 and the 28 as "ideal for boys and women," especially beginners. Nothing could be farther from the truth. The small bores *are for experts* who don't mind handicapping themselves. Shot patterns in these light guns are proportionally smaller in diameter than those of the 20, 16 and 12. A full choke barrel further adds to the handicap so that game birds on the wing can be hit consistently only by an expert wing shot, who can make up by shooting skill for the lack of power and the small shot pattern.

This is not to say that any idea you may have had about buying a 28 or .410 should be discarded, but the limitations of these shotguns should be considered along with their light recoil and general light weight.

I once lived for four days on ruffed grouse, shot in the wilderness north of Moosehead Lake, where birds were extremely tame and would sit for easy ground or limb shots. I took these birds with a .410 and had no trouble feeding myself. However, compare these grouse with those of southern Vermont or Pennsylvania and you will soon conclude that the .410 is inadequate in these areas where grouse may well flush 50 yards ahead of the hunter.

At the other extreme is the 10 gauge, the biggest bore permitted by federal law for migratory bird hunting. For long-range shooting it has proved its worth, although I used to hunt black ducks with a friend who used a 10 gauge for lack of any other gun and though he was a fair shot with it, he never seemed to knock down many more ducks than did the 12s and 16s used by other hunters in the party.

There's no question, though, that the 12s and 16s are the best all-round gauges, suitable with varying loads for ducks, grouse, skeet, or trap.

Shot Sizes

The tremendous versatility of the modern shotgun really becomes impressive when you consider that one standard shell may fire as many as 731 pellets, each .08 inches in diameter, or that a single one of nine pellets, .33 inches in diameter, could well bring down a 200-pound buck. Both loads can be fired from the same shotgun.

No. 12 shot is used in .22 shot shells and I know of no shotgun shells loaded with the tiny pellets. In general use, however, is No. 9 shot for use on light game birds such as quail, woodcock and doves, as well as on the skeet field. Heavier shot, such as No. 2, No. 4 and BB, the largest of the "bird shot," are popular as loads for heavy game birds like the turkey and for high-flying geese. The type of shot, in loading, is governed by the powder load with regular-velocity shells usually handling smaller shot while the heavy-duty shells are armored with the bigger pellets. Within this range of shot size and powder loads there is some overlapping due to varying preferences of hunters for one size shot over another.

The following table will give you some indication of the general acceptance of certain shot sizes for specific tasks. Shotgunners, like riflemen, enjoy disagreeing among themselves, and all may not agree with this table's suggestions!

Suggested Shot Sizes

Game	*Shot*
Crows	6, 7½
Doves	6, 7½, 8
Ducks	4, 5, 6, 7½
Fox	BB, 2, 4
Geese	BB, 2, 4
Grouse	5, 6, 7½, 8
Jacksnipe	8, 9
Pheasant	5, 6
Quail	7½, 8, 9
Rabbit	4, 5, 6
Squirrel	5, 6
Turkey	BB, 2, 4
Woodcock	7½, 8, 9
Trap Shooting	7½, 8
Skeet	9

The number of pellets in a shotgun shell is indicated in ounces rather than by the number of pellets. Following is a chart showing the number of pellets in various loadings.

A favorite among old-time shotgun hunters, buckshot, which is large bird shot, ranges in size from No. 4, .24 inches in diameter through No. 00, .33 inches in diameter. This is used on larger shotgun game up to and including deer and black bear. It's at its best in dense growth and on running game, as is often the case in southern hunting where hunters are posted along deer runways while the latter are driven by dogs. Northern hunters are inclined to sneer at this kind of deer shooting, but the thick growth and the game's speed make rifles impractical.

Objection to buckshot generally lies within the limited capacity of a shell loaded with shot of this size. A 12 gauge 2¾-inch shell carries only nine 00 pellets and even a 3-inch Magnum load

Pellet Size

No.	*Pellet Size*							
Ounces	*9*	*8*	*7½*	*6*	*5*	*4*	*2*	*BB*
1⅞					318	252	168	93
1⅝				366	276	219	146	81
1½				337	256	203	135	
1⅜				309		186	124	69
1¼	731	513	438	281	213	169	113	63
1⅛	658	461	394	253	191	152	101	
1	585	410	350	225	170	135	90	
⅞	512	359		197	149	118		
¾	439		263	169	128	101		
½	293		175	113	85	68		

Shot Size, Diameter and Weight

No.	12	9	8	7½	6	5	4	2	BB
Diameter in Inches	.05	.08	.09	.09½	.11	.12	.13	.15	.18
Number per Ounce	2385	585	410	350	225	170	135	90	50

totes only fifteen. Another 3-inch Magnum shell propels 41 No. 4 buckshot pellets.

However, when you consider the comparatively few critical areas on a deer's body, and the small size of these areas, the chances of a quick and humane kill from a scattergun load of pellets at 40 yards are limited. The possibility of wounding and losing a deer is great, except at close range. After all, the initial velocity of buckshot is approximately the same as that of the .22 rim-fire, and, certainly, the .22 can't be considered a deer or bear load, even if a half-dozen shots are sprayed with an automatic! Buckshot has its place where no other type of load is suitable, and sportsmen in these areas certainly can't be criticized for using it, but if you hunt deer where slugs or rifles are permitted, by all means, use them in place of buckshot.

Choke and Pattern

The "choke" in a shotgun barrel is the degree of constriction at the muzzle which governs the shot distribution or spread. The result of this is the gun's "pattern."

The standard for determining choke is the percentage of pellets which a gun will fire into a 30-inch circle at 40 yards. Some shotgun manufacturers offer three "standard" degrees of choke: full, modified and improved. Others offer a fourth, skeet. Still others include "cylinder," actually an absence of constriction, hence its name. "Improved" modified and cylinder are also included by some. At first, this is confusing, but the table below may help to clarify these various chokes:

Choke	*Percentage of Shot Within 30-Inch Circle at 40 Yards*
Full	65 to 75 per cent
Improved Modified	55 to 65
Modified	45 to 55
Improved Cylinder	35 to 45
Cylinder	25 to 35
Skeet	30 to 35

These are "paper specifications" and actual shooting tests usually reveal that these choke specifications overlap considerably and, too, apparent discrepancies appear. The fact is that not all gauge or bore dimensions are exactly alike among the various makers of guns, nor are the choke dimensions. Add to this the great variance in loads that are used and you can then well see why guns don't always "pattern" according to choke charts. Generally speaking, today's shotguns tend to "shoot tighter" than their choke specifications might indicate. Some attribute this to the new-type wadless crimp. (The old-type crimp rolled the edge of the shell mouth inward against a round paper wad, the latter having been discarded.) No matter the reason, the only way you can determine the exact choke with which your gun is equipped is to pattern it. Most shooters today are "overchoked" and patterning your gun will, I believe, bear me out.

To do this, pin a large sheet of paper on a board fence. Fire one shot at the paper from the 40-yard line and then draw a 30-inch diameter circle encompassing the densest part of the shot pattern. Although it's a tedious job, count the number of pellet holes in the paper within this circle. Consult the pellet tables in this chapter to learn the number of pellets contained in the shell. Divide the pellet table figure into the number of holes counted within the 30-inch circle and you have the percentage which will tell you the degree of choke *actually* encompassed with the muzzle of your gun.

If, in your test you fired a 12 gauge shell loaded with 1⅛ ounces of No. 7½ shot, the table will indicate that such a shell contains an average of 395 pellets. Assuming your count within the circle was 229 pellets, your percentage is 58, placing your gun in the modified to improved-modified class, *no matter what is stamped on the barrel!*

Remember that this test is made at 40 yards. What happens, then, at 20 or 30 yards? The shorter the range, the more heavily concentrated will be shot so that you may have, in effect, a "full choke" barrel at these ranges. The spread of shot can be figured roughly at slightly less than one inch per yard of range, so that at 20 yards, your shot spread or pattern is likely to be less than 15 to 17 inches in diameter.

Now, if the gun is going to be used solely at 40-yard ranges, it may be completely suitable. But what happens when shooting at shorter ranges? You will need to become an expert wing shot to connect consistently on flying game birds such as quail, grouse and woodcock. However, a direct hit on these small birds with such a concentration of shot will blow them to a messy pulp! In other words, you may have a gun suitable at 40 yards but quite impractical at, say, 20 to 25 yards, common ranges in upland shooting.

The reverse of this situation is also true. A gun whose shot pattern "opens up" suitably at 25 yards is likely to shoot a wide, much too thin pattern at 40. In other words, with a permanent built-in choke, a shotgun has only one range at which it will pattern anywhere near perfectly. All other ranges must be compromises.

In order to determine what your gun will pattern at various ranges, you will have to repeat the patterning process at shorter distances, probably at 20 and 30 yards. Ten-yard ranges are impractical and even if you could catch a bird off guard at this range, it's best to allow it to fly a short distance or else you will pulverize it. Ranges beyond the 40-yard mark are also generally impractical because the pattern then becomes erratic with "holes" in it, through which a flying bird might well escape. Longer shots can be made successfully, but luck contributes much.

Another reason for patterning your shotgun—and actually a more sound one—is to determine the distribution of the shot within the 30-inch circle. This is a more accurate definition of "pattern." If the shot is concentrated in one area of the circle with open sections containing no shot, or too few, your pattern is poor—sometimes termed "blown." You should try another brand of ammunition or another loading until you find one that patterns *evenly*.

The problem of fixed choke is alleviated somewhat in double-barreled shotguns which may, for example, have one barrel bored full-choke and the other modified or improved. A shooter may then use the more open bore for his first shot at comparatively close range. If he misses, or if a second shot presents itself at a longer range, he then fires the full-choke barrel with its longer-range possibilities. A gunner with a single-barrel shotgun, such as a pump or automatic, may purchase two or three barrels for his gun, all interchangeable and all bored differently, so that one gun may well serve for geese and ducks, upland shooting and skeet or trap. While these barrels can be changed in a matter of minutes, it's not practical to carry the spares along in the field during actual hunting and, of course, the cash outlay for shooting equipment is increased considerably. A less expensive way of accomplishing the same effect is to install a "choke," or variable choking device.

Chokes

Recommending a choke to a shooter is like recommending a woman to be his wife. The end result may be a friend for life or a dedicated enemy! Nevertheless, there are a number of excellent chokes on the market which will perform pretty much within the claims of their manufacturers. Remember, however, that the number of variables involved each may affect the per-

hood that the right mechanical choke can cure it. The basic purpose of these chokes, though, is to make available varying degrees of muzzle constriction within one barrel.

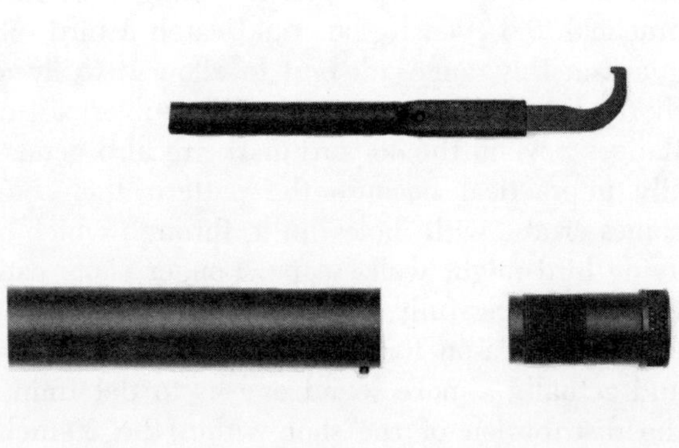

The Win-Choke consists of three interchangeable tubes of various constrictions, inserted or removed with a compact spanner wrench. This type of choke does away with distracting "bulge" at the muzzle. (WINCHESTER ARMS CO.)

The Poly-Choke, which affords various degrees of muzzle constriction simply by turning a sleeve with fingertips. (POLY-CHOKE CO.)

The number of chokes on the market is growing so that it's difficult to keep up with new models. Most manufacturers issue well-detailed literature describing their wares and you should read as many of these as possible before deciding. Some of the booklets are an education in shot behavior, with most of them sticking to reasonable and plausible claims. Steer clear of the choke makers who make wild or exaggerated predictions regarding the improvement in your shooting with one of their chokes. No choke is *that* good! Since libel laws protect the unscrupulous as well as the honest, I can't make my warning any clearer than this!

Generally speaking, there are two types of choking devices. The most popular is a constricting tube, or hollow and slightly tapered cylinder having longitudinal slits which allow it to be pinched together at the forward end by means of springs or a collet. Turning a selector sleeve on the outside of the instrument constricts or expands the interior sleeve which, in turn, governs choke. A new variation of this allows the choke to be fired with one degree of constriction following which the device automatically tightens the setting for a fuller choke. This allows the shooter then to set the choke at an open bore setting for a close-up shot, after which the choke automatically gives him a full-choke setting for the longer second shot.

Another type of choke device utilizes a number of interchangeable sleeves or tubes, each of which contributes a different degree of muzzle constriction. The newest of these is Winchester's Winchoke which consists of three interchangeable tubes that thread into the muzzle of the shotgun by means of a small spanner wrench provided with the device. Since the tubes are small and compact, the entire set can be carried afield and interchanged in a matter of two minutes. Winchester shotguns in 12, 16 and 20 gauge are available with the Modified tube installed, plus a Full and an Improved Cylinder tube to make up the set. When I tested the units in 1971—the first time I had seen the Winchoke—I was able to make the changes quickly and with ease. And I liked the resulting shot patterns. This type of

formance of any shotgun, with or without a mechanical choke. Velocity of shot, gas pressures, wad structure within the shell, size of shot, powder load—all these affect a gun's ability to pattern well. If your shotgun gives you trouble with poor patterns, there's more than a good likeli-

choke maintains the streamlined appearance of the barrel, eliminating the forward bulge which I have always found disconcerting when using the variable-type choke. However, there's much to be said for the variable-type, especially for its ability to shift choke constrictions quickly in the field, the hunter merely pausing to twist a calibrated collar.

The best known of the variables is the Polychoke, available for single-barrel shotguns in 12, 16, 20 and 28 gauge. It provides nine settings covering all shot patterns desirable in the field. The Polychoke requires permanent installation by one of more than two hundred dealers in the United States. A special skeet choke is also available in 12 gauge, dispersing shot in a 36-inch pattern at 40 yards, ideal for skeet, as compared to a 30-inch dispersal for upland hunting.

Polychoke also offers a combination installation of a ventilated rib with its choke.

Perhaps as well known as the Polychoke is the Cutts Compensator, produced by Lyman. Other shotgun producers which offer their own chokes with their guns include High Standard, Savage, and Mossberg.

The chokes themselves, though, offer more than a psychological advantage and today's single-barrel shotguns waste much of their potential hitting ability when not equipped with a good choke. The variable choke puts the gun's owner in the same favorable position as the wealthy gun owner with six or eight models, or an assortment of variously bored barrels at his disposal.

Critics of shotgun chokes are quick to point out that the added weight at the end of the barrel makes the gun slower to swing and, in theory, this may be true. However, the weight of most chokes is figured within a few ounces and this is substantially offset by the weight of the portion of the barrel which is removed.

Shot String

Shot string is the distance between the first pellet to arrive on target and the last, since not all of them reach the target at the same time. The shot string may be as long as 12 to 14 feet at 35 to 40 yards. Some experts claim that the "head" of the shot string must bring down fast-flying birds, because the "tail" will arrive too late, the bird having then flown by. One writer, though, pointed out that the tail end of the shot string can well bring down a bird which has been missed by the "early arrivals"! Theoretically, and in some instances, these conjectures might well be true but I feel they're a little far-fetched. Today's modern loads are excellently engineered to overcome every possible deficiency in pellet flight and I doubt that "shot string" has little effect, favorable or otherwise, on hits. Marksmanship does!

Powder Loads

A rifle or pistol shooter, accustomed to thinking of powder loads in terms of grains, may be puzzled by the shotgun powder designations of "drams equivalent." This is a holdover from the days of black powder which was measured in drams, each weighing 1/16 ounce. Powders today are of the "smokeless" variety—of much greater power output. Therefore, a smaller amount of the newer powders is used to deliver the same force formerly activated by the black powder. For example, "3½ drams equivalent" means that enough smokeless powder has been loaded to equal the power of 3½ drams of black powder. It's an antiquated and confusing designation but it persists. It has nothing to do whatsoever with reloading shot shells. It's simply a designation for identifying powder loads in commercially loaded shells.

Magnum Loads

Here again, a rifle shooter may be puzzled by the shotgun shell "Magnums." Magnum loads for rifles are usually those including a heavier bullet at greater velocity. This is not completely true in the case of shot shells. It means simply that some 20 per cent more shot has been placed in the shell and powder burning retarded slightly to build up pressure needed to drive the heavier shot charge out through the barrel. Velocities in shotgun Magnums are not greater than those in the full or "maximum" loads, but the shot charge is.

The purpose of the Magnum load in a shotgun is to place a greater number of pellets on target. Using them to increase killing range usually fails, except of course, that *some* of the extra shot may penetrate beyond normal shooting distance for a kill. Actually, 40 yards is roughly the shotgun's maximum *consistent* killing range and Magnum loads increase the killing potential at this range by placing more shot in the target area. At longer ranges, pellet velocities fall off as fast with Magnum loads as they do with any other.

Rifled Slugs

These are solid lead slugs, hollow at the base for expansion and available in 12, 16, 20 and .410 gauges for hunters who prefer a solid projectile to buckshot for use in shotguns. They may be used in full-choked barrels or in guns to which choking devices have been attached, but this muzzle constriction will deform them somewhat. I doubt, though, that this seriously affects accuracy, especially at the short ranges usually involved in the shooting of these. However, slugs are at their best in improved cylinder-bore guns such as the special "slug guns" made by Ithaca, Remington, High Standard, Browning, Mossberg, and Savage, all equipped with rifle sights.

Any single-barrel shotgun normally used for upland wing shooting can be converted into a slug gun for deer and bear hunting by the addition of a temporary "Slug Site," an interesting device produced by John Ebeling of Des Moines, Iowa. The Slug Site is a one-piece front and rear sight combination, about 7 inches long, which attaches to the receiver of the shotgun by means of a pressure adhesive which sticks well during field use, yet can be peeled off easily when reverting to wing shooting.

Shotgun slugs have a notoriously poor trajectory but when used with such a sight (or in slug guns) at ranges up to 80 or 100 yards, they are ideal for use on deer where high-power rifles are not permitted. At 40 to 50 yards, slugs are as deadly as many center-fire rifles.

Slugs have spiral grooves along their sides—the counterparts of the spiral rifling in a rifle or handgun barrel—supposedly to impart a spinning effect to the slug as it is projected through a smoothbore barrel. No doubt, *some* spinning effect is imparted to the slug but I suspect that with most the lateral stability is due to the fact that the forward end of the slug is heavier than its tail. Rifling on the surface is simply a means of decreasing pressures and cutting down bearing surface.

The Slug Site makes it possible to aim a shotgun rather than merely pointing it. It is attached to the receiver by means of a built-in adhesive, is easily removed. (SLUG SITE CO.)

A visual demonstration of the accuracy of rifled slugs fired in a special "slug gun." Here is a 1¾-inch group of five slugs at 40 yards by the Ithaca "Deerslayer."

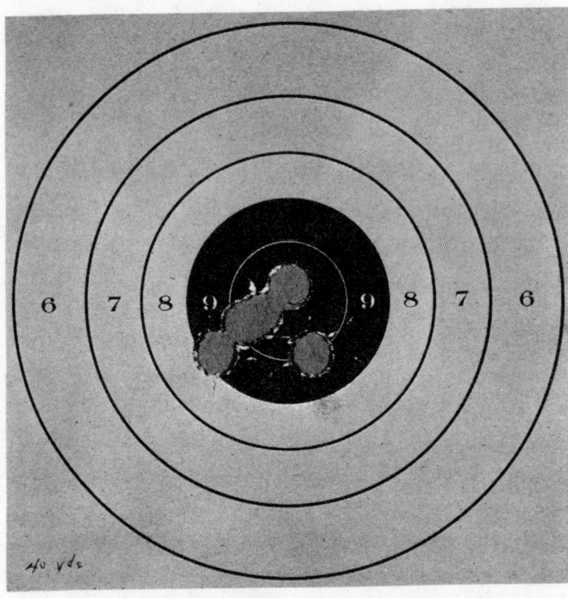

Nevertheless, the accuracy of a rifled slug is impressive. The 12 gauge slug is capable of 4- or 5-inch groups at 50 yards and it has a 100-yard

Shotguns with rifle sights make sense when smoothbores are used with rifled slugs for short-range big-game hunting. These include: Harrington & Richardson Model 162 single-shot cylinder bore, Mossberg Model 500S pump action, Mossberg three-shot 12 gauge bolt-action slug gun, Remington pump in 12 and 20 gauge, Savage Model 30 pump also in 12 or 20 gauge, Winchester Model 1200 pump in 12 gauge, Winchester Model 1400 Auto Mark II Deer gun in 12 gauge.

mid-range trajectory of about 3 inches—a formidable missile when you consider that such a slug weighs a full ounce and has a muzzle velocity of 1600 foot seconds. Tests by the Ithaca Gun Company, which makes the Deerslayer slug gun, produced a 5-shot 1¾-inch group at 40 yards!

The 16 gauge slug, also excellent for woods and brush hunting, weighs ⅞ ounce while the 20 gauge missile has a weight of ⅝ ounce, each with a muzzle velocity the same as that of the 12 gauge slug. Both the 16 and 20 are suitable deer loads.

The .410 gauge rifled slug has greater velocity —somewhat over 1800 foot seconds—but its ⅕-ounce pee-wee weight makes it quite unsuitable for deer and black bear. I once saw a yearling deer hit in the shoulder by a .410 gauge and escape, only to be brought down later by a .38 Special. A shoulder shot on such a small deer with almost any other weapon would have knocked it down, but the .410 failed. It is *not* a suitable deer load.

Long or Short Barrel?

The best length for barrels on an all-round shotgun is between 26 and 28 inches. Duck and goose hunters, as well as many trap shooters, lean toward longer barrels, up to 32 inches on 12 gauge guns. Hunters of upland game and skeet shooters have a tendency toward 28-inch barrels and possibly 2 inches longer for waterfowl hunting. The most popular barrel length for 16 gauge guns for upland shooting is 26 to 28 inches, with an average of 30 inches for ducks and geese. In figuring barrel length, any choking device is included.

The Shotgun Rib

The shotgun rib is a sighting plane set atop the single-barrel gun or raised slightly between the barrels of double-bores. Ribs vary from ¼ inch to 5⁄16 inch in width and run the entire length of the barrel(s), usually ending flush with the rear of any mechanical choke. The narrow band of metal, usually matted or faintly corrugated to kill light glare, forms a natural channel for the eye to follow in sighting. A sighting bead is usually mounted atop the rib at the muzzle end. Today's ribs are "ventilated," mounted "bridge-like" on lightweight supports spaced along the barrel so that air can circulate under them. These serve to keep the rib cool even when the gun is fired steadily for long periods. Keeping the rib cool prevents the formation of heat waves which would distort sighting.

12-20 Danger

It's likely to happen only once to a shooter, but if he accidentally places a 20 gauge shell into a 12 gauge gun, the 20 will slip neatly into the barrel and lodge. Firing a 12 gauge shell with the 20 in the barrel spells disaster! The gun barrel will burst with a fifty-fifty chance of injury to the shooter.

The Federal Cartridge Company is to be commended for the introduction some time ago of its "Golden 20" shell which, because of its distinctive color, stands out prominently among the common reds and greens of 12 gauge shells, helping to eliminate the possibility of accidental double loadings of 12 and 20 shells.

A 20 gauge shell isn't always the culprit, however. Using modern high-pressure loads in Damascus or "twist" steel barrels often results in a burst barrel. Damascus or twist barrels were designed for black powder loads, not today's high-pressure shells. An obstruction of any kind, even in modern barrels, will also cause an accident.

The Single-Barrel Shotgun

"'Tis far better to hunt with a single-shot gun than not to hunt at all" pretty well sums up the reason for owning a single. As with the .22 single-shot, you'll soon train yourself to make the first—and only—shot count, for there'll be no second shot at a darting grouse or scuttling rabbit! Some may sneer at the single-barrel gun and its limitations, pointing smugly to the beauty of the double, the efficiency of the pump and the speed of the automatic; but unfortunately not all of us can lay out a month's grocery money for a better shotgun. My first shotgun, now close to forty years old, was a single-barrel Model 37 Winchester which I wouldn't trade for any other gun although its actual cash value is probably less than $10. It was this gun that taught me more about New England grouse than all of the shotguns I've owned since, and for that reason it has a permanent resting place in my gunrack.

Most of the single-shot shotguns are of the break-open type, some with visible hammer, and usually with an automatic ejector. They may be taken down easily for storing or carrying. The least expensive of all shotguns, many are available in youth models for junior shooters who cannot handle full-size versions. As with single-shot .22s, these are the safest for beginners, and good teaching instruments. Most have full-choke barrels, although a few are available in Modified.

The Ithaca version varies in that its action is lever-activated.

Pioneered by Mossberg, the bolt-action shotgun seems incongruous since wing shooting calls for fast handling, yet the bolt action is the slowest of all! However, these guns have found their place at about half the price of pump or automatic actions.

Not to be confused with the inexpensive beginners' guns are the single-barrel trap guns. Their prices, soaring into the $1000 bracket, are an indication of the difference between the two. These single-shot trap guns fill a demand for a lightweight model which will stand the almost continuous shooting at clay birds. In order to ease the physical strain on the shooter the mechanics of these guns are phenomenally smooth and easy to operate. Many are custom-made although several manufacturers offer stock models. Design features usually include a forearm that protects the shooter's hand from a hot barrel, a full-length ventilated rib and an extremely fast lock. The stock invariably is of the highest grade to withstand the punishment of trapshooting.

Ten years ago I wrote that "the double-barrel shotgun is definitely on the way out." This prediction can be likened to the ones that put Thomas E. Dewey in the White House and foretold great things for the hula hoop! I was wrong. Absolutely and irrevocably wrong. True, at the time, doubles were at a low ebb and seemed headed downhill. But good sense among American upland shooters wouldn't allow a fine field piece to die. They brought back the double.

And for good reason. At the risk of seeming snobbish, the double is a "gentleman's gun." Two shots at a duck, grouse or quail are enough. If the game evades these, it deserves to live for another day. But there are more practical aspects to the double's resurging popularity. It is rugged. Minimum common-sense care will maintain it for years. There's little to get out of order.

Single-Shot Shotguns

Make	*Model*	*Action*	*Gauge*	*Choke*	*Youth Model*
Glenfield (Marlin)	50	Bolt	12–20	Full	
H & R	158	Break-open	12–16 20–.410	Full Mod.*	
H & R	490	Break-open	20–.410	Full Mod.*	Yes
H & R	198	Break-open	20–.410	Full Mod.*	
Ithaca	66	Lever	12–20 .410	Full Mod.*	Yes
Mossberg	173	Bolt	.410	Full	Yes
Rossi		Break-open	12–16 20–28 .410	Full	Yes
Savage	94	Break-open	12–16 20–.410	Full Mod.*	Yes
Savage	220L	Break-open	12–16 20–.410	Full	
Savage/Stevens	51	Bolt	.410	Full	Yes
Winchester	370	Break-open	12–16 20–28 .410	Full	Yes

* Modified chokes usually available only in 20 gauge but may vary among manufacturers.

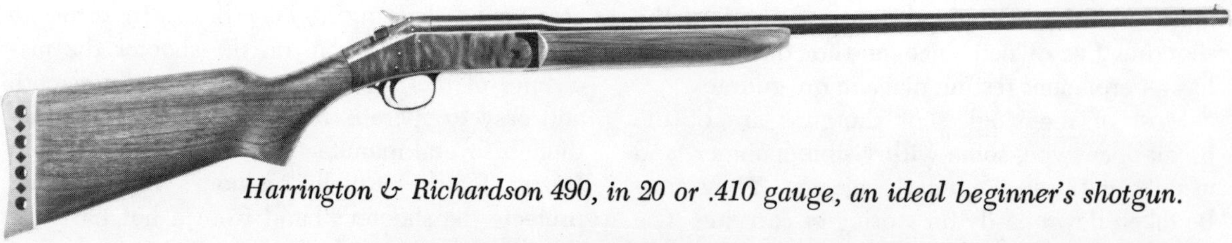

Harrington & Richardson 490, in 20 or .410 gauge, an ideal beginner's shotgun.

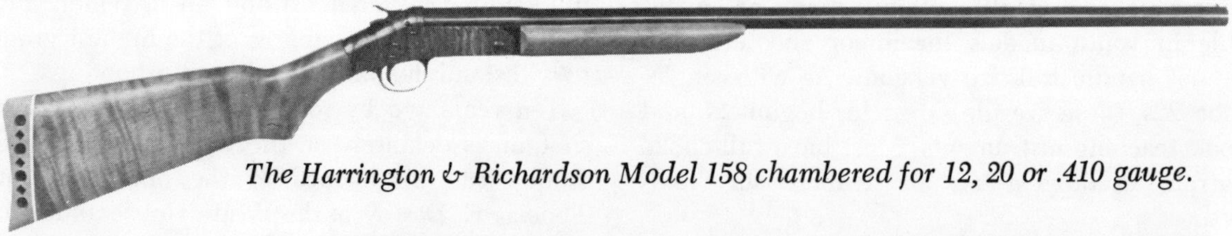

The Harrington & Richardson Model 158 chambered for 12, 20 or .410 gauge.

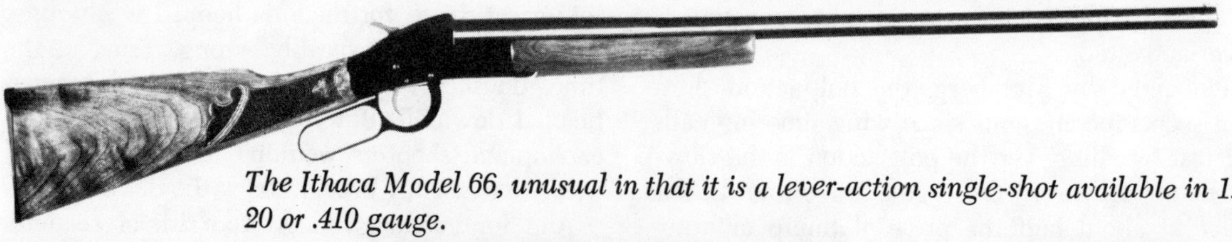

The Ithaca Model 66, unusual in that it is a lever-action single-shot available in 12, 20 or .410 gauge.

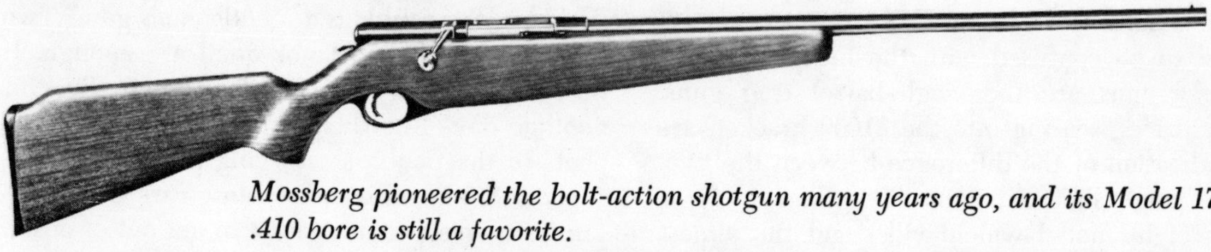

Mossberg pioneered the bolt-action shotgun many years ago, and its Model 173 in .410 bore is still a favorite.

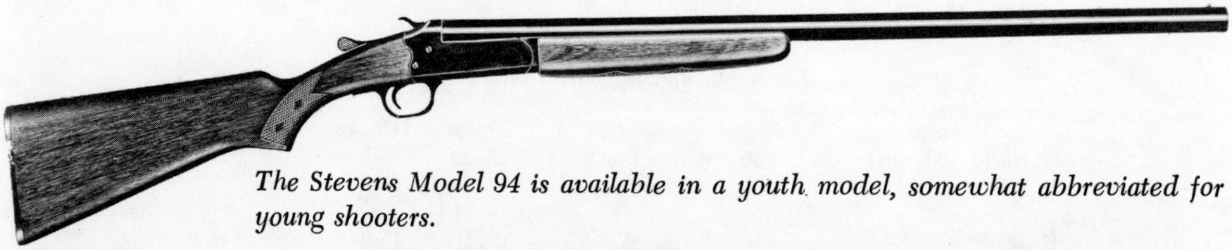

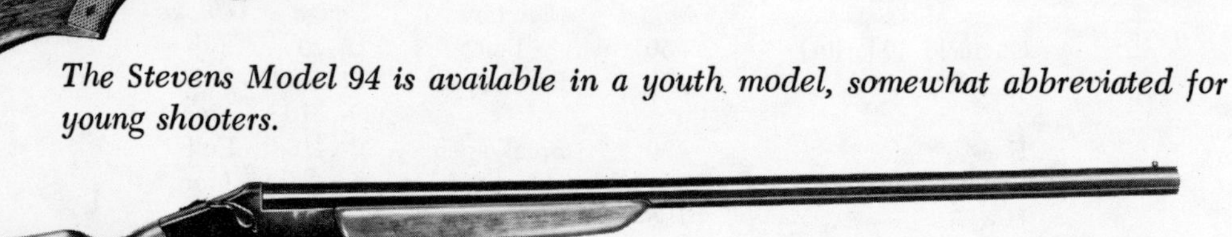

The Stevens Model 94 is available in a youth model, somewhat abbreviated for young shooters.

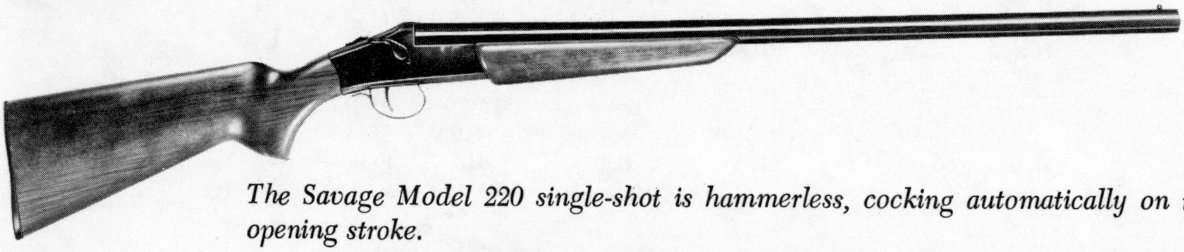

The Savage Model 220 single-shot is hammerless, cocking automatically on the opening stroke.

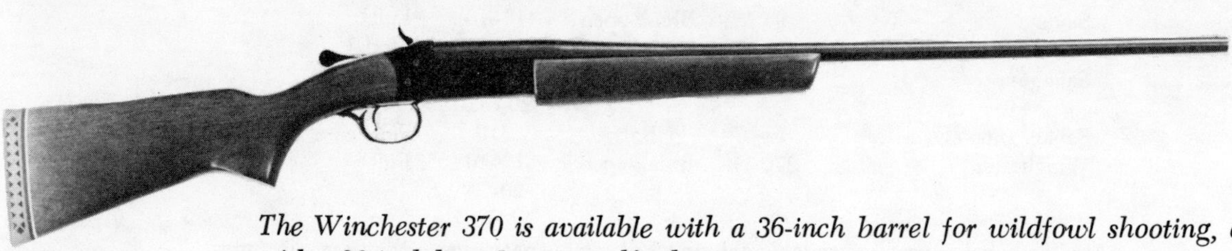

The Winchester 370 is available with a 36-inch barrel for wildfowl shooting, or with a 26-inch barrel as a youth's shotgun.

Bolt-action repeating shotguns: Glenfield Model 50 in 12 or 20 gauge, Marlin Model 55 Goose Gun in 12 gauge with 36-inch barrel, Mossberg Model 183D a three-shot 410 gauge with detachable choke, Mossberg Model 395K in 12 gauge with C-Lect Choke, Stevens Model 59 in 410 gauge with tubular magazine, Savage-Stevens Model 58 in 410 gauge, Stevens Model 58 in 12 gauge.

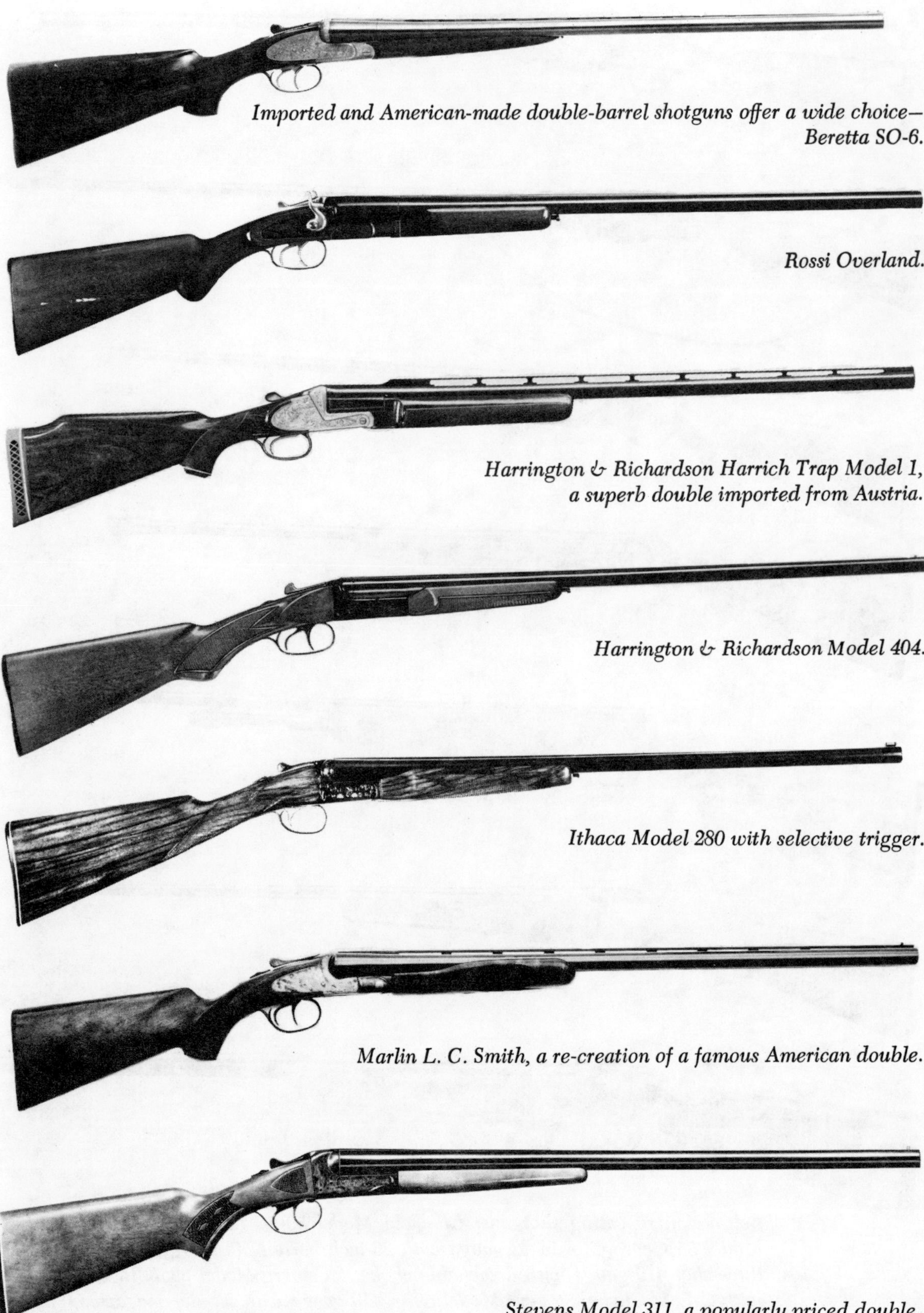

Imported and American-made double-barrel shotguns offer a wide choice—Beretta SO-6.

Rossi Overland.

Harrington & Richardson Harrich Trap Model 1, a superb double imported from Austria.

Harrington & Richardson Model 404.

Ithaca Model 280 with selective trigger.

Marlin L. C. Smith, a re-creation of a famous American double.

Stevens Model 311, a popularly priced double.

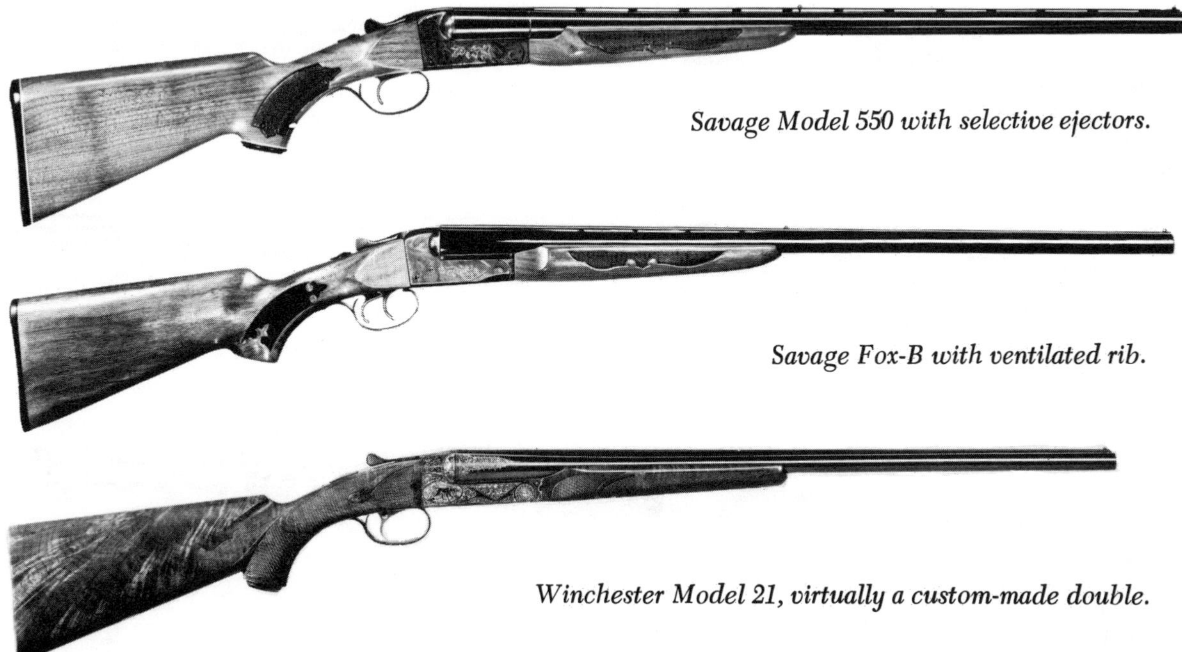

Savage Model 550 with selective ejectors.

Savage Fox-B with ventilated rib.

Winchester Model 21, virtually a custom-made double.

It is relatively light, handles well in the field and is equally adapted to hunting or skeet.

What's more there is a tremendous variety of doubles available. Less expensive models have two triggers—one for each barrel—and even some of the lower-priced doubles have "automatic selective ejectors." The latter means simply that when you break open the gun, an empty shell will be popped out, but an unfired shell will simply be lifted from the chamber so that you can remove it.

Among the more sophisticated doubles, you can have a "selective trigger" which may be pre-set to fire either barrel first. Currently, American-made doubles can be purchased for about $100, but if you have the means, inclination and desire, you can invest from $1200 to $3900 for a Winchester Model 21 which includes a gold-plated trigger. Needless to say, the action is as smooth as an otter slide!

Double guns are available with the barrels side by side in the traditional manner, or as "over-and-under" models, the latter probably contributing most to the double gun's continued popularity. Doubles are sold in all the standard gauges with the full variety of choking available, although, of course, variable chokes cannot be attached to these. Depending upon the grade and manufacturer, they are chambered to handle the 2¾-inch or 3-inch shells.

The Winchester Model 12 was recently reintroduced after a 15-year lapse. Considered the world's finest pump-action shotgun of which more than two million were produced. William Fasula, foreman in charge of Model 12 production at New Haven (left) pointed out features to the author at the Winchester plant.

Over-and-under doubles are increasingly popular: the fine Beretta SO-2; Mauser Model 620, a high-grade import; Mauser 71E, made for the popular American market; Savage Model 440 with selective trigger and extractors; the new Savage Model 333 trap gun; Winchester Model 101 with extra barrel sets.

Pump-action repeating shotguns are equally at home in a duck blind or on the skeet field: Harrington & Richardson Model 440; Marlin 120 Magnum with ventilated rib; Mossberg Model 500 APR, a 12 gauge "pigeon-grade gun"; Mossberg Model 500E with choke; Remington 870, available in many versions; Savage Model 30-D, also available in several grades; Winchester 1200; Winchester Model 12, probably the most famous American pump shotgun, reintroduced in 1972.

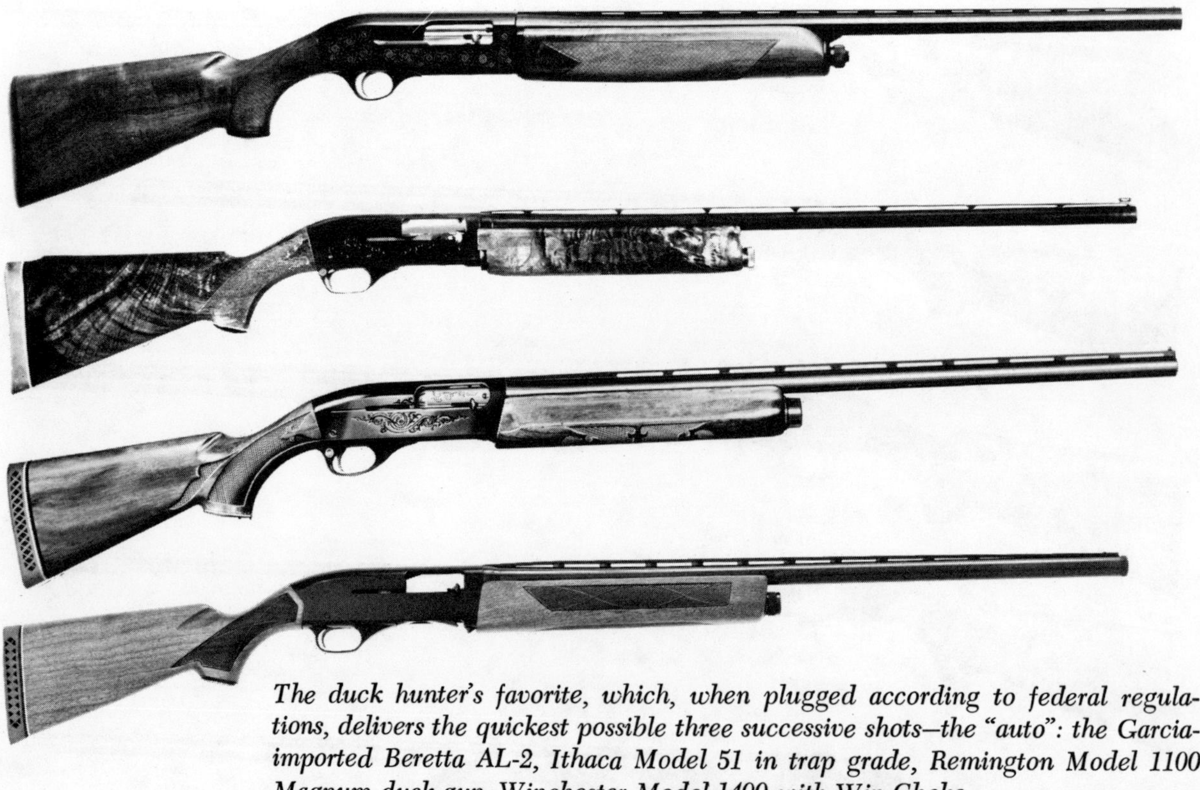

The duck hunter's favorite, which, when plugged according to federal regulations, delivers the quickest possible three successive shots—the "auto": the Garcia-imported Beretta AL-2, Ithaca Model 51 in trap grade, Remington Model 1100 Magnum duck gun, Winchester Model 1400 with Win-Choke.

Pump and Automatic Shotguns

The ease and speed with which these shotguns can be fired has already been explained with regard to similar actions in rifles with much the same qualities applying to both. Shooters who use a pump- or slide-action rifle are prone to using this type of shotgun and there's a similar choice for automatic rifle users. Keep in mind, however, that pump-action and automatic shotguns are limited to three-shot capacity when being used on migratory birds governed by federal law, including woodcock, ducks and geese. Magazine capacity is temporarily cut back to three by the insertion of a plug, easily removed for full magazine capacity on other types of game.

Many favor the automatic, not only because of its speed, but because apparent recoil is absorbed somewhat by the operation of the action. A further advantage of the auto and the pump is that it is excellently suited to the use of the variable choke.

The variety of pump-action shotguns available is a wide one, with most American gunmakers offering a number of models.

Chapter XIV

HANDLING THE SHOTGUN

When you lift your brand-new shotgun from its box for the first time you'll find instructions for assembling and cleaning it, along with directions for loading and firing. There'll be an inspector's slip and quite likely some advertising material describing the manufacturer's other products. Even with the finest shotgun, however, you'll find no guarantee that you can hit anything with it! This comes only with practice.

Before I bought my first shotgun, I read every book and magazine article dealing with the scattergun that I could find. The more I read, the more confused I became and when I finally acquired the gun I couldn't hit the side of a barn—even from the inside! The writers hadn't agreed among themselves and each had a "new" approach or gimmick that made shotgun shooting infallible—or at least easier. They described necessary lead on ducks and "snap shooting" at quail or grouse. Mathematical formulas were dragged in to prove (or disprove) that a game bird can (or cannot) fly into (or out of) a shot string, or that a field load with 1⅛ ounces of No. 7½ shot ahead of 3 drams equivalent powder in 12 gauge is superior firepower for early season woodcock, but that the hunter should shift to No. 9 shot with 3¼ drams equivalent powder after the first full moon in October. My derision may be a little exaggerated, but if these writers set out to impress me with their great knowledge and to confuse me, they succeeded.

Without referring to theories regarding lead, discussions of shot string, gimmicks or "sure-fire" methods, any man or woman, with near-normal reactions and with practically any shotgun, can become a good shot, given enough practice. The process, however, can be speeded up by using a well-fitting shotgun and following a few—a very few—simple rules.

Gun Fit

A shotgun that fits is one that comes up easily, smoothly and gracefully. The butt cradles into your shoulder almost automatically, your cheek settles along the comb or stock naturally, and your shooting eye looks out over the barrel(s) without undue strain of the neck muscles or awkward tilting of your head. Your trigger finger slips into the trigger guard without searching. If this happens when you "try" a gun to your shoulder, you've found a gun that *fits.*

There are formulas and theories for arriving at such a fit and the shooter who can lay out $500 to $1000 for custom work may have dimensions tailored to his needs, but the average shooter must go into a sporting goods store and pick out a gun for himself. Here, he must try gun after gun, possibly every one in the store as long as the clerk believes he *is* going to buy one. Eventually, he'll find one that fits him. I have never bought a shotgun in any other manner. Either a gun "felt good" and fitted, or it didn't!

General Shooting

You will, of course, pattern your new shotgun, as explained in Chapter XIII. While you're doing this, try a few shots under simulated hunting conditions, bringing the gun up as if you were about to swing on a grouse or pheasant. Shoot, however, at a large sheet of paper. This may surprise you. It's possible that the center of your shot pattern is exactly where you pointed the gun (shotguns are rarely *aimed* in the true sense of the word). However, you may also discover that your center of impact or pattern is high or low. In other words your shot isn't going where you think you're pointing.

Not getting cheek low enough on comb usually results in shot pattern overshooting target.

Shooting high usually is the result of not getting your cheek down on the comb or stock closely enough. Looking over your barrel as you shoot, the muzzle appears high enough but the stock is down; hence your shot pattern will be higher than your actual "aim." "Crowding" the gun too closely with your face and cheek can well result in a reverse situation—shot pattern too low—though it is less likely to occur.

As you bring up the shotgun your shooting eye should look over the barrel *at the target*. You may close one eye, or shoot with both open, the latter being called "binocular shooting." Despite the fact that you'll be looking over your barrel, you will see little of its detail. At this writing, I became curious regarding the type of bead-front sight on my pet 12 gauge pump which I've used for several years. Surprisingly I couldn't recall and checked my gunrack to discover that the bead is a rather soiled gray one, although I'd been half ready to believe it was red! Shotgun "sighting" boils down to following the target with your eyes and "pointing" the gun with your arms and shoulders. Co-ordination between the two comes with practice.

There are dozens of volumes discussing shotgun shooting stance and its importance to accuracy. Such material *is* helpful, if you can keep it in mind while shooting. However, rather than trying to conform to a set of anatomical rules, you'll be just as well off to adopt a comfortable, unrestrained position. One point, which I've rarely seen discussed, is flexibility of the body, acquired through physical fitness. A man who exercises little, except for an occasional shooting trip, can rarely become any more than a mediocre shot. The torso especially should be supple as possible so that you can pivot at the waist and hips as well as with your feet. Good shooting form calls for swinging the gun with the body instead of with just the arms and shoulders. Using the latter as hinges will disturb the position of your shooting eye in relation to the barrel.

Most beginners are prone to shoot and look afterwards, especially on such game as grouse, pheasant, quail, and woodcock which "erupt" suddenly, sometimes literally from under the hunter's feet. Most instructors urge that shooters try to avoid being startled by these sudden game eruptions, but after some 30 years of New England grouse hunting, the "pa'tridge" still gives me a start, as do Minnesota pheasants. My early reactions were to bring up the gun quickly and fire before the game got out of range, a theory that led to more misses than hits. Only when I learned to "simmer down" did I realize that I was not bringing my gun up fully. The game bird does not exist that can outfly a load of No. 7½ shot, so take an extra second to bring up the gun to full shooting position.

Initial practice with a scattergun isn't always possible on game birds. During off-seasons, have a friend stand behind you and toss tin cans in long arcs over either of your shoulders. Practice on these "going-away" shots, first trying to hit them as they reach the peak of the arc, then as they descend. Later have the cans thrown from either side, so that they arc in front of you from left to right or vice versa. Cans are ideal since their travel is comparatively slow and hits are clearly visible.

Later, try clay birds thrown from a hand trap from stations in back of you as well as to the side.

These will whirl through the air considerably faster than did the cans and they more nearly approximate the speedy flight of game birds.

If you miss consistently and can't seem to improve within a reasonable time, chances are you're a "gun stopper." This is the shooter who estimates where his target and charge of shot will meet. He then follows the target with the barrel, overtakes it, stops and shoots. The secret to hitting consistently is to *follow through* with your swing.

This consists of swinging the barrel along the path of flight of the target or bird, coming abreast of the quarry, pulling the trigger and *continuing the swing*. None of these are completely separated motions. They are continuous and co-ordinated. Continuing the swing as you pull the trigger will keep you on target. If you stop the swing, your own reaction time and even the gun's lock time will give your target a chance to continue its flight out of your pattern's range. Overlook every other rule of shotgun shooting, if you will, but don't ignore this one! Follow through!

The woods are full of charts and tables illustrating the speed of flying game birds and recommendations for suitable lead. One trouble with these is that the theoretical or paper examples all too often don't occur in the field as they were illustrated. After all, at how many angles can a duck fly in relation to the hunter's blind? How can you chart on paper the whirling and darting of a ruffed grouse dodging among trees? These paper discussions are interesting and most of the suggestions are sound, but they're not a substitute for practice.

"Lead" is the distance at which you fire ahead of a flying object, so that the target's path of flight and the shot charge will meet. The faster the target the greater the amount of lead needed. Lead, however, is further affected by the direction of flight of the target.

The simplest illustrations involve targets moving at right angles to the shooter's line of fire and it is with these shots that lead is most pronounced. However, what about going-away shots, and targets that are soaring at various angles from your shooting position?

A game bird, flying directly away at a very gradual rate of climb, will require little if any lead since its path of flight lies along that of your shot charge. It's simply a case of the shot overtaking the bird. On an incoming bird, flying directly at you, as frequently happens over decoys, the bird will fly into your shot pattern.

A going-away shot in which the bird climbs rapidly requires lead *over* the bird, since in its upward climb it will fly into the shot pattern if you've held correctly. Shooting directly at the bird may dust its tail feathers but chances are the shot will pass harmlessly beneath. If you've ever seen a black mallard erupt from a quiet slough or backwater, you've no doubt noted that its climb is almost vertical, with the bird literally jumping out of the water.

As we've seen, birds flying at right angles require the greatest apparent lead. A sudden swerve from this flight path to one approximating 45 degrees away would, in theory, cut that lead in half and the sharper the path of flight away from you, the less lead you'll need. Undoubtedly a mathematician could devise a chart indicating the necessary lead for all species flying in all directions at all speeds, but you'd need an IBM machine in the duck blind with you!

The only rule I have to suggest regarding lead is an old adage among shotgunners, especially among the old-time practical shooters. "Give it enough lead so you think you'll hit it—then double it!" And, I might add, don't forget to follow through! On these two premises rest all of the other shotgun rules.

Trapshooting

Trapshooting evolved from early English sport of live bird shooting, with birds released from traps or cages, one at a time. Later, the targets were glass balls fired from tubes by means of spring releases. Still later the "clay" pigeon, a saucer-shaped target, was developed and modern versions of these are today's trap targets.

A trap layout consists of a low trap house which houses the target release mechanism or "trap." Sixteen yards back from this are five shooting stations. According to the rules, clay pigeons may be released at any angle from the trap house up to 65 degrees right or left. Many clubs and associations now limit the release area to 47 degrees. The shooter has no way of knowing in which direction his next bird will fly.

Five "handicap" positions are located directly back of the five primary shooting stations. The more skillful shooters may then be placed as far back as 25 yards from the trap house.

In trapshooting, a shooter takes his position at one of the five front or primary stations. He then may "mount" or raise his gun to firing stance and when he is ready he calls "Pull!" This is the signal for the "trap boy" to release a target. A seasoned trapshooter doesn't try to guess or anticipate the coming bird's path of flight. Instead, he poises his gun so that it points just over the trap house and he does not start his swing until he has established the path of his target. Guessing at the target's flight usually means a false swing and the necessity of starting over from an off-balance position.

While it might appear that the variety of shots in trapshooting is limited, the opposite is true. Every angle of going-away shot is possible, ranging from the right-angle flight to a full "straightaway," depending upon which of the five stations the firing is being done from. Firing the course, a shooter is required to shoot from all five stations. Generally speaking, trapshooting is a longer range sport than skeet (see below), since the shooter is stationed at least 16 yards from the trap. By the time he has noted the flight path and completed his swing, the target may well have reached the 30-yard mark. Because of this, many of the specially made trap guns have full chokes. Trap shot, too, is usually small, No. 7½ and 8 being popular.

The Amateur Trapshooting Association has a huge layout at Vandalia, Ohio, where regional and national championship competition is conducted every year. Vandalia is the group's national headquarters.

Skeet

Skeet shooting differs from trapshooting in that *two* trap houses, one high and one low and 40 yards apart, are used. They fire birds over a fixed course, the path of flight never being varied. Instead, there are eight shooting stations, seven of which are on the perimeter of a semicircle running between the trap houses. Because skeet firing is done at short range—as close as 5 yards and up to 22—most skeet guns are bored-cylinder or with a special skeet bore. No. 8 or 9 shot is used.

A "round" of skeet calls for 17 "single" birds to be shot with the balance of 8 fired as doubles, to complete a 25-bird course. In the doubles, two birds are thrown simultaneously. Skeet shooting allows the use of any gauge, including the .410 in some matches, although shot loads are governed by varying regulations.

Skeet and trapshooting fill a very definite need among shooters who would become experts with the scattergun. Limited by comparatively short hunting seasons, few could become truly expert as a result of game shooting alone. Being an expert at skeet or trap, however, is no guarantee that you'll be equally skillful on game birds, but it will go a long way toward helping. Besides, you'll acquire a love for the smell of burning gunpowder, the camaraderie of competitive shooting, and the feel of a shotgun in your arms.

Chapter XV

SHOT-SHELL RELOADING

As a boy, too young to have a gun, I sublimated my gun-owning urge by picking up vast quantities of red and green empties, or fired shot shells, at local trap and skeet fields. Nowadays, an empty is snapped up almost as it hits the ground, to be reloaded, or sold to reloaders. An empty shell on the ground is a rare sight, except for an occasional one in the grouse woods or pheasant fields, overlooked in the excitement of retrieving a bird.

During black powder days, brass shot shells were commonly reloaded, but the advent of the inexpensive paper shell almost put a complete end to this. The rising price of shot shells and the simplification of bench reloading tools, coupled by a growing interest in shotgun shooting, revived shot-shell loading during the days immediately after World War II. The hobby has been growing in scope ever since.

Shot-shell reloading can be accomplished at a cost of about half the over-the-counter price of similar shells. Frequently claims of 75 per cent savings are made, but these are rarely based on fact, especially when you consider the price of reloading equipment. In figuring cost, this is usually disregarded, as is the reloader's time. Even at that, a 50 per cent saving, coupled with the pleasure afforded by this hobby, more than makes it worthwhile. In addition, a reloader can devise loads for special purposes, or which will deliver better patterns in *his* gun than he might possibly be able to obtain in a sporting goods store. Gun shops now recognize shot-shell reloading for the popular hobby that it is and sell components, as well as ready-to-fire shells.

Although shot-shell reloading may appear more complex than the loading of rifle or pistol cases, it's actually easier since you'll be dealing with comparatively soft cases which can be reformed and crimped with little manual effort. At the same time, a greater number of components is involved, but when you understand the purpose of each of these, the matter of reloading shot shells will simplify itself in your mind.

Reloading shot shells can start with the saving of your own factory cases, picked up after a shooting session, or you can purchase new or used empties. New shells are now available, and many trap and skeet clubs sell used shells which are picked up on the shooting grounds. These used shells are usually "once-fired" and suitable for five or six more loadings. How often you can reload a shell depends much upon its condition at the time you sort them. Claims of up to a dozen reloadings are somewhat optimistic, a safer estimate being five before the shell must be discarded because of one or more critical structural failures.

Sorting

The first step is to sort the empties according to brand and interior base height, assuming of course they've already been sorted according to gauge.

With regard to sorting—and later use—there is much confusion regarding the terms "high brass," "low brass," "high base," and "low base." High and low brass refer to the height of the sides of the base cup or metal rim that forms the cup. Actually, the "high" designation is a misnomer since these are no longer made in the U.S. So-called high-brass shells are really medium brass and they are loaded with high-velocity and Magnum loads. Low brass is used for standard or field loads.

Not to be confused with high and low *brass* are the terms high and low *base*. These are *interior* designations, referring to the height of the filler wad or base wad that is built into the shell. These vary in height according to the load, even among shells put out by the same factory. The height of the base is determined by the bulk of the powder charge to be used and that of the shot charge, allowance being made for crimping.

It's important to sort the shells according to the height of their interior bases, as you will not be able to load bulky powder charges into high-base shells for lack of room. On the other hand, care should be taken that you don't try to double-charge a low-base shell with a powder of high density occupying less room.

Besides being sorted, the shells should be examined for defects. Any sign of separation between the metal base and the paper wall, pinholes, cracked mouths, loose interior bases, thinned or softened walls, deformed primer pockets, and paper that is generally "beat up," all call for discarding the shell. Load only those which are in perfect condition.

You can probably expect up to about twenty reloadings with the compression-formed plastic cases; with paper cases, many less. In either instance, however, the number of reloadings must depend upon the condition of the shells. Check them closely.

Decapping and Priming

A shotgun primer differs from a rifle shell primer in that a cap, similar to the center-fire primer itself, is contained within a "battery cup" which extends into the base of the shot shell. The entire battery cup containing the primer itself may be punched out and replaced as a unit, and this is the most common method, especially among newcomers to reloading. Some savings can be effected, however, by reloading the battery cup with a fresh cap, but this is not an easy operation and involves rather exact seating of the anvil.

Decapping procedure in a shot shell is much the same as with a rifle shell, except for the varying mechanics of different reloading tools. The same is true of priming the shells. In either instance, decapping and priming remain the first basic steps, except that shells which have been fired in a gun other than your own, may need resizing. With shot shells, little manual force is required for this because of the softness of the shell's paper.

Before purchasing primers for reloading, study the various reloading manuals and recommendations and the catalogs of component manufacturers. Some primers are designed for certain shells and will work poorly or not at all in others. Also, there is a relationship between the primer, powder type and load, and the shot load, so far as performance is concerned. However, by sticking to recommended loads you should experience no difficulty. As you progress in experience and try for improved loads for your gun, a thorough knowledge of primers in relation to powder loads will come to you.

Powder Charging

Shotgun powder terminology is confusing to those who have dealt only with rifle or pistol powders, mostly because of the "drams equivalent" designation on shot-shell boxes. As I pointed out earlier, this term ***has nothing to do with reloading***. It's simply a standard adopted by all shot-shell manufacturers and it refers to velocity and pressure of loads. Powders used for reloading shot shells are measured in grains by weight, except when a bulk powder may be used. Reloading manuals explain the use of various powders and the procedures for loading them. Shotgun powders may be weighed in a powder scale or measured in a powder drop, the latter usually a part of the shot-shell reloading tool.

Wads

Powder loads for rifle and pistol cases rarely fill the cartridge. In the case of shotgun shells, the powder must be compressed under some pressure by means of a tight-fitting "over-powder" wad, the latter having pressure applied against it by the reloading tool. Above the powder wad are placed one or two "filler wads."

The over-powder wad, known as nitro-card, is a greaseproof, snug-fitting disc of .070, .135 or .200 inch thickness. Most reloaders prefer to use one .135-inch wad, although some lean toward using two .070-inch wads. Generally considered best for filler wads are those of hair felt, although also available at some savings are those made of paper and wood fiber. The filler wads are usually lightly greased, which helps to seal the powder charge and to lubricate the gun barrel when the shell is fired. Because the over-powder wad is greaseproof, it prevents the greased filler wad from contaminating the powder.

The total length or height of the combined wads is known as the "wad column," and its purpose lies in providing a firm and uniform confinement for the powder charge, in sealing gases from the shot charge, and in cushioning the shot against the sudden blow of the powder discharge.

The over-powder wad must be compressed against the powder at a given pressure which is indicated on the container in which the powder is packed by the manufacturer, or in the printed literature describing his powder and its uses. Most reloading tools have a spring-compression unit or plunger which may be set at a certain pressure for lodging the over-powder wad. Even bathroom scales may be used for applying the correct pressure, simply by inserting the wad against the powder, adding the plunger unit and bearing down upon the scale until the required pressure is attained. Pressure should be applied against the powder wad only, before the filler wads are inserted.

The length of the wad column will vary according to the recommended powder and shot charge, since sufficient room must be left for these and allowance also made for crimping. Loading manuals indicate this information for various loads and shells.

Two-piece plastic wad column includes an over-powder wad with a cushioning pillar and a shot cup, the latter protecting the shot from distortion as it travels through the barrel. (FEDERAL CARTRIDGE CORP.)

Shot Charging

This may be accomplished by means of a dipper, after the shot charge has been weighed. Many tools, however, have built-in shot chargers which will "throw" a pre-set quantity of shot. It's a good plan, though, occasionally to check these automatic chargers against a scale. If you have charged the proper amount of powder, the correct wad column and the required weight in shot, there should remain only enough of the shell wall to form a perfect crimp, or closure of the shell's mouth.

While conventional over-powder wadding continues in use, the shot sleeve or cup is growing in popularity. This varies in design among various makers, but essentially it is a plastic cup which holds the shot within the shell. Upon firing, the cup or sleeve is projected with the shot, protecting the latter from abrasion against the gun barrel. Upon leaving the muzzle, the sides of the cup or sleeve open. The shot continues on its course; the cup or sleeve drops to the ground.

Some of these plastic sleeves or cups have a built-in over-powder wad at the base; others use a separate cushioning pillar. Winchester and Remington factory loads use a one-piece wad/cup, while Federal loads utilize a two-piece unit. Reloaders have a choice.

Crimping

Most of today's shells use a star crimp, except those loaded with rifled slugs which still use the old-fashioned roll crimp. The star crimp, when correctly formed, looks like a miniature pie which has been marked for cutting. In using shells that have been fired once, crimping dies will fold the shell mouth along the lines of the original crimp. With new shells, which have never been crimped, a crimp-starter unit is sometimes required and these are usually part of the reloading tool. When the crimp has been started, it is then transferred to the crimping die, which then completes it under some pressure.

Shells that are to be used in wet weather, or exposed to dampness, should be sealed with a small dab of wax. Some reloading tools have a heating element which melts and distributes the wax over the star-crimp area, thus making the shell as waterproof as a new factory shell.

The roll crimp requires a different unit which rolls the edge of the shell mouth over itself so that it bears against a thin wad placed over the shot charge. Few of these are in use today, however, except to hold rifled slugs.

The crimping operation determines whether or not you have properly loaded your shell. If the crimp will not close fully and bulges upward, chances are you have an overcharge of powder, too much shot or too great a thickness of wadding. In some instances, where this bulge is not very pronounced, you may reinsert the shell into the crimping die and apply additional crimping pressure to level it. Care must be taken, however, that too much pressure doesn't bulge or split the side of the shell.

In the event the crimp sinks too deeply, the shell probably hasn't been properly filled with one or another of the interior components. Double-check your powder weights, shot weights, and wad column to make sure they are correct.

Don't let a poor crimp "get by," hoping the shell will function properly. The crimp might open accidentally and spill its shot charge. This might occur in your shotgun, following the recoil from another shell.

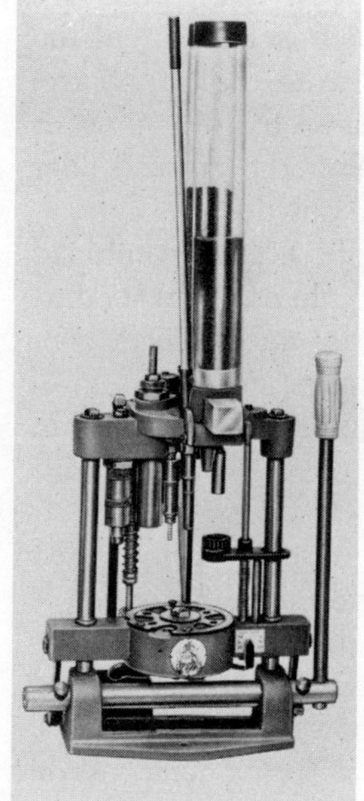

Each stroke of the lever produces a completed shot shell at a rate of up to 600 per hour with this "Polar Bair" reloader. (BAIR COMPANY)

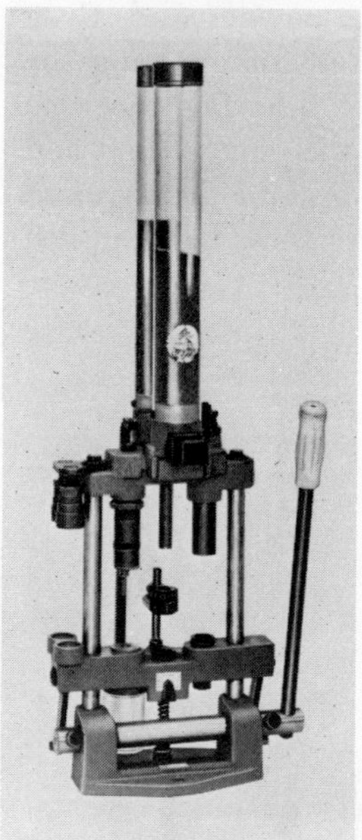

A three-station shot-shell reloader, capable of 250 shells per hour. (BAIR COMPANY)

Reloading Tools

All reloading tools will perform the tasks I've just described in pretty much the same sequence and manner, the principal difference between tools being the speed and ease with which the operations can be performed.

An example of the speed and efficiency with which a bench-mounted reloading press can be operated is the Model 600 "Polar Bair," produced by the Bair Company of Lincoln, Nebraska. This unit is rated at six hundred reloads per hour! That's ten shells per minute. The tool has rotating stations into which "empties" are placed. As these work their way around with each stroke of the lever, the complete decapping, sizing and reloading operation is performed. Each lever stroke produces a completed shell. Such production is at its best with two operators, one running the tool and the other feeding in empties and removing reloads. There's no reason why an individual who shoots a great deal can't utilize such a reloader, of course, but two or three shooters owning and operating it jointly will pro-

The "Honey Bair" reloader handles plastic or paper shells, has a wad-pressure indicator that is adjustable.
(BAIR COMPANY)

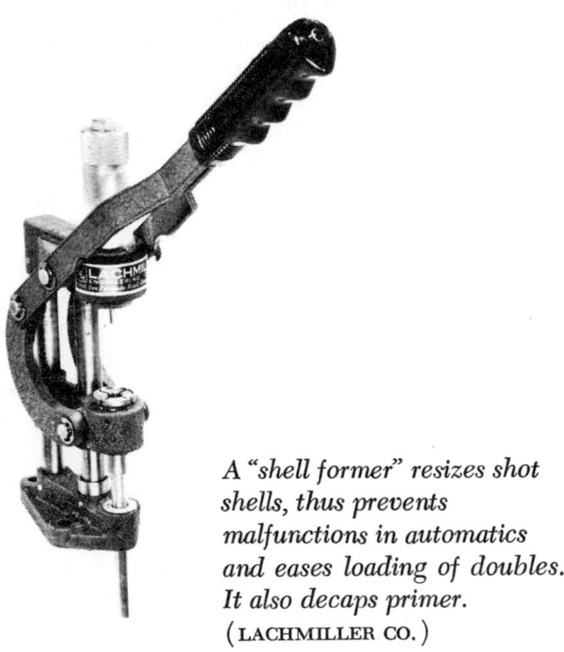

A "shell former" resizes shot shells, thus prevents malfunctions in automatics and eases loading of doubles. It also decaps primer.
(LACHMILLER CO.)

Lachmiller "Super Jet" (above) handles dies for all gauges from .410 to 10 gauge magnum.
(LACHMILLER ENGINEERING CO.)

duce more than ample reloads for their use while sharing the cost of its purchase and operation. Gun clubs, too, find such machines to their advantage.

The Bair Company has other multiple-operation units which produce shells at a rate of 225 to 250 per hour.

Pacific's Model DL-366 is also capable of six hundred reloads per hour, with a basic three-step operation. The operator inserts the shell case, the wads, and pulls the lever. The machine does the rest. Pacific's Model DL-266 similarly turns out 240 shells per hour.

Perhaps the ultimate in home reloading presses for shot shells is the Ponsness-Warren Model 800B, capable of 800 shells per hour with one operator, up to 1200 with the help of a partner. Except for pulling the lever this machine is virtually automatic even including a cam-operated wad carrier that swings out to receive the wads, including the new plastic sleeves. Another Ponsness-Warren machine, the Model 375, while somewhat less sophisticated, is capable of three hundred reloads per hour.

Such multiple-operation reloaders are for heavy users of shot shells. The occasional shotgun shooter really has no need for such a unit unless he shares the ownership and use with one or more partners. Prices for these range from about $125 up to close to $500.

Such semi-automated efficiency is impressive and certainly useful to those who shoot hundreds of rounds weekly, or to those who can stock up shot shells by the thousands during the off-season. Also, I might point out that the per-hour "rated" production speeds which I have cited are manufacturers' claims. I have no doubt that expert reloaders can attain such production efficiency, but I have never been able, personally, to achieve it. However, this is most likely an indication of my lack of practice and not misrepresentation by the manufacturers. It takes practice, and I neither reload nor shoot that much! I feel that if I can reload a half-dozen boxes of shells during one evening, I have done well.

If you're not seeking to match Winchester/Remington/Federal in the production of shotgun shells, look into the less exotic reloaders—far less expensive, requiring greater finger manipulation, longer hours at the reloading bench—but capable of superb loads at a cost roughly one third that of factory ammunition.

The Lyman Easy Shotshell Reloader, for example, sells for less than half the price of the least expensive multiple-action press. A simpler machine, it decaps the fired shell, primes and charges the powder, seats the wad to a pre-determined pressure, crimps and resizes the case, each step requiring moving the empty by hand. Yet, with practice, 150 shells per hour are not impossible!

Then look at the Lachmiller Super Jet, about which the manufacturer makes no speed claims. That's up to you, I presume. The tool handles paper or plastic shells, wad pressure is governed automatically and it crimps beautifully. It does all that higher priced, faster reloaders do. It simply requires somewhat more effort on the part of the user. And its cost is half that of the least expensive "super-loader."

All of the tools which I described briefly have such standard features as built-in powder and shot measures, wad pressure gauges and wad feeders. My omission of any tool from this description is not an inference that it is inferior in any way. It's simply that there's a limit to the number of shot-shell tools with which one can become familiar!

The best way to buy shot-shell reloading equipment is first to watch one in operation in the hands of a friend. He'll point out little idiosyncrasies which he's found—and which *all* reloaders discover in their tools. Some may be advantageous, others detrimental; and that's why it's best to "ask the man who owns one." A dealer who handles two or more brands is usually a sound consultant on the subject.

Chapter XVI

AIR GUNS

With roughly half our population living in cities or in compact suburbs, shooting a .22 "out back of the barn" on the spur of the moment is no longer possible for millions. Americans still enjoy using firearms, but, increasingly, this involves travel to a suitable area.

Which explains the growing popularity of the air gun. These can be used indoors, even in a living room, attic, garage, and certainly within the confines of a suburban back yard.

Air guns are quiet, almost silent, their report a mere "phfft!" except for some pneumatic models which may approximate the report of a .22 Short when pumped to maximum pressure. Otherwise, even apartment dwellers can shoot without disturbing neighbors.

A heavy plastic sheet, or canvas, draped loosely will stop pellets fired from the less powerful air guns. A cardboard box stuffed with newspapers or magazines is more than adequate as a backstop for maximum-power air guns. More sophisticated pellet traps are inexpensive.

Restrictions on air guns are relatively few. Most municipalities prohibit their indiscriminate use out of doors, such regulations aimed at curbing vandalism, but responsible shooters encounter no problems using these guns on their own property or within their homes. In those areas where stringent handgun laws exist, a permit to buy or possess an air-type handgun may be required. Usually, however, even in strict communities, buying an air gun is far less complicated

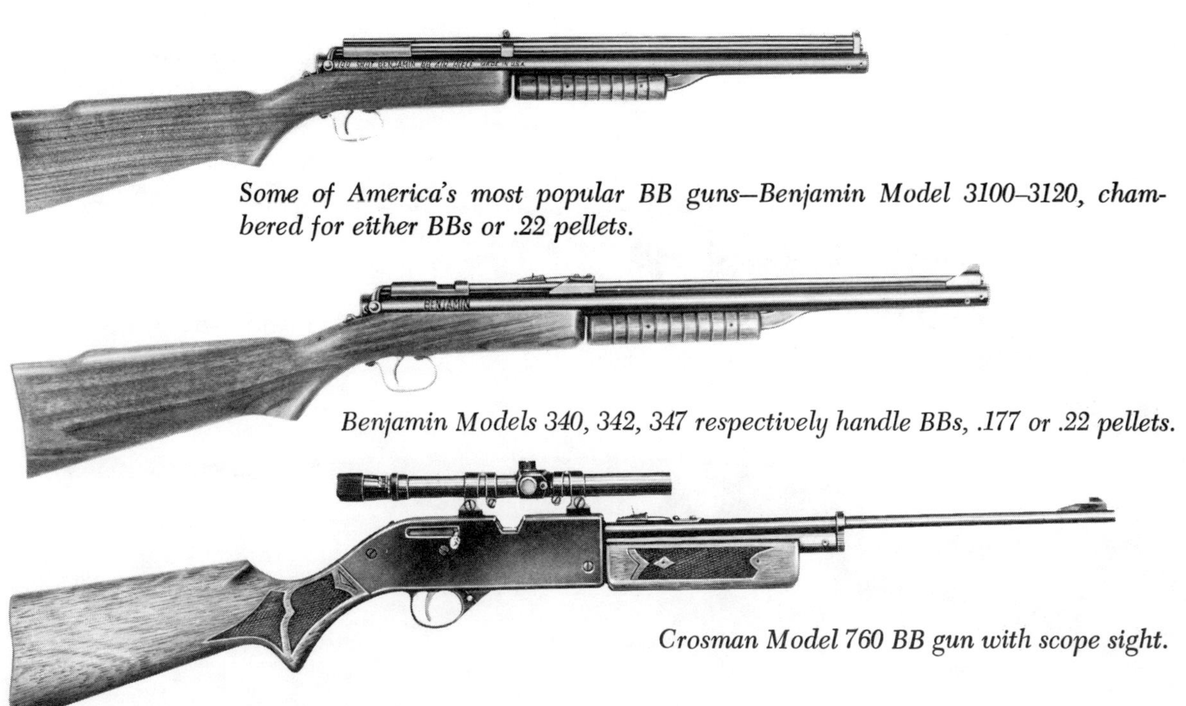

Some of America's most popular BB guns—Benjamin Model 3100–3120, chambered for either BBs or .22 pellets.

Benjamin Models 340, 342, 347 respectively handle BBs, .177 or .22 pellets.

Crosman Model 760 BB gun with scope sight.

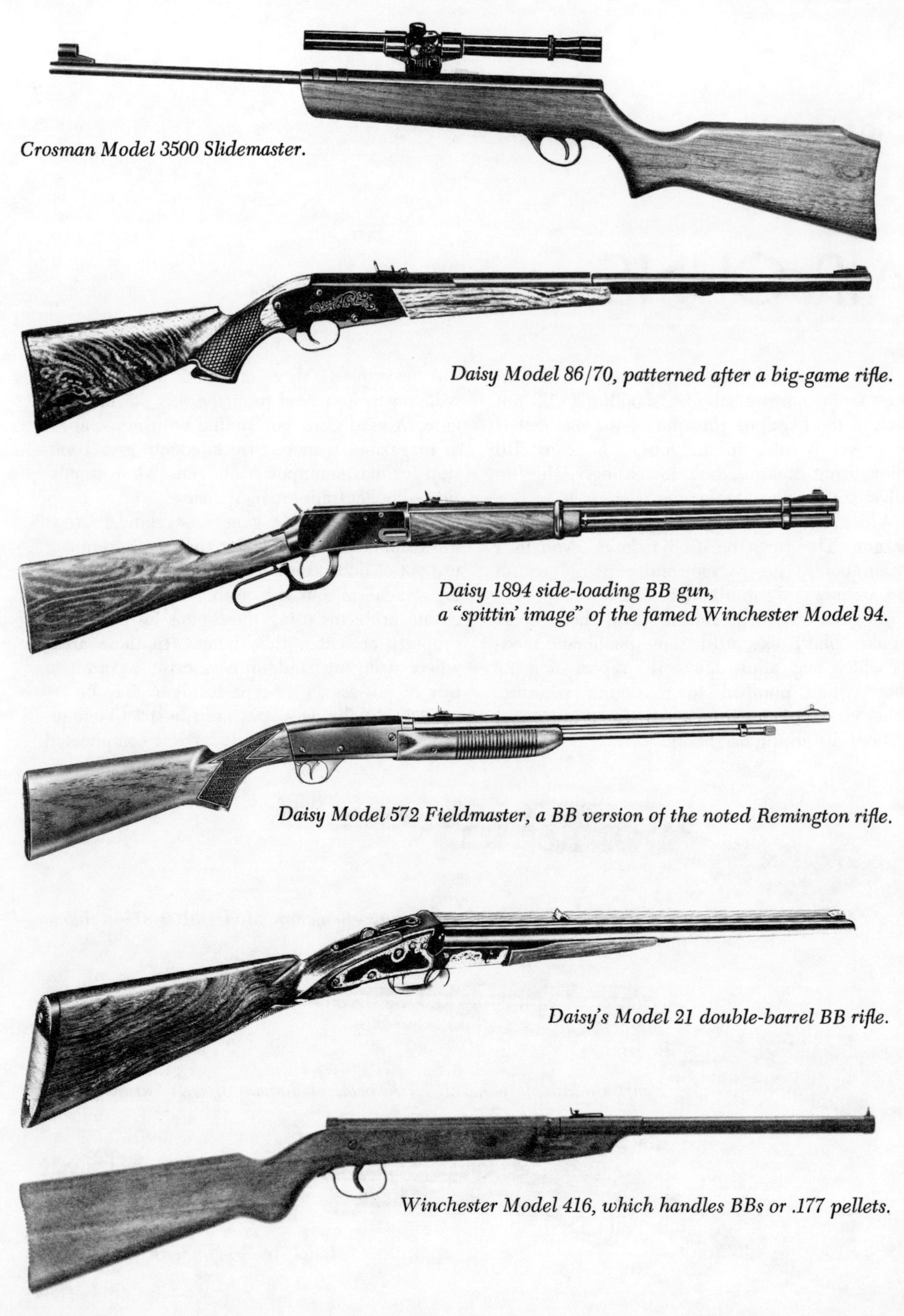

Crosman Model 3500 Slidemaster.

Daisy Model 86/70, patterned after a big-game rifle.

Daisy 1894 side-loading BB gun, a "spittin' image" of the famed Winchester Model 94.

Daisy Model 572 Fieldmaster, a BB version of the noted Remington rifle.

Daisy's Model 21 double-barrel BB rifle.

Winchester Model 416, which handles BBs or .177 pellets.

than purchasing a firearm. Dealers will enlighten you regarding local codes.

While some air guns are little more than toys, many are precise arms, capable of ½-inch groups at 40 feet. Some of the more refined models will shoot "one-hole" groups!

Virtually every refinement applied to powder-burning guns has been adapted to air guns: adjustable trigger pulls, telescope sights, iron sights adjustable for windage and elevation, heavy forearms and match stocks, automatic cocking and safeties.

Many are single-shot models but there is a wide choice of repeaters, including semi-automatics. Some handguns, and at least one rifle, feature a six-shot rotating cylinder.

Velocities are respectable, 300 foot seconds or more for BBs, more than 750 foot seconds for pneumatic guns. Since pellets weigh a mere 5½ to 14 grains, impact energy is limited. These *will* break windows and inflict painful flesh wounds where carelessness prevails, and, of course, being struck in the eye obviously has serious consequences. There is no more justification for the sloppy handling of an air gun than there is for the foolhardy use of a .22 powder burner. But with common sense the danger from air guns is inconsequential.

Some experts suggest air guns for small-game hunting, pointing to trophies such as squirrels, rabbits, even raccoons and wildcats. In the hands of a skilled stalker and shooter, the air gun may be adequate but it is generally at its best as a target and plinking arm.

Economy is appealing. The initial outlay can be well below $30 for a rifle, about the same for a handgun. More sophisticated versions run up to about $70, and you can invest $200 in an international match model. But $40 will likely get you a superb air gun for home or suburban shooting.

Ammunition costs are trifling. Steel BBs, about 1250 to the pound, sell for less than $1.50 at this writing. Lead pellets used in pneumatic guns cost about ½ cent per shot.

Projectiles

Once you have examined the various projectiles, the workings of air guns are more easily understood.

The BB gun fires a spherical steel pellet, .175 inch in diameter, although these may vary slightly, up to .177 inch. Don't mistake these for powder-burning shotgun BB loads which are charged with .180-inch pellets. These may stick in an air rifle barrel. Some steel BBs may be lead- or copper-coated. Opinions regarding these vary. Lead minimizes barrel wear and helps to seal in compression behind the BB as it travels through the barrel. On the other hand, lead BBs are easily deformed, thus decreasing accuracy. All-steel BBs appear to have the edge.

Guns designed to handle BBs are usually smoothbores, hence the term "air rifle" is a misnomer, since there is no rifling. There is no point to setting a spherical BB to spinning.

The other type of projectile is the pellet, a lead bullet not unlike a .22 Short, except that its nose is generally blunted and its waist often constricted for a "Coke bottle" appearance. These are used in pneumatic and CO_2 guns, whose barrels *are* rifled.

Two calibers are common, the .177 and the .22, although one gunmaker bores rifles and handguns for 5 mm (.20 caliber) pellets which he supplies. Certain BB guns will also handle .177 pellets.

Power Systems*

Power systems for air guns are of three types: a spring/air combination, compressed air (pneumatic), and compressed gas (CO_2, carbon dioxide cartridges).

The spring/air system is common among BB guns. Working the action compresses a spring which draws back a piston within a cylinder. A sear then holds the latter in poised position until released by the trigger. The spring then expands and drives the piston forward, compressing air ahead of it. This is then released through a valve into the "firing" chamber, projecting the BB through the barrel.

The system is inexpensive and requires only

* Standard reference works on air guns include: *The American BB Gun,* by Arni Dunathan, A. S. Barnes Co., Cranbury, N.J., 1972; *The Complete Book of the Air Gun,* by George C. Nonte, Jr., Stackpole Books, Harrisburg, Pa., 1970; *Smith's Standard Encyclopedia of Gas, Air, and Spring Guns of the World,* by W. H. B. Smith, Book Sales Inc., Secaucus, N.J., 1957.

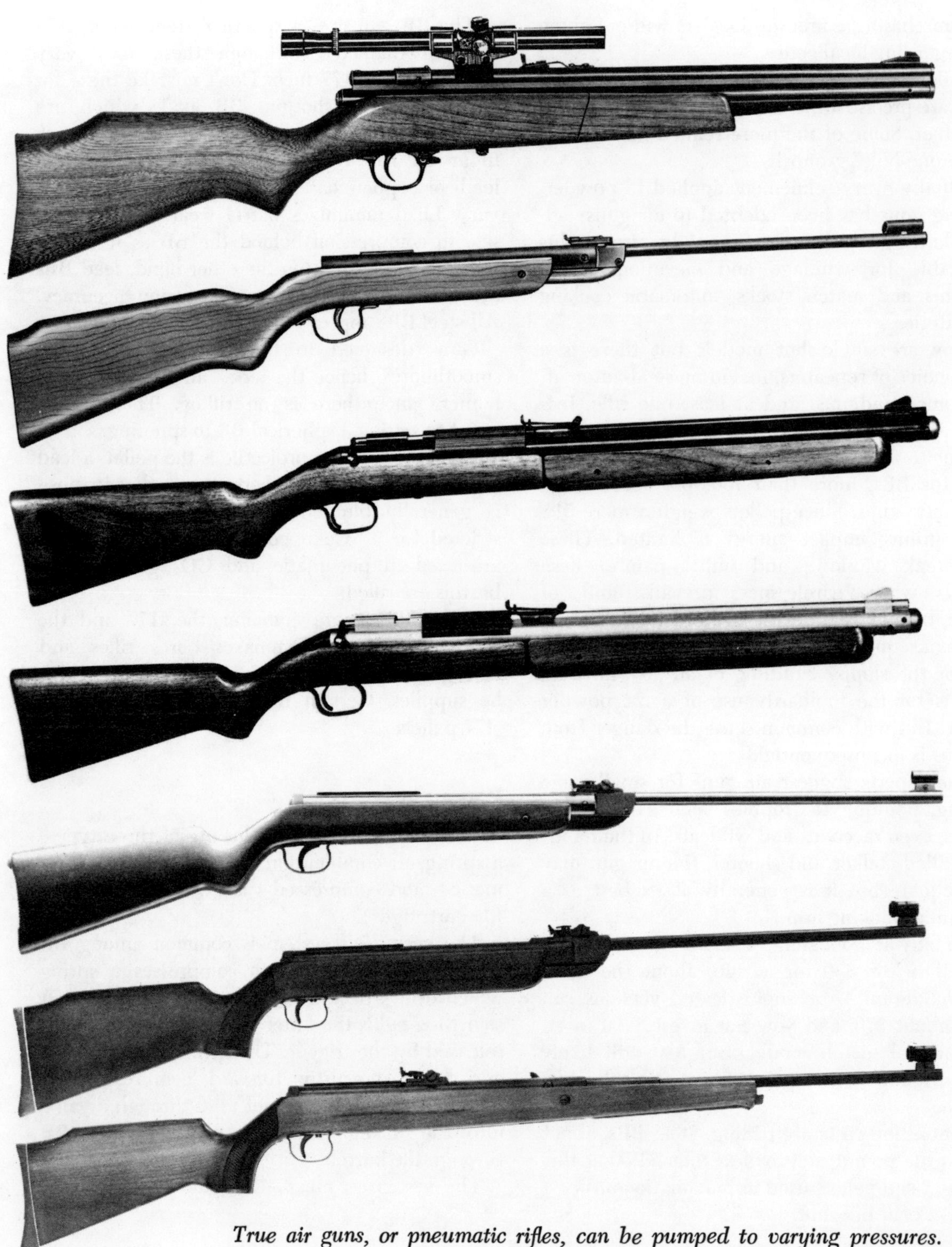

True air guns, or pneumatic rifles, can be pumped to varying pressures. These fire lead pellets. Crosman single-shot Pumpmaster handles a .22 pellet, Daisy Model 230 is also a .22 air gun, Sheridan's Blue Streak is a single-shot 5 mm (.20 cal.) rifle, Sheridan Silver Streak is a somewhat more sophisticated version of the Blue Streak, Winchester Model 427 has an adjustable trigger pull, Winchester Model 435 is a steel-barrel target model, Winchester Model 450 has an interchangeable front-sight assembly.

one movement of the action fully to compress the spring. Power is consistent. The action is the simplest of all used in air guns.

Disadvantages occur too. There is a definite recoil which may start before the BB has left the barrel. Some of the better BB guns compensate for this. Power cannot be varied except in a few refined models which provide for a low- and high-power discharge. While most BB guns are repeaters with magazine capacities running as high as seven hundred shots, a reserve supply of compressed air is not built up or retained. The action must be worked for each shot.

At 20 feet, BB penetration into a soft-pine board can be as much as ¾ inch, but generally the BB will barely bury itself.

As for accuracy, shooting a BB rifle at the standard 15-foot NRA target is comparable to shooting a target .22 at the NRA 50-foot target. The BB provides competition-level accuracy. The Boy Scouts of America, the Junior Chambers of Commerce, the National Rifle Association and the Daisy/Heddon Company are involved in a vast BB-shooting training program which has taught more than 20 million youngsters since 1946. In addition, the Jaycees and Daisy/Heddon annually co-sponsor the International BB-Gun Championships which attract young shooters from thirty-five states and Canada.

The second source of power used in air guns is compressed air, attained by manual pumping various types of actions, hence the term "pneumatic" gun. This system is used in guns propelling BBs and lead pellets, the latter in three calibers: .20, .177 and .22. Essentially, repeated strokes of a lever or slide action build up pressure in a reservoir, the pressure governed by the number of strokes.

These are the air rifles that compete in national and international precision matches: Anschutz Model 335, Anschutz Model 236, Daisy Model 150 Feinwerkbau, Winchester Model 333.

"Air rifles" that require no pumping, power being supplied by a CO_2 cartridge: Benjamin Model 3030, Crosman Powermatic 500, Daisy $CO_2$300.

This variable pressure has advantages. A shooter soon learns how many strokes will deliver optimum accuracy and which pressure best suits shooting conditions. The excellent Crosman Model 760, for example, will drive a .177 pellet at about 200 foot seconds with two strokes so that it can be fired in a relatively small room. Up the number of strokes to twenty, however, and velocity climbs to 575 foot seconds, more than adequate for longer range shooting, indoors or out.

The pneumatic gun can, of course, be "fired up" for greater velocities than are possible with the spring/air gun. What's more, there is no appreciable recoil. Some shooters, however, consider repeated pumping a nuisance, since most of these guns require at least a half-dozen strokes for maximum efficiency.

With this in mind, some air-gun shooters choose the CO_2 power system since it provides repeated shots without pumping. Technically, a CO_2 gun is not a true "air" gun, but rather a "gas" gun, since CO_2 is carbon dioxide, a harmless, odorless and non-flammable gas used to add "fizz" to mixed drinks. The cartridge is inserted into the gun where its mouth is pierced but its pressure controlled by a valve system. When the gun is cocked and the trigger pulled a pre-set pressure is released to fire the pellet.

The CO_2 gun has definite advantages over both the spring/air and the pneumatic types. Cartridges are easily obtained. The guns are simple to operate and they function much like firearms. Power and velocity are more consistent than those of pneumatic guns. Accuracy may be enhanced too since the CO_2 shooter need not tire his arms by repeated pumping.

On the other hand, CO_2 convenience increases the cost of shooting. Compressed air pumped by hand is free; CO_2 cartridges cost money, albeit not a great deal. Generally, too, velocities and penetration of CO_2-powered pellets fall short of those attained by pellets fired in a pneumatic gun.

Types of Air Guns

Pick out almost any favorite powder-burning gun—Winchester, Remington, Savage, Colt or Smith & Wesson—and you will find a counterpart among the air guns. Many are visual replicas of famed guns often difficult to tell apart at 15 feet. This lends much appeal to air-gun shooting. Add to this authentic weights and sizes.

It is not my intention to influence a shooter's choice of one brand over another, but initiative and imagination deserve recognition.

The Daisy Model 1894 is authentically patterned after the famed Winchester Model 94, even to a side port loading of BBs. Daisy's 1894 is so much like the Winchester 94 and 9422 that the three are difficult to tell apart across a large room.

And you will have to take a second look to tell the Daisy Model 572 Fieldmaster from its powder-burning cousin, the Remington Model 572 Fieldmaster.

Then there is the Daisy Model 21, bringing to a shooter's mind the venerable Winchester Model 21 double-barrel shotgun. And this is just what the Daisy Model 21 is—a double-barrel BB gun, with double triggers firing one barrel, then the other.

Savage fans react to the number "99." This model number applies to one of the most famous of all hammerless lever-action big-game rifles, the Savage Model 99. Daisy's version looks not one whit like the original M99 but the magic of the number is there to help popularize the Daisy Model 99 Target BB rifle.

Among handguns, Daisy's Model 179 is a twelve-shot BB pistol, strikingly similar to Colt's hogleg Peacemaker. And Daisy's Model 177 BB handgun and its CO_2 Model 200 closely resemble the beloved Colt Woodsman.

Target pistols that are "fired up" by pumping closely resemble powder-burning counterparts: Benjamin Model 130 is available in BB, .177 or .22 caliber, Crosman Medalist II is a single-shot .22 pellet gun, Winchester's Model 363 is a .177 caliber target model designed especially for competitive shooting.

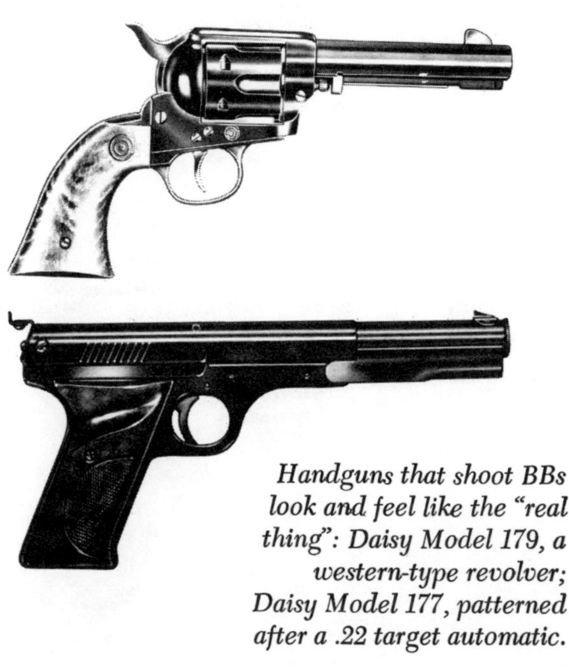

Handguns that shoot BBs look and feel like the "real thing": Daisy Model 179, a western-type revolver; Daisy Model 177, patterned after a .22 target automatic.

Benjamin does not strive for replica realism but it does offer bolt-action models. Its Model 340, 342 and 347 shoot BBs, .22 or .177 pellets respectively. The bolt closes the breech and cocks the action. Benjamin's CO_2 rifle resembles no powder burner, but being labeled Model 3030, it is automatically associated with the world's most popular firearm caliber.

Benjamin's ten-shot CO_2 pellet pistol, at a glance, is the "real thing." Each time the trigger is squeezed, a .22 pellet is fed into the breech for another shot. The finest Browning or Colt can do no more.

Sheridan is the single-shot specialist. Its line includes no repeaters, nor do its guns resemble specific firearms. Sighting and power are Sheridan's forte. Its rifles, all pneumatic, are available with Williams receiver sights, Bushnell or Weaver scopes. These are all chambered for .20 caliber (5 mm) pellets.

Crosman's M-1 Carbine bears a striking resemblance to the military M-1 but it is a slide-action spring/air gun with a magazine capacity of twenty-two BBs. The Model 622 has the general appearance of popular pump guns but its magazine is unique, consisting of a six-shot, removable rotating clip that handles .22 pellets. It is powered by Crosman's oversized 12.5-grain CO_2 cartridge.

The Crosman Powermatic 500 is a semi-automatic fifty-shot repeater, also powered by a CO_2 cartridge.

The two Crosman handguns, the Model 38 Target and the Model 38 Combat, are modeled after well-known Colt and Smith & Wesson revolvers. Powered by CO_2, each has a six-shot rotating cylinder and can be fired either single- or double-action.

And there is even a shotgun! The Crosman

A close second look is needed to tell these CO_2-powered handguns from true firearms: Benjamin semi-automatic .22; Daisy Model $CO_2$200 semi-automatic BB handgun; Crosman Peacemaker, a single-action .22 counterpart of the famous Colt; Crosman Target 38, which bears a striking resemblance to the famed Smith & Wesson K-38; Crosman Frontier Model 36, another authentic western type; Crosman Mark I, which looks like the famed Luger.

Trapmaster "1100" has the lines of a fine automatic or pump shotgun, with a .380-cylinder bore barrel. A single-shot CO_2 gun, it has a power selector for varying ranges. Shot shells are available with No. 8, No. 6 or No. 4 lead shot, and there is even a reloading kit which brings shooting cost down to about 1 cent per shot.

Savage's single-shot Model 250 Anschutz match air rifle is built along the lines of the famed Anschutz Model 1407 Match 54 .22-caliber target rifle. It fires a .177 pellet and has a recoil compensation mechanism. Some indication of its sophistication as a target gun lies in its weight: 11 pounds!

Savage's Model 335, also a single-shot .177 gun, has a break-open action. Although in no way resembling any powder-burning target guns, its 7-pound weight is an indication of its suitability as a target air gun.

Of Winchester's six air rifles, only one is a smoothbore, the Model 416, designed to handle BBs or .177 pellets interchangeably. This is a beginner's gun.

The Winchester Model 450, although lacking a bolt (it has a recessed lever action), looks remarkably like the Winchester Model 70, at least at first glance. This is probably more than coincidence. Since it weighs 7¾ pounds and fires the .177 pellet, it is intended for precision target work as well as field shooting.

Winchester's prime target model is its M333, weighing 9½ pounds and equipped with a double-piston action to eliminate recoil.

Two target pistols are included in the Winchester line. The Model 353 is calibered for either the .177 or the .22 pellet, while the 363 handles only the .177. Both have adjustable trigger pulls and micrometer rear sights. What famous powder burner do they most closely resemble? The Remington XP-100 Fireball!

I have cited only a few of the many air/gas rifles and handguns that are available, those most popular among American shooters. The variety is far greater than this. A city-bound shooter should have no problem finding a gun best suited to his pocketbook and shooting facilities.

Chapter XVII

SHOOTING ACCESSORIES

Shooting accessories are *not* necessities but they do contribute much to the more efficient use of today's rifles, shotguns and handguns. Many of us like to think of our early shooting days in the light of the barefoot boy prowling pasturelands with his pet Stevens Favorite, completely unencumbered by devices or gadgets. Maybe that boy was a happier shooter—but I'll wager that one of today's youngsters could shoot circles around him, with a strong assist from what we call accessories.

While an accessory to one shooter may be a necessity to another, in most instances they're in the nature of special equipment designed to help in a particular type of shooting. They would not necessarily be employed by *all* shooters.

Binoculars

While the spotting scope has come to be used by big-game guides and trophy hunters to spot game, a pair of binoculars is still a definite aid for this purpose. The varmint shooter, too, can use them to advantage to locate small game and predators. Deer, antelope and elk hunters of the open country of the West use them to locate resting or skulking game and to size up "trophy possibilities." About the only rifle hunter who really has little use for binoculars is the whitetail deer hunter, seeking his quarry in dense woodlands.

The optical qualities of binoculars are much the same as those of scope sights, already described. Lest the numerical designations of binoculars, such as 7×35 or 8×40, puzzle you, the first number indicates the power or magnification, while the second applies to the diameter of the objective lens, given in millimeters. Binoculars and "field glasses," incidentally, are not the same. Field glasses are, in effect, two side-by-side small telescopes which, while they may be focused individually, may not always be adjustable laterally to fit the distance between the iris of each eye. Binoculars use a prism system, for transmitting the image to the eye, including mirrors which reflect the image from the widely spaced objective lenses to the eye-fitting ocular lenses. Binoculars won't allow you to see any farther than you can with the naked eye and on this basis, some advertising is misleading. They merely bring "nearer" the object being viewed, according to the magnification. An eight-power glass, for example, brings an object eight times nearer (optically, of course) than it actually is.

Properly set, a pair of binoculars will not show you the image within two overlapping circular areas, as is so often shown in the movies! Correctly adjusted, the view is confined within a single circular plane.

The optical qualities of a pair of binoculars—or the lack of them—become most apparent when three or four pairs are examined at once. Even a poor glass will seem quite efficient compared to the naked eye. It's much like trying out a three-year-old car after having driven an eight-year-old model. The newer one seems so much better that its deficiencies are hidden by comparatively improved performance.

Don't buy glasses that are *too* powerful for your purpose. Binoculars, like scope sights, magnify body tremors. Most shooters can hold seven- or eight-power glasses sufficiently steady for effective use. Binoculars of greater power will have to be used with a rest. Glasses that are too powerful can also prove a hindrance in seeking hidden game in brushy or wooded areas, at least until you become well accustomed to them.

When I worked as a forest fire lookout, tower men were issued seven-power glasses because more powerful glasses sometimes caused them to look right through a "smoke" without seeing it!

Nearly all manufacturers and importers issue booklets describing suitable qualities in binoculars. Some of these offer sound advice in much greater detail than can be given here, although most slant the copy and advice toward their own product. Read several of these booklets and then make your own judgment without being awayed by ad copywriters!

The Hutson Chromatar spotting scope has a 45-degree-angle eyepiece for convenient use during shooting. Power ranges up to 45X. (HUTSON CORP.)

The Unertl 100 mm Team Scope's 32X maximum power unit for long-distance spotting of center-fire rifle matches. (J. UNERTL OPTICAL CO.)

Spotting Scopes

These are used primarily by pistol and rifle shooters to save walking to the target after each shot. Handgun shooters usually mount a spotting scope on the cover of their shooting boxes for a steady rest, these boxes being designed for this purpose. Riflemen, shooting prone, use the spotting scopes on low tripods. Since spotting scopes are usually of at least twenty-power, holding them in a shooter's hands is out of the question due to extreme magnification of even the slightest body movement.

Scopes come in two types, the prismatic and the draw-tube, with the former design, like prismatic binoculars, using a set of reflective prisms to conduct the image to the viewer's eye. The draw-tube is not unlike the old-fashioned "pirate's telescope," which is focused by sliding one tube within another.

Most spotting scopes are of the 20X to 30X range, although interchangeable eyepieces can vary the scope's power up to 60X! How well do they work? A 20X scope, of good quality, will easily point out .22 bullet holes in the bull's-eye at 100 yards.

Most are designed in the conventional "straight-look-through" system, while a few have a 45-degree eyepiece which allows the shooter to peer through an eyepiece *projecting to the side.* With such an eyepiece, a rifleman can use his scope merely by turning his head slightly and without shifting his body position.

Just as with telescope sights, the field of view decreases with magnification, with a 20X scope equipped with a 60-mm objective lens having a field of about 12 feet at 100 yards. Many spotting scopes, however, are rated at 1000 yards with the field then designated at 120 to 125 feet.

While the prismatic scope is by far the best, it is more costly. However, certain non-prismatic models are excellent. Bushnell's 9X to 30X variable spotting scope, for example, boasts a 40 mm objective lens and an instant-focus device, along with its ability to zoom in for close-ups. In 1971 its price was about $30, when the better prismatic scopes were selling four to five times that price.

You have probably noted that the field of view in spotting scopes is much narrower than those of the scope sight and binoculars but this should cause no concern. A spotting scope, filling its

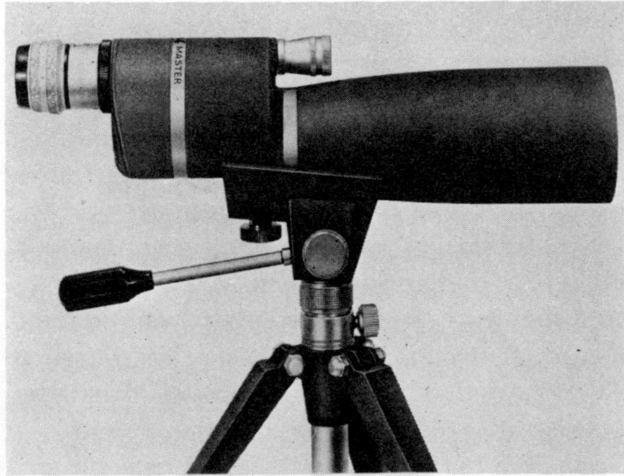

The Weatherby Sightmaster can zoom from 20X to 45X with a twist of the dial. (WEATHERBY, INC.)

purpose, is aligned on a target before use and is not touched until shooting is finished. The narrow field of view is more than ample to cover a target. When used for other purposes the narrow field of view is, of course, a handicap. Scanning a distant view with one will require that you "pan" very slowly.

Shooting Glasses

Shooting glasses serve to protect a shooter's eyes from blown primers, escaping gas, barrel bursts, blow-backs, stray shot and even bits of clay birds on the trap or skeet field. They help a gunner utilize the greatest possible light on a cloudy day, and inversely they eliminate harmful glare under a bright sun. Few professionals shoot without them, whether with rifle, pistol or shotgun.

I'm not referring to the drugstore variety of sunglasses but rather to optically corrected lenses, designed for shooters. Sunglasses offer token protection, but the lenses are usually flimsy and the color or tint of the glass is offered for its eye-appeal rather than for its protective qualities.

Yellow or amber lenses are considered best for dull or cloudy days when every possible bit of available light is needed for fine shooting. Green, on the other hand, seems best for turning back the harmful infrared and ultraviolet rays. Lenses for shooting glasses may be ground to a shooter's prescription and if he uses corrective lenses for reading or everyday use, this is generally recommended for his shooting glasses also.

Recoil Pads

While these can only loosely be considered accessories, many shotguns and most rifles are sold without them. A few shooters can withstand the incessant pounding from a 12 gauge shotgun through an afternoon's shooting, but rarely without a recoil pad. A high-power rifle, also, can punish a shooter, creating an inclination toward flinching as a result. The answer is a recoil pad, a perforated or slotted replacement of the gun's butt plate. Most recoil pads are ¾ inch, ⅞ inch or 1 inch thick and made of rubber, firm enough to hold its shape and soft enough to absorb much of the recoil and to cushion the blow from the shooter's shoulder. A recoil pad sometimes serves to lengthen a gun's pull also.

Unless used for this purpose, however, bear in mind that a corresponding thickness must be removed from the gun butt before attaching a pad. Otherwise the stock may prove too long for most efficient use. The pad replaces the metal or fiber butt plate with which shoulder guns are equipped and attaching such a pad is a simple matter which anyone can accomplish with a screwdriver, barring the need for cutting the stock, of course. A slip-on pad, of all rubber, is available, made to fit snugly over the butt like a rubber glove over a physician's hand. It can be removed at will.

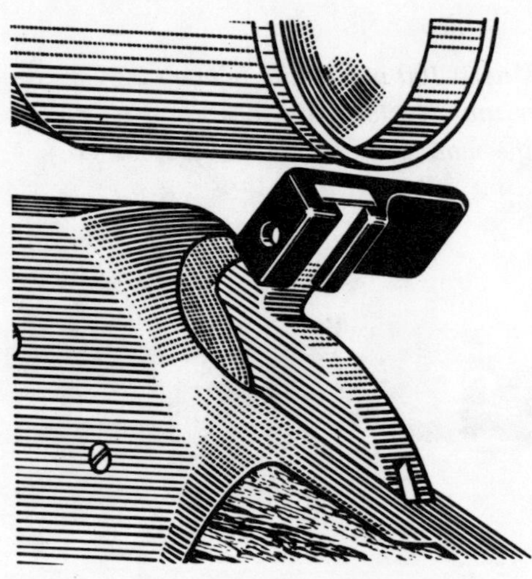

Williams Auxiliary Hammer Extension for use on rifles with low-mounted scopes. (WILLIAMS GUN SIGHT CO.)

Hammer Extensions

Such rifles as the Winchester Model 94 and Model 9422, and the Marlin 336 and 39 may prove difficult to cock when a low-mounted scope sight extends back over the hammer. The Williams auxiliary hammer extension, which can be attached to the hammer by means of a small setscrew, widens the hammer, either to the right or left, so that it protrudes to the side of the scope tube, eliminating fumbling for a quick shot.

The Williams swivel adapter makes it possible to attach a sling to a tubular magazine rifle. (WILLIAMS GUN SIGHT CO.)

Detachable Sling Swivels

A rifle sling, so handy on the target range or in open-country shooting, can be a nuisance in brush or heavy forest cover. Removing the sling with conventional swivels isn't always easy. The hooks too often won't pass smoothly through the swivel eyelets. Williams Quick Detachable sling swivels eliminate this problem and allow a sling to be removed, or replaced, in a matter of seconds. A push button releases the swivel and the sling from the stock screw almost as quickly as I can tell about it. Such swivels are available for attaching to wooden forearms, or with metal bands for attachment to the barrel, in the case of a slide-action gun. This is done with a band encircling the barrel. With such a rig, it's possible to use the sling for carrying the gun into the hunting area and removing it quickly for actual hunting.

The Guide Strap

Probably because I now do little target shooting, I rarely use a sling in the recommended manner, with the loop about my left arm. In hunting, this is too much trouble and too slow. A simplified sling is the Williams Guide Strap, a one-piece sling which can be adjusted for length by means of a single keeper button. On

Williams Guide Strap, a one-piece simplified sling that is easier and faster to use than conventional slings. (WILLIAMS GUN SIGHT CO.)

the target range, the military or Whelen sling is superior but for hunting, the Williams model is simpler, easier and faster. For offhand hunting shots, it should be pre-set as to length so that you can quickly "climb into it." A shift in the keeper button's position, a matter of five seconds, then lengthens the strap for gun toting.

Pistol Grips

Few handguns come from the factory with grips that fit the purchaser. Most of them are too small, seemingly made for children and women. A few of the huskier revolvers, such as the Magnums, have more ample stocks, but even these don't necessarily fit well. Shooters with big hands or long fingers particularly have difficulty with factory grips. I once owned a .32 revolver which I had to hold in my fingertips in order to get my trigger finger into position!

Custom grips eliminate this holding problem. In addition, their use helps control recoil of heavy handguns. Most have a thumb rest and a heel flare that keeps the gun firmly aligned despite recoil. Proper grips on a revolver—and some automatics—make cocking a smoother operation. Too, custom grips lend a gun some degree of individuality.

Not all such grips are really custom-made. While some firms, notably Herrett's of Twin Falls, Idaho, carves grips to order, working from a hand outline for mail customers, others carry a vast variety of molded stocks or grips in all shapes for nearly all handguns made in America today. The latter are, of course, less costly than the custom-carved models but since such a wide choice is available, a shooter can generally buy a pre-molded set of grips that will fit perfectly. A set of grips, carved to your personal hand-fitting specifications will, of course, be even more satisfactory. At any rate, you'll rarely see a factory set of grips on the firing line of an important match!

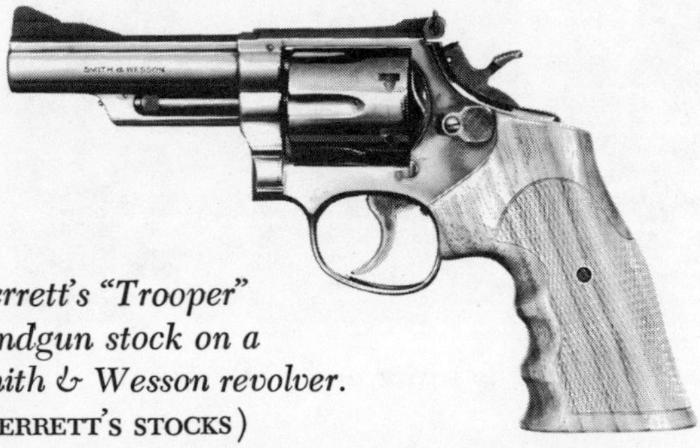

Herrett's "Trooper" handgun stock on a Smith & Wesson revolver. (HERRETT'S STOCKS)

Carved grips are usually of walnut although you may have these made from any hard and stable material. Molded grips are of a plastic material which is moisture- and perspiration-proof, the latter at about one third the cost of customized grips.

Trigger Shoe

A trigger shoe is a little-known accessory, except among expert handgun shooters who appreciate the importance of correct trigger behavior. The shoe is attached to the trigger by means of a tiny setscrew. The shoe, in effect, widens the trigger so that pull is directly backwards despite any tendency on the part of the shooter to pull sideways. Also, some trigger shoes have an adjustable "stop" which eliminates trigger "backlash," which occurs with the continued travel of the trigger after the shot is fired. Such trigger shoes, however, cannot be attached to guns having wide, target-type triggers.

Grip Adapter

The revolver grip adapter increases the heft of the butt where it joins the frame, thus placing the weight of the gun more firmly upon the middle finger and raising the height of the gun in the hand slightly, so that cocking is easier. The adapter is held in place by a spring clip which fits over the butt frame after removal of the wood grips. The latter can be replaced, over the spring clip, without cutting or altering. Two minutes with a screwdriver will accomplish the addition of a grip adapter, and better scores will result.

Carbide Lamps

Despite the many improvements in guns and the innumerable gadgets that go with shooting, nothing seems to have been devised to improve upon the miner's or carbide lamp for blackening the sights of a handgun. Blackened sights are essential in cutting down minor reflections or glare, especially on the front sight. Holding the sight close to the flame of a burning carbide lamp coats the sight with a fine layer of dull jet-black soot which causes the sight to stand out solidly and clearly defined even under the most difficult light conditions. These little lamps will fit in a shooter's hand and take up little room, along with a season's supply of carbide, in his gun box.

Bullet Traps

While there are bullet traps that will safely stop a .30/06, .357 or .44 Magnum, most of them are used in home basements with .22 rim-fire rifles and handguns. These traps make possible year-round shooting, no matter what the weather may be. They're made of steel-plate construction and contain a centrifugal channel that guides the bullet in a circular motion until its power or velocity is dissipated and it falls into a hopper. Some shooters retrieve the bullets, melt them down and cast more with the lead. This type of trap eliminates the need for sand, baled cotton or log backstops, although some provision should be made for stopping an occasional "stray" which may miss the trap aperture, in front of which is hung the target. Some of these traps are easily portable, weighing as little as 17 pounds. For as little as $20 and a couple of light bulbs, many a home basement can be converted into a shooting range for .22 pistols or rifles.

Heavy-duty traps are available, too, for guns of greater velocity or energy, but using these guns in home ranges isn't practical, unless the members of your family or the neighbors have no objection to noise!

Traps

Handtraps make possible inexpensive and interesting shotgun shooting, especially if your partner who operates the unit is bent upon convincing you that you're not the deadly shot you'd have him believe. A simple unit, the handtrap clasps a clay bird and is operated by swinging back the thrower's arm and then thrusting it forward in a wide arc, completing the motion with a snap of the wrist. This frees the bird and it soars into the air. Direction and angle of flight are entirely up to the trap man. These traps are ideal for training shotgun beginners, since the clay bird's arc of flight can be kept within easy, yet varying, shooting range. For more expert shooters, some handtraps will throw "doubles."

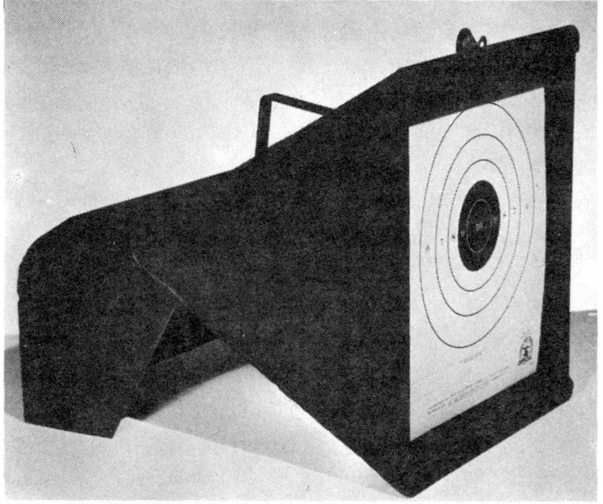

Bullet trap of steel construction makes year-round shooting possible indoors. (DETROIT BULLET TRAP CO.)

Bullet trap eliminates need for elaborate sand, baled cotton or log backstops. (SHERIDAN PRODUCTS, INC.)

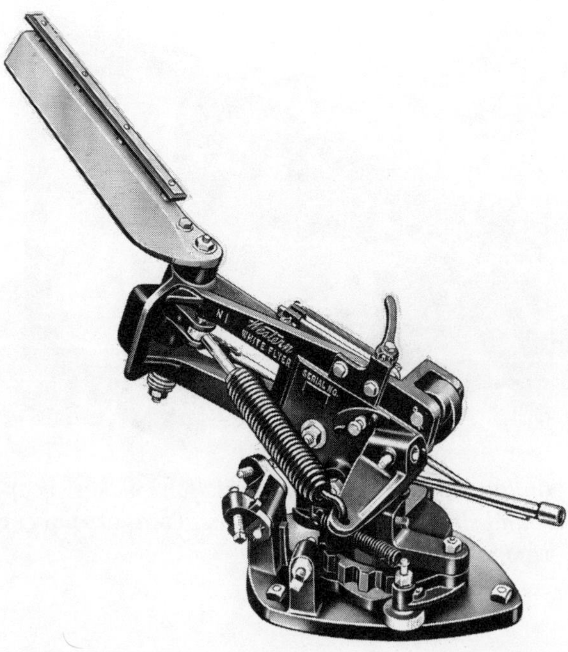

Winchester/Western "White Flyer" trap popular at shooting clubs throws clay birds at all angles. (WINCHESTER/WESTERN)

The Trius Trap can trigger singles or doubles with the pull of a string. (TRIUS PRODUCTS, INC.)

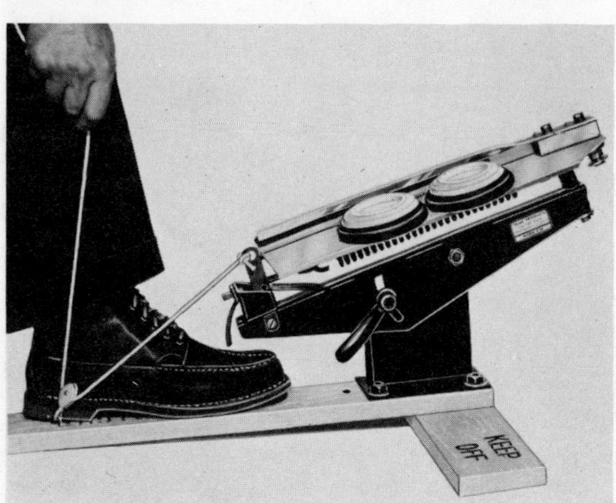

For more elaborate setups, such as at shooting clubs, private estates or even the rear deck of a cabin cruiser, there are spring and electrically powered magazine feeding traps which release birds at the touch of a button. These, too, can be adjusted for angle of flight and some are capable of firing doubles.

Handgun Cases

Fine target handguns should not be carried in a holster, particularly if they're equipped with adjustable sights. Serious handgun target shooters acquire a handgun case at about the time they purchase a spotting scope. Such cases hold three to five guns, either revolvers or automatics, in padded brackets. A tilt-up lid is generally equipped with a bracket for holding the scope. The case is then set up on a shooting table or stand at the firing line with the scope directed to the target. Although handgun cases vary in size and design, they're generally equipped with drawers or compartments to hold ammunition, carbide lamp, shooting glasses and gun tools. When closed, they encompass not only the gun but the scope and look not unlike a small suitcase with a carrying strap or handle. A Pachmayr model features an adjustable bridge that will fit snugly any type of handgun, so that tipping or even dropping the box accidentally will not disturb the guns.

Handgun case holds pistols securely against damage, has room for ammunition and serves as a spotting scope stand. (PACHMAYR GUN WORKS, INC.)

Game Calls

Calling devices, either mouth- or hand-operated, are in use on practically all game animals. The idea isn't new, by any means, having been used by the Indians, and more recently by moose-hunting guides. In the case of game birds and animals, the calls imitate the love, mating or feeding sounds, while those used to attract predators imitate the screech of a dying rabbit, the standard diet of carnivorous animals.

Great skill is required in the use of these calls—it's easy to frighten the quarry away with a sour note! However, my first attempt at crow calling resulted, quite accidentally, in a sky full of cawing and craning black devils. Never having used a crow call before, I hid in a pine thicket and began sending out what I believed were a series of seductive bits of crow conversation. Quite by chance, I apparently sounded a bewitching and appealing call to the crows, for in a matter of minutes, some five or six dozen crows appeared overhead, wheeling about as they peered into the pines to locate the source of the calls. Unfortunately, I'd chosen my blind too well. I couldn't shoot through the thick screen of pine branches and I was never again that successful at calling!

Observing and listening to an expert caller will teach you more about the use of these calls than reading all of the several books that have been written on the subject. Transposing animal and bird calls onto paper has never been successfully done. You must *hear* them to learn them. Some sportsmen's clubs conduct off-season calling contests where you can pick up some sound pointers. The next best possibility is to purchase recordings which all game-call manufacturers offer.

Most calls are mouth-operated, with the caller not actually blowing into the call but rather "talking" the animal's or bird's "language" into it. This is the most difficult type to learn to use.

A call easier to master is one which has a rubber bellows, known as a Scotch call. It resembles a regular mouth call, except for the addition of the bellows unit. Shaking or depressing the rubber unit creates the calling sound. A surprisingly authentic "quack" can be rendered when calling ducks, simply by swinging the bellows loosely. By opening and closing the mouth of the call with the palm of the hand, the chuckling or chortling call of a contentedly feeding duck can be effected. The bellows-type call is used very successfully on predators and squirrels.

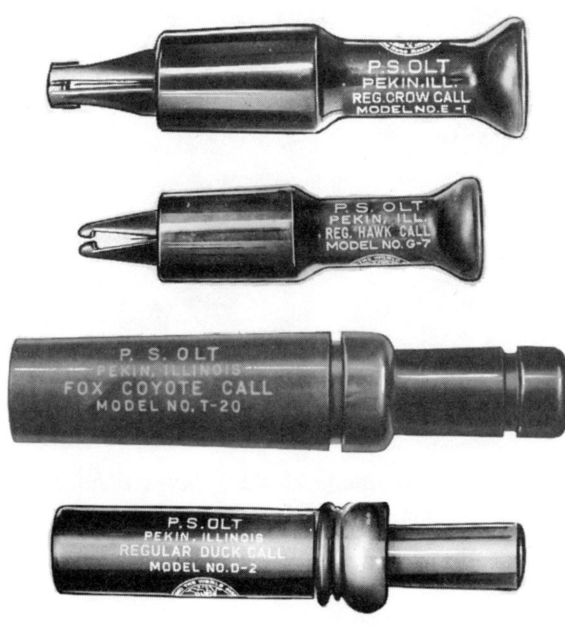

A few of the many calls available for attracting game. These are operated by the caller "talking" into the call. Pictured here are calls for crows, hawks, ducks, foxes and coyotes. (P. S. OLT CO.)

The bellows-type game call operates by shaking or depressing the rubber bellows. Pictured here are squirrel calls by P. S. Olt Co. and Lohman Call Co. The predator call is by Scotch Game Call Co.

Camouflage clothing helps a hunter blend into the background. (SCOTCH GAME CALL CO.)

Camouflage Suits

Having done my early shooting in Maine and New Hampshire, traditionally the home of the big-checkered shirt, I scoffed for some time at camouflage clothing. I ate crow during an odd-ball Minnesota duck hunt, however.

At the height of the November duck flights, every slough and waterhole seemed to be rimmed with duck hunters, so we sought out a farmer's flooded cornfield, at the edge of which we posted ourselves among some leafless and scraggly willows. My two partners were each clad in camouflage parkas and we all wore waders or boots. However, in place of a parka, I wore a green and black checkered shirt with hunting cap to match. As we called to ducks circling the area, they darted toward our water-hole, but always flared away before coming into range. My partners decided I was the culprit and insisted I return to the car, a half-mile away, to don a spare camouflage parka. Grumbling against this new-fangled nonsense, I plowed through knee-deep water to the road and put on the parka. Twenty minutes later I was back to my station. Ducks then began to plunge into our underwater cornfield, completely oblivious to us until too late. I bought a camouflage suit the next morning!

Two types of camouflage material are made. One is a solid, hard weave which is not only a disguising material that blends with brush or woods, but also protects its wearer against wind. A lighter weight type is of netting, for warm weather use.

Using camouflage clothing does not make you invisible. It merely helps you blend with the background; so while you wear it, be sure you *do* blend. Don't stand so that your figure is silhouetted against the sky, for example. Also, any premature movements made as the game approaches will likely be spotted. Remain quiet until you're ready to shoot. The mottled gray-brown-green and tan patterns will prove effective during the hunting of varmints, deer and crows. During the winter, with snow on the ground, the conventional pattern is out of the question, of course, and you must then wear white to blend with a snow background. In a pinch, even a discarded bed sheet will serve.

Dedicated crow hunters go so far as to wear face masks and gloves of material matching their clothing. This may seem a little farfetched at first, but consider how a man's white face and hands must stand out against a background of darker colors! Crow shooters think from the point of view of the crow!

Chapter XVIII

HUNTING HINTS

Predator Calling

Predators will come running to investigate the anguished squeal of a dying rabbit. Object: stealing and eating said rabbit. The surest way to hunt predators, therefore, is to bring them to you by imitating the rabbit cry. Predators, depending upon the part of the country in which you live, may include fox, coyote, bobcats—and even house cats gone wild. Fox, however, may be protected in some regions, as a game animal.

Imitating the rabbit is most easily done with a predator call as explained in the last chapter. Don't underrate these—gray foxes have been known to leap into a predator hunter's blind and hawks have swooped down upon a caller!

Some calls, however, are pitched too low, sounding not unlike the blat of a sheep or young deer. Better calls have adjustable reeds which can be pitched a note or two higher. Anyone who has heard the screech of a dying rabbit will know what I mean. The sound usually starts with two or three relatively low moans, then rises to a crescendo of piercing screams that will prickle your spine. The call ends with a wavering moan. It can't be described with words. You'll have to listen to one, either in real life or on a recording.

Calling should be done from a blind of brush or other material which will afford good cover and which overlooks a fairly wide area, *upwind* of the stand. January to May, when food is scarce and animals must forage farther afield, is the best time of year. August, when the young start to roam, is also good. Late afternoon and evening are more productive than the broad daylight of high noon. A quiet day will allow your call to carry farther since you must consider that wind will cut down the range of sound.

Many advise "Don't smoke while hunting," and this is a sound rule though not as important as generally supposed. It makes little difference if you're hunting upwind, and the danger of a tip-off lies in some critter's sharp eyes seeing the drift of smoke rather than smelling it. Some go so far as to advise garlic under the armpits, or balsam fir needles in your pockets to overcome the man smell. This advice results in a hunter's smelling like a man with garlic or balsam overtones. A man smells like a man to a wild animal.

Animals most likely to respond to calling are the foxes, either red or gray. Once you start calling, watch closely every bit of cover, especially along the edge of clearings, ravines, or ditches, as approaching game will take advantage of these. Keep your rifle or your shotgun at ready. A pair of binoculars will be helpful. If you see nothing within ten to fifteen minutes after your initial call, try another and if nothing appears within a quarter of an hour, move on to another stand, at least a half-mile away.

If a fox appears but keeps his distance, use a "mouse call," something relatively new which imitates the squeak of a mouse. Few foxes can resist this appetizing call.

Wildcats, as well as wild house cats, are stealthy hunters, pussyfooting an inch or two at a time until they're ready to pounce on their prey. For cat hunting, stick to a blind at least a half-hour.

Rabbit Hunting

The smallest of our true game animals, the cottontail rabbit, is helpless against predators, except for its peculiar zigzag bobbing pace. However, it has the good sense to duck into brush piles or abandoned dens of other animals and thus survives well. A prolific animal, the female may reproduce at six months and have as many as twenty young in a year. A mother cottontail will literally give the shirt off her back, often lining her nest with fur plucked from her own hide! The cottontail doesn't like to swim but is perfectly capable of it if necessary. One eluded our dogs during a cold February day and plunged belly-flop into an open stream, swimming determinedly across. In admiration, we called off the dogs and didn't shoot.

Like the grouse, it will lie close, then suddenly pop into high gear, throwing the hunter completely off guard. If chased by dogs, it frequently holes up.

You'll get the most sport simply by walking along in cottontail areas, usually swamps or low hillsides that have been logged over, and kicking at every brush pile, blowdown or stump. Don't travel stealthily. If a rabbit doesn't pop out after a kick, wait a moment. It takes a rabbit a few minutes to make up its mind sometimes! Very cold days when there is fresh snow on the ground are best, since you can locate new tracks easily. The cold weather cuts the tularemia rate, considerably. Humans can be infected by handling ailing rabbits with bare hands, especially if there are skin breaks or cuts. Wear rubber gloves when dressing suspected rabbits and cook them well. White or yellow spots on the liver or spleen indicate the rabbit is diseased and one that acts sluggishly is probably also infected. Well cooked, however, rabbit meat is not only safe but delicious. To field-dress a rabbit, slit the belly, grasp the forelegs in one hand and the hind legs in the other and snap the animal away from you without letting go. The entrails will pop out.

Running shots are the order of the day usually, so a shotgun in any gauge is well suited. A semiautomatic or pump .22 rifle will give you some fast sport if you're careful about the direction in which you spray lead.

The snowshoe rabbit is really the "varying hare," and he's bigger than the cottontail as well as smarter and faster. Because he turns white in the winter, some call him the "white rabbit," and in some parts of the East he's known incorrectly as a jack rabbit. He's equally at home in alder and softwood swamps or high on mountainsides and he's best hunted with dogs. I like slow trailers in preference to dogs that run the snowshoe rabbit so fast the latter forgets to circle back and leaves the county! A slow-running dog will push a rabbit at the latter's own pace so that he'll circle at least once or twice. This circular course brings the rabbit back to the hunter, or very close by.

Unlike the cottontail, the snowshoe rabbit seldom holes up and will keep running as long as the dogs trail him. This doesn't mean that he's helpless, for he has nearly as many tricks up his fur-lined sleeve as the fox. He may backtrack his own trail when pressed hard, or leap suddenly to one side and run parallel to his earlier course. Later, he'll swerve quickly and run at right angles to it. I've known a snowshoe rabbit to circle within a 10-foot area, clockwise and then counterclockwise, leaving a mass of tracks and scents that few dogs can decipher. On powdery, dry snow, he's likely to get "cold feet," so that he leaves tracks not as lusciously scented as those of the cottontail.

Nature sometimes plays a dirty trick on the snowshoe rabbit, turning him white before snow falls. He then stands out on the bare ground, looking not unlike a small but speedy polar bear and a much easier target! Shotguns are best weapons, because a snowshoe in high gear is a difficult target, although a fast-shooting .22 rifle provides great sport.

The jack rabbit—not to be confused with the snowshoe—is a big-eared, long-legged variety of the western plains who is so fast he seems to outrun bullets! At other times, he sits in an apparent stupor, an easy standing shot. You'll need a long-range rifle with a scope, preferably a varminter-type rifle.

The jacks are rarely plentiful enough to warrant hunting them entirely on foot. Best technique is to ride the roads slowly while a partner "glasses" the area with binoculars. When you spot a rabbit in the distance, park the car and stalk on foot. Depend on long-range shooting skill rather than your stalking ability, however. Most jacks have eyes comparable to those of hawks and your chances of getting close are slim.

The Woodchuck

Also known as groundhog, the woodchuck digs a burrow with two entrances. Farmers don't like him because he's fond of clover, beans and even young cornstalks. He's been known to climb leaning apple trees! Hibernating in the winter, he likes to get out early and romp on spring snowbanks.

Hunting is best before spring grasses have grown tall enough to hide the dirt mounds that identify his den. Also, he's less wily then, after long months of hibernation. You'll find him in hayfields, orchards, in the woods bordering fields, and along stone walls. Alert to any suspicious movement, he's best hunted from behind hedges, clumps of brush, knolls or stone walls, quite often by crawling on your stomach.

A hard-hitting rifle in the varminter class is needed, with a six- to eight-power scope. He must be killed instantly, or he'll crawl into his hole and die a lingering death from his wounds—hence a .22 is unsuitable, in fact, cruel. If one doesn't offer a clear shot, give a sharp whistle between your fingers. He's a whistler himself and this will usually bring him to an erect position for a moment—but not for much longer! Woodchuck meat is delicious and a New Hampshire farmer on whose land I used to hunt, preferred them to chicken, of which he had thousands!

Crows

It's practically impossible to walk within shotgun range of a crow, and stalking one with a rifle isn't easy either! You'll have to call them in to your blind. There you can shoot them to your heart's content and you'll hear nary an objection from anyone. The crow is the worst of predators. He loves the eggs of ducks, quail, pheasant, grouse and he likes freshly sown grain.

Calling from a blind is the only consistently successful hunting method. For further attraction, however, rig a stuffed owl—preferably a great horned owl—not over 15 yards from the blind. Crows hate owls, even stuffed ones, and they'll come for miles to plague one. A mechanical owl that flaps its wings at the pull of a string from the blind makes crows lose all sense of caution. A live owl or hawk, not necessarily in a cage, will do an even better job. The crows won't actually attack it, merely darting and swooping at it. A tame hawk or owl should be tied to a tree limb, however.

Cat lovers will howl in protest, but a live house cat in a cage, or tethered by a collar, will prove a great crow attraction. The cat won't get hurt, but its spitting and snarling will enrage the crows and they'll again throw caution out the window to become easy targets. A live pet crow sometimes helps, providing he's properly trained not to give an alarm signal.

Let the first crow to arrive get a good look at your decoy rig but don't shoot him. He'll call the others much more efficiently than you can do it! After you've killed at least four, however, and activity dies down a little, tie two crows at each end of an 8-foot string and flip them over a limb so that they dangle in the breeze near your decoy. This will bring more crows!

A shotgun is necessary, of course, since most of the shooting is on the wing, but have a .22 rifle in the blind, too, for potting the "sitters" which will light in nearby trees to watch. Trap loads, because of their dense patterns, are well suited, although some hunters prefer high-velocity loads of 7½ or 6 shot. Strangely, the firing of guns won't frighten the crows unduly, if they don't see you. After the first barrage they'll leave but will come back when you resume calling. Some flocks make three or four return trips.

The Porcupine

There's an old woodsman's belief that porcupines should be protected because they're the only animals which a man can overtake and kill with a club when he's lost and faced with starvation. Foresters counter with the claim that a single "porky" will ruin $6000 worth of lumber in its lifetime, by girdling trees as it eats bark. Hunting-dog owners aren't fond of them either, since many a dog has learned that a porcupine, while it can't throw its quills, is mighty fast about flipping its tail! Also, these walking pincushions will gnaw such items as ax handles, canoe paddles, camp furniture, kitchen sideboards, picnic tables, and even privy seats! They have few natural enemies, with only the bobcat, lynx, and fisher having learned to flip porky over before gutting its unprotected belly.

Porcupines are hard to kill. The first one I ever shot took *nine* .22 slugs from my handgun and I never again used a .22 on one. By strange contrast, a sharp rap on the nose with a stick will often kill one. However, use a high-power rifle or handgun on them for a quick, humane kill. They're found usually near rocky ledges where there are small caves, and quite often near abandoned buildings.

The Bobcat and Lynx

Much has been written about these two wilderness killers by writers who've never seen one outside of a zoo. To know and understand the cats of the wild, you have to live among them!

They feed on all small game up to and including animals as large as deer. Some naturalists say cats kill deer "occasionally." During one morning, I once found three deer carcasses which had been brought down the night before by cats! Such killings are easy to identify. The cat gnaws around the rump and hind quarters and then makes a token attempt to bury the remainder by scraping up grass, leaves or forest duff around it.

Cats have other interesting habits, too. Among them is a curiosity about man. They'll follow a man through the woods for great distances and I've proved this to myself by circling back and finding cat tracks running parallel to mine! Cats love to walk along fallen logs and they'll investigate anything that moves in the woods. Hence they're susceptible to traps. The first time you hear one scream, you'll want to go rescue the woman who's being tortured—for that's what a cat often sounds like! Cats are generally credited with an average of 20 pounds, but northern species I've seen average closer to 30. In 1954, a 61-inch, 41-pounder was shot near Kezar Lake, Maine, and the unofficial New Hampshire "big cat" weighed in at 51 pounds! Bobcats and lynx should not be construed as the same animal. They're not the same, the latter somewhat larger and rarer than the bobcat. I've seen only one lynx in the woods during thirty years, other than those caught in traps, of course.

Bobcat hunting is best done with dogs which trail the cats until the latter tree. Shooting one down is then easy. Trailing, however, is rugged sport, usually done in the winter and on snowshoes. Lacking good "cat dogs"—and these are rare—calling them as described earlier is the most effective. A .22 handgun is usually all that is needed when hunting with dogs, but in calling, you'll need a rifle of the varminter class for long shots.

Ruffed Grouse

This is the king of the upland birds in the minds of many and he is an interesting quarry. He plunges deep into snowbanks to keep warm in the dead of winter; he loves apples that have been touched by frost; he "dusts" himself on gravel roads during early fall mornings; and he can be shot with a handgun, despite his reputation as a rocketing aerial target.

Knowing its feeding habits will help you locate the grouse. He has adapted himself to semi-agricultural environment so that he haunts abandoned farms yet still retains his more primitive feeding habits, being fond of chokecherries, blueberries, wild grapes, pa'tridge berries and beechnuts. In the winter he feeds on the buds of poplar, alder, hazel, willow, beech and maple. In turn, he's among the finest eating of our wild birds.

I've already pointed out that in wilderness areas, the grouse may stand for several handgun shots but in areas more heavily hunted, you'll need a staunch dog and some skill with a shotgun, the 16 gauge being a favorite, loaded with No. 6 or 7½ shot. The 12 or 20 gauge are also suitable, but not the .410. The grouse flushes with a sudden eruption of beating wings that will startle you, flying among trees at seemingly reckless speeds, dodging and twisting and he has an uncanny habit of quickly placing a large tree between himself and a shotgun!

The Raccoon

A black stripe across his face lends the raccoon the look of a masked bandit and the stripes on his tail would indicate that he's been caught and is serving time! He'll wash his food in water before eating it, and this may include anything from fish to birds, nuts, fruits and his favorite, sweet corn. The coon is supposed to hibernate, but I have seen a number abroad in the dead of winter.

Coon hunting is done at night, with trained dogs running the masked quarry until it trees. Dogs, clamoring at the foot of the tree, try to keep him there until the hunter appears. This doesn't always work, since many a coon has escaped by jumping from one tree to another, or even into the scrambling dogs. Most states where coon hunting is permitted allow the hunter to carry a .22 handgun or rifle, or possibly a shotgun, along with a flashlight. A .22 is handiest to carry and will do the job amply—if the coon waits in the tree for you. The fur has value, though this depends greatly upon the current market. The meat is excellent but should be soaked overnight in soda and water before cooking.

Quail

The quail or "bobwhite" is to the South what the grouse is to New England. He's smaller than the grouse and he's a bird that lives close to man. This doesn't make the quail any less sporty to hunt. It's a bird of the open clearings and fields adjacent to wood lots and briar patches. Flush a covey of quail and they will scatter, only to regroup. A well-trained dog is almost a necessity, although quail may be hunted, like grouse, by "jump shooting."

This calls for walking in quail habitat and shooting as they flush before you. Don't shoot the first bird, for chances are he'll unravel your nerves and you'll miss. Use this first bird as a warning, since a flock rarely flushes all at once. Other birds will follow in a moment or two. This is work for the scattergun, of course, with an open-bore 16 or 20 considered ideal with No. 9 shot.

The Badger

There's a strong case for the badger as a beneficial species, for he helps keep down the population of rodents such as mice, rats, gophers and prairie dogs. His abandoned dens offer shelter from predators for such game as rabbit, quail and some grouse. In country where horses are still used, he's hated and killed off because he litters the countryside with dangerous holes. A vicious fighter, he's in a class with the wildcat when it comes to scrapping. A member of the weasel family, he weighs 17 to 18 pounds and is up to 30 inches long. His sharp claws allow him to dig at a rate that makes him seem to disappear into the ground!

You'll need a varminter-class rifle with a scope, as the little .22 is inadequate. A pair of binoculars will help you locate him in open country, although he's changing his habits somewhat and is frequently found in timbered areas.

The Opossum

Because of its nocturnal habits, the 'possum is hard to hunt. It nests in abandoned game holes, small caves and underbrush heaps and is primarily an animal of the South, although it is found as far north as New York. I've never seen one in New England. It likes to clean up highway kills. Some southern cooks reportedly can concoct culinary delights with 'possum meat—but others classify it with the skunk and coyote because of its carrion-eating habits.

Fox

Biologists are fast concluding that the fox, as a predator, makes little difference in the population of small-game species, providing these have "escape cover." Most advocate the removal of fox bounties where these still exist, but it's not a popular belief in areas where hunters make a sideline business of bounties.

The traditional method of hunting fox, of course, is with hounds. The fox, like the rabbit, will return close to the point where he was "jumped" by the dog or hunter. The latter has only to post himself strategically for a shot during the "round trip." The fox likes to run along the top of stone walls, or along ravines and stream beds and he'll take advantage of the cover afforded by brush or woods. For this hunting, a full-choke 12 gauge shotgun loaded with No. 2 shot is best, since the fox will probably be loping by at a good clip. Keep yourself out of sight when "on stand" and don't make any unnecessary or sudden moves until you bring up the gun to shoot. You'll have to shoot fast. I once missed one at 12 yards because when he "was comin', he was also goin'," seemingly having turned himself inside out to escape.

In the Middle West, where much of the farm country is blocked off in mile squares or "blocks," hunters use civilian-band short-wave radio to converge their forces, once a fox has been spotted. They use no dogs and shoot with varminter rifles and scope sights. Calling fox, as explained earlier, is growing in popularity and is probably the most effective method.

Coyote

These are increasing their range as evidenced by a stepped-up program in New York state in

1956 to cut down depredations there. More than 20 were trapped or shot in Maine during 1972. Calling coyotes is about the only way to get them within shooting range, as explained in the predator calling section. You'll need a flat-shooting, long-range varminter rifle.

Cougar

The only authentic record of a cougar's being killed in the East in recent years was that of a big cat trapped in northwestern Maine in 1938, in country where I used to roam extensively. During the summer of 1960 I took part in a number of Minnesota cougar hunts, following alarms by neighboring farmers. Invariably we uncovered large dog tracks.

Cougar hunting is a western sport, of course—one that requires a trained hound pack, good horses and a clever guide. Once the cat is treed or cornered by the dogs, a .22 handgun will take care of the situation, despite tall tales of great danger that have come out of too many cougar hunts.

The Pheasant

The great grain belt of the Middle West and the prairie states forms the nucleus of America's ring-neck pheasant shooting and there you'll rarely locate this exotic bird far from a grain field, especially corn. However, he's also found over a widespread range in the East and Far West—again close to a grain supply. The pheasant is changing its habits somewhat, however. He's harder to flush than he was twenty-five years ago and he has taken to running ahead of the dogs and hunters.

To counter this, the best hunting method is to have three or four or more hunters walk through a cornfield parallel some 15 to 20 yards apart. Post hunters at the far edge of the field so that the birds are gradually squeezed between the two lines of hunters. When the pheasants reach the posted hunters, they must then flush.

One or two hunters can work a field alone and may get a few shots, but the above method will guarantee more shooting. A 12 gauge pump or automatic is a favorite gun, although the double is still popular, either using No. 6 shot. Most states allow the shooting of cocks only, easily distinguished by their brilliant plumage and white ring about the neck.

The Mourning Dove

It surprises me that sixteen or seventeen of the northern tier states don't have an open season on mourning doves. The birds merely fly south to furnish sport in the southern states. Also, game biologists report that we're not harvesting a sufficient crop of the doves, despite an increasing population.

Slightly smaller than a quail, the mourning dove is a sporty target, literally leaping into the air from the ground. Since their requirements include water, grain, and trees, they're fairly easy to locate. Watch the flights during the day to see where they're feeding—likely some farmer's barley, wheat or oat field. As evening approaches (the best time for hunting), notice the direction of the flights for this is when they head for water. Locate the waterhole, post yourself under some cover, and wait. You'll get some shooting—not unlike pass shooting for ducks. Any gauge shotgun is suitable, with No. 9 shot the most effective.

The Woodcock

Also known as "timberdoodle," the woodcock is slightly larger than a quail and has a 2½-inch bill designed for probing into the earth in search of worms, the bird's standard diet. It's said he can eat his weight in worms daily! His "corkscrew" flight foils many a beginner with the shotgun!

His favorite hangout is a low-lying and damp alder run although he's found, too, among hillside birches and poplars, his presence advertised by the limelike white splotches on the ground. Northeastern states have a native population and they're visited in the fall by flight birds, coming from eastern Maine and Quebec.

Woodcock have a ghostly quality about their travel habits. A run may be full one day and barren of birds the next, or vice versa. The only way to keep track is to check a known woodcock area daily during the hunting season. A bird dog is a big help but "jump shooting" is also sporty. An open-bore 20 or 16 gauge shotgun loaded with No. 9 shot is a frequent and suitable choice of armament.

The Wild Turkey

When it comes to wild turkeys, I want to bow to another hunter who worked more than fifty years to save the gobbler from extinction and who has supervised the raising of some 60,000 pure-bred wild strains. He is Henry P. Bridges and his book on turkeys is *The Woodmont Story.** All there is to know is contained in this book.

Because of his wariness the wild turkey is thought of as big game and it takes a hunter with a knowledge of his quarry to hunt the gobbler successfully. Some eighteen states report some success with restoration efforts, although not all have an open season. Hunting, where legal, may vary from calling turkeys that have purposely been scattered by dogs to awaiting in a blind with a light rifle. For flight shots, a full-choke 12 gauge loaded with No. 2 or 4 shot is recommended.

Antelope

Popularly known as the "pronghorn," the antelope is, in turn, the pixie of the prairie, a fading ghost, an arrogant brute and a greyhound. He may stand and stamp his feet at you—or he may streak away at 70 miles per hour, or at least so some claim.

His actual speed is probably nearer 40. He's not a large animal, weighing 110 to 135 pounds dressed. I've managed to stalk within a hundred feet of antelope, when carrying a camera. With a rifle, it seems I've always needed binoculars! A six-power scope will help on these long shots and you'll need a long-range, flat-shooting rifle. Use natural cover in stalking, following gullies or washes and always keeping behind knolls or brush. You'll need skill as a "belly stalker," crawling on your stomach, rifle cradled in your arms, inching forward slowly with an eye on the quarry. Chances are, he'll have two on you!

Ducks and Geese

A well-rigged decoy set will pull in more ducks, but for action I'll take "jump shooting." This consists of two hunters prowling a marsh in a canoe, one shooting from the bow seat and the other poling stealthily from the rear, or paddling. With this method you can hunt areas otherwise seldom hunted and you can actually stalk ducks by sound. The shooting is fast!

However, decoys and a blind are not only traditional but they will produce more ducks. I've hunted from blinds that were merely tall grass or reeds gathered about me and from luxurious enclosed blinds that were heated, with 150 decoys set out in front! A blind, simple or expensive, should blend with or seem a part of its natural location, must afford quick and easy shooting and be rigged so there's no chance that two hunters, shooting together, will endanger each other or interfere with each other's aiming and firing.

A dozen properly set decoys will do a better job than a hundred badly scattered blocks. Try setting three or four Canadian goose decoys slightly upwind of your duck blocks. "Honkers" are among the wariest of waterfowl and their presence will give incoming ducks more confidence that your rig is the real thing. Don't buy your decoys with all of their heads in erect position. This is a sign of alertness, sometimes even nervousness. Adding a few "feeding heads" with necks arched downward will indicate that your decoys are relaxed and enjoying themselves, tantamount to an invitation to drop in.

Early morning, of course, is best but if the weather is cold and blustery, the ducks may fly all day. Bluebird weather keeps them down and few will fly as a rule. On a quiet day, when decoys will be lifeless, use a feeding duck rig. Attach a fine neutral-colored line to the bill of at least one duck, run this down through a smooth ring attached to the anchor, and then to your blind. Pulling on the string will tilt the duck head-down, in feeding position, lending "life" to your blocks.

A duck call is a must—and the skill to use it well. Duck calling is a fine art which can't be learned by reading. Hunt with an experienced caller if possible, or buy a recording which will include not only calls but instructions for making them.

Geese are more wary than ducks and generally fly much higher. Snow geese will sit in the middle of a lake all day but late in the afternoon, they'll take off for a neighboring grain field, usually within two to four miles. Hunters often follow them in a car to locate the "lunch-

* A. S. Barnes Co., New York, 1953.

rooms." Once the field is found, hunters split up and stalk the feeding flock from several sides until within shooting range. At a signal, all hunters stand and the geese, of course, erupt into flight, to run the gamut of No. 2 shot.

Canada geese or "honkers" are also taken in grain fields, but usually with decoys. Pits are dug around a known feeding area so that hunters are hidden below ground level. Goose calling is then performed, a finer art even than duck calling. Shooting is much like that of ducks coming in to water-borne decoys.

A 12 gauge pump or automatic is the favorite of duck hunters as well as goose hunters.

Deer Hunting

I know a deer hunter who hunted one week each season for eighteen years *without even seeing a deer!* Some 50 per cent of hunters are unsuccessful each year, and among those who do connect, I'll warrant that 90 per cent were just lucky, blundering upon a deer or vice versa. The reason for this poor average is that few hunters take the trouble to learn deer habits.

The first thing to learn is that deer are nocturnal critters, feeding by night and bedding down by day. The trick is to learn *where* they're feeding and where they bed down and then posting yourself somewhere in between at the right time. At the risk of being accused of proposing a formula for successful hunting, the surest way of connecting with venison on the hoof, is to learn the deer's feeding habits and where it's likely to bed down for the day. While grouse hunting, early one morning, I blundered into a handsome buck to the consternation of both of us, for I caught him with a big McIntosh apple in his mouth. We gawked at each other for a moment before he wheeled away. Three days later I saw what I believed was the same buck, headed toward the abandoned orchard where we had met. Somewhat over a week later, after the deer season opened, I guided an Ohio hunter to the edge of the orchard and we arrived just as the gray light of morning became strong enough to reveal the buck, feeding under an apple tree, completely unaware of our presence some 60 yards away. A shot from the Ohio hunter's .35 Remington brought the buck down. The hunter thought I was a wizard as a guide but the credit really should have gone to the buck himself—and his regular feeding habits.

Deer like more than apples, however, and in their diet will include mushrooms—the coral mushroom that grows on hard maple—beechnuts, the shoots of yellow birch, white maple, beech, sarsaparilla, raspberry buds and even acorns. Locate these foods in the woods and you can be sure there are deer nearby.

If you investigate carefully, you'll find that the neighboring deer will be bedded down close by during the day, quite often within a quarter-mile of a feeding area. Deer, like men, won't travel far on a full stomach.

Mule deer and the black-tail have similar habits and food tastes, plus a number of other feed varieties native to their own habitat. These may include the snowberry, cliff rose, serviceberry, blackberry, and even mistletoe. Unlike the white-tail, they prefer broken country that is fairly open but containing thickets and small timber stands where they may bed down during the daylight hours. I once watched four mule deer lying in the shade of a tiny clump of ponderosa pine, the thicket barely 30 feet across!

"Still hunting" is the most exciting, although the term is a misnomer. A hunter does *not* stand still but rather walks quietly and stealthily along old woods roads and swamps, or skirts apple orchards and heavy softwood clumps. If you look for an animal that stands out, clearly silhouetted, you'll probably fail. Look instead for a bit of snowy white hair or tawny brown hide that doesn't quite "belong." A pair of ears, quite often a single eye peering from back of brush, will reveal the presence of a wily buck who's watching you and hoping you'll blunder on by. Walk slowly, observe *every* bit of cover and listen for the slightest rustle of leaves that signals a deer skulking around you!

Tracking deer on snow is productive. Many hunters think of two or three inches as "trackin' snow." It is, I suppose, but I prefer six to eight inches. This depth will muffle your footsteps while a shallower depth will create a "crunch" that is audible for quite some distance, especially to the sharp ears of a deer.

Most hunters, taking a shot at a deer and seeing the white flag flying in what appears to be wild leaps of desperation to get away might be surprised to learn that a deer rarely runs more than a couple hundred yards before stopping to look back! Most amble away a shorter distance and await "developments," watching carefully over their own trail. When this happens to you, don't try to follow directly or too speedily. Instead, circle *downwind*, trying to approach the deer from another angle. If the deer sees or hears you first—and this is more than likely—whistle loudly! This will often stop a deer long enough for a quick shot.

Deer calling is still comparatively unknown—and certainly badly understood—among hunters. Excellent deer calls are available but it requires skill to use them successfully. Your blind must be perfect, or else you must take a well-hidden position in a tree in an area where deer travel between feeding and bedding grounds. Your call should be muted by folding one hand over its mouth. Blowing a "Baaaa" sound into it for one half to three fourths of a second at a time at intervals of about ten minutes will usually attract a deer. Some advocate more frequent calls, but I believe that the fewer calls the better since no man-made sound can perfectly imitate a deer's "language."

A favorite trick of Texas hunters is rattling a pair of antlers and striking the ground occasionally with a stout stick, to imitate a fight between two bucks. Don't overdo these tricks however. Deer won't come to a three-ring circus!

Probably the most effective hunting method is trail watching. Post yourself on a deer run, and if you have the patience to sit long enough, you'll get some shooting. It may take only ten minutes or it may take two days—but it *will* happen. Another method, though less productive, is to paddle quietly along a stream that flows through a deer area, especially early in the morning and again just before dark. This is best done with two hunters, one paddling and the other poised in the bow with a rifle. Keep the canoe close to shore, avoiding the center of the stream where you'll be exposed to easy view. Go around a bend in the stream on the *inside* of the bend, poking the canoe cautiously around the turn.

Incidentally, so-called deer scents are next to useless, despite glowing claims—some of them downright misleading—by advertisers. Some may contain an essence attractive to deer but if the deer can smell the stuff, it can smell you, too!

Skilled deer hunting is a matter of experience, and since you might just as well be successful while acquiring this experience, be sure to hunt upwind at all times and hunt where the deer are likely to be—not where they were last night. Find the feeding areas and work these carefully at the crack of dawn and again at dusk. Not that noontime hunting will go without its rewards. If there are other hunters in the area, they may keep the deer on the move when they would otherwise be bedded down.

Bear

The black bear is rarely shot except by deer hunters who blunder into bruin accidentally. Only once was I ever successful in overtaking a bear by tracking and this was a large she-bear with two cubs. I got too close, actually, and had to shoot when the she-bear decided to investigate me!

It *is* possible to shoot bear, however, without tracking them. Some hunters, posing as sportsmen, have shot them while bear were feeding at a town or camp dump and, of course, a number of them are trapped and finished off with rifles. There's a more sporting method. If you have the patience and perseverance to sit on a beech ridge long enough, a black bear will come along, although it may take several days before your presence—and the bear's—coincide. Abandoned farm orchards are also good hunting spots, since bruin, too, is fond of apples.

Don't be surprised to see bear tracks in the snow. They frequently roam during the early winter, going into hibernation only after the first sharp cold spell. A bear's weight will seldom exceed 300 pounds, contrary to newspaper reports and those of hunters. A 500-pound black bear is most unusual and bear weights, on an average, will approximate those of buck deer.

The bear is a wily animal who gives man a wide berth in the woods and presents no danger to the hunter except in such cases as mine, where I crowded a she-bear too closely. Also, the impression that bear are difficult to kill is erroneous. They can be knocked down with any suitable deer rifle and cannons are not necessary. Probably more black bear have been killed with the .30/30 than with any other caliber.

In some areas, black bear are run by dogs, just as are wildcats and cougars. The sport here is not in the shooting but in the chase. Following the dogs will test a hunter's stamina.

Chapter XIX

GUN SAFETY AND CARE

A weekend guest at my home once picked up a .32 revolver from my open gunrack, looked into the muzzle—and pulled the trigger! I figure I saved that woman's life—long before she appeared on the scene—by making empty guns in my home a habit. I'd always been cautious, but I was doubly so after *that* escapade!

The "Ten Commandments" of gun safety which appear in nearly all gun publications amply cover the field of accident prevention, but like their biblical counterparts, they're occasionally overlooked or deliberately ignored. By way of proof of this, a friend of mine once sent a .22 bullet into the kitchen ceiling while cleaning a rifle which was "unloaded." The following Saturday night, repeating the cleaning process, his gun fired again and struck a relative!

A member of the Massachusetts Camp Perry rifle team, whom I was guiding on a deer hunt in Maine one fall, fell and drove the muzzle of his .30/06 into the snow. He pulled the muzzle toward him, planning to blow out the snow. A twig caught the trigger and the 180-grain slug missed him so closely that he suffered powder burns and was deaf in one ear for several hours. A deer hunter, also in Maine, shifted the weight of his rifle in his arm and shot off the right leg of another hunter walking ahead of him. A midwestern youngster, finding a loaded revolver in his father's car, pointed the gun at his younger brother, pulled the trigger, killing the victim instantly. A tired bear hunter on the slope of Kennebago Mountain, near the Canadian border, sat down with his rifle leaning against his shoulder. When we found him, he had blown off the top of his head. A young squirrel hunter leaned his .22 rifle against a tree which he climbed to retrieve a dead squirrel that had lodged in a branch. The rifle fell and shot the young hunter's companion in the stomach.

These are not incidents which I culled from newspaper reports, nor are they remote "it happened to some other fellow" accidents. They occurred to people whom I knew and in some instances while I was at hand or in the vicinity. All were close to home.

Why do these accidents continue, despite the clear admonitions of the "Ten Commandments of Gun Safety"? Each and every one of these ten rules is a sound and reasonable one but the weakness of the ten lies in their number. *Ten rules are too many for most shooters to memorize!* Few will take the trouble to read them through and fewer yet will memorize them.

Before reading any further, can you repeat them?

1. Treat every gun with the respect due a loaded gun.
2. Guns carried into camp or home, or when otherwise not in use, must always be unloaded.
3. Always be sure barrel and action are clear of obstruction.
4. Always control the direction of the muzzle, even if you stumble.
5. Be sure of your target before you pull the trigger.
6. Never point a gun at anything you do not want to shoot.

7. Unattended guns should be unloaded.
8. Never climb a tree or fence or jump a ditch with a loaded gun.
9. Never shoot a bullet at a flat, hard surface or the surface of water.
10. Always avoid alcoholic drinks before or during shooting.

Frankly, I don't believe we need *ten* such rules especially since many duplicate each other and others overlap. One rule—one of the commandments, in fact—would do the work of the other nine and could easily be dinned into the minds of all shooters. This is No. 6. I would word it as follows:

"NEVER POINT A GUN AT ANYONE OR ANYTHING YOU DON'T INTEND TO SHOOT!"

All of the other nine commandments, while they give sound advice, especially regarding alcoholic drink and unloading guns, have as their meat the prevention of an accidental shooting. This is summed up most clearly and impressively in Commandment No. 6. Shooters who pay little attention to the ten can easily memorize, and remember upon suitable occasions, the forceful command of the sixth law!

Hunting accidents always get a big play in news reports and these cover two types of gun accident, the self-inflicted shooting and the shooting of another person through accidental discharge or through the "I thought he wuz a deer!" premise!

The self-inflicted accident is certainly a flagrant violation of the common sense put forth in Commandment No. 6. Whether you're crossing a fence, climbing a tree, jumping a stream or just resting in the woods a few minutes, if you hold or place your gun in such a manner that the muzzle is pointing at yourself, you may be violating one or two of the other commandments, but you are primarily ignoring No. 6! The same is true if your muzzle endangers someone else besides yourself.

So far as the mistaken-identity accident is concerned, I can bear little sympathy for the shooter. In some thirty years of hunting, I've never seen a deer—or any other animal—that remotely resembled a man. It's been conclusively proven that deer don't wear red britches! A hunter who shoots another "accidentally" violates Commandment No. 5, but he also violates No. 6! In fact, if you will examine reports of gun accidents you'll find that the person involved violated *one* of the *other nine* commandments—but *always* he has violated No. 6!

Therefore, any shooter who doesn't want to bother to memorize—and observe—ten rules, can accomplish the same end by remembering to NEVER POINT A GUN AT ANYONE OR ANYTHING YOU DON'T INTEND TO SHOOT, for most certainly, *this* is the law of all the prophets!

While *all* gun accidents are tragic enough in themselves, the one for which there is the least plausible reason is the mistaken-identity accident. A hunter who makes such a shot, at a slight movement in the bushes, at an unidentified sound or at a "deer" which he can't see clearly, is a fool to the *n*th degree. How can he properly place a bullet into an animal? A skilled hunter *places* his shot, in the head or chest area, for a quick kill. Any hunter who takes this precaution will never have to report to his best friend's wife that she is a widow thanks to his scatter-brained marksmanship.

The legal penalties which follow such shootings are often ridiculous. The careless driver of a car who kills or maims a person on the highway may well be required by civil action in a court to pay the victim or his family several thousand dollars. A hunter who kills another because he "thought he was a deer" is fined up to $300 in Maine and similar lukewarm penalties exist in most other states! In fact, I've often considered that the safest place in which to commit murder is in the deer woods, if the would-be killer can induce his victim to go hunting. If the motive can be hidden or disguised, many states will let the murderer off with a fine smaller than that assessed against an unarmed burglar.

Conservation departments work constantly to cut down accidents, of course. Several states now require that deer hunters wear red, either a cap or jacket or both. Red is a poor choice since it tends to look much darker in poor light, often appearing to be a dark brown or black at a distance. Luminescent red stands out much more clearly but as long as there are trigger-happy hunters in the woods, bright clothing only helps searchers to find a shooting victim!

Luminescent yellow and blaze orange devised during World War II for life rafts, is visible at much longer ranges, and up-to-date safety authorities recommend this in place of red. In some states it is mandatory. Maybe it's because I'm getting crotchety in my advancing age but I resent being asked—or required—to look like a billboard beer advertisement in order to stay alive in the woods!

Getting Lost

Another facet of hunting that often produces tragedy is the susceptibility to getting lost. Any hunter who protests that he has never been lost is either a liar, or he hasn't been hunting long enough for the law of averages to catch up with him. Getting lost is a hunter's occupational hazard.

Man does not have a natural sense of direction, and this is true of Indians as well as whites. The former can get just as "badly twisted" in the landscape as any white man once he leaves country with which he is familiar. The same thing can be said of a professional guide, if he's careless about his landmark observations.

Getting lost doesn't have to be tragic, or even harrowing—not if a hunter keeps his head when he discovers that the "strange tracks" in the mud are his own, or when he encounters a hardwood ridge where, a few hours earlier, there was a swamp. He'll get into trouble only when he gives way to panic which *is* a prelude to tragedy.

The most heart-rendering case of panic I ever encountered occurred while I was a member of a search party that beat the puckerbush for five days near the Maine-Canada border. We never found the hunter. We did, however, find his cap, his hunting jacket, his rifle and finally the last bit of eloquent proof of the man's complete loss of reason—one of his boots! Over a year later, a fisherman found a similar boot some miles away, with part of a human foot in it.

The search most vivid in my mind, however, occurred while I was with the U. S. Border Patrol. It started with a phone call from the local game warden, asking for help in a search for a lost hunter. We were underway within ten minutes. Other wardens and patrolmen joined what proved to be a three-day search on snowshoes in 30 inches of fresh-fallen snow. The hunter had started out in a snowstorm on Monday morning and never returned. I'll omit the details of the agony of three days on snowshoes, but on the third day I heard signal shots a half-mile from where I was beating my way along the edge of a wilderness meadow. When I arrived at the scene, a hunter lay on his back in the snow, his .30/30 alongside. He was dead.

His story was clearly recorded in the snow, his tracks showing where he had zigzagged crazily toward his end. His rifle was in excellent working order and he still had shells, although we'd heard no answer to our early signal shots. I tried one of the two dozen matches he was carrying and it flickered into a robust flame. He lay near the foot of a huge dry pine stub containing enough easily ignited firewood to last him a week. Less than a hundred feet away stood the remnants of an abandoned tar-paper trapper's shack which he could have fired to attract the attention of the search plane that had worked with us. We met the medical examiner as we were bringing out the body. "Exhaustion" was his verdict after an examination. "Must have run himself to death," the doctor added! What do you say to a man's wife and to his children, standing stunned on a camp porch, when you drag in his body on a toboggan? There's a notable lack of comfort in the words "He panicked" —even if it's the truth.

Panic builds up gradually, at first a slight annoyance that you're not sure of yourself. It's like seeing the last bus pull away from the curb late at night and four miles out in the suburbs. Then, you begin casting about with your eyes, wondering where you made the wrong turn. You go back a few yards, seeking something familiar, something associated with the pleasant hunting you were enjoying only a few minutes ago. The trees stand indifferent to your plight and soon they even take on a hostile cast. Your heart begins to beat rapidly and soon you can hear it pounding above the crunch of your hurrying footsteps. You quicken your pace and a gut-gnawing and overwhelming fear takes possession of your mind and your body. This is panic.

It's useless, of course, to advise a hunter who has never been lost that he should keep his head and that there is nothing in the woods at night that wasn't there during the day when he was enjoying the hunting. Yet there are hunters who have little serious trouble if they do get lost, while others as I've shown you, go to their deaths. What, then, is the difference?

Experience. Experts get lost, too. I've worked and lived with professional woodsmen, guides, foresters, timber cruisers, trappers and game wardens, and I don't know a single man among these who has not, at some time or other, been lost in the woods. When a professional gets lost, it rarely makes the headlines because he's found his way out by the time a search party gets underway and long before the reporters hear of it. I've never known a woodsman to panic, which leads me to believe that experience in the woods eliminates this fear of the unknown which develops in the once-a-year hunter who runs into strange country and can't find his way out. As a result of this experience, the woodsman manages to keep calm so that he can *reason his way out!*

The woodsman stays calm because he knows he has nothing to fear. If he can't get out before nightfall he accepts his fate and makes the best of the night with a companionable campfire, possibly a lean-to and a bough-bed. Smoking his pipe, he awaits the dawn, much as if he were in a bus depot awaiting the next bus.

Any hunter can attain an equal degree of composure under the same circumstances by building up confidence in his ability to care for himself in the woods in an emergency.

This you can do by going into the woods, even park areas close to home, as often as you can, for short hikes, day-long excursions or even overnight trips. In connection with this conditioning, assemble yourself a small survival kit. When entering the woods, whether close to home or in a vast wilderness area, bear in mind that you could well get lost. It's a universal human failure. Once reconciled to this fact, it will hold less terror for you. In fact, anyone interested in conducting a personal experiment in this field will find it interesting—and a revelation!

Pick a wooded area anywhere, possibly a state park or forest. Enter the woods in late afternoon, and deliberately lose youself—possibly by walking in circles or by wandering erratically about. Give yourself enough time to make a rough camp before dark, including time enough to build a small fire, gather firewood and set up a small shelter of some kind. Pick an area small enough so that you can safely walk out by compass route the next morning—but don't look at your compass until morning. Spend the night out, keeping as comfortable as possible under these simulated "lost" conditions. Listen to the night noises, decipher the shadows about you, but keep busy feeding the fire, smoking a pipe or even just observing the stars. Undergo this experience once, and you'll never again be afraid of staying alone in the woods at night. You may get lost but your chances of giving way to panic will have melted away, like the smoke from your campfire during your "dry run."

The survival kit will go far toward building your confidence, so much so that you might well *enjoy* being out overnight! A plastic sheet, possibly 6 feet by 10 will fold compactly and fit into a hunting jacket pocket, yet it will make an excellent lean-to to keep off rain and to reflect heat from your campfire. Have a good supply of waterproof matches, saving these for emergencies—not lighting cigarettes! Carry a packet of dehydrated soups or meat and a small can or metal cup in which to cook. Raisins or chocolate bars make a fine dessert. To this equipment, add a tiny wire saw, about 18 inches long and which looks like miniature barbed wire. One of these weighs less than two ounces but it'll cut a four-inch softwood tree in two minutes! Firewood will then be no problem. This entire kit can be supplemented by a pipe and tobacco or a supply of cigarettes and the entire unit will weigh less than two pounds! You will have shelter, warmth and food. These produce confidence!

If you find that you *are* lost and you have several hours of daylight ahead of you, it's reasonable to try to find your way out. However, if it's getting on toward the time when shadows lengthen in the woods, make a comfortable camp and plan to *enjoy* the night out. Remember that a search party will be looking for you in the morning, so stay put, building a signal fire of smoky materials to help the searchers. Remember, too, that when you *are* found they will either encounter you comfortably set up in camp coolly awaiting help, or if you panic, they may have to overtake you and take you out by sheer force! Your fellow hunters will rib you thoroughly for getting lost—that's standard protocol in the woods—but you'll have their admiration for keeping cool if you do so. If you panic, you'll get sympathy and a considerable loss of face to boot. Even pride can help you.

You're probably wondering why I've approached the subject of getting lost by describing possible results rather than by pointing methods for not getting lost. The reason for this is that, even with precautions, it is still possible to get so badly turned around that you'll be "a half-mile away from your own tracks!" A hunter who's intent upon a trophy buck is likely to forget that he's supposed to observe landmarks and trail signs and to make note of compass directions—especially if he sees a big buck skulking around the back side of a spruce thicket! Take precautions to avoid getting lost by all means, but at the same time plan on the possibility!

If you're a complete beginner at woods travel and plan to hunt alone, buy a Geological Survey map of the area in which you'll hunt. Study the map beforehand—even before you leave on the hunting trip so that notable landmarks will be inscribed in your mind. These maps are, in effect, aerial photos, although the size and shape of hills, knolls, mountains and valleys will be indicated by contour lines. When you arrive on the scene for the start of your annual hunt, note your starting position on the map and follow your travel through the woods *on the map* even marking it with a pencil, if you want to be doubly sure. In this way, you'll know exactly where you are at all times and getting back to camp will be a simple matter of retracing your steps or picking out a shorter route. From there on the degree of skill you acquire in woods travel will depend upon how often you can make similar jaunts into woodland areas.

Up until now, I have not mentioned the compass, because most hunters who religiously carry one have little *practical* knowledge of its use. They know that if they've traveled north into an area, they must retrace their steps southward to return to camp and the compass will help them do this. But unless a hunter knows where he is exactly, or even approximately, the compass is next to useless. It does not point the way back to camp! It mutely, yet eloquently, points to magnetic north! It does no more than this.

If you use the map—and possibly the pencil—as I've suggested, you probably won't need the compass. If somehow, though, you *do* get turned around (most woodsmen don't "get lost," they get "turned around") the compass can help you locate yourself on the map. It can, in fact, pin-point your location by a process I call "reverse triangulation."

First you'll need to orient your map. At the bottom of this and on most maps, there is an offset *V* symbol, with one leg pointing to magnetic north and the other to true north on the map. In the East, the *left* leg points to magnetic north, while on the West Coast, it's the *right* leg. This is the declination symbol with the variation usually shown in degrees also.

Place your map and compass on a flat spot, such as a stump or ledge, or even on the ground. When the compass needle comes to rest, rotate the map under the compass until its needle lies parallel to the *magnetic* leg of the declination symbol. Your map now lies in correct relation to the geographical features which surround you.

You must have a compass, however, that is marked by 360 degrees about the outer rim of its face. A compass without these is really of little real value. Pick out a prominent landscape feature, a mountain, a butte, or possibly a forest fire lookout tower which you can see from your position. Orient your compass so that the number of degrees between the needle and the true north point on the compass face coincides with the number indicated on the declination symbol. If the map's declination calls for 20 degrees, then there should be 20 degrees between the compass needle and its true north.

Now take a bearing on the landscape feature you've chosen, possibly a fire tower. Assume the tower is located on a 40-degree bearing from your position. Now, place the compass directly over the tower's location on the map and take a bearing in the *opposite* direction from the 40-degree bearing. This will be, in this instance, 220 degrees. With a pencil or even a piece of charred wood or match stick, draw a straight line from the outer edge of the compass *along this* 220 bearing. Your actual position on the map is somewhere along this line.

Phase two of the "find-yourself" process, is a repetition of the first, but using *another* prominent landmark which may be a mountain or hill in the distance. Follow the procedure up to and including the final drawing of the line with pencil or charred wood. *Where the two lines cross on the map is your location.* Knowing your location should make it easy to take another bearing that will lead you back to camp.

Don't wait until you're lost to try out this system. You'll probably have forgotten it by then. Instead, practice it occasionally during neighborhood hunting trips or short family hikes. What I've pointed out is probably the most complicated phase of compass use any sportsman will ever have to contend with. If you understand the reverse triangulation process, you may get turned around, but you'll never be seriously lost!

Hunter Training

Organized training courses for young shooters are available in most parts of the country, usually under the sponsorship of a local sportsmen's club or high school physical education department, in co-operation with the National Rifle Association.

In some instances, hunter training courses are offered and these accent gun safety in the field, rather than the formal ready-aim-fire type of target shooting. A youngster who does not get this hunting training will be handicapped when he takes his gun into the field for there's little resemblance between target shooting and hunting.

The best training comes from *actual hunting,* under supervision. I started my own son when he was eleven, in the woods near our camp in Maine. At first, he was allowed to carry a single .22 shell *in his hand* while he walked ahead of me in the woods. When game was sighted, he was then allowed to load and fire. Only then was he given a second cartridge.

This technique resulted in a small game bag but it served several more important purposes. It allowed him to make mistakes in the handling of his .22 rifle, a single-shot model, *while it was empty.* Each time he erred, such as swinging the muzzle toward me, he was reminded of his error. Gradually, he learned not only safety but sound hunting technique. A boy anxious to have his gun loaded won't repeat his mistakes! This type of training also taught him the value of the first shot.

As his proficiency and good woods manners improved, he was allowed to carry the single shell in the firing chamber with the gun uncocked. Later, as he progressed still more, he was permitted to cock the rifle and carry it on safety. Since that day, I've never worried about his ability to keep himself and his hunting companions safe from his gun.

Although I used a single-shot rifle to teach my son, a repeater will serve just as well, since these can also be loaded one shot at a time.

This type of woods training is far more valuable than the formal and regimented target range instruction where youngsters are under constant supervision. A boy, accustomed to this, is somewhat at a loss when he's on his own in the woods where, too, he encounters conditions completely unlike those on the firing line.

Gun Care

Whenever I think of gun care I think of Hoppe's No. 9 which I can recall smelling in my home seemingly as far back as the diaper stage! As a boy, with my first .22, I used it to clean the bore; I wiped the bolt with it and even polished the stock. I've long since given up using Hoppe's on the "handle," but I continued its use elsewhere for many years. My guns never rusted nor did pitting ever develop in a rifle, handgun or shotgun bore. This may sound like a commercial "plug," and I suppose it amounts to one, but I'm simply pointing out that gun care pays off, whether you use Hoppe's or any other good solvent!

Necessary implements for keeping a sporting armory in shape are few and inexpensive—a solvent for cleaning the bore occasionally; a light gun oil for working parts and exterior surfaces; cleaning patches; an old toothbrush; and, of course, a cleaning rod.

Any one of the commercial solvents will work well at keeping the bore of your gun clean. In the case of a rifle or handgun, apply it solely with a cleaning patch, preferably of cotton flannel that contains no sizing. Commercially made patches are excellent and usually cut to fit the bore. A small slot at the end of the cleaning rod holds the patch while you swab the gun. Running a half-dozen patches through a bore will do the work, the last three or four being run through dry to wipe out excess solvent. These will appear soiled and so will the twentieth if you use that many, but what appears to be dirt or powder residue is more likely to be only excess solvent. Always clean from the breech end if possible. If not, be careful in running the rod into the muzzle that you don't create excess wear of the muzzle by rubbing it with the rod.

It might appear that a soft metal, such as aluminum, would be best for a rod because of the danger of throat abrasion. This isn't so. Soft metals pick up bits of dirt which have an abrasive effect on the bore. Steel rods are best.

In the case of a shotgun, wire brushes are sometimes used to remove leading which occurs. Always dip the brush in solvent or pour a few drops on it. Finish the job with patches or a soft cloth brush.

A light gun oil is necessary, for protection of the action, including all moving parts and those adjacent. This can be applied directly from the can through the tiny spout and then wiped or brushed into recesses with a toothbrush. For exterior surfaces I keep an oil-saturated chamois cloth or skin and I've gotten into the habit of giving my guns a quick wipe every few days as I happen by the gun case. Wiping them this often isn't needed, though, and I probably perform the chore for the sheer pleasure of picking up the guns, but it keeps them in fine condition.

How often the guns should be cleaned depends, of course, upon how often they're used and where you live. Although modern smokeless powder and non-corrosive primers have eased the job of gun care, I still like to clean my guns after each use, although there is no danger in waiting a day or two *in a dry climate.* If you live close to the sea, where salt air can reach the guns, clean them often—or at least wipe them often. This is true of guns in humid areas. In dry mountain air, there's little danger of atmospheric moisture causing rust.

Guns that have been cared for in this manner are rarely injured by being carried in the rain except, of course, that the stock may absorb some moisture. If your gun gets wet, wipe it as dry as possible after use, then apply a light wiping of gun oil.

Incidentally, if you have guests in your home who pick up your guns to admire them, it's a good plan to wipe the guns with an oiled chamois or cloth—although you can wait until the guests have gone! The moisture from human hands is corrosive to fine gun metals.

One point to remember is that excess oil in the barrel of any gun will cause the first shot to be a bit wild, and in the case of a shotgun, the first shot's pattern may well be erratic. Always wipe out excess oil. A thin coating is all that is needed for regular or routine maintenance.

For long-time storage, use a special gun grease which may be applied in the same manner as the oil or solvent. Make sure that *all* parts receive at least a light coating.

This is the shortest chapter in this book for the simple reason that modern ammunition has eliminated the old bugaboos of barrel corrosion caused by early powders and primers containing potassium chlorate. Modern powders and primers make it possible to overlook cleaning for a few days without harmful effect. A lover of fine guns, however, will see that his rifle, handgun or shotgun gets the best of care as soon as possible!

Glossary of

SHOOTING TERMS AND ABBREVIATIONS

Action—The unit, including the firing mechanism and bolt or breechblock, which handles a cartridge or shell.

Aperture—Peep hole in rear receiver sight through which a shooter looks at a target.

Auto-Loader—A self-loading or semi-automatic gun which fires once with each pull of the trigger. Also called an automatic.

Automatic—A truly automatic gun fires continually as long as the trigger is held back—really a machine gun, although the term is popularly applied to semi-automatic sporting weapons.

ACP—Automatic Colt Pistol, the .45 caliber cartridge for automatic pistols.

Ballistics—The science of projectiles.

Ballistic Table—Charts issued by ammunition manufacturers indicating the performance of various loads.

Battery Cup—The unit containing the primer cap in a shot shell.

Base Wad—The bottom wad in a shot shell, surrounding the primer and battery cup, varying in thickness according to the shell's load.

Beavertail—A wide, hand-filling forearm, usually on a rifle.

Bedding—Refers to the fitting of a stock to a gun's action and barrel.

Bench Rest—A specially devised shooting table, usually having a rest for the gun's forearm.

Berdan—A European-type primer, utilizing twin flash-holes. Not interchangeable with American or Boxer primers.

Big Game—Generally applied to animals of the deer and black-bear size and larger.

Bolt—Usually associated with bolt-action rifles. The unit which houses the firing pin and which drives the cartridge into the firing chamber and locks it into place for firing.

Bore—The caliber of a rifle or handgun and the gauge of a shotgun. In the case of rifled barrels, the bore diameter is measured from the top of the lands although occasionally the groove diameter is given.

Boxer—American-type center-fire primers, using a single flash-hole in the cartridge base.

Breech—Opening at the rear of the barrel through which ammunition is loaded and empty cases ejected.

Breechblock—Serves the same purpose as the bolt. Sometimes the terms "bolt" and "breechblock" are used interchangeably.

BT—Boat tail, a streamlined bullet having a tapered heel.

Bullet—The projectile fired by a rifle or handgun.

Caliber—The bore-diameter designation of a rifle or pistol, usually given in hundredths or thousandths of an inch, such as .30 caliber or .300 caliber. Except for English loads, foreign ammunition caliber is designated in millimeters such as 8 mm.

Cannelure—Circular grooves about a bullet into which the mouth of the shell may be crimped or, in the case of cast bullets, into which is placed the lubricating grease.

Cant—Tilting a gun slightly to one side or the other while aiming.

Carbine—A short rifle, usually having a barrel 18½ to 22 inches long. Designed originally for cavalry but now popular among hunters.

Cartridge—A complete load including shell, primer, powder and bullet.

Case—Popular term among reloaders and applying to an empty rifle or handgun shell.

Center-Fire—Refers to cartridges with primers located in the center of the base.

Center of Impact—The center of a group, averaged between the most widespread hits on a target. Wild shots are usually discounted.

Chamber—The reamed-out part of the barrel from which a cartridge is fired, hence the "firing chamber." Also applies to the holes in a revolver cylinder which hold cartridges.

Chilled Shot—Shot made of lead and antimony. Probably will soon be replaced by non-poisonous iron or steel shot to eliminate lead poisoning suffered by waterfowl which eat lead shot found in shallow water, mistaking it for food.

Choke—The degree of constriction of the muzzle of a shotgun barrel to govern the spread of shot. Also applied to a mechanical device which varies this degree of constriction.

Clip—A container holding cartridges which fits into a magazine.

Comb—That portion of the gunstock upon which a shooter's cheek rests while sighting. Usually raised somewhat.

Corrosive Primers—Primers containing potassium or other salts that are harmful to gun barrels. No longer in use generally.

Cupronickel—A copper-nickel alloy from which bullet jackets are made.

Crimp—The tight constriction of the mouth of a shell to hold a bullet in place. Also, the folding of the mouth of a paper or plastic shotgun shell to hold the shot.

Cylinder Bore—Cylinder bore is actually an absence of constriction of the muzzle of a shotgun. Arbitrarily, cylinder bore results in 25 to 35 per cent of a shell's shot load remaining within a 30-inch circle at 40 yards. This and other "choke" designations overlap to a great degree and are not to be relied upon until the gun is actually patterned.

Cylinder—A cylindrical magazine for revolvers, holding five to nine shots depending upon caliber, and which aligns itself automatically with the barrel as the hammer is cocked.

Decapping—The process of removing the fired primer from a rifle, pistol or shotgun shell.

Decapping Pin—A thin rod, located within a reloading die, which punches out a fired primer.

Die, Loading—A reloading implement which can be described as a female mold, which "reforms" a fired shell, prior to reloading.

Double Action—The firing of a revolver, and some automatic pistols, by pulling the trigger and without benefit of manual hand cocking.

Drift—The deviation of a bullet from its intended course, usually caused by wind.

Drop-at-Heel—The pitch of shotgun or rifle stock, designated by the distance between the heel (top of the butt plate) and a line drawn from the top of the barrel straight back over the stock.

Drop-at-Comb—Same as drop-at-heel, except that it is measured at the comb.

Drop Shot—Lead shot dropped from a height through a sievelike plate, into cold water. See Chilled Shot.

Ejector—The unit which ejects an empty shell after firing, usually automatic.

Elevation—Sight adjustment which raises the trajectory of a bullet to compensate for range.

Enfield—A .30 caliber infantry rifle used in World War I by both American and English troops. Often called the British Enfield '17.

Energy—The power developed by a gun charge, expressed in foot pounds.

Erosion—Wear within a barrel.

Eye Relief—The distance between the rear lens of a telescope sight and the shooter's eye.

Exit Pupil—By holding a telescope sight a foot or so away from the eye, you will see a concentration of light in the center of the eyepiece. This is the exit pupil.

Expander Nipple—Located above the decapping pin within a reloading die, this serves to expand the neck of a cartridge shell so it will accept a bullet during the reloading process.

Extractor—The unit which extracts a fired shell from the firing chamber.

Field of View—Target area and surroundings seen through a telescope sight.

Firing Pin—The pin which strikes the primer, discharging a gun.

Flash-Hole—Aperture in the base of a cartridge through which the primer ignites the charge.

Flinch—The tendency on the part of shooters to recoil from the expected "kick" of a gun.

Foot Pounds—Expression of energy generated by a gun charge. One foot pound will move a one-pound weight one foot.

Foot Seconds—Expression of a bullet's velocity: The number of feet a bullet will travel in one second.

Fore-End—The part of a gun stock located under the barrel. Also called "forearm."

Full Choke—The fullest constriction of a shotgun barrel muzzle which will contain 65 to 75 per cent of the shot within a 30-inch circle at 40 yards.

Garand—A .30 caliber M-1 gas-operated semiautomatic battle weapon of the U.S. armed forces during World War II.

Gauge—The bore of a shotgun barrel, indicated by the number of lead balls per pound which would fit a particular barrel. For example, a 12 gauge shotgun has a bore diameter equal to that of a lead ball which would weigh 12 to the pound. This application is used on all gauges except the .410, which is the bore diameter in thousandths of an inch.

Groove—The spirals that are cut or pressed into a rifle or handgun barrel.

Groove Diameter—The diameter of a gun barrel, measured from the bottom of the grooves.

Group—A cluster of bullet holes in a target.

Hammer Spur—Thumb piece on gun hammer.

Hammerless—A term applying to guns which do not have visible hammers.

Head Space—The slack space in a firing chamber between the bullet and the walls of the chamber.

Heel—The upper part of the rifle or shotgun stock butt.

Improved Modified—Constriction of a shotgun barrel muzzle to keep 55 to 65 per cent of the shot within a 30-inch circle at 40 yards.

Improved Cylinder—Similar constriction, though not as pronounced, since it will keep only 35 to 45 per cent of the shot within a 30-inch circle.

Ignition Time—The time interval required for the primer to touch off the powder charge.

Jacket—The metal covering of a lead bullet to control, or eliminate, expansion of the bullet upon impact. Also reduces leading and deforming of the bullet in a barrel.

Lands—Barrel surfaces between the spiraling grooves in a rifled barrel.

Lead—The distance in front of running or flying targets or game at which a gun is fired in order for the target to "run into" the shot charge, or bullet.

Lebel—French military rifle caliber 8 mm.

Lock Time—Same as Ignition Time.

Magazine—Container of cartridges or shells from which they are fed into the firing chamber.

Magnification—Enlargement of the field of view through a telescope sight or binoculars.

Magnum—In rifle and handgun loads, this refers to those of unusual velocity and energy. In the case of shotgun shells, an increased number of pellets over the standard or field loads.

Mauser—Popular European action used for sporting and military rifles. Originated by Paul Mauser at Obendorf, Germany.

Middle Sight—An open sight, having a *V*, *U* or square notch and located just forward of the rifle receiver.

Mid-Range Trajectory—The height of a bullet's path above the line of sight halfway between the muzzle and its target.

Minute of Angle—Adjusting a rifle or handgun sight one minute of angle shifts the point of impact one inch at 100 yards. One minute subtends one inch at that range.

Modified Choke—Shotgun barrel constriction restricting 45 to 55 per cent of the shot to within a 30-inch circle at 40 yards.

Mushroom—Popular expression applying to the expansion of a bullet upon impact.

Muzzle—Exit end of a gun barrel.

Muzzle Energy—Actually measured a few feet in front of the muzzle, it applies to the power developed by a bullet as it leaves the barrel.

Muzzle Velocity—Similarly, this applies to the bullet's rate of travel as it leaves the barrel.

Objective Lens—The front lens in a telescope sight or binoculars.

Pattern—The distribution of shot, usually gauged by the number and even distribution within a 30-inch circle at 40 yards.

Peep—The sighting aperture in a receiver sight.

Penetration—The ability of a bullet to plow its way into game flesh. Experimental shooting sometimes involves a number of one-inch pine boards with penetration indicated by the number of boards pierced by the bullet.

Pistol—Usually applied to handguns which do not have revolving cylinders, including single-shot and automatic guns.

Primer—A highly sensitive explosive unit which

ignites the powder charge, upon being indented by the firing pin.

Primer Pocket—A pocket at the center of the base of a shell where the primer is located.

Proof Mark—A stamping, usually on the barrel or receiver, indicating that a gun has been tested and released for sale by its manufacturer. Like western cattle brands, no two are alike.

Pull—The distance between the trigger and butt plate. Also, the weight or pressure required to release a trigger, hence "trigger pull."

Pump—Slide or "trombone" action, activated by pulling and pushing forward the forearm of a rifle or shotgun.

Radius, Sighting—The distance between the front and rear sight.

Receiver—That part of a rifle or shotgun which houses the bolt or breechblock and the firing mechanism.

Recoil—Backward reaction of a gun set up when it is discharged. Often referred to as "kick."

Relative Brightness—A measure of the scope sight's (or binocular's) light efficiency. Obtained by dividing the glass's power into the diameter of the objective lens and then squaring the answer.

Rem.—Remington.

Resizing—The re-forming of a shell to its original dimensions by forcing it into a die.

Reticle—Also spelled "reticule," this is the sighting unit within a telescope sight, generally a pair of cross hairs, post or a dot, or a combination of these.

Revolver—A handgun having a revolving cylinder which turns as the trigger is pulled or the hammer cocked.

Rib—A metal sighting plane atop a shotgun barrel, sometimes used on double-barrel shotguns.

Rifle—A shoulder arm having spiraling grooves cut or pressed into the inner surfaces of the barrel.

Rim-Fire—A cartridge having the primer within a thin rim about the base of the cartridge.

Rimless—A cartridge case having a recessed rim which is flush with the sidewalls. It is *not* actually rimless.

Sav.—Savage.

Sear—Holds the hammer or striker in firing position after cocking.

Seating, Bullet—The process of inserting a bullet into the mouth of a shell during reloading.

Sectional Density—Technical term applying to a bullet's diameter in relation to its length.

Semi-automatic—A gun which fires and reloads one shot automatically with each pull of the trigger.

Shell—Cartridge container, sometimes called a hull or case.

Single Action—Applies to revolvers which must be cocked manually before each shot.

Sizing—Same as resizing.

Skeet—A shotgun shooting course, requiring 25 shots from varying positions at clay targets projected by two mechanical traps set at different heights.

Slide Action—Same as pump action.

Slug, Rifled—A solid shotgun missile, designed for use on deer and black bear primarily. Grooves, corresponding to the rifling in a rifle barrel, are cast along its sides.

Smoothbore—A shotgun barrel which has no rifling on its interior surfaces.

Springfield—The .30/06 military rifle used in World Wars I and II, named after the Springfield, (Mass.) armory, although it was also manufactured at the Rockford, Ill., armory.

S & W—Smith and Wesson.

Swaging, Bullet—The cold forming of bullets from soft lead wire or slugs by forcing them into a swaging die.

Tracer—A bullet which burns in flight, indicating its trajectory to the shooter. Primarily of military value.

Trajectory—A bullet's path of flight.

Trapshooting—A shotgun shooting course, fired from five different positions at 16 yards from a single trap which may project clay birds at unexpected angles.

Trombone Action—Same as slide or pump action.

Twist—The number of inches required for one complete spiral of the grooves in a rifled barrel. For example, a 1-in-12 twist, indicates a complete spiral every 12 inches.

Varminter—A flat-shooting, long-range rifle adapted to the shooting of "varmints," usually equipped with a scope and special stock and possibly a semi-heavy barrel for greater accuracy.

Wad—Circular disc used in shotgun shells to separate powder and shot compartments. Also used as a filler.

Wad-cutter—A low-velocity target type of bullet

with a flat nose, known for the neat round holes it cuts in paper targets.
W.C.F.—Winchester Center-fire.
Win.—Winchester.
Windage—Lateral adjustment of rear sights to compensate for bullet drift.
W.R.F.—Winchester Rim-fire.
X—Scope-power designation symbol, for example: 4X indicates four power.
X-Ring—A ring within the bull's-eye of a target. Tie scores are broken by counting the number of hits within the "X-ring."
Zero—Range at which a rifle is sighted.

DIRECTORY

Manufacturers and Importers of Firearms, Air Guns, Ammunition, Reloading Equipment and Accessories

Alcan Company, Inc.
Seminary Rd.
Alton, Ill. 62002
(Reloading components)

Bair Company
P. O. Box 4407
Lincoln, Neb. 68504
(Reloading equipment)

Bausch & Lomb Optical Co.
635 St. Paul St.
Rochester, N.Y. 14605
(Scopes)

Benjamin Air Rifle Co.
807 Marion St.
St. Louis, Mo. 63104
(Air guns)

E. C. Bishop & Son, Inc.
P. O. Box 7
Warsaw, Mo. 65355
(Gunstocks)

Bonanza Sports Mfg. Co.
412 Western Ave.
Faribault, Minn. 55021
(Reloading equipment)

Browning Arms Co.
Rt. 1
Morgan, Utah 84050
(Handguns, long guns)

Maynard P. Buehler
17 Orinda Highway
Orinda, Calif. 94563
(Scope mounts, accessories)

Bushnell Optical Corp.
2828 East Foothill Blvd.
Pasadena, Calif. 91107
(Scopes)

Charter Arms Corp.
265 Asylum St.
Bridgeport, Conn. 06610
(Handguns)

C-H Tool & Die Corp.
P. O. Box L
Owen, Wis. 54460
(Reloading equipment)

Colt's Small Arms Div.
150 Huyshope Ave.
Hartford, Conn. 06102
(Handguns, rifles)

Crosman Arms Co., Inc.
Fairport, N.Y. 14450
(Air guns)

Daisy/Heddon
Rogers, Ark. 72756
(Air guns)

Charles Daly, Inc.
90 Chambers St.
New York, N.Y. 10007
(Shotguns)

Federal Cartridge Corp.
2700 Foshay Tower
Minneapolis, Minn. 55402
(Ammunition, components)

Garcia Corp.
329 Alfred Ave.
Teaneck, N.J. 07666
(Gun importers)

Harrington & Richardson, Inc.
320 Park Ave.
Worcester, Mass. 01610
(Handguns, long guns)

Herrett's Stocks, Inc.
Box 741
Twin Falls, Idaho 83301
(Handgun stocks)

High Standard Sporting Firearms
1817 Dixwell Ave.
Hamden, Conn. 06514
(Handguns, long guns)

Hornady Mfg. Co.
P. O. Box 1848
Grand Island, Neb. 68801
(Bullets)

Hutson Corp.
P. O. Box 1127
Arlington, Texas 76010
(Scopes)

Ithaca Gun Co. Inc.
Ithaca, N.Y. 14850
(Shotguns, rifles)

Lachmiller Div.
P. O. Box 97
Parkesburg, Pa. 19365
(Reloading equipment)

Leupold & Stevens, Inc.
P. O. Box 688
Beaverton, Ore. 97005
(Scopes)

Lyman Gun Sight Co.
Rt. 147
Middlefield, Conn. 06455
(Scopes, sights, reloading equipment)

Marlin Firearms Co.
100 Kenna Drive
North Haven, Conn. 06473
(Rifles, shotguns)

Mauser-Bauer, Inc.
34575 Commerce
Fraser, Mich. 48026
(Importer, rifles, shotguns)

O. F. Mossberg & Sons, Inc.
7 Grasso Ave.
North Haven, Conn. 06473
(Rifles, shotguns)

Norma-Precision
South Lansing, N.Y. 14882
(Ammunition, components)

Nosler Bullets, Inc.
P. O. Box 688
Beaverton, Ore. 97005
(Bullets)

Pachmayr Gun Works
1220 South Grand Ave.
Los Angeles, Calif. 90015
(Reloading equipment)

Pacific Gun Sight Co.
Box 4495
Lincoln, Neb. 68504
(Sights, reloading equipment)

Poly-Choke Company
Box 296
Hartford, Conn. 06101
(Shotgun chokes)

Ponsness-Warren, Inc.
P. O. Box 861
Eugene, Ore. 06033
(Reloading equipment)

RCBS
P. O. Box 1919
Oroville, Calif. 95965
(Reloading equipment)

Redfield Gun Sight Co.
5800 East Jewell Ave.
Denver, Colo. 80222
(Scopes)

Remington Arms Co., Inc.
Bridgeport, Conn. 06602
(Rifles, shotguns, ammunition)

Savage Arms Corp.
Westfield, Mass. 01085
(Rifles, shotguns)

Jay Scott, Inc.
81 Sherman Place
Garfield, N.J. 07026
(Handgun grips)

Sheridan Products, Inc.
3205 Sheridan Rd.
Racine, Wis. 53403
(Air guns, bullet traps)

Sierra Bullet Co.
10532 S. Painter Ave.
Sante Fe Springs, Calif. 90670
(Bullets)

Sloan's Sporting Goods, Inc.
88 Chambers St.
New York, N.Y. 10007
(Importers, guns)

Slug Site
3835 University
Des Moines, Iowa 50311
(Shotgun sight)

Smith & Wesson
P. O. Box 2208
Springfield, Mass. 01101
(Handguns, holsters, rifles)

Speer, Inc.
Box 896
Lewiston, Idaho
(Bullets)

Sturm-Ruger & Co., Inc.
Southport, Conn. 06490
(Handguns, rifles)

Tasco Sales, Inc.
Box 878
Miami, Fla. 33138
(Importers, scopes)

Trius Products, Inc.
Box 25
Cleves, Ohio 45002
(Shotgun traps)

John Unertl Optical Co.
3551 East St.
Pittsburgh, Pa. 15214
(Scopes)

Weatherby, Inc.
2781 Firestone Blvd.
South Gate, Calif. 90280
(Magnum rifles, scopes, ammunition)

W. R. Weaver Co.
El Paso, Texas 79915
(Scopes)

Williams Gun Sight Co.
7300 Lapeer Rd.
Davison, Mich. 48423
(Scopes, gun accessories)

Winchester/Western
275 Winchester Ave.
New Haven, Conn. 06504
(Rifles, shotguns, ammunition)